THE
NEW LEVIATHAN

OR

MAN, SOCIETY, CIVILIZATION
AND BARBARISM

BY

R. G. COLLINGWOOD

LL.D., ST. ANDREWS
SOMETIME PROFESSOR OF METAPHYSICAL
PHILOSOPHY IN THE UNIVERSITY OF OXFORD
AND FELLOW OF MAGDALEN COLLEGE

Martino Publishing
Mansfield Centre, CT
2014

Martino Publishing
P.O. Box 373,
Mansfield Centre, CT 06250 USA

ISBN   978-1-61427-555-8

© *2014 Martino Publishing*

Cover design by T. Matarazzo

Printed in the United States of America On 100% Acid-Free Paper

THE
NEW LEVIATHAN

OR

MAN, SOCIETY, CIVILIZATION
AND BARBARISM

BY

R. G. COLLINGWOOD

LL.D., ST. ANDREWS
SOMETIME PROFESSOR OF METAPHYSICAL
PHILOSOPHY IN THE UNIVERSITY OF OXFORD
AND FELLOW OF MAGDALEN COLLEGE

OXFORD
AT THE CLARENDON PRESS
1942

Oxford University Press, Amen House, London E.C.4

FIRST EDITION 1942

PREFACE

A READER may take the title of this book in whichever way he pleases.

If he is one of those who think of Hobbes's *Leviathan* as the classical exposition of a classical type of despotism, namely seventeenth-century absolutism, the portrait and anatomy of 'that great LEVIATHAN called a COMMON-WEALTH, or STATE (in latine CIVITAS) which is but an Artificial Man; though of greater stature and strength than the Naturall',[1] he may take it to mean that I have set out in this 'New *Leviathan*' to portray and anatomize the new absolutism of the twentieth century, based (like that which Hobbes described) on the will of a people who in thus setting up a popular tyrant gave into his hands every right any one of them has hitherto possessed. For the immediate aim of this book is to study the new absolutism and inquire into its nature, causes, and prospects of success or failure; success, I mean, in either destroying all competitors and becoming the political form of the future, or at least contributing to the political life of the future some positive heritage of ideas and institutions which men will not forget.

If he thinks of the *Leviathan* as a book which is unique in dealing with the entire body of political science and approaches its colossal subject from first principles, that is, from an examination of man, his faculties and interests, his virtues and vices; a book dealing first with man as such, then with political life as such, then with a well-ordered political life or a 'CHRISTIAN COMMON-WEALTH', and lastly with an ill-ordered political life or 'KINGDOME OF DARKNESSE'; then he may take my title to mean, not that I have in fact dealt with these vast subjects exhaustively, but that in this book I have set out to deal with the same groups of problems in the same order, calling the four parts of my book 'Man', 'Society', 'Civilization', and 'Barbarism'.

Readers of the second school (though I have no quarrel

[1] Hobbes, *Leviathan*, p. 1. Here and throughout I quote the pages of the first edition, which are given marginally in the Clarendon Press reprint.

with the others) will of the two be nearer to my own way of thinking. It is only now, towards the middle of the twentieth century, that men here and there are for the first time becoming able to appreciate Hobbes's *Leviathan* at its true worth, as the world's greatest store of political wisdom. I say that this is only now beginning to happen. From the time of its publication, when it impressed every reader with a force directly proportional to his own intelligence as the greatest work of political science the world had ever seen, but pleased nobody because there was no class of readers whose corns it left untrodden upon or whose withers it left unwrung, it fell more and more deeply into disfavour beneath a rising tide of ethical and political sentimentalism. Hardly a single political writer from the seventeenth century to the present day has been able so to clear his mind of that sentimentalism as to look Hobbes in the face and see behind those repellently grim features what manner of man he was; or to see behind the savage irony of his style how deeply he understood himself and his fellow men.

But war, says Thucydides, is a stern teacher. The wars of the present century have taught some of us that there was more in Hobbes than we had supposed. They have taught us that, to see political life as it really is, we must blow away the mists of sentimentalism which have concealed its features from us ever since the beginning of the eighteenth century. I believe that I am not reporting my own experience alone when I say that the dispelling of these mists by the almost incessant tempest through which we have precariously lived for close on thirty years has revealed Hobbes's *Leviathan* as a work of gigantic stature, incredibly overtopping all its successors in political theory from that day to this.

My own book is best to be understood as an attempt to bring the *Leviathan* up to date, in the light of the advances made since it was written, in history, psychology, and anthropology. The attempt was undertaken, and the writing of the book begun, almost immediately after the outbreak of the present war; when first it became evident that we did not know what we were fighting for, and that our leaders were unable or unwilling to tell us.

But the preparation for the attempt had been going on for

twenty years before that. It was on returning to my studies in 1919, from such service as I was able to do, in what we now call the Four Years' War, that I realized, dimly and incompletely, what the situation was that had been confronting us; namely what I should now describe as a new form of barbarism. It was now that I began to think out the fundamental ideas of the present book, thereafter revising and elaborating them year after year in experimental forms, accumulating as time went on I will not say how many thousand pages of manuscript on every problem of ethics and politics, and especially on the problems of history which bore on my subject; and imparting my results, when I seemed to reach any that were worth imparting, in lectures to my juniors and in manuscript to such of my colleagues as seemed interested.

The book which is now offered to the reader is not what I should call a finished work. It has been so far finished as time and health permitted during a space of nearly two years; the earlier part of this time, so far as it was not occupied in teaching, being devoted to writing the manuscript in Oxford, in Bath, and in London. The later part, ever since April 1941, was spent at Streatley, in Berkshire, on the manuscript.

I seem to remember something that Bernard Bosanquet once said about the loss to professional thought from the fact that it is always done by cowards. I do not claim to be an exception; but it was said in a letter to Malvolio that 'some are born great, some achieve greatness, and some have greatness thrust upon them'; and some degree of greatness, though I hardly know what, might be ascribed to a book written in great part not (as Hegel boasted) during the cannonade of Jena, but during the bombardment of London.

R. G. C.

SOUTH HAYES,
STREATLEY, BERKSHIRE
16 *January* 1942

CONTENTS

PART I. MAN

PART II. SOCIETY

PART III. CIVILIZATION

PART IV. BARBARISM

PART I

MAN

I

BODY AND MIND

1. 1. WHAT is Man?

1. 11. Before beginning to answer the question, we must know why it is asked.

1. 12. It is asked because we are beginning an inquiry into civilization, and the revolt against it which is the most conspicuous thing going on at the present time.

1. 13. Civilization is a condition of communities; so to understand what civilization is we must first understand what a community is.

1. 14. A community is a condition of men, in which are included women and children; so to understand what a community is we must first understand what men are.

1. 15. This gives us the scheme of the present book: Part I, an inquiry into man; Part II, an inquiry into communities; Part III, an inquiry into civilizations; and Part IV, an inquiry into revolts against civilization.

1. 16. About each subject we want to understand only so much as we need in order to understand what is to be said about the next.

1. 17. We know, or at least we have been told, a great deal about Man; that God made him a little lower than the angels; that Nature made him the offspring of apes; that he has an erect posture, to which his circulatory system is ill adapted, and four incisors in each jaw, which are less liable to decay than the rest of his teeth, but more liable to be knocked out; that he is a rational animal, a risible animal, a tool-using animal, an animal uniquely ferocious and malevolent towards his kind; that he is assured of God, freedom, and immortality, and endowed with means of grace, which he prefers to neglect, and the hope of glory, which he prefers to exchange for the fear of hell-fire; and that all his weal and all his woe is a by-product of his Oedipus-complex or, alternatively, of his ductless glands.

1. 18. Each of these themes would fill this book: but which of them would advance the inquiry whose lines I have laid down?

1. 19. We of the twentieth century hold ourselves bound to the tradition in these matters laid down by Bacon and Descartes in the seventeenth: to speak not merely 'to the subject' but 'to the point'; to divide our subject into parts, to arrange the parts in such an order that what is said about each prepares the way for what is said about the next; and to say about each not all we know but only what need be said for the sake of that preparation.

1. 2. Of all the things we know or have been told about Man, which is the one thing that concerns us at the present stage of our inquiry?

1. 21. I answer: *The division between body and mind.* For civilization is a thing of the mind, and a community, too, is a thing of the mind. It follows that the 'Man' into which we are inquiring in order to prepare for our account of civilization is a 'Man' of the mind.

1. 22. If Man, as they say, consists of body and mind, our inquiry demands that we should dismiss research into man's body as alien to our purpose and concentrate on the study of man's mind: not all about it, but so much of it as will advance us towards the study of community.

1. 3. Man's body is made of *matter* and the study of man's body belongs to that group of studies which are concerned with 'the material world': what are called the natural sciences.

1. 31. To say that, separately considered, the several parts of man's body are 'matter' is to say that they behave according to laws investigated by physicists and chemists.

1. 32. Whether these are two sciences or one is a question we need not here raise.

1. 33. Collectively considered, these same parts are an *organism*: that is to say, a thing whose special characteristic it is to be alive.

1. 34. What being alive is, I leave to the physiologists.

1. 35. If anybody were to ask me: 'What is life?' I should reply: 'It is what physiologists investigate.'

1. 36. Whether physiology is the same as physics and

chemistry, or different from one or both of them, is another question we need not here raise.

1. 4. Some reader may think it strange to define matter in terms of physics and chemistry (1. 31) and life in terms of physiology (1. 35); and may think it better to define physics and chemistry in terms of matter, and physiology in terms of life.

1. 41. 'Physics and chemistry', he may say, 'is the Science of Matter; and everyone knows what matter is. Physiology is the Science of Life; and everyone knows what life is.'

1. 42. Egregious blunder! A beginner in physics or chemistry does not know what matter is, and if he thinks he does it is the duty of his teacher to disabuse him; but he knows what physics or chemistry is; it is the stuff in this red text-book, or the stuff old So-and-so teaches, or the stuff we have on Tuesday mornings.

1. 43. The beginner *has in his head a definition of the science*; a childish definition, perhaps, but still a definition; of the science's subject-matter he has *no definition at all*.

1. 44. Only the hope of a definition. 'I don't know what life is, but I hope I shall when I have studied physiology for long enough.'

1. 45. 'That is true for a beginner in physiology; but for a master in physiology the reverse is true; a master in physiology has found out all that it can tell him and knows what life is. A beginner in physiology does not; for him physiology is definable and life as yet, except in the language of hope, indefinable.'

1. 46. A man ceases to be a beginner in any given science and becomes a master in that science when he has learned that *this expected reversal is never going to happen* and that he is going to be a beginner all his life.

1. 47. A physiologist who has learned that lesson can certainly offer a definition of life; but this will only be *an interim report on the progress of physiology to date*. For him, as for the beginner, it is the nature of physiology that is relatively certain; the nature of life that is relatively vague.

1. 48. For each, life is definable (so far as it is definable at all) only in terms of physiology; never physiology in terms of life.

1.5. To think that physics or chemistry ought to be defined in terms of matter or physiology in terms of life is more than an egregious blunder; it is a threat to the existence of science.

1.51. It implies that people know what matter is without studying physics or chemistry, and what life is without studying physiology.

1.52. It implies that this non-scientific and pre-scientific knowledge concerning the nature of matter or life is perfect and final, so far as it goes, and can never be corrected by anything science can do.

1.53. It implies that, if anything scientists imagine themselves to have discovered about matter or life or what not is inconsistent with anything contained or implied in this non-scientific and pre-scientific knowledge, the scientists have made a mistake.

1.54. It implies that, if they have made the mistake by using (for example) experimental methods, it is experimental methods that are at fault and must be abandoned.

1.55. It implies that, if they have made the mistake by arguing logically, it is logic that is at fault and must be abandoned.

1.56. It implies that any scientist who will not yield to persuasion and confess the supremacy of non-scientific or pre-scientific knowledge over all possible scientific inquiry must be made to yield by any means that can be devised.

1.57. At one blow, by enunciating the apparently harmless proposition that physics or chemistry is the science of matter, physiology the science of life, or the like, we have evoked the whole apparatus of *scientific persecution*; I mean the persecution of scientists for daring to be scientists.

1.58. In whose interest is such a persecution carried on? Who stands to gain by it? The nominal beneficiary differs from time to time: sometimes it is religion, sometimes statecraft, and so on. None of these has ever in fact gained a ha'porth of advantage. The actual beneficiary has always been *obsolete science*.

1.59. A given science, in its progress down to the year y_1, has reached certain conclusions which we will call c_1. Later, in the year y_2, it has demolished these and arrived at the conclusion c_2. At the time y_2 religious or political authorities who learned the doctrine c_1 at school and have never learned anything else (or perhaps never even in their youth learned what scientists were then teaching, but only something which had been taught long ago) learn to their horror that scientists are now teaching the doctrine c_2.

1.6. Their loyalty to the long-dead scientists who taught them to believe in c_1 boils over, and they call upon all the powers of Church and State to suppress this new doctrine c_2, whose only fault is that while it was growing up they were asleep. Their persecution succeeds, as John Stuart Mill long ago remarked that persecution generally does; and who is the gainer? The scientists who taught c_1? But they are dead. The gainer is their obsolete doctrine.

1.61. Man's mind is made of *thought*.

1.62. What this statement means I shall explain in the sequel; I will not linger over it now.

1.63. I will only say two things: first, that thought is both theoretical and practical.

1.64. Theoretical thought is, for example, thinking about the cold, or thinking about the difference between cold and hot, or thinking that yesterday was even colder than to-day.

1.65. Practical thought is, for example, thinking whether to light a fire or thinking that you will go back to bed, or thinking: 'Why should I have the window open?'

1.66. Secondly, that thought is primarily practical; and only in the second place theoretical, because it is in the first place practical.

1.67. Its theoretical forms depend more completely on its practical than its practical do upon its theoretical; without theory there would only be a few rudimentary types of practice, but without practice there would be no theory at all.

1.68. It would be a more disastrous mistake in the science of mind to forget that thought is always practical than to forget that it is sometimes theoretical.

1.7. There are sciences which investigate mind; but they have certain peculiarities distinguishing them from the 'natural sciences'.

1.71. Their principle is that whereas from a natural

science a man often learns something utterly new to him, the sciences of mind teach him only *things of which he was already conscious.*

1.72. Any form of consciousness may be reflected upon; that is, it may become the object of another form of consciousness.

1.73. Let a man have a certain form of consciousness, C_1. Let him reflect on this: let him, that is to say, call into being in himself another form of consciousness, C_2, the consciousness of C_1.

1.74. Whatever a science of mind can tell him about C_1 is something of which he was already conscious in the state C_2.

1.75. This does not mean he already knew it, whether by the organized or systematic knowledge called 'science' or by the random, unsystematic knowledge called 'experience',[1] which is the raw material out of which 'science' is made by arranging it in systematic form.

1.76. But when it has been thus worked up every element in the resulting product is derived from the original raw material; for every question has been asked and answered 'with your eye on the object', where the object is C_1 and the eye C_2.

1.77. The answer to any question in any science of mind is provided by reflection. Any man who answers that question must already have reflected on the function he is studying, or he could not answer it. Any man who understands (let alone accepts or rejects) the answer must have reflected on the same function, or he could not understand it.

1.78. The two are exactly on a level so far as the materials for the science are concerned.

1.79. The only advantage the first has over the second is in deciding what questions to ask.

1.8. Whatever questions he asks, the answers depend on the extent of his own reflection; not on distant travel, costly or difficult experiment, or profound and various learning.

1.81. The second has exactly the same resources for checking the answers as the first for giving them.

1.82. The only way in which the first can establish an

[1] A name for 'propositional thinking' (11. 22).

ascendancy over the second is by talking so obscurely that the second does not know what he is talking about. This is the infallible mark of one who deals with the sciences of mind in the spirit of a charlatan.

1.83. Man as body is *whatever the sciences of body say that he is.* Without their help nothing can be known on that subject: their authority, therefore, is absolute.

1.84. Man as mind is *whatever he is conscious of being.*

1.85. The sciences of mind, unless they preach error or confuse the issue by dishonest or involuntary obscurity, can tell us nothing but what each can verify for himself by reflecting upon his own mind.

1.86. Any lesson which he is too poor a hand at reflection to verify he cannot learn at all; the most he can do is to repeat parrot-wise the words in which it was taught.

1.87. A man who wants to know what he is in his capacity as mind has no need to ask a specialist, and no specialist has any right to demand his acceptance of any particular answer.

1.88. The general form of answer to any such question is: *In teipsum redi.* You have the makings of the answer in your own consciousness. Reflect, and you will find what it is. In the meantime I offer you the fruits of my own reflection, so that 'the pains left another, will onely be to consider, if he also find not the same in himself. For this kind of Doctrine, admitteth no other Demonstration.'[1]

---

[1] *Leviathan,* p. 2.

II

THE RELATION BETWEEN BODY AND MIND

2. 1. MOST people, probably, have thought of man's mind as inhabiting his body somewhat as he inhabits a house.

2. 11. Traditional folk-lore is full of stories that testify not only to the past prevalence of this belief but to its permanent hold over men's minds.

2. 12. For as long as the story expressing a belief is still told the belief is alive, though the people in whom it is alive may know that it is childish and would be quick to disown it.

2. 13. Childish it certainly is; for nothing can inhabit a house made of matter except something else made of matter.

2. 14. Nobody can entertain this ancient belief, therefore, except either a person who does not know enough about man's body to know that it is made of matter, or a person who does not know enough about man's mind to know that it is not.

2. 15. A story that can only survive by ignorance of its subject-matter can have no scientific interest. Let us call it an *old wives' tale*.

2. 2. Suppose a man who had lately believed this old wives' tale grew dissatisfied with it.

2. 21. Suppose he said: 'The mind is more intimately connected with its body than an inhabitant with his house.

2. 22. 'There seems to be a sympathy between the two. Hardly anything happens to the mind without a corresponding thing happening to the body, and vice versa.

2. 23. 'This correspondence between body-events and mind-events I will call (for I like long words, especially when derived from the Greek) *psycho-physical parallelism.*'

2. 24. Has this man taken the step from old wives' tales to scientific theory, or has he only moved from one old wives' tale to another?

2. 25. 'Psycho-physical Parallelism' is another old wives' tale. If a mind does not really live in its body it does not really run parallel to its body, and what is more nobody thinks it does.

2. 26. Parallelism is a geometrical idea presupposing a

space of at least two dimensions in which two lines run, each preserving its equidistance from the other, not meeting.

2. 27. Psycho-physical Parallelists do not really think that mind-events and body-events occur in pairs at equidistant places. They do not even want to be regarded as thinking so. They would be rather vexed than flattered if you took them so seriously as to ask: 'What is the unvarying distance between any mind-event and the corresponding body-event?'

2. 28. They would protest that this was breaking a butterfly upon the wheel. They use the word 'Parallelism' only because it is long and sounds learned. They don't mean anything by it; at any rate, not what they say; all they mean is that there is a one-one relation between a mind-event and its corresponding body-event, and that this is not a causal relation.

2. 29. 'One-one relation' sounds more up-to-date than 'parallelism': less mellifluous, more appropriate to an age of rubber truncheons. But it is just as evasive. It hints mathematical implications which it does not mean you to take seriously. You are told that a single mind-event is never correlated with a group of body-events, or vice versa: but if you thought you were meant to believe this, you would find that you had only been listening to another old wives' tale.

2. 3. One bids farewell to 'Psycho-physical Parallelism' with regret. It is a pity that so nice a derangement of epitaphs should turn out to mean simply nothing at all. But if sadder we are wiser. We have learned that polysyllabic phrases do not necessarily conceal profound significance; they may conceal a desire to persuade the simple that there is significance where there is none.

2. 31. Alternatively, a man who grows dissatisfied with the first old wives' tale may say (priding himself a little, perhaps, on being too clever to fall into psycho-physical parallelism): 'Anyhow, body-events and mind-events do not form two parallel series, proceeding each on its own way without mutual interference.

2. 32. 'For there is mutual interference. The pain which occurs as a mind-event when a kick on my shin occurs as a body-event cannot be traced to any origin in the mind-series; it is a mind-event, due to a body-event.

2.33. 'The kick with the pain it produces is a breach of parallelism. It is a case of *interaction*; a case where body acts on mind.

2.34. 'Similarly there are cases where mind acts on body. The movements of my hand as I write these words are not due to previous body-events, though no doubt previous body-events such as eating my breakfast are more or less indispensable conditions of them; they are due to mind-events, namely my wish to write the words.'

2.35. Here is a third old wives' tale called, no less pompously than the second, and for the same discreditable motives, *Psycho-physical Interactionism*. The idea is that mind acts on body and body on mind.

2.36. How body acts and is acted upon it is for the physicist to tell us. Different schools of physicists have answered in different ways; but all schools have agreed that however one body acts it can only act upon another body, and however one body is acted upon it can be acted upon only by another body.

2.37. Challenge any Psycho-physical Interactionist to put forward any account of Psycho-physical Interaction which any school of physicists will accept as regards the physical end for anything except nonsense, and you will find no takers.

2.38. You will find that the Psycho-physical Interactionist already knows his own ideas to be what any physicist would call nonsense, and will counter-attack by maintaining that physicists know nothing about physics; in fact, by what I have called evoking the apparatus of scientific persecution (1.57).

2.39. Who, in this case, is the beneficiary? The man who wants to palm off an old wives' tale as a theory of the relation between body and mind.

2.4. The truth is that there is no relation between body and mind. That is, no direct relation; for there is an indirect relation.

2.41. 'The problem of the relation between body and mind' is a bogus problem which cannot be stated without making a false assumption.

2.42. What is assumed is that man is partly body and partly mind. On this assumption questions arise about the relations between the two parts; and these prove unanswerable.

2. 43. For man's body and man's mind are not two different things. They are one and the same thing, man himself, as known in two different ways.

2. 44. Not a part of man, but the whole of man, is body in so far as he approaches the problem of self-knowledge by the methods of natural science.

2. 45. Not a part of man, but the whole of man, is mind in so far as he approaches the problem of self-knowledge by expanding and clarifying the data of reflection.

2. 46. The natural sciences have already made some progress towards describing man in their own way. Friends of these sciences believe that this progress will continue if natural scientists are allowed to go on working.

2. 47. Some who profess to be friends of the human mind, and show their friendship by showing enmity towards natural science, one of the human mind's most triumphant successes, hope it will stop because, they fancy, whatever in man proves recalcitrant to explanation by the natural sciences will prove itself to be not body but mind; if nothing does, the inference will be that man is all body and therefore has no mind.

2. 48. Nothing could be sillier. In the natural sciences, mind is not that which is left over when explaining has broken down; it is what does the explaining. If an explanation of mind is what you want, you have come to the wrong shop; you ought to have gone to the sciences of mind.

2. 49. The 'indirect relation between body and mind' (2. 4) is the relation between the sciences of body, or natural sciences, and the sciences of mind; that is the relation inquiry into which ought to be substituted for the make-believe inquiry into the make-believe problem of 'the relation between body and mind'.

2. 5. Not that these make-believe inquiries are valueless. Hobbes, noticing the fictitious character of academic discussions, made the famous remark: 'I say not this, as disapproving the use of Universities: but because I am to speak hereafter of their office in a Common-wealth, I must let you see on all occasions by the way, what things would be amended in them; amongst which the frequency of insignificant speech is one.'[1]

[1] *Leviathan*, p. 4.

2.51. This is scolding little girls for giving dolls' tea-parties with empty cups and little boys for playing with wooden swords. Academic discussions and the frequency of insignificant speech belong to the world of *make-believe*.

2.52. One chief pursuit of the immature animal, human or other, is to prepare itself for the dangers of real life, while its elders are protecting it from them, by making believe to face them; and this is the greater part of education; so that the office of universities in a commonwealth is to provide an unfailing flow of insignificant speech.

2.53. For speech is man's weapon against the dangers of his own world, and insignificant speech is what he teaches his cubs as his fellow creatures teach theirs to bat without clawing and nip without biting.

2.54. Man's world is infested by *Sphinxes*, demonic beings of mixed and monstrous nature which ask him riddles and eat him if he cannot answer them, compelling him to play a game of wits where the stake is his life and his only weapon is his tongue.

2.55. That is why men teach their offspring to use their tongues in a kind of puppy-play where all speech has to be as insignificant as a doll's teacup is empty or a boy's sword harmless; where the talk is only pretence talk or what is called *academic discussions* and the problems talked about are only pretence problems or what are called *academic problems*; where the supervisors of these childish sports set for discussion 'academic' questions such as: 'Compare the merits of Psycho-physical Parallelism and Psycho-physical Interactionism', not because they fancy them significant but because they know them for nonsense.

2.6. I have mentioned two approaches to the problem of self-knowledge: the natural sciences and the sciences of man (2.44–5). I have suggested that the relation between them is one into which inquiry ought to be made (2.49).

2.61. I shall not undertake it. There is only one thing about it which has to be said here.

2.62. Each is valid. Each is a search for truth, and neither goes unrewarded.

2.63. Each, therefore, has its own problems and must solve them by its own methods.

2. 64. Neither can do anything but harm, either to itself or to its fellow, by trespassing on its fellow's hunt.

2. 65. Of these two different forms of science, *the one that has started a hare must catch it.*

2. 66. The reason is plain. You can only solve a problem which you recognize to be a problem.

2. 67. The same methods, therefore, which led to the asking of a question must lead to the answering of it.

2. 68 If they cannot, at least no others can; for others will involve the recognition that the question needs an answer.

2. 7. Here you are in the middle of a problem. The same horse that got you into it must get you out again.

2. 71. No amount of admiration for some other horse must betray you into the FALLACY OF SWAPPING HORSES.

2. 72. If the wretched horse called Mental Science has stuck you in mid-stream you can flog him, or you can coax him, or you can get out and lead him; or you can drown, as better men than you have drowned before.

2. 73. But you must not swap him even for the infinitely superior horse called Natural Science.

2. 74. For this is a magic journey, and if you do that the river will vanish and you will find yourself back where you started.

III
BODY AS MIND

3. 1. MAN's 'body' as known to the physicist, the chemist, and the physiologist, whether these sciences are three or two or one, is by definition something other than his mind; for these sciences are natural sciences.

3. 11. Our inquiry has to do with man's mind (1. 21). We must refuse, therefore, on pain of falling into the fallacy of swapping horses (2. 91), to let ourselves be side-tracked by any siren-song describing the delights of physics, chemistry, or physiology, and the horrors awaiting the rash voyager who would air his ignorant opinions about thought without troubling to inform himself, for example, upon the all-important subject of cerebral physiology.

3. 12. But it does not follow that there is no sense in which a discussion of man's 'body' can be of value for an inquiry into his mind.

3. 13. There is another sense of the word 'body': a sense neither physical nor chemical nor physiological but *psychological*.

3. 14. This sense is closely connected with our present inquiry, and we must not ignore it.

3. 15. First, however, we must assure ourselves that it exists: I mean that there is in ordinary, everyday, well established usage a sense of the word 'body' in which, surprising though it may seem, the body is part of the mind.

3. 2. For this purpose I shall ask the reader to reflect on three phrases: '*bodily appetite*', '*bodily pleasure*', and '*bodily exertion*'.

3. 21. I think he will admit that they are in common use. I want him to ask what sort of a 'body' it is to which they refer.

3. 22. If he thinks that question implies an attempt to get more meaning than they actually contain out of popular phrases, I shall remind him that the phrases have a respectable ancestry: they come down to us from Plato and Aristotle, and anything we say about their meaning in current English can be checked and shall be checked by research into their pedigree.

3. 3. When hunger is called a *bodily appetite* the word 'bodily' is not otiose; at that rate curiosity might be called an appetite but not a bodily appetite.

3. 31. I should not care to say that 'bodily' conveys a reference to the physiological body and that curiosity is not a 'bodily appetite' because physiology cannot give any account of it. I should not be at all surprised to find that, when cerebral physiology and the physiology of the endocrine system were taken into account, it could; and very much surprised to find out that it never hoped to.

3. 32. Hunger is, at any rate in part, a certain group of *feelings*; for example, a 'gnawing' sensation at the stomach, a general organic sensation of weakness or lassitude, with an inability to see clearly and a tendency for things to go black, and an emotional feeling of gloom or depression.

3. 33. There is nothing corresponding to these in the case of curiosity, or if there is I have never noticed it, perhaps because I have never suffered from curiosity as acutely as I have suffered from hunger.

3. 34. I make bold to say that there is a characteristic group of feelings (sensations and emotions connected with them) whereby a man knows that he is hungry, and none by which he knows that he is curious.

3. 35. The adjective 'bodily' when used of hunger refers to the presence of this group of feelings.

3. 4. I turn to the phrase *'bodily pleasure'*. The pleasure of lying in a hot bath is called a bodily pleasure; the pleasure of reading Newton's *Principia* is not.

3. 41. 'Bodily' here does not mean 'physiological' in the sense that physiology could offer an account of the one and not of the other; if it could explain either, I do not doubt that it could explain both.

3. 42. The difference is that in the case of the bath the pleasure is the pleasure of feeling in certain ways: the pleasure of warmth on the skin and so forth; in the case of the *Principia* the pleasure is the pleasure of thinking in certain ways.

3. 43. If my pleasure in reading the *Principia* were derived from the actual look and smell and feel of the volume in my hands and under my nose and before my eyes I should call that, too, a bodily pleasure.

3.44. A 'bodily' pleasure means a pleasure arising out of 'feelings', that is, sensations and the emotions directly connected with them.

3.45. I do not call hunger, fear, or love a feeling, though each is rich in elements of feeling; hunger I call an appetite, fear a passion, love a desire or an appetite according to whether it does or does not involve the recognition that 'this is love'.

3.5. Why is digging called '*bodily exertion*' and following a mathematical argument not?

3.51. Not because physiological strains are present in the former case and not in the latter.

3.52. Anyone who knows anything about blood-pressure knows that they are often present in the latter.

3.53. It is because in digging my consciousness of effort either is or is closely bound up with motor sensations in, for example, the muscles that I use when I dig.

3.54. Once more, then, 'bodily' means 'connected with feelings, i.e. sensations and the emotions directly connected with them'. This is what I call the '*psychological sense of the word body*'.

3.6. This sense of the word 'body' goes back through the New Testament to Aristotle and Plato.

3.61. 'Body' in the New Testament (σῶμα) is often used to mean 'feeling' in this sense of the word; sometimes, but by no means always, with some further (Gnostic) suggestion that what is so called is inherently evil and a source of sin, though not its only source.

3.62. Here are a few references, to which others might be added. Mark v. 29, 'she felt in her body that she was healed of that plague'; Luke xi. 34, 'the light of the body is the eye'; Romans vi. 6, 'knowing this, that our old man is crucified with him, that the body of sin might be destroyed'; vii. 24, 'who shall deliver me from the body of this death?'; viii. 10, 13, 'if Christ be in you, the body is dead because of sin . . . but if ye through the Spirit do mortify the deeds of the body, ye shall live'; 1 Corinthians ix. 27, 'I keep under my body, and bring it into subjection.'

3.63. In Plato the expressions 'bodily pleasure' and 'bodily appetite' are common, and Plato is careful to tell us that they are not his own invention ('the so-called bodily pleasures', αἱ περὶ τὸ σῶμα καλούμεναι ἡδοναί, *Republic*, 442 A, where *pace* Adam I suppose 'so-called' to qualify not 'pleasures' but 'bodily'); but are currently used as implying a special sense of the word 'body'.

3.64. The 'so-called bodily pleasures' are (ibid.) the pleasures of eating, drinking, and sex. Now these according to Plato himself (*Rep.* 580 E) are the pleasures, or some of the pleasures, of 'The Acquisitive'; and 'The Acquisitive' is one of the three 'forms' (εἴδη) or 'parts' (μέρη) which go to make up the mind (ψυχή).[1]

3.65. 'The Acquisitive' is that part or form of the mind to which sensation belongs.

3.66. That pleasure is a mental thing is nowhere to my recollection said outright by Plato himself (Adam says it occurs in *Timaeus*, 64 B, but I cannot see it there). Plato does, however, say (*Philebus*, 35 C) that appetite is a mental thing, and Aristotle says the same of pleasure (*Eth. Nic.* 1099ᵃ8, τὸ μὲν γὰρ ἥδεσθαι τῶν ψυχικῶν).

3.67. But Aristotle does not hesitate to speak like Plato of 'bodily pleasures', evidently with the same implied gloss on 'body' as here meaning a part of mind which includes among its functions that of sensation.

3.7. The thing that first concerned us at the beginning of our inquiry, I said (1.21), was the division between body and mind.

3.71. The inquiry is concerned with mind. We must exclude from it all inquiry into 'body' where 'body' means matter, or what is studied by natural science.

3.72. It has now become clear that sometimes 'body' means not matter but feeling; and that when it does it means something which we must not neglect.

3.73. I have already said (1.61) that man's mind is made of thought; but here comes something else, *feeling*, which seems to belong somehow to mind. Let us consider it.

---

[1] 'Soul' is our conventional translation for ψυχή; but the word 'soul' is obsolescent or obsolete in modern English, except in a few special contexts, and 'mind' has taken its place.

IV

FEELING

4. 1. A *feeling* consists of two things closely connected: first, a *sensuous* element such as a colour seen, a sound heard, an odour smelt; secondly, what I call the *emotional charge on this sensation*: the cheerfulness with which you see the colour, the fear with which you hear the noise, the disgust with which you smell the odour.

4. 11. Does every feeling consist of these two elements? I do not know. Generalization about feelings is impossible (5. 55). All I can say is that those which I can recollect examining have done so, and that I assume the rest are, and have been, and will be like them.

4. 12. Does 'sensation' mean the *object* of seeing or the like (the colour, the sound, &c.) or the *act* of seeing it, hearing it, &c.? The question is not answerable without first clearing up the confusions it involves. I shall attend to this later (5. 2).

4. 13. Man's mind is made of thought (1. 61), but feeling seems to belong somehow to mind (3. 73); how?

4. 14. There are two senses in which one thing 'belongs' to another: as a *constituent* or as an *apanage*.

4. 15. One thing belongs to another as a constituent in the way in which a man belongs to a family or a plank to a boat or a page to a book.

4. 16. One thing belongs to another as an apanage in the way in which an estate belongs to a family or a mooring to a boat or a card in the library catalogue to a book.

4. 17. A mind has both constituents and apanages.

4. 18. The essential *constituent* of mind is *consciousness* or thought (practical and theoretical) in its most rudimentary form. In addition, many minds have other constituents in the shape of various specialized forms of consciousness. Forms of consciousness are the only constituents, so far as I know, possessed by any mind.

4. 19. Feeling is an *apanage* of mind. It is an apanage of simple consciousness, namely its proper object, what there is consciousness of.

4. 2. Man as mind *is* consciousness, practical and theoretical, both in its simplest form and also in specialized forms; he *has* feeling, both in its simplest or purely sensuous-emotional form and also in specialized forms.

4. 21. These specialized forms of feeling arise through the practical work of consciousness, which is always bringing into existence new types of feeling and then, reflecting on the situation its practical work has created, making it an object to itself in its theoretical form.

4. 22. Consciousness in its simplest form finds feeling in its simplest form, and consciousness in any specialized form finds feeling in a correspondingly specialized form, 'there', 'ready-made', 'immediately given', as soon as it begins to operate theoretically.

4. 23. Whether this means that feeling already exists 'unconsciously' before that happens is a question I will postpone (cf. 5. 8).

4. 24. Simple feeling is the 'proper object' (4. 19) of simple consciousness: that is, the only thing simple consciousness in its theoretical form does is to apprehend simple feeling, and the only way in which simple feeling is apprehended is by simple consciousness. And similarly with the relation between a specialized form of feeling and the corresponding specialized form of consciousness.

4. 25. A man will describe himself as 'conscious of seeing a red colour', 'conscious of hearing a loud noise', and so forth. This is normal usage of the word 'conscious' or the equivalent word 'aware'.

4. 26. There are abnormal usages: 'I am conscious of a flaw in this argument', 'I am conscious of the dangers by which I am surrounded', where it is not implied that a logical fallacy or a danger is a feeling.

4. 27. These abnormal usages are what grammarians call 'figures of speech', recognized and licensed inaccuracies which deceive no one. These are either '*synecdoche*', mentioning only one part of a thing when you wish to be understood as referring to the whole of it, or '*ellipsis*', saying outright only one part of what you wish to be understood as meaning.

4. 28. It does not matter which they are. It makes no difference whether you call them inaccurate in the same way or in different ways, so long as you recognize them as in-accurate and are not deceived by them.

4.29. People often say 'I am conscious of' or 'I am con-scious that' when they mean 'I know'. 'I am conscious of an impending change in the weather' is a short way of saying 'I am conscious of a peculiar pain in my shoulder: I recognize that as rheumatism; I know by experience that I get rheuma-tism when the weather is going to change', or something like that. What is important is that nobody should suppose the man to be seriously implying that a future change of weather is an object of consciousness.

4.3. Consciousness is the root of knowledge, but it is not knowledge. Knowledge is a highly specialized form of consciousness containing many elements which are not pre-sent in simple consciousness.

4.31. In order to know anything I must not only be conscious, I must reflect on that consciousness. This reflection on simple consciousness I call *second-order con-sciousness*. Until consciousness is made an object of reflection there can be no knowledge, because there is no know-ledge without, first, the performance of certain specialized operations of thought and, secondly, consciousness of these operations as having been actually performed: which is a second-order consciousness.

4.32. Of these specialized operations I will mention three. First, where *x* is the thing I want to get knowledge about, and begin with mere consciousness of, I *make suppositions about x.*

4.33. For example, as I write, I hear a roaring noise. Having fixed my attention on it by an act of second-order consciousness whose practical aspect is what I call *selective attention* or the *focusing* of my consciousness on that noise and away from other things, I consider whether I shall suppose it to be a noise in my head or a noise made by something outside me, and choose the latter.

4.34. Next, I *ask questions about it.* These are logically connected with the suppositions. In this case, having decided to suppose that the noise is made by something outside me, I ask: 'What makes it?'

4.35. Thirdly, I *answer the questions.* In this case,

having compared the noise with what I recollect of other noises I have heard, I answer: 'An aeroplane: to be precise, a Hurricane fighter.'

4. 36. All this time I keep 'my eye' or rather my ear 'on the object'; that is, retain my consciousness of the noise by an act of second-order consciousness; and also watch myself to make sure that I am conducting with sufficient care and in the proper way the various operations of thought which go to convert my simple consciousness of the noise into knowledge about the noise.

4. 37. So much for a rough description of the relation between feeling and consciousness. Now let us turn to some characteristics of feeling itself.

4.4. A feeling is a *here-and-now*. What I feel is something that exists when I feel it and where I feel it. There are place-differences and time-differences within what I feel but they are differences within my here-and-now, not between what is inside it and what is outside it.

4. 41. Just now I see the green of the grass and the blue of the sky; I hear the song of the blackcap and the thrush, the roar of the aeroplane, and the rustle of the leaves in the wind: I feel the warmth of the sun on my head. All these things are parts of one and the same here-and-now.

4. 42. A learned man may assure me that the sun is so many miles away and its light takes so many seconds to reach me; but, although I gladly take his word for it, I note that he agrees with me that it does reach me; and that what I see and feel is the light as it ends the journey, not as it begins it.

4. 43. Within my here-and-now there are place-differences and time-differences (4. 4); it is not a point-instant; it has spatial and temporal bulk; it contains distinctions of *there* and *there*, distinctions of *then* and *then*, positional differences as well as qualitative differences—between colour and sound and between one colour and another, intensity-differences between louder and softer sounds, brighter and dimmer colours, and so forth.

4. 44. The here-and-now has a *focal region* where, generally speaking, both precision and intensity are greatest, and a *penumbral region* where they decrease in every direction until,

in some outer zone of the penumbra, dimness and confusion are such that you no longer know what it contains, nor whether it contains anything at all, nor even whether it is still going on.

4. 45. What the here-and-now does not possess is an *edge*. Its spatial and temporal penumbra fades away into gathering mists.

4. 46. These mists are haunted by ghosts of feelings: colours fancied but not seen; sounds fancied but not heard; and so on. Even in the focal region these ghosts walk in daylight; far more in the outward parts where nothing is clear.

4. 47. Take any feeling and ask whether it is a real feeling or only the ghost of a feeling. I do not know on what principles you can find an answer. A man who was privileged to take part in the late J. S. Haldane's[1] experiments on colour-vision might have been excused if he jumped to the conclusion that there are no real feelings, only ghosts of non-existent feelings.

4. 48. He would at any rate have Hobbes on his side, who wrote that 'Sense in all cases, is nothing els but originall Fancy.'[2]

4. 5. Within a here-and-now, thus equivocally peopled, distinctions are made by the act of *selective attention*. The act is a practical one: you 'turn your attention' one way or another, creating by that act a situation in which your consciousness is concentrated on one object (one feeling) or another. In order that there should be such an act there must already be a here-and-now of diffused feeling and a diffused consciousness of it; unless there were both these there could be no selection, for selection implies that you have before you all the things from which the selection is to be made.

4. 51. The act heightens and sharpens your consciousness of the object on which you focus it, and muffles or blunts your consciousness of the rest. This muffling or blunting your consciousness of the objects away from which you turn your attention is called by psychologists *repressing* those objects.

4. 52. This practical directive or selective act 'makes', as we say, the distinctions between what we attend to and what

[1] See his *Philosophy of a Biologist*, 1935, ch. ii.   [2] *Leviathan*, p. 4.

we attend from or 'repress'. People sometimes talk so vaguely that they speak of making things when they mean finding them ready-made; but not so here.

4. 53. When I attend to a red patch in my here-and-now, my act of attention really makes the edges of that patch. Edges nowhere exist in the here-and-now as actually 'given'. They have to be made by the various acts of attention that cut it up in various ways.

4. 54. When once they are made they are there, and an act of reflection subsequent to the cutting-up will find them there; but only because the act of cutting it up has been done, namely by attention.

4. 55. Suppose attention isolates a red patch in a green field. What was the field to primitive consciousness before the act of isolation took place? Every painter can tell you that, because the training of a painter largely consists in 'recovering the innocence of the eye', learning to re-establish the primitive consciousness in such cases.

4. 56. The visual field which selective attention cuts into a red part and a green part was pervaded all over by a sort of vibratory or 'dazzling' quality of a peculiar kind. Selective attention can analyse this as produced by a juxtaposition of red and green in the same visual field; but that is putting the cart before the horse; it is the juxtaposition of red and green that is produced by attending selectively to the vibratory field.

4. 6. Out of the tangle or confusion of the 'here-and-now' in which feeling-elements of all kinds are given to simple consciousness in their simplest form, overlapping and interpenetrating and mixed up together, selective attention gradually makes a pattern; or rather an infinite variety of different patterns, according as it reduces this confusion to order in an infinite variety of different ways; each way at first imposed by an act of practical consciousness and then affording an object of contemplation to theoretical consciousness.

4. 61. One way is by making what I called (4. 43) *positional* distinctions; distinctions of place or time (if those are really different; a question I shall not go into); and in the first instance distinguishing positional distinctions from *qualitative* distinctions.

4. 62. Then the distinction is made between *sensations* and their *emotional charges*.

4. 63. Then sensations are distinguished into seeings, hearings, smellings, and so forth; and what I see, what I hear, and the rest.

4. 64. And emotional charges into qualitatively distinct emotional types.

4. 65. What has positional differences within it, as well as positional differences between it and something else, is measurable in so far as those differences are reduced to quanta or units.

4. 66. Even positional differences are not always measurable, but only so far as they are reduced to common units. Qualitative differences are never measurable, because they are never reducible to quanta.

4. 67. Thus, all qualities have *intensity*; e.g. the brightness or the saturation of a colour, the loudness or pitch of a sound; and in respect of their intensities they are *comparable* (this colour is brighter, this sound higher, than that) *but never measurable*.

4. 68. Some measurable difference is often associated with a difference of intensity (e.g. a difference in vibrations per second with a difference of pitch), but this does not imply that the difference associated with the measurable difference is itself measurable.

4. 7. Of the statements I have made about feeling, some are true of other things as well.

4. 71. Feeling is a here-and-now immediately given to consciousness; from which it follows that any characteristics that feeling may have are discoverable by simply reflecting on that consciousness, and any characteristics that a particular feeling may have are discoverable by reflection on that particular feeling as given to theoretical consciousness after being distinguished from the here-and-now in which it occurs by the act of selective attention.

4. 72. There is *nothing to argue about*. Have I a headache? Do not weigh pros and cons; do not reason about it; simply consider how you feel. Can I hear the squeak of a bat? Do not reason about it; go out of doors when bats are flying, and listen.

4.73. The fallacy of arguing about questions like this is what I call the FALLACY OF MISPLACED ARGUMENT; which may be defined as the fallacy of arguing about any object immediately given to consciousness.

4.74. Feelings are not the only objects about which it is fallacious to argue. A man convinced by a piece of mathematical reasoning is immediately aware of conviction. Whether he is convinced or not is a question on which to argue would be to indulge the Fallacy of Misplaced Argument. Yet conviction is not a feeling. It is a highly developed form of consciousness.

4.75. Yet that form is an object immediately given to another form of consciousness in which a man reflects upon it. Whatever is thus immediately given is removed from the sphere of argument.

4.76. I have spoken of emotional charges on sensations; but there are also emotional charges on other things.

4.77. Every immediate object, so far as I know, carries one.

4.78. Take any form of consciousness, however highly developed, it always has an immediate object, and the immediate object always carries an emotional charge.

4.79. Again, feeling is not the only thing that has degrees of intensity, or the only thing that carries a charge of pleasure.

4.8. Feeling itself and the various kinds of feelings which have been the subject of discussion in this chapter have all been left undefined. Why is this? It is because feeling is indefinite.

4.81. However strong it may be, it is not clear; additional strength does not make it clearer, it only makes it dazzling.

4.82. This has been already said, emphatically enough, by two great men whom it is an honour to follow: Plato and Leibniz.

4.83. For Plato, sensations and emotions cannot be knowledge because they lack the precision which knowledge must have.

4.84. For Leibniz, feeling in general is *confusa cognitio*.

4.85. I do not accept either view in its entirety. Plato thought that knowledge cannot even rest on a foundation of feeling, because feeling is too vague; knowledge must be the work of pure thought operating all by itself.

4. 86. But what a foundation needs is *strength*, and *strength is what feeling has*.

4. 87. Leibniz thought feeling was confused knowledge, and to clear up the confusion is to purge it of what makes it feeling and leave it knowledge.

4. 88. But feeling is not knowledge at all; it is feeling; and if you could purge it of what makes it feeling there would be no residue.

4. 89. Yet each was right in saying that feeling is confused or indistinct. That is why one should not try to define it or any kind or element of it; but only to give examples and say: 'This is the sort of thing to which the word refers.'

V

THE AMBIGUITY OF FEELING

5. 1. KNOWLEDGE 'rests on a foundation of feeling' (4. 85), and this is possible because feeling, though indefinite (4. 8), is strong (4. 86). This chapter will elaborate those statements.

5. 11. It is a commonplace that thought rests on a bodily foundation. 'Bodily' is used here in its psychological sense; it does not refer to anything in the physico-chemical world or to anything in the physiological world; it refers to sensations and the emotions associated with them. A foundation is not a constituent part of a building, like a wall, a roof, a door, a window; it is an apanage of the building that rests on it; a device for distributing the strains set up by the building in such a way that the ground will take them.

5. 12. All thought has a certain degree of *difficulty*; that is, it sets up *emotional strains* in the mind. In extreme cases these lead to the condition called *insanity*, which is compatible with a high degree of intellectual precision and clarity, but involves sensuous hallucinations and emotional disturbances so violent that the mind is disorganized.

5. 13. The intellect's ability to do its proper work does not depend solely on its horse-power and on the accuracy with which it is made and assembled. It depends also on the engine's being so solidly bolted down on so strong a foundation that it cannot shake itself to pieces.

5. 14. The solidity or robustness of a man's sensuous emotional nature, whereby it affords a sane basis for his thinking, consists in two kinds of strength in his feelings, which I will call compression-strength and tensile strength. Compression-strength in feeling is *vividness*: tensile strength is *tenacity*.

5. 15. Vividness in a colour is brightness, which has several different forms: it may be highness of key or intensity of illumination, it may be purity or freedom from admixture of different colours, it may be intensity of saturation. Vividness in a musical note may be loudness, or it may be a matter of pitch (shrillness is one form of it), or it may be a matter of quality; that is of the way in which harmonics are combined with their fundamental. Vividness in toothache is the well-known quality that distinguishes a really bad toothache from a milder one.

5. 16. Let these suffice for examples. An intelligent reader will see what I mean and think for himself how vividness presents itself (always in a variety of alternative forms) in other feelings. An unintelligent reader, forgetting (or never having understood) my warning in 4. 8, will complain that, vividness never having been defined, it is my fault that he does not know what I mean.

5. 17. Tenacity is the quality in a feeling which does not so much make it hard to forget and easy to remember (for no feeling can be remembered, 5. 54), as make it linger in the mind, be slow to vanish, and be easily revived when occasion permits. This is not the same as vividness; many feelings which are notably vivid are notably brittle. Nor is it the same as the power of memory, which is an activity of thought presupposing in its objects (which are never feelings) a certain degree of tenacity.

5. 18. These are the only characteristics of feeling which are indispensable to its function as the foundation of thought.

5. 19. There is a saying, *nihil est in intellectu nisi quod prius fuerit in sensu*. If this were true, the precision or definiteness which is characteristic of thought would already be characteristic of feeling. Many people try to persuade themselves that it is; but they are mistaken. They regard feeling as a constituent of knowledge; but it is only an apanage of knowledge: an indispensable apanage, but an apanage and no more.

5. 2. *Are there objects of feeling or not?* I do not know. Nobody knows. Some have said there are, some have said there are not. As the question is unanswerable on *positive* grounds I answer it on *methodological* grounds (5. 39).

5. 21. That there are objects of feeling was asserted by Locke. It was a scholastic doctrine which Descartes had denied; Locke gives no reason for reasserting it, and perhaps it was just a bit of youthful scholasticism which had somehow escaped his bonfire.

5. 22. Since Locke's time it has been cherished, I suppose

out of patriotic fervour, by English, Scotch, Irish, and American writers: not one of them, so far as I know, offering to defend it against its Cartesian rival; merely taking it for granted.

5.23. The doctrine is this. *Seeing* is an activity which has a proper object, namely *colours*. *Hearing* has a proper object, namely *sounds*. As a general name these objects may be called *sense-data* or *sensa*.

5.24. They are immediate or first-order objects to sensation, and hence second-order objects to simple consciousness, consciousness in its most primitive form, whose immediate or first-order object is the activity of sensation itself.

5.25. Even if feeling has no objects this may stand as an explanation of the terms first-order object, second-order object, which I shall use again.

5.26. Let a man have a certain form of consciousness, C_1 (cf. 1.73). To that form of consciousness let x, y, z, be immediate objects. Let him call into being in himself another form of consciousness, C_2, the consciousness of C_1. Then to C_2 (i.e. to him in that form of consciousness) C_1 is what I call *first-order object* and x, y, z *second-order objects*.

5.27. It is commonly believed (whether correctly or not I do not know; because I do not know whether by the word *percipere* Berkeley meant *seeing, hearing, and so forth*, as most of his readers and interpreters suppose, or *consciousness of seeing, hearing, and so forth*, as a comparison of his terminology with that of the Cartesians from whom he was borrowing would suggest) that Berkeley found this doctrine implicit in Locke and having made it explicit, proceeded to ask a question arising out of it: namely (as people say nowadays) 'what is the status of objects of sense-perception?'

5.28. Berkeley answered: 'their *esse* is *percipi*'; meaning, if the first interpretation mentioned above is right, that the being of a colour is its being seen, the being of a sound is its being heard, and so forth.

5.29. The things whose *esse* is *percipi* are in his language 'ideas', which are non-mental things, not constituents of mind like the activities of seeing or hearing, but apanages of mind and in particular inert or passive things, products of these activities.

5.3. If there are such things (which neither of them seriously asked, merely assuming the affirmative answer) Locke argued not without solid grounds that some of them, and Berkeley that all of them, must be products of the activity (whether a sensuous activity or an activity of consciousness) whose objects they were.

5.31. Among others Professor G. E. Moore, beginning from the same assumption, has of late expressed the opposite opinion, namely that any such object 'is precisely what it would be if we were not aware [of it]' ('The Refutation of Idealism', reprinted in *Philosophical Studies*, 1922, p. 29).

5.32. Neither Moore nor any of the numerous contemporaries who hold the same opinion give reasons for it; they praise it, rather, as derived from a faculty in man called 'common sense' towards which they inculcate an attitude of submission.

5.33 The notion of 'common sense' is not always used in an obscurantist spirit, and not always (though deplorably often) for the rehabilitation of long-exploded errors; but the admission of such a faculty always opens the door to scientific persecution (1. 57), and if nothing slips through no thanks are due to those who opened it.

5.34. The Cartesian answer to the question: 'Are there objects of feeling or not?' (5. 2) was negative. This does not mean that Descartes was such a lover of paradox as to deny that when I raise my eyes above the table at which I am writing I see a blue colour. What it means is that Descartes denied the blue colour to be the object of a transitive verb *to see*, as a dog may be the object of a transitive verb to kick.

5.35. It means that for Descartes the grammar of the sentence 'I see a blue colour' is not like the grammar of 'I kick a bad dog' but like the grammar of 'I feel a transient melancholy' or 'I go a fast walk'. The colour, the melancholy, the walk, are not objects of an action, they are *modes* of an action; their names have an *adverbial* function in the sentences in which they occur.

5.36. If the Cartesian answer is right, the question which Berkeley answered in one way ('sensa are mind-dependent') and Moore, like so many others in the present century, in the opposite way ('sensa are not mind-dependent') is a nonsense question: a question to which no possible answer is right because it arises logically from an assumption that is not made.

5. 37. On the Cartesian view there is feeling; feeling is at once sensuous and emotional; in both capacities it has modes; in neither case are these modes objects to it, though in both cases they are objects to the consciousness of it; a blue colour is a feeling of which I am conscious exactly as a slight exhilaration is a feeling of which I am conscious; in neither case is there any object of feeling; in neither case, therefore, is there anything of which it is other than idiotic to ask whether its *esse* is *percipi* or not.

5. 38. Either view fits the facts. Neither is inherently nonsensical. It is true that the adoption of the Lockian view in this country has led to an awkward situation: If there are sensa, is their *esse percipi* or not? For a long time people accepted Berkeley's reasons for saying 'yes', now they are tending to accept an unreasoned 'no'; it seems rather like the Bigendians and the Littlendians. If we accepted the Cartesian view, the controversy would be at an end; but do not fancy that everyone would be pleased; everyone whose professional honour, pride, or emoluments were concerned in there being such a controversy would be furious.

5. 39. *Entia non sunt multiplicanda* (runs Occam's Razor) *praeter necessitatem*. Following this rule I answer the question: 'Are there objects of feeling or not?' by what I call a *methodological negative*. Feeling must on any view have modes; even Professor Moore allows sensation the single uniformly sustained mode he calls 'transparency', which is (of course) infinitely differentiated into different cases of transparency by the variety of the occasions on which it is exhibited and therefore, for the purposes of Occam's Razor, must be regarded not as one entity but as an infinity of entities. The question is whether a theory of feeling needs objects as well as modes. The Lockian theory does; the Cartesian does not. By Occam's Razor the Cartesian theory is preferable.

5. 4. *Is feeling active or passive?* Once more I do not know, and here I cannot give even a methodological answer. Between these alternatives feeling, to quote Plato (*Republic*, 479 E), 'wanders about' without coming to a decision.

5. 41. Locke, for example, says that ideas of sensation are 'caused in the mind' by the operation of 'external causes', that is, by physical things acting on our sense-organs 'manifestly *by Impulse*, the only way we can conceive Bodies operate in' (*Essay*, II. viii).

5. 42. Having thus formulated a causal theory of sensation, Locke goes on to apologize for doing so. 'I have in what has just gone before engaged in physical Enquiries a little farther than perhaps I intended.' He originally proposed 'to consider the discerning Faculties of a Man, as they are employ'd about the Objects they have to do with' (I. i, § 2) and expressly renounces physical inquiries, recognizing that by indulging what I call the Fallacy of Swapping Horses he could in no way advance his purpose.

5. 43. The Fallacy of Misplaced Argument (4. 73) must also be avoided here. The question whether when I feel I am doing something or having something done to me is a question that cannot be settled by appeal to argument any more than it can be settled by considerations drawn from the natural sciences as Locke tried to settle it.

5. 44. The only way of settling it is by appeal to reflection upon the immediate, unphilosophical, unargumentative consciousness of feeling. The question is: 'How does feeling present itself to a man immediately conscious of it? As something he does or as something done to him?'

5. 45. The immediate consciousness of feeling will not answer this question; immediate consciousness of a thing never answers questions about it; questions can be answered only when they have been asked, and questions about a thing are asked only at a higher level of reflection upon it; but immediate consciousness alone can 'provide' the answer (1. 77).

5. 46. The only legitimate procedure, then, is to keep your eye fixed on feeling as immediately present to the consciousness of feeling; don't allow yourself to be trapped into argument, or into physical, chemical, or physiological considerations; and then ask: 'Is feeling something I do or something I undergo?'

5. 47. When I ask myself this I get no answer. I can only say that feeling is more like being active than some experiences I could mention which are definitely experiences of being passive; but more like being passive than some which are definitely experiences of being active. I could easily be bounced or cajoled or argued into admitting that it was active, or that it was passive, by a man who was determined to make me admit such a doctrine, but when I sat down in a cool hour I should regret it.

5.48. If I stuck to being honest and to answering the question on the facts as I found them in actual consciousness I should say: 'I am aware of seeing the sky blue, and feeling the sunshine warm. I am not aware of feeling them actively as opposed to passively or passively as opposed to actively.'

5.49. I might become a little pompous and add: 'Nor is it possible I should; for the distinction between activity and passivity involves the distinction between oneself and what is not oneself, and this distinction, as I shall explain later on (chapter viii), is first made at a far more highly developed stage of mental development than that which we are now exploring.' But I should be sorry for thus pandering to your weakness. A man who will not recognize that a thing is so until he knows why it is so is a man who will never come to any good.

5.5. Another ambiguity about feelings is that they are *evanescent*. They are things that begin to perish as soon as they begin to exist. They may be described as one of his princes, we are told, described the life of man to King Edwin: 'like the swift flight of a sparrow through the hall wherein you sit at supper with your commanders and ministers, a good fire in the midst, while storms of rain and snow rage abroad; the sparrow, flying in at one door and out at once from the other, vanishes from your eyes into the dark winter night from which it came. So the life of man appears for a short space, but what went before, and what is to come after, we know not at all' (Bede, *Hist. Eccl.* II. xiii).

5.51. The tenacity of a feeling (5.17) may stave off the time of its vanishing, as the strength of a man may stave off the hour of his death; but the time is only postponed, not cancelled.

5.52. The evanescence of feeling is recognized both by the Lockian theory (where the here-and-now is multiplied into two, one of feeling and one of consciousness) and the Cartesian. On either theory the only feeling actually present to you is what you now feel.

5.53. By reflecting upon this and asking questions about it you may for a time be able to 'evoke' (see below), not the feeling itself (that is dead long before questions about it can be asked) but some ghost or caricature or abstract of it; but only for a time; when the feeling's tenacity is exhausted this can no longer be done.

5.54. It follows that *feelings cannot be remembered*. People who think they remember a feeling are deceived, never having been careful to make the distinction, by the fact that *a proposition about a feeling can be remembered*. You cannot remember the terrible thirst you once endured; but you can remember that you were terribly thirsty.

5.55. It follows, too, that *there is no generalizing about feelings*; that is, no framing universal propositions about them and assuring oneself that these are true, or (alternatively) omitting to do so because one is too lazy. People who think this is possible are deceived, never having been careful to make the distinction, by the fact that *to think inductively about feelings is quite possible*.

5.56. To think inductively is to assume, because this x has (or some x's have) a certain characteristic, that other x's have or would have the same characteristic. Such an assumption is not a proposition; it is not true or false; it is likely or unlikely (more or less likely), and to make it is more or less reasonable; it is (as some inductive logicians have confessed) a 'leap in the dark', a 'step from the known to the unknown', and leaps in the dark or steps into the unknown are not divisible into true and false, they are divisible into wise and rash, sensible and foolish, or the like. What are called 'inductive methods' are precautions for reducing the risk to one that a sensible man will take.

5.57. And though it is quite easy to think inductively about feelings (to think 'I shall always love this woman as I love her now, and indeed I always did; and so, no doubt, does everybody else'), it is impossible to do it sensibly; for that, one has to think not about feelings but about propositions about feelings.

5. 6. Another ambiguity about feelings is a *numerical ambiguity*. No feeling is ever a single feeling, none is a complex consisting of a determinate number of feelings. Nor is it ever a whole; for a whole would have edges and a feeling has none.

5. 61. Feeling as we are actually conscious of it is a *field*, a here-and-now extended in space and time (4. 43), having a focal region and a penumbral region (4. 44), but no edge.

5. 62. Sensations with their emotional charges (whether one emotional charge goes to one sensation or to one complex of sensations is a nonsense question of the type to which I am now objecting) interpenetrate all over this field.

5. 63. How selective attention cuts up such a field into distinct feelings (sensations distinct from emotions, visual sensations distinct from auditory sensations, red patches distinct from green patches, and so on *ad infinitum*) I have already said (4. 5 seqq.).

5. 64. I will repeat it only so far as to say that anybody who supposes 'this red patch' to be immediately given in or by sensation to consciousness has overlooked the numerical ambiguity of feelings.

5. 65. The red is actually given in feeling to consciousness as a quality transfusing all the rest of the same field; only a man who indulges in the practice of selective attention segregates it into a patch.

5. 66. I have just shown that feeling is ambiguous with regard to the Kantian 'categories' of unity, plurality, and totality, the 'categories of quantity'. It would be easy to show that it is equally ambiguous with regard to the 'categories of relation' (substance and attribute, cause and effect, interaction) and those 'of modality' (actuality, possibility, necessity).

5. 67. I will leave the reader to do this, if he cares to have it done, for himself, and pass to the 'categories of quality'. For he may think that qualitatively at least a feeling must be determinate: if it is a colour, for example, it must be a definite colour, red and not blue, and a particular shade of red at that. This is quite wrong.

5. 7. The qualitative indeterminacy of feelings is not the same as the indeterminacy of the language by which we mention them. No one, I suppose, thinks that by 'red' we mean anything determinate; everyone who has thought at all must recognize that it is only a way of referring to any colour that falls between orange and purple and brown, the limits being left quite vague. It costs us nothing to say 'We won't argue about whether *this* and *this* and *this* are red or not; anyhow *that* is.'

5. 71. The point is not that our names for colours and so on are vague, but that *the colours themselves as we actually see them are vague*; and so with sounds, smells, emotions, &c. We never see anything exactly any colour. However carefully we look at a colour it remains ambiguous. Indeed, looking at it carefully creates a new ambiguity; for the eye becomes fatigued and a complementary after-image interposes itself between the eye and the colour at which one is looking, so that the mere looking at a colour dims it.

5. 72. But this ambiguity has limits. The colour may be indeterminate, but it falls between points on a colour-scale. We can always fix these limits as closely as we need; a painter, for example, fixes them far more closely than another man; but the ambiguity is only restricted, it can never be removed.

5. 73. And not only in the case of sensations, but of emotions. This is how Robert Louis Stevenson apologizes for the crudity of his account of a young girl's emotions when she begins to fall in love. 'It is to be understood that I have been painting chaos and describing the inarticulate. Every lineament that appears is too precise, almost every word too strong. Take a finger-post in the mountains on a day of rolling mists; I have but copied the names that appear on the pointers, the names of definite and famous cities far distant, and now perhaps basking in sunshine; but Christina remained all these hours, as it were, at the foot of the post itself, and enveloped in mutable and blinding wreaths of haze.'[1]

5. 8. I will end this brief list of ambiguities with what, frankly, I consider a typical case, but what for civility's sake (5. 93) I will call a peculiarly difficult one, namely *whether feelings can be unconscious*.

5. 81. In this discussion the word 'unconscious' is always

----

[1] *Weir of Hermiston*, ch. vi.

used passively (= that of which something else is not conscious), not actively (= that which is not conscious of other things).

5. 82. I have called feeling the proper object of consciousness (4. 19). If all a man can find out about his feelings is derived from his consciousness of them, as I have said, no man can know (and *a fortiori* no other can know about him) that he has feelings of which he is unconscious.

5. 83. It seems to follow that no feelings can be unconscious. Psychologists, however, have long taken the opposite view. That does not settle the question, because psychologists are no more infallible than other men; if even the greatest of all physicists, Newton, believed in things called 'forces' which now every physicist allows to be 'occult entities', scientifically inadmissible, and only believed in by Newton because he made a blunder in method, it is conceivable that psychologists have been wrong to believe in things called 'unconscious feelings'.

5. 84. The question, however, is not about possibilities but about facts. What have psychologists actually said about unconscious feelings?

5. 85. In nineteenth-century psychology the term was freely used for feelings so lacking in strength that they 'lay below the threshold of consciousness' and the person who felt them was unaware of them. These were occult entities, and whatever excuse people had for talking about them, the fact remains that they were talking nonsense.

5. 86. In 1912 Freud dropped that sense of the word and put forward a new one. His practical work had brought vividly to his notice the importance of *repression*, the negative side of attention. Whenever attention is directed towards some element or complex of elements E_1 in a field of feeling it is directed away from some other element or complex of elements E_2 in the same field.

5. 87. This withdrawal of attention from E_2 Freud called the *repression* of E_2, which in consequence, to quote his own words 'seems to be cut off from consciousness'. He insists that it is not really cut off from consciousness; and rightly, because I could not repress a thing unless I were conscious of it.

5. 88. The Freudian patient in post-hypnotic suggestion does not even, by repressing E_2, obliterate all the consciousness of it which he began by having. He is conscious of his repressed feelings as something, he knows not what, that urges him to do something. The strength of E_2 is thus not repressed at all, though its other qualities are. As Freud says, 'We learn by the analysis of neurotic phenomena that a latent or unconscious idea is not necessarily a weak one': in other words, that its strength is by no means 'latent or unconscious', even if everything else about it may be so described.

5. 89. If, in spite of this rather quaint usage of words, we acquiesce in Freud's decision to mean 'repressed' by 'unconscious', the methodological grounds (5. 82) for denying that there can be unconscious feelings disappear and we can agree with Freud that there is valid experimental reason for believing in them, which there can be just because 'unconscious' no longer means what it says.

5. 9. In 1923 Freud stated a new position. 'We obtain our concept of the unconscious from the theory of repression. . . . We see, however, that we have two kinds of unconscious—that which is latent but capable of becoming conscious [the so-called *Preconscious*] and that which is repressed.' The Preconscious is 'only unconscious in the descriptive, and not in the dynamic sense'.

5. 91. This again is fully in agreement with the view of mind I am here expounding. Forms of consciousness are the only constituents of mind (4. 18). But no man is conscious of any given form of consciousness, even though it is operating in him, until he 'reflects' on it or 'calls into being in himself another form of consciousness, C_2, the consciousness of C_1' (1. 73) the form of consciousness with which we started.

5. 92. Any form of consciousness, practical or theoretical, call it C_x, exists in what Freud calls a preconscious condition unless and until it has been reflected upon by the operation of a form C_{x+1}.

5. 93. I called this question peculiarly difficult (5. 8) out of deference to Freud because he says that a person who thinks of mind as constituted solely by forms of consciousness should find it so. Why he says this I do not know. That is how I think of mind myself, and I find no difficulty.

5.94. My quotations from Freud's works are from the 1912 articles on 'the unconscious' in *Gesammelte Schriften*, v. 433–42 and from *das Ich und das Es* (ibid. vi). For the reader's convenience I have quoted only passages which appear in John Rickman's *General Selection from the Works of Sigmund Freud*, and in the words in which they are there given.

VI

LANGUAGE

6. 1. By 'language' I mean not only speech, that is, language consisting of movements in the mouth-cavity producing sounds; I mean that chiefly, because that is the most highly developed kind of language men possess: but I also mean any system of bodily movements, not necessarily vocal, whereby the men who make them *mean* or *signify* anything.

6. 11. A language is an abstraction from *discourse*, which is the activity by which a man means anything; a language is the system adopted, the means employed, the rules followed, in this activity.

6. 12. Discourse is continuous; even the 'rests' or 'pauses' of silence, immobility, or the like which punctuate it are significant parts of it, not interruptions of it. But selective attention breaks it up into *words*; vocal words if it is a discourse in speech, gesture-words if in gesture, and so on.

6. 13. Words are not units out of which discourse is built up like a mosaic, any more than colour-patches (5. 64) are units out of which a visual field is built up like a mosaic.

6. 14. Discourse begins by being a continuous activity, and is only afterwards dissected into parts, just as a visual field begins by being a continuous feeling and is only afterwards dissected into colour-patches; in each case the dissection is done by the same agency, viz. an activity of selective attention.

6. 15. It is a lexicographer's business to *define words*: that is, to determine the meaning which a given word bears whenever it is used or (more often) the various meanings some one of which it bears whenever it is used.

6. 16. He does this by studying occasions on which it is used correctly; hence the definitions he gives rest on correct usage as already existing; they cannot be guides to correct usage except for persons ignorant of the language in question.

6. 17. The phonetic or other *vehicle* of discourse (the flow of sounds, gestures, &c.) is 'bodily' (6. 1); but in what sense? Not the physical or chemical or physiological sense (chapter iii). The vehicle of discourse is a succession of feelings, or sensations with their emotional charges, 'produced' by the activity of speech or the like.

6. 18. The sensuous vehicle of discourse, sound or the like, is not discourse. To discourse is to *mean something* by the sounds (or what not) you make. A language is not a system of sounds or the like; it is a system of sounds or the like as having meanings. A word is not a sound or group of sounds (the question 'How does a word get its meaning?' or 'Why did people decide that this word was appropriate for this meaning?' is nonsense); it is a sound or group of sounds having its own meaning, namely what a person using that word means by making that sound.

6. 19. Discourse is thus two things at once. It is the activity of *meaning something* (*a*) *by something else* (*b*), where meaning *a* is an act of theoretical consciousness, and *b* is a practical activity, the production in oneself or others of a flow of sounds or the like which serve you as the vehicle of that meaning.

6. 2. Feeling (4. 19) in its simplest form is 'the proper object of consciousness in its simplest form, what there is consciousness of'; consciousness (4. 22) finds feeling 'there', 'ready-made', 'immediately given' to it, as soon as it begins to operate theoretically.

6. 21. But what is the *modus operandi* of this finding? If feeling is 'given' to consciousness, what is the procedure by which consciousness receives the gift? How does a man make himself conscious of his feelings?

6. 22. By talking about them, whether in speech or in any other language.

6. 23. For example, a man is cold. He may be cold 'preconsciously' (5. 9); not that he represses the feeling of cold, but just that he 'hasn't noticed it'.

6. 24. Take the case when, after being in this condition, he comes to notice it. Is there anything he does, any practical activity of his own, that marks or brings about the change?

6. 25. Certainly there is. He *names the feeling*. Perhaps he uses the language of speech and says 'cold'. Perhaps he uses the language of gesture and gives an expressive shiver. This shiver is the name in gesture-language of the same feeling whose name in English is 'cold'.

6. 26. To name the feeling awakens his consciousness of the feeling. There is a tendency to put the cart before the horse and fancy that consciousness of the feeling comes first and finding a name for it afterwards; but that is a mistake due to false analogy with cases that are essentially different, e.g. when an explorer sees an unrecorded mountain and then finds a name for it, or when you or I, out for a walk, see a little pink flower and wonder what its name is.

6. 27. Rid yourself of these misleading analogies, fix your mind on the point at issue, and you will see that the practical act of naming your feeling is what sets you off being conscious of it.

6. 28. Until you name it, the feeling is preconscious. When you name it, it becomes conscious. This does not mean that the act of naming it becomes conscious; it does not, either as an act of your own or even merely as the sound of your voice or the like. It remains preconscious until you reflect upon it.

6. 29. This is the difference between linguistic activity in general and that reflective, critical form of it which is called 'literature' or 'poetry' or in general 'art'. The artist or poet, like other men, achieves consciousness of his feelings only so far as he finds words for them; but he is conscious not only of the feelings but of the linguistic activity, and works at performing this activity as well as he can.

6. 3. 'If a man becomes conscious of a feeling only through finding a name for it, is not that a way of saying that his consciousness of the feeling is not immediate, as you said (4. 22), but mediated through language?'

6. 31. The consciousness of B is mediate if you can only be conscious of B as an abstraction from something else, A, of which you are conscious.

6. 32. Let A be something of which you are immediately conscious; then A is a first-order object and B, the abstraction from it, a second-order object (5. 25), and the consciousness of B is mediated through the consciousness of A.

6. 33. This is only one case. B may be a third-order

object and A the second-order object from which it is an abstraction; and so on.

6. 34. In general, to say that the consciousness of B is mediated through the consciousness of A is to say that A is an object of the nth order and B an object of the $(n+1)$th order abstracted from it.

6. 35. But the feeling is not an abstraction from the name of the feeling.

6. 36. The man who names his feeling thereby becomes immediately conscious of it; he is not conscious of his name for it until he reflects on the act of naming it, and he proceeds to think of the name he has uttered in abstraction from that act.

6. 4. It has long been known that language is an indispensable factor in social life, the only way in which knowledge can be communicated from one man to another. But it was long believed that within the precincts of the individual mind the processes of thought could go on without language coming into operation.

6. 41. It would be hard to find an advocate for that belief to-day. It is a commonplace with us that language is not a device whereby knowledge already existing in one man's mind is communicated to another's, but an activity prior to knowledge itself, without which knowledge could never come into existence.

6. 42. To discover this truth was one of the greatest achievements of Hobbes. After observing that 'the Invention of Printing, though ingenious, compared with the invention of Letters, is no great matter', whereas letters were 'a profitable Invention for continuing the memory of time past, and the conjunction of mankind, dispersed into so many and distant regions of the Earth', Hobbes goes on thus:

6. 43. 'But the noblest and most profitable invention of all other, was that of SPEECH, consisting of *Names* or *Appellations*, and their Connexion; whereby men register their thoughts; recall them when they are past; and also declare them to one another for mutuall utility and conversation; without which, there had been amongst men, neither Common-wealth, nor Society, nor Contract, nor Peace, no more than amongst Lyons, Bears, and Wolves.'[1]

[1] *Leviathan*, p. 12.

6. 44. So far Hobbes is describing language as hardly more than a factor in social life. But let us skip a little and continue. 'The generall use of Speech, is to transferre our Mental Discourse, into Verbal; or the Trayne of our Thoughts, into a Trayne of words; and that for two commodities; whereof one is, the Registring of the Consequences of our thoughts . . .'[1] as if there could be any 'mental discourse' without at least the inward use of language when a man talks to himself; or as if a train of thoughts could proceed at all, unexpressed in a train of words.

6. 45. But a page or two later Hobbes begins to unmask his heavy guns. Some kinds of mental discourse, he tells us, among them those which go to the making of science, cannot proceed at all except as 'registered' in a train of words.

6. 46. 'But the use of words in registring our thoughts, is in nothing so evident as in Numbring. A naturall foole that could never learn by heart the order of numerall words, as *one*, *two*, and *three*, may observe every stroak of the Clock, and nod to it, or say one, one, one; but can never know what houre it. strikes. . . . So that without words, there is no possibility of reckoning of Numbers; much lesse of Magnitudes, of Swiftnesse, of Force, and other things, the reckonings whereof are necessary to the being, or well-being of man-kind.'[2]

6. 47. Since mathematics, for Hobbes as for Descartes, is the basis and type of all science; and since the word 'science', for Hobbes as for Descartes, refers not to knowledge of the natural world alone but to knowledge of any kind so long as it is knowledge not of isolated 'facts' but 'of the Consequence of one Affirmation to another'; his doctrine is clear. From being an indispensable means to the diffusion of knowledge, language has become the precondition and foundation of knowledge, so far as knowledge is scientific.

6. 5. Notice has been taken of Hobbes's innovation in the theory of language, a notice more significant for being unsympathetic, by an accomplished scholar, the late W. G. Pogson Smith, in his essay on 'The Philosophy of Hobbes', prefixed posthumously to the Oxford type-facsimile reprint of the *Leviathan* (1909).

[1] *Leviathan*, pp. 12–13.　　　　[2] Ibid., p. 14.

6. 51. 'Hobbes emphatically asserts that it is . . . reason . . . which marks men off from the brutes. . . . And yet if we look more narrowly we shall find that this marvellous endowment of man is really the child of language. . . .

6. 52. 'This bold paradox is a masterpiece of tactics. Speech is ushered in with the fanfaronade, and lo! reason is discovered clinging to her train. Instinct says, reason begets speech: paradox inverts, speech begets reason.

6. 53. 'Man acquires speech because he is reasonable [is opposed by] man becomes capable of reason because he has *invented* speech. A wonderful *hysteron proteron*.'[1]

6. 54. If a paradox means something unexpected, paradox it is; one that deserves to be remembered beside the paradox of Copernicus that the earth goes round the sun; the paradox of Newton that what keeps the planets in their orbits is the same as what makes an apple fall to the earth; or the paradox of Darwin that animal and vegetable species are not a repertory of types fixed for ever, but change as the course of the world's life unfolds itself.

6. 55. If an *hysteron proteron* means a decree that what was last shall be first, and the first last, *hysteron proteron* it is; but to call it so is not a reproach.

6. 56. 'Instinct' may say if it likes that you must first be conscious of a feeling before you can fit it with a name; experience teaches that this is a vulgar error (6. 26). The experiment, I confess, is not easy to make, because normally the act of naming is preconsciously done (6. 28). When I succeed in reflecting on it I find that Hobbes was right.

6. 57. It is true, of course, and Mr. Smith may have been confused by it, that man begins to speak like a rational being only when he is one; and if you think that the word 'language' ought to be used only of rational language, you will find Hobbes's doctrine surprising. What Mr. Smith failed to consider was that language is not always reasonable.

6. 58. Language in its simplest form is the language of consciousness in its simplest form; the mere 'register' of feelings, as wild and mad as those feelings themselves; irrational, unorganized, unplanned, unconscious. As consciousness develops, language develops with it. When

[1] Op. cit., p. xx.

consciousness becomes conceptual thought (7. 21), language develops abstract terms.

6.59. When consciousness becomes propositional thought language develops the indicative sentence as the standard verbal form in which to state the proposition. When consciousness becomes reason (14. 1) language becomes demonstrative discourse wherein sentences are so linked together as to state verbally 'the Consequence of one Affirmation to another'.

VII

APPETITE

7. 1. THERE are things which often receive the name of feeling by synecdoche or ellipsis (4. 27), though in fact they are not feelings at all but complex things consisting of feelings and ghosts of feelings (cf. 7. 37) combined into a certain pattern by the practical work of consciousness.

7. 11. Such a thing is *hunger*. Some of the feeling-elements which go to make up one typical case of hunger have been already described (3. 32).

7. 12. Hunger is often called a feeling or a group of feelings; the expressions are synonymous because of the numerical ambiguity of feeling (5. 6), but it is properly not a feeling but an *appetite*.

7. 13. Feeling as given is always contained within the impalpable but inviolable limits of its own here-and-now (4. 4); so that, if hunger were a feeling, a hungry man could think of nothing that is not contained in the same here-and-now as his hunger.

7. 14. But actually a hungry man thinks of two different feeling-states, compares them to the disadvantage of the one and the advantage of the other, and struggles to escape the one and realize the other.

7. 15. The one is a feeling-state that involves emptiness; the other a feeling-state that involves repletion.

7. 16. The first is his here-and-now, and this contains all the feelings of which he is conscious as given; the second I shall call a *there-and-then*, containing (to speak paradoxically) feelings that are not 'given' to him at all.

7. 17. The expression 'there-and-then' does not necessarily refer to any special place and any special time; merely to a place that is not here, and a time that is not now.

7. 18. The paradox (7. 16) is not merely verbal. It serves to express a real problem about appetite, in fact the problem of appetite. How can a man compare given feelings with ungiven feelings, and how can he struggle to escape the one and realize the other?

7. 19. If he remained at the stage of feeling and con-

sciousness of feeling, he could not. If mental development
went no farther than that, there would be no appetite. But
there is appetite; we are immediately conscious of it, and
a sensible man will not allow himself to be bounced out of his
belief in it by the fact that it is difficult to explain. Any
argument directed to so bounce him, he knows, involves the
Fallacy of Misplaced Argument.

7.2. A man emerges from the state of feeling and consciousness of feeling in the same way in which he enters that
state: by an act of practical consciousness; only of course a
different act.

7.21. In this case the act is one of *conceptual thinking*.

7.22. 'But that is an act of theoretical thinking!' No.
Concepts or abstractions are not things lying about in the
world, ready-made, like blackberries, for the sedulous
micher to find; they are things that man makes (and perhaps
not man alone, but man alone is what we are studying) by an
act of practical thinking; and if he then finds them ready-
made it is because that act has made them.

7.23. We have already met with conceptual thinking
under the name of *selective attention* (4. 5).

7.24. A man is conscious (because he has found language
of some kind by which to 'mean' it: necessarily a very primitive, illogical, ejaculatory sort of language) of a confused
mass of feeling. That is the first stage of mental life. Then
he 'attends to' some element or group of elements in this
mass of feeling. That is the second stage of mental life.

7.25. It is useless to ask why he takes this or any other
of the steps which initiate the various stages of mental
development.

7.26. If 'Why?' means: 'With what intention?' the
answer is that these steps are not intentional. Intention
begins to exist only when the development of mind has
brought it to choice (chapter xiii). Until then mind has
been developing (so to speak) in its sleep.

7.27. If 'Why?' means: 'Guided by what law of development or progress?'

7.28. There are no laws of development or progress.
Occasions arise when certain kinds of progress, certain steps
in development, are possible for a mind.

7. 29. They are never necessary. Whether the mind takes the step that is possible for it depends entirely on the mind's practical energy.

7. 3. The act of attending is not merely a doing something to yourself, focusing your consciousness on a certain part of the field and repressing (4. 51) the rest; it is also a doing something to the object: circumscribing it, drawing a line between it and the rest of the field.

7. 31. For example if the field is a visual field this act converts the part 'attended to' into a patch of colour. It is fashionable to describe colour-patches as if they were given in sensation and not (as they really are) made by selective attention; but that is only because those who so describe them have penetrated in reflection no further than the level at which these things are found ready-made, stopping short of the deeper level at which the work of making them is done, and still further short of the level at which it has not begun.

7. 32. With the delimiting of the patch or other *selection* (a word by which I mean either an act of selecting or, as here, what is selected; a double usage of a single word very common in English and all other European languages from Latin onwards, and perplexing only to a person who knows none of these languages) goes the act of *evocative thinking*: the act of arousing in yourself by the work of thought feelings you do not find as 'given' in yourself.

7. 33. These I call *evocations*; they form a *context* inseparable from any selection and are connected with it by logical relations, logic being the science which studies the structure of concepts (7. 39) or, which is the same thing, the relations between them.

7. 34. Any logical relation may preside over the birth, from a given selection, of an evocation forming part of its context; and to compile a list of logical relations, if it were possible (as it is not, though Germans have thought it so), is a business foreign to my purpose.

7. 35. I will mention one as a sample: that of contrast. Whenever a selection has a certain character, its context includes evocations having variously contrasting characters.

7. 36. A selection coloured in a certain way, for example, is accompanied by evocations contrasting in colour; what

contrasts with what being determined by an act known as *comparison*.

7.37. Evocations are feelings felt but not given; they are taken without being given; produced in a man by the act of evocative thinking. This gives them a ghost-like quality; the distinction hinted at above, between feelings and ghosts of feelings, is in fact the distinction between given feelings and evoked feelings.

7.38. As not given but abstracted from the given, a selection is a product of practical consciousness; in cutting it off from the rest of the datum you have not only circumscribed it (7.3)—in your mind of course, not with a pencil; everything we are discussing goes on in your mind—you have also clarified it; in the above case (7.33) you have eliminated the green out of what was given as a red-green colour-contrast, and selected the red for attention. What you attend to is pure red, and this pure red is nothing found, it is something made: made by the practical act of attention, and afterwards found ready-made by reflection on the consequences of that act.

7.39. A selection together with its context of evocations is a *concept* (*notion*) or a number of them; it does not matter whether the relation between, for example, good and bad is called a relation between one concept and its opposite or a relation between contrasting elements in a single concept.

7.4. We are now ready to explain what appetite is. By selective attention a man isolates in his present state of feeling a group of feelings consisting of a gnawing sensation at the stomach, a general organic sensation of weakness and lassitude, and so on (3.32), the whole carrying an unpleasant emotional charge.

7.41. These form a selection from his here-and-now, which as a product of selective attention is a concept or part of a concept and requires a context provided by evocation.

7.42. This must be a there-and-then of feelings comparable with those of the selection and contrasting with them as pleasant with unpleasant.

7.43. The man is attracted away from the here-and-now towards the there-and-then not by pleasure itself but by the abstract notion of pleasure, or rather of the *pleasure-potential* attached to the there-and-then, its superiority in pleasure to the here-and-now.

7.44. His practical movement of escape from the here-and-now towards the there-and-then, as instigated by this notion of pleasure-potential, is *appetitive action* or *doing what you want*; and the initial stage of this movement is *appetite* or *wanting*.

7.45. The pleasure-potential of the there-and-then, as abstractly conceived, is *satisfaction*.

7.46. No man wants pleasure as such; what he wants is satisfaction, the satisfaction of appetites he has.

7.5. Appetite is blind. Nobody in a condition of wanting knows what he wants or is conscious of wanting anything definite; only when he comes to reflect on his appetite is he even conscious of wanting at all.

7.51. This is what I mean in the preceding paragraphs by emphasizing the word 'abstract'.

7.52. A man in a condition of appetite wants a feeling-state contrasting with the one he has, but one which, so far as the appetite goes, is otherwise indeterminate. He wants to escape from a feeling-state contrasting with the one he wants; but otherwise, so far as the appetite goes, indeterminate.

7.53. A man who reflects on appetite is conscious of himself as wanting one feeling-state and wanting to escape from another; but he is not conscious of either as having any determinate characteristics: except that each contrasts with the other.

7.54. If someone asked him: 'What do you want?' all he could say is: 'Something I have not got.' If someone asked him: 'What have you got?' all he could say is: 'Something I want to get rid of.'

7.55. The fact of appetite is the immediate or first-order object 'given' to a man who thus reflects: the initial point and the terminal points of appetite, what it tends from (the unsatisfactory) and what it tends to (the satisfactory) are conceived by abstraction from the process of appetite itself.

7.56. Like all abstractions they are conceived as determinate only in some ways; in others as indeterminate.

7.57. A triangle abstractly conceived, for example, is conceived as determinate only in having three straight sides;

except for what is implied in this, everything about it is conceived as indeterminate.

7.58. So an object of appetite is conceived by a man reflecting upon appetite as determinate only in being the thing that will satisfy him; everything else about it is indeterminate.

7.59. A man actually in the condition of appetite and practically engaged in doing what we have just conceived him as reflecting on, is directing his appetite on something (namely an evocation), making it the thing that will satisfy him, but otherwise leaving it vague.

7.6. Appetite is what thought makes out of feeling when thought develops by its own activity from mere consciousness to conceptual thinking. It is both a specialized form of consciousness (namely conceptual thinking) and a specialized form of feeling produced out of simple feeling by that form of consciousness.

7.61. In this partnership thought is the active partner. It is thought which by generating abstractions converts its apanage, feeling, into the feeling-side of appetite, itself becoming the intellectual side of appetite.

7.62. Some people talk about abstractions as if they were nasty things with which a wise man would have nothing to do.

7.63. But as soon as thought develops beyond its most primitive embryonic stage as mere apprehension of the given it begins making abstractions. However far it pushes the process of development it never leaves off.

7.64. To fancy that when thought begins making abstractions it condemns itself to live in a world of abstractions and turns its back on reality is as foolish as to fancy that an unborn child, when it begins building itself a skeleton, turns its back on flesh and blood and condemns itself to live in Ezekiel's Valley of Dry Bones.

7.65. The life of a vertebrate is a symbiosis of flesh with bone; the life of thought is a symbiosis of immediate consciousness with abstractions.

7.66. It is a further development of the same foolish fancy when people obsessed with this fancy (like F. H. Bradley in the late nineteenth century and H. Bergson in the early twentieth) look forward to a divine event whereby thought shall not only return into the womb but there digest its own skeleton.

7.67. The cure of these nightmares and nightmarish hopes is to recollect that abstractions are only second-order objects made by the mind out of its immediate or first-order objects as naturally and as unconsciously as bees make honey out of flowers; and that a wealth of abstractions indicates not poverty in immediate consciousness but abundance of it, as a wealth of honey in the comb shows, not that the bees have left off visiting flowers, but that they have visited flowers to some purpose.

7.68. I will not ask whether (as is commonly supposed) non-human animals have appetites. I will only observe that, if they do, it is a mistake to suppose (as is commonly supposed) that their minds are unequal to conceptual thinking. For appetite is a product of conceptual thinking.

7.69. Appetite is a name for the inherent restlessness of mind. The blindness of appetite means that this restlessness drives it unconsciously from an indeterminate here-and-now to an indeterminate there-and-then in quest of a future not so much dark as blank: a quest due to no choice, guided by no reason, directed on no goal. Choice and reason and goal are not among the sources or conditions of appetite, they are among its products.

VIII

HUNGER AND LOVE

8. 1. IF I had been studying appetite physiologically I should have divided it into a very large number of kinds: the appetite for food, for drink, for air, for rest, for exercise, for sunshine, for scores of other things.

8. 11. But the distinction between these is mainly physiological and does not concern me. When I consider appetite as a mental thing, partly a matter of thought and partly a matter of feeling (7. 6), I find it falling into two types and no more.

8. 12. These are the hunger-type and the love-type, or as I shall call them hunger and love.

8. 13. In all appetite there is an incipient (7. 44) movement from an unsatisfactory feeling-state (a selection from the here-and-now, 7. 32) to a satisfactory feeling-state contrasting with it, an evocation (7. 33) forming the most prominent feature in the context (7. 33) of that selection by reason of the pleasure-potential (7. 43) which is its emotional charge.

8. 14. The self in the unsatisfactory feeling-state I call the *actual self*; the self in the satisfactory feeling-state I call the *ideal self*; observing (*a*) that a man in a state of appetite as such has no idea of himself; how that idea arises we shall see in this chapter; (*b*) that I use the word 'ideal' with no implications other than appetitive ones, and mean by it simply 'what a man wants'.

8. 15. Hunger in the psychological sense (8. 12) is wanting to be *strong*. The actual self of hunger is a self with which you are dissatisfied because it is *weak*. The ideal self of hunger is a strengthened self. How much strengthened? Just strengthened; the appetite specifies no limit; we must say, indefinitely or infinitely strengthened.

8. 16. Love in the psychological sense (8. 12) is wanting to be *attached*. The actual self of love is a self with which you are dissatisfied because it is *lonely*. The ideal self of love is a self which has achieved a relation with something other than itself (I will call it a *not-self*) of such a kind that the dissatisfaction is removed.

8. 17. This relation is called *having*. The idea of possession is an abstraction from the idea of loving. Reflection on loving reveals it as an appetite in which the satisfaction aimed at is to be found in the establishment of a relation between the self and a not-self; and to establish that relation (which of course is conceived as indeterminate, 7. 56, and differs for every different kind of appetite covered by the name 'love') is to 'have' the not-self.

8. 18. It is only the activity of loving that establishes the distinction between the self and the not-self, and only reflection on the same activity that apprehends the distinction as something ready-made.

8. 19. But not as something 'given'. In spite of much misapprehension, neither self nor not-self is ever immediately given as a first-order object of consciousness. Each is an abstraction correlative to the other; and the two abstractions are made together in a single act, namely the reflection on loving for which they are second-order objects.

8. 2. *Hunger* (to expand this outline) starts with a feeling of defect or weakness; not defect relatively to a standard, but defect as such; not, for example, feeling weaker than usual but just feeling weak; with a craving to annul that feeling.

8. 21. Its satisfaction would be the feeling of this defect removed. In the type-case the defect was bodily lassitude due to an empty stomach; the satisfaction would be the feeling of this lassitude dispelled by repletion.

8. 22. In affiliated cases the defect is inability to get rid of anything that irks you: the irking of fatigue or cold or lust or an itch or an ache; what makes the case one of 'hunger' is that you dislike, not the mere feeling itself, but the weakness that makes you unable to dispel it; when you find means to do so you get a feeling of relaxation, smoothness, plumpness, akin to that of a nicely filled stomach.

8. 23. When you are hungry in any of these ways, or even when you reflect on it, you are not necessarily conscious of the hunger as your own.

8. 24. On the contrary, you tend to regard the hunger as a thing that pervades the whole world; as every reader knows who can remember what it is to be really tired or really thirsty.

8. 25. Hunger as a quest after indeterminate or infinite strength (8. 15) is what Hobbes calls that 'generall inclination of all mankind', the 'perpetuall and restless desire of Power after power, that ceaseth only in Death'.[1]

8. 26. The ideal self which is the object of a hungry man's appetite is a *god*. Being an infinitely strengthened man, it may be called an anthropomorphic god. Being the infinitely strengthened self of the man who worships it, it may be called an *idiomorphic* god.

8. 27. The ancients said that fear made the gods; and this old error has been refurbished of late with general applause by Rudolf Otto.

8. 28. The first notion of a god which arises untaught in every man's mind is much older than fear. It is born of hunger. It is the notion of what a hungry man is pursuing: the infinitely magnified image of himself.

8. 29. From this crude beginning the idea of God has a long path to travel; but it never loses its first features. No religion quite forgets that, whatever else its God may be, he is first and foremost the infinite satisfaction of man's hunger: man himself become omnipotent.

8. 3. To love a thing you must think of it, in the first place, as something other than yourself; in the second place, as something in contact with which you will overcome the loneliness that is the source of your present dissatisfaction.

8. 31. Loneliness is a kind of weakness, and attachment (8. 16) is a kind of strength; but a special kind. Strength as such, the strength that a hungry man wants, is his own strength, the strength of a self *which he is*. This new kind of strength is a strength he borrows from something else, the strength of *something he has*.

8. 32. In the language of love this other thing is called his 'second self'. The idea of a second self is the abstract idea of anything, no matter what, to which his practical relation is that he looks to it to cure his loneliness; he wants a satisfaction, no matter what, which he expects it to supply.

8. 33. The type-case here is sex; but sexual love is not the mere desire for sexual union, or even for sexual union with a certain mate; that is lust, and lust is not a kind of love but a kind of hunger. Sexual love is looking to a member of the

[1] *Leviathan*, p. 47.

opposite sex to supply one with certain satisfactions; those of sex among others, but not those alone.

8. 34. Even sexual love is not lust, though lust is an important element in it; and there are many kinds of love containing little or no lust, for example a man's love for other men, children, non-human animals, flowers, places, rivers or mountains or the sea. There are schools of psychology that have won a *succès de scandale* by exaggerating the sexual elements in these and others like them; but no light is thrown on the nature of love by showing that it often contains an element of lust and that many people are ashamed or unconscious of this element; even when it is true.

8. 35. Love is a modification or development of hunger. The hungry man wants to be his own idiomorphic god (8. 26). The lover still has the idea of an idiomorphic god, but only to reject it. What he wants is to have an *heteromorphic* god: an *object* of love, something not himself to which he looks for satisfaction.

8. 36. Whatever is loved is an heteromorphic god to its lover. Human lovers worship each other, and that not only in the modern or 'romantic' tradition of sexual love, whose origin has been studied by C. S. Lewis (*The Allegory of Love*, 1936), but always and everywhere so far as sexual love has been distinguished from lust; parents worship their children, as Christians can never forget; people who love cats or dogs, flowers or trees, rivers or mountains, worship (whether they reflect on the fact or no) cat-gods or dog-gods, flower-gods or tree-gods, river-gods or mountain-gods, and so on.

8. 37. This is the religion of satisfied love, or love that hopes to be satisfied. It is the 'feeling of dependence' that Schleiermacher identified with religion in general.

8. 38. But there is also a religion of unsatisfied love, where the not-self on which the lover fixes his affections is not accessibly lodged in the world, an 'immanent' god whose many addresses the worshipper knows, with whom he can take tea, and whom he can hope to find about his path and about his bed; but utterly and fatally 'transcendent', ἐπέκεινα τῆς οὐσίας, so that he cries into the dark and gets no echo because there is nothing there.

8. 39. This religion has found an historical form. It is called Christianity; not the comfortable pseudo-Christianity of sentimentalists, but the very different thing to which that name ought to be confined.

8. 4. Love is called a *passion*. A passion is an activity (10. 12) wherein a man reacts to the action upon him of something not himself.

8. 41. To call love a passion is to say that what we love has in itself a power to make us love it.

8. 42. This power is called *beauty*; and the theory of beauty as the power to stimulate love is familiar from Plato and a long line of Platonists.

8. 43. It is false. Beauty is in the eye of the beholder; that is to say the beauty which is, no doubt, characteristic of all beloved objects is the effect, not the cause, of somebody's loving them.

8. 44. Unlike hunger, which is an appetite for an object it can neither find nor create, an omnipotent self, love is an appetite for a relation with an object it can and does create, a beautiful not-self.

8. 45. The establishment of this relation, or even of a struggle towards it, is the origin both of the not-self which is thereby created, and of the self which in creating it establishes itself as a focus of activity with an identity of its own, unique and different from everything else, that is, from every not-self.

8. 46. It is only in retrospect from this development that the object of hunger can be called an omnipotent 'self'. Apart from this newly established distinction between self and not-self it is just omnipotence in the abstract, an omnipotent nothing-in-particular.

8. 47. Until this distinction is made by the self which brings itself into existence by making it, there is neither self nor not-self; only a chaos of consciousness and feeling in which works the restlessness called appetite.

8. 48. I have called this chaos 'mind' (7. 69) because all I know about it is learned by studying the most primitive levels of what are called minds; but in many ways the name is inappropriate, though not so decisively inappropriate as any other I can suggest.

8. 49. Once the distinction between self and not-self has been made by the practical act of loving, it is there as a *fait accompli* to be reflected upon. Love is a first-order object of immediate consciousness to one who loves and reflects on loving; the self and the not-self are abstractions from this. Neither can ever be a first-order object; neither is ever immediately 'given'; what is given is the act (loving) in which the one creates the other and establishes itself.

8. 5. How does love come into existence? It is not a question of repeating a mythical story already current about the Birth of Love or of inventing a new one; it is a question of psychological inquiry into a process that is always going on, in myself and others.

8. 51. Love is a modification of hunger (8. 35); it is the quest for a satisfaction derived from relation to a not-self (8. 32) instead of, as in the case of hunger, the heaping-up of 'Power after power' in oneself (8. 25). How does the modification come about?

8. 52. A hungry man wants to become omnipotent (8. 25). That is impossible; he cannot become omnipotent without ceasing to be himself.

8. 53. He cannot come to know this except at a level of mental development far beyond what we have reached; he cannot at this stage say to himself: 'I see I have been aiming at the impossible; I must school myself to aim at something less.'

8. 54. What he can do is to *suffer repeated disappointments in his quest for omnipotence until blind appetite despairs of that quest and embarks upon another*; being too resilient, adaptable, resourceful, to lie down and die because it fails to get what it first wanted.

8. 55. The power to satisfy its wants, which at first it sought in a strengthened self, but now despairs of finding there, it now seeks in something not itself.

8. 56. What sort of a something not itself? No answer is possible, for the not-self is an abstraction, determinate only in being other than the self; in all else indeterminate, as (for that matter) the self is.

8. 57. What is being sought is a not-self that will satisfy. What kind of a not-self will satisfy is a question to which no answer can be given *a priori*: only partial and provisional answers by trial and error, as this or that selection from the ambient chaos is found to afford, or not to afford, a partial and provisional satisfaction.

8. 58. The birth of love is the act of *limiting your demands*: substituting for the quest of absolute satisfaction (the demand for omnipotence) the quest of many partial or incomplete satisfactions, each derived from a specialized relation to this, that, or the other specialized not-self.

8. 59. For the distinction between the self and the not-self involves the distinction from one another of innumerable not-selves, and of innumerable relations in which the self may severally stand to them; thus in effect the conversion of hunger into love means that *hunger is put into commission*, the one final absolute satisfaction for which appetite in its primary form is the quest is cut up into an infinite number of partial, temporary satisfactions. To enjoy any one of these satisfactions is to 'love' the thing that affords it in the Christian sense of 'love': ἀγάπη, 'contentment' with what falls short of perfection.

IX
RETROSPECT

9. 1. THE account of man as mind given in this first Part, the account of community to follow it in the second, and the account of a civilized community to be given in the third, are all constructed on what Locke called the 'historical plain method'.

9. 11. The essence of this method is concentration upon *facts*. 'Facts' is a name for what history is about: *facta*, *gesta*, things done, πεπραγμένα, deeds.

9. 12. *Facta* has also a secondary sense, πεποιημένα, 'things made'. A making is a deed; a thing made is the result of a deed. To know about deeds is to know about their results; but you can know about the results without knowing about the deeds.

9. 13. It is a *fact* in the proper sense that Bishop Poore built Salisbury Cathedral. You cannot know about that fact without knowing about Salisbury Cathedral.

9. 14. In a secondary sense Salisbury Cathedral may be called a 'fact': a 'fact' which may be known in abstraction from the *fact* that it was built by Bishop Poore.

9. 15. The results of deeds are abstractions from the deeds; the historical method involves studying both deeds and their results: in this case, both mental activities and their results, for example concepts (7. 39).

9. 16. A study of mind on the historical method involves two renunciations. First, it renounces with Locke all 'science of substance'. It does not ask what mind is; it asks only what mind does.

9. 17. You can have your cake and eat it too by holding that mind is 'pure act', so that the question *what mind is* resolves itself without residue into the question *what mind does*; but whether this is defensible I shall not ask.

9. 18. Secondly, it renounces all attempt to discover what mind *always and everywhere does*, and asks only *what mind has done* on certain definite occasions.

9. 19. Once more, you can have your cake and eat it too by holding that what mind has done on a certain definite occasion is typical of what it always and everywhere does; but once more I shall not ask whether this is defensible.

9.2. As a devotee of the 'historical plain method' all I want to know about mind is what it has done on certain definite occasions; not everything it has done, but enough for my purely practical purpose, deciding how to deal with the present attack on civilization.

9.21. Whatever I need know for this purpose is about the *modern European mind*; for that is what has produced in itself the thing called modern European civilization (or 'civilization' for short) and also the revolt against it.

9.22. All this knowledge is about modern European history, the *gesta* of the modern European mind, including my own mind; not that my own is peculiarly interesting, but that it is peculiarly accessible to myself for certain kinds of study.

9.23. What I have to say is entirely matter of history; but much of it is undocumented by reference to history-books, partly because 'the history of what passes in a man's mind' (as Locke has it), though history, and important for my purpose, is little noticed by their authors; and partly because much of it is too familiar to need documentation.

9.24. The mind of man, as I am studying it in these chapters, means the modern European mind; and that only as revealed in its *gesta*.

9.25. How far this is typical of human mind at large, and how far my results apply to non-human minds, are questions not to my purpose.

9.3. The modern European mind is a highly complex fact: I mean, a complex not of many *gesta* (though it is that too) but of many *functions*, where function means not a single act but a type of activity.

9.31. An individual act may include in itself more than one type of activity; for example the individual act which I call 'seeing my inkpot ten seconds ago' includes a function or group of functions belonging to sensation, and also a function or group of functions belonging to thought.

9.32. The account of the modern European mind which I aim at giving is a *catalogue of its functions* as exemplified in its practical and theoretical working.

9. 33. One can easily begin such a catalogue and expand it to considerable length; but it will never be completed, because a catalogue is not completed until the maker is able to say that it is complete; and this can never happen: he can never be sure that he has not omitted something; in fact, the more trouble he takes, the more certain he becomes that he has.

9. 34. What is required is not that the catalogue should be complete, but that the compiler should bear steadily in mind the purpose to be served by compiling it and should make it as full as that purpose requires.

9. 35. If there is properly speaking no purpose, only the idle purpose of compiling an exhaustive list, the question falls to the ground; without a practical purpose no scientific work can be done; only pseudo-scientific work.

9. 36. When the catalogue is as full as it need be, how ought the items to be arranged? The answer is: 'Serially'; that is to say, each term should be a modification of the one before it.

9. 37. In the *series of integers*, for example, every term is generated by the addition of one to the term before it; so that we have not only a series but a *regular* series, one in which the development is governed by a rule.

9. 38. A series of numbers may be an *irregular series*; for example, the series 7, 8, 9, 12, 13, 15, 17, 18, 19, 21; which are the depths in fathoms obtained by starting at a point I will call A on the first chart I pick up at random, and sounding at every *x* yards on a line running south-west.

9. 39. There is a rule for determining the positions at which soundings are to be taken; none for determining the depths of water that will be found.

9. 4. *The series of mental functions is an irregular series.* Let its terms be called, if you like, consciousness, second-order consciousness, third-order consciousness, and so on: the rule here is only a rule specifying the successive positions to be taken up for using the lead-line; it does not tell you, and no rule can tell you, what water you will find.

9. 41. 'I do not see why it should be so.' Consider, then, that mind has apanages, namely feeling and its forms, as well as constituents, namely consciousness and its forms.

Now the depth of water obtained by sounding at 'consciousness' is simple feeling; but the formula 'find out what it is that is given to mere consciousness' will not tell you what feeling is like. If you want to know you must put yourself into that position by a practical effort[1] and find out.

9.42. The depth of water obtained by sounding at 'second-order consciousness' is appetite; but the formula 'find out what becomes of feeling at the position of second-order consciousness' will not tell you what appetite is like; you must find out.

9.43. *The development of mind is not predictable.* This is 9.4, restated so as to suggest the connexion between a series or logical development (where any two terms A and B, in that order, are so related that B renders A necessary, 'presupposes' A as that out of which it develops while A does not render B necessary) and a temporal development (where A comes into existence at one time and its modification B at a subsequent time). For 'prediction' suggests time-sequence, though in correct usage it need not imply it.

9.44. A temporal development is called a *progress*; the opposite, where the terms of a series cease to exist at time-intervals, beginning with the highest, is called a *regress* or *degeneration*.

9.45. Let there be a series ABCD where each term is related to the next as A is to B in 9.43. Let there be a time t_1 at which A exists alone: a subsequent time t_2 at which A and B exist; and so on. That is progress.

9.46. Let there be a time t_1 when ABCD all exist; a subsequent time t_2 at which ABC exist; then t_3 at which AB exist; lastly t_4 at which A exists alone. That is regress or degeneration.

9.47. Unlike progress, &c., *development does not imply time*. Development is a logical process in which B 'presupposes' A, C 'presupposes' B, and D 'presupposes' C. This takes no time to happen, or no more time than A,B,C,D take to exist.

9.48. In a development of mental functions ABCD,

[1] An effort of selective attention (4.56) to the element of mere consciousness which, by the Law of Primitive Survivals (9.6), is contained in every higher mental function.

whether merely logical (the functions coexisting in a single act) or temporal (the functions coming to exist at successive times) there is nothing in A to necessitate B; nothing in $A + B$ to necessitate C; nothing in $A + B + C$ to necessitate D. Given $A + B + C$, the mind in question goes on to D if it has the energy to do so; if it has not, the development stops at C or else, if even that demands more energy than is available, gives place to a regress. This I call the LAW OF CONTINGENCY: *the earlier terms in a series of mental functions do not determine the later.*

9. 5. I will close this retrospect by stating another principle that I have assumed throughout: I call it the LAW OF PRIMITIVE SURVIVALS. It runs as follows.

9. 51. *When A is modified into B there survives in any example of B, side by side with the function B which is the modified form of A, an element of A in its primitive or unmodified state.*

9. 52. Evolutionary cosmologists assume such a law. There is a cause at work, they think, converting inorganic matter into living matter. But in the world as we know it some inorganic matter exists in its primitive state side by side with some matter in its living form. Apes have evolved into men; but there are still apes.

9. 53. I do not recollect that they offer to justify so curious an assumption and explain why the whole of the inorganic world, for example, does not come alive. But it is easy to see why, if there is a development of mind through its various functions, there must be such a law. Take any two functions, A and B, the second a modification of the first; without such a law there could be no development.

9. 54. For example, let A be consciousness and B second-order consciousness or reflection; and suppose that reflection is a modification of consciousness. Unless a man reflecting had in him a primitive survival of mere consciousness, he would have nothing to reflect on, and would not reflect.

9. 55. If appetite, passion, and desire form a series, each is a modification of the one before; but any individual example of passion contains, over and above the appetite which has been modified into passion an element of appetite pure and simple: any example of desire contains a primitive

survival of passion and also one of appetite: and so, as the series goes on, the structure of the functions grows more complex.

9.56. Thus we know why in the development of mind there must be, as Herbert Spencer says there is in the evolution of the material world, a process from the relatively simple to the relatively complex.

9. 57. When hunger develops into love (8. 35) hunger does not disappear; it survives after being 'put into commission' (8. 59) in its new form as love.

9. 58. But it also survives in its primitive form as a tendency one has learned to resist or reject (8. 35).

X

PASSION

10. 1. I AM not going to discuss passion in its literal sense, but in the sense in which the word is used in ordinary speech.

10. 11. Literally it means this: when A does *x* to B, *x* is A's action and B's passion.

10. 12. In ordinary speech a 'passion' means not simply *having something done to you*, but *doing something else* (*y*) *when something* (*x*) *is done to you*.

10. 13. Something does something (*x*) to you. For example a knot baffles your efforts at untying it; and in 'response' to that 'stimulus' you do something else (*y*), for example, you become angry or 'fly into a *passion*'.

10. 14. Reflecting on this you find the fact of becoming angry immediately given to you as a first-order object.

10. 15. From this first-order object the self (you, who become angry) and the not-self (something that makes you angry) are abstractions.

10. 16. Having only an abstract and therefore indeterminate (7. 56) idea of the latter, you do not know what it is that makes you angry (and in fact people often make mistakes about this); still less what the particular thing is which it does to you to which your anger is a response.

10. 17. All you can learn about it from reflection is that it is something not yourself you know not what, which by acting somehow upon you, you know not how, provokes that reaction in you.

10. 18. Passion is the power of the not-self; reflection on passion is the discovery of that power.

10. 2. Like appetite (8. 11), passion has two forms, *fear and anger*.

10. 21. 'Feare', says Hobbes, 'is Aversion' (that is, 'the Endeavour fromward something') 'with opinion of *Hurt* from the object'.[1] This is a rationalistic account in the seventeenth-century manner, making a thing out to be rational which is not rational. It accounts for fear by reference to our

---

[1] *Leviathan*, p. 35 ('aversion', p. 23).

supposed reasons for being afraid. Spinoza makes the same mistake.[1]

10. 22. It is a mistake because, although some fears can be partly explained in this manner (for example my fear of a poisonous snake or something I believe to be a poisonous snake), some cannot be thus explained (for example a woman's fear of a mouse or a boy's fear of the dark, where there is no 'opinion of *Hurt* from the object', or if there is it is a rationalization of the fear, not a constituent of it or a cause of it), and none can be wholly thus explained: for if there is belief in danger the right reaction is to keep calm and avoid it, not to fall into that strange paralysis of mind which is called fear.

10. 23. If Hobbes and Spinoza were right, a man frightened of a bull would begin by deciding that it was a bull and knowing how bulls can hurt men, and then argue syllogistically that this bull can hurt him, in these ways. If he is capable of thinking like this, he is capable of planning how to avoid the bull.

10. 24. But a man really frightened can neither syllogize nor plan. His mind goes numb. A regress (9. 45) occurs in it; the fear which is normally resisted (9. 58) or kept in check by higher functions, rational and other, but by the Law of Primitive Survivals (9. 5) never entirely ceases to exist, breaks bounds and, as I call it (13. 67), 'takes charge' and prevents these higher functions from coming into play.

10. 25. In fact a man frightened of a bull begins by being frightened. Next, if he is able to reflect (which if he is frightened enough he cannot do), he recognizes that he is frightened, and that something is frightening him. If he is able to reflect further, he may ask: 'What is it that is frightening me?' and may identify this with some definite feature of his situation, the bull.

10. 26. Fear contains an intellectual element, an element not of propositional thinking (as Hobbes and Spinoza thought: 'this may hurt me') but of conceptual thinking: the idea of a not-self. There is also the idea of myself, and the idea of a contrast between them.

10. 27. The relation between them is simply one of

[1] *Ethica*, iii, prop. 39, *schol.*, and *Affectuum definitiones*, xiii.

contrast. What the object does to me that frightens me is simply to contrast with me. My fear of it is a practical reaction to this contrast.

10. 28. What are the things a boy is afraid of? Anything that contrasts with his idea of himself. He is afraid of other boys because they are boys like him but different boys. He is afraid of girls because they are female; their femininity is a menace to his sex. He is afraid of babies because their babyishness is a menace to his boyishness. He is afraid of grown-up people because their maturity is a menace to his immaturity. He is afraid of non-human animals because they are animals like him but alien in species and behaviour. He is afraid of the dead because they are not alive. He is afraid of 'rocks, and stones, and trees' because they are not organisms, not even dead organisms.

10. 29. Not that all these fears are permanently active. It is only when one of the situations out of which they arise impresses upon him forcibly the contrast between something else and himself that he has a twinge of fear for that thing; perhaps a very mild twinge; otherwise he is not frightened of it at all.

10. 3. Love turns into fear when a man starts thinking of the not-self no longer as existing for the satisfaction of his own appetites but as having an independent character of its own: as being, so to speak, *alive*.

10. 31. This is the old tale of the sorcerer's apprentice who conjures up a spirit and then finds that the spirit refuses his inexpert control: a frightening story because it tells in a myth the origin of fear.

10. 32. The theme of the story is constantly re-enacted in real life when a lover finds the object of his love no longer content with the passive role of accepting adoration, but behaving like a real person or whatever it is.

10. 33. Fearfulness, like beauty, is in the eye of the beholder. The object of fear, the terrible object, is made such by fear itself: which (like love) is a form of consciousness arising spontaneously in the mind of man and creating for itself appropriate objects: for it is not the object's being alive (10. 3) that frightens you but your thinking it alive, whether it is or not.

10. 34. Here as elsewhere, the Law of Primitive Survivals (9. 6) holds good. All fear contains in itself a trace of the love out of which it has developed.

10. 35. Popular psychology recognizes something called *hatred* which it regards as the opposite of love; it regards this combination of love and fear as a combination of love and hatred.

10. 36. The word 'hatred', however, is also used as a name for anger; or for loathing or aversion (11. 22); or for the impulse to torment or persecute what we love in order to satisfy ourselves of our power over it, which is a common, perhaps an essential element in love; or for any confusion or combination of these.

10. 37. There is nothing of which 'hatred' is the right name; and psychologists might be well advised to drop the word and use various different ones for the various different things they now mean by it; except when they mean by it a confused state of mind.

10. 4. Hobbes defines *anger* in terms of fear: which when accompanied by 'hope of avoyding that Hurt (10. 21) by resistance' becomes 'COURAGE'; and 'Sudden Courage' is 'ANGER'.

10. 41. Spinoza defines it in terms of hatred: 'odium est tristitia concomitante idea causae externae' (*Affectuum definitiones*, vii); 'ira est cupiditas qua ex odio incitamur ad illi quem odimus malum inferendum' (ibid. xxxvi).

10. 42. These are rationalistic accounts of anger, parallel to the rationalistic accounts mentioned above (10. 21) of fear, and subject to the same criticisms. Anger is no more rational than fear; there is what may be called a rational anger, namely a deliberate attempt to overcome resistance offered by its object to some enterprise of your own: but just as 'rational fear' lacks the special characteristics of fear, namely what I have called a 'paralysis of mind' (10. 22), so this 'rational anger' lacks the special characteristics of anger, namely the uncontrollable, spasmodic aggressiveness of that 'brief madness'.

10. 43. In anger you have no consciousness of being angry; that comes only with reflection upon anger; what you are aware of is simply a contrast between yourself and something (you know not what) other than yourself. This is the intellectual element in anger. It is identical with the intellectual element.in fear.

10. 44. The difference is purely practical. You conceive yourself as 'contradicted' or 'contrasted with' by the not-self (10. 27). The simplest thing to do is to lie down under this menace. That is fear. The alternative is to rebel against it. That is anger.

10. 45. I do not mean that there is a choice between the two alternatives. There is not. The first thing a man feels inclined to do, when he encounters opposition, is to give way to it. And this is what everybody begins by doing. But there is a difficulty about doing it. Just as hunger is insatiable, being a quest for an omnipotence inconsistent with the being of the finite creature that wants it (8. 52), so fear is insatiable because yielding to it completely would be self-annihilation. The impulses of pure fear include no attempt at resistance or even escape; they are impulses to cower, to obliterate yourself, to throw yourself over the precipice or under the train, to jump down the snake's throat. But so complete a submission is an escape from submission, though undesigned; a too thorough cowering frustrates the very impulse to cower.

10. 46. The impulses of fear are self-contradictory; and the flight from self-contradiction is far older than reason: here, as in the case of hunger (8.54), it arises from despair: the blind and purely practical abandonment of an unrewarded search, combined with the resilience or adaptability which enables the unsuccessful effort to find a new outlet.

10. 47. Thus passion turns from fear into anger: invents a new response to the old stimulus, renews the combat against the not-self instead of accepting defeat at its hands.

10. 48. This involves fighting on two fronts. You have to fight not only the victorious not-self but the self which has been frightened into treachery. The renewal of the war against the not-self is *anger*: the renunciation of the cowardly self is *shame*.

10. 49. What a man is ashamed of is always at bottom himself; and he is ashamed of himself at bottom always for being afraid.

10. 5. Shame, which is the critical point in the process converting fear into anger, is in a larger sense a critical point in the whole development of mind: for unlike a man in a condition of appetite a man in a condition of shame knows what he wants: he wants to be *brave*; not devoid of fear, but triumphant over fear.

10. 51. The importance of anger as a bridge from the lower levels of consciousness where thought is at first merely apprehensive, capable of taking what is 'given' to it, and then merely conceptual, capable of framing abstractions from what is 'given', to the higher levels of consciousness where thought is first 'propositional', capable of discriminating good from evil and truth from error, and then 'rational', capable of understanding both itself and other things, has been long ago expounded in many different forms.

10. 52. I will mention two: one in Plato, one in the Bible; attested, as it happens, by documents nearly contemporary.

10. 53. In Plato's doctrine of the so-called 'tripartite soul' (cf. 3. 6–63) the 'irascible' is intermediate between the 'appetitive' and the 'rational'. Anger, that is to say, is intermediate between the lowest mental functions, of which appetite is typical, and the highest, of which reason is typical. If there is a progress of the soul from appetite to reason, it passes through anger.

10. 54. Old Testament literature records a progress from a religion of fear, where 'the fear of the Lord is the beginning of wisdom' (Proverbs ix. 10), ('wisdom' being the activity whereby man makes for himself a good life, the same activity whereby God created the world), to a religion of anger.

10. 55. There was a man in the land of Uz, says the story, whose name was Job; and that man was perfect and upright and one that feared God and eschewed evil; and being afflicted was taught by the religion of fear that he was afflicted by God's permission and reminded by his 'comforters' of what that religion had long ago taught him, that all affliction was God's just punishment for sin.

10. 56. But Job has been brought by his sufferings to a point at which the religion of fear no longer contents him. He 'taketh liberty to expostulate with God'. 'Thou knowest that I am not wicked,' he says; 'remember, I beseech thee, that thou hast made me as the clay; and wilt thou bring me into dust again?'

10. 57. The reply of his third comforter calls forth his open anger against all who preach the religion of fear. 'No doubt but ye are the people, and wisdom shall die with you. But I have understanding as well as you; I am not inferior to you: yea, who knoweth not such things as these? I am as one mocked of his neighbour, who calleth upon God, and he answereth him: the just upright man is laughed to scorn.' 'Hold your peace, let me alone, that I may speak, and let come on me what will.'

10. 58. What comes upon him is that the fear of God in which he has been trained turns to anger with God. 'Wherefore hidest thou thy face, and holdest me for thine enemy?' Undeterred by everything an omnipotent creator can do, his creature turns against him in accusation.

10. 59. And God, as a character in the story, takes it. 'The Lord said to Eliphaz the Temanite, my wrath is kindled against thee, and against thy two friends: for ye have not spoken of me the thing that is right, as my servant Job hath.'

10. 6. In Christianity this conversion of the Old Testament fear-religion into an anger-religion is a *fait accompli*.

10. 61. It is more than a commonplace of Christianity, it is the essence of Christianity, that the God who made Adam and gave him a woman; and forbade them to eat of a certain tree; and exposed them to temptation by another of his creatures, the serpent; was responsible for Adam's sin and was the agent who brought sin into the world and all our woe.

10. 62. It is the essence of Christianity that (as savages beat the gods who fail to answer their prayers) so Christians should vent their wrath and, as the poem of Job has it, with God's own approval, upon God's own wounded head.

10. 63. When we show in our churches the likeness of our God scourged with rods and crowned with thorns and suffering the death of a criminal, and in the central rite of our worship commemorate, as some of us say, or as others say actually repeat that doing to death, we prove to the world that we hold God responsible for whatever evil there may be in the world; and think we cannot serve him better than by wreaking on him our inevitable wrath.

XI

DESIRE

11.1. THE word 'desire' is sometimes used as a synonym for 'appetite'. But when properly used it means *wishing* as distinct from wanting. In appetite or mere wanting a man does not know what he wants, or even that he wants anything; in desire or wishing, he not only knows that he wants something, but he knows what it is that he wants.

11.11. How does this happen? Knowing a thing is more than merely being conscious of it. Knowing involves asking questions and answering them.[1]

11.12. Asking a question implies contemplating alternatives. A question that offers no alternatives is a bogus question. The technique of knowing proper, or what is called scientific method, depends on replacing questions which, being vague or confused, are unanswerable, by real questions, or questions which have a precise answer.

11.13. The vague question: '*What* do I want?' is thus replaced by the precise or real question: '*Which* do I want, *a* or *b*?'

11.14. Reflection upon appetite tells a man that he wants something; but does not tell him what he wants. The experience of passion gives him the idea of alternatives, which is an idea arrived at by abstraction from the experience of fear and anger as two alternative reactions to the menace of the not-self.

11.15. This is why the experience of passion must necessarily occur between appetite and desire. Without it, a man would not have the idea of alternatives which is originated by the experience of passion and is presupposed by the characteristic question of desire: 'Which of two things do I want?'

11.16. Reflection upon love as an appetite yields the

---

[1] In this chapter I use the word 'knowing', as people often do, for something that is, strictly speaking, rather less than knowing; what, later on, I call *propositional thinking*. For the distinction between propositional thinking and knowing, see 14. 22.

idea of a not-self; but love as a desire only comes into existence through the experience of passional relations towards that which appetite renders attractive.

11. 17. Every young man is sexually attracted by women. Being inexperienced he does not know what he wants of the woman who attracts him. If he is an Englishman, the custom of his country leaves him to find out for himself. This is done by passing through an emotional process of fear and anger, in that order: impulses of self-abasement before the woman and impulses of aggression towards her. A baby when confronted by the nipple for the first time may visibly pass through the same process until at last it attacks the thing in a rage. Tired or hungry persons are commonly depressed and then quarrelsome. It is the normal process whereby men find out what they want; and perhaps it is what Freud meant when he said that hatred is older than love; for anger is one of the things people mean by 'hatred'.

11. 18. It is important for the conduct of practical life to realize that *coming to know what you want is not to be done by reflection*; not because your appetites are repressed as too vile to contemplate; but because they remain preconscious until they have changed into passions and so into desires.

11. 19. Trying to force oneself or another to identify the object of an appetite by reflection ('come, come,'—one knows the hectoring voice—'think; tell me what you want') can only do untold damage. Already the vulgarized Freud, Jung, and Adler which constitutes our popular psychology warns us against the danger of repressing desires; but not against the far worse danger of abating appetites by never letting them grow into desires.

11. 2. If a man wants *a* his attitude towards it is one of appetitive attraction. If he does not, his attitude towards it is one of indifference.

11. 21. Appetite has no negative form in relation to a given object, there are only its presence and its absence.

11. 22. But desire has a negative form, aversion or loathing. This is because desire involves (and here we meet it for the first time, except in shame, which is a form of it) *propositional thinking*; and a proposition is an answer

to a question; and a question offers alternatives (11.12); so desire asks and answers the question: 'What do I want?' which it begins by converting into: 'Which do I want, *a* or *b*?'

11.23. Accepting one alternative means rejecting the other. The appetite which attracts you to *a* is indifferent to *b*; but when they are put before you as alternatives your knowledge or even your unfounded belief that there is in you an appetite attracting you to *a* implies that the same appetite attracts you away from the alternative *b*.

11.24. Appetite and absence of appetite, converted into objects of knowledge by asking and answering the question: 'Which do I want, *a* or *b*?' thus become respectively *desire* and *aversion*.

11.25. You loathe a person, or a dish, or a book, when you are forced by inopportune solicitation to ask yourself 'Do I love this person (or whatever it may be) or not?' and find yourself obliged to answer 'no'. The question has converted indifference into loathing.

11.26. That is why a wise man, hoping for a woman's love, never asks her whether she loves him until he knows she does. If she does not, she may come to do so if he leaves her alone; but an untimely question will convert indifference into loathing.

11.27. It does not fol low that desire and aversion are equally easy to achieve.

11.28. Grant that I have an appetite for *a* and none fo r *b*, it is easier, I think, to know that I have no appetite for *b* than to know that I have an appetite for *a*.

11.29. To know the latter is to achieve aversion from *b*; to know the former is to achieve desire for *a*, a much harder thing to do.

11.3. Another distinction between appetite and desire is the contrast between *true desires* and *false desires*, to which nothing corresponds in the case of appetite.

11.31. A true desire for something is 'really wanting' it. A false desire is 'thinking you want it, but being mistaken'.

11.32. Let a man have an appetite for *a*. Let him ask himself: 'Which do I want, *a* or *b*?' Whichever answer he gives is a statement of fact which may be true or false.

11.33. If the object of his appetite were a first-order object immediately given to consciousness he could not make a mistake about it; his pronouncement would be infallible; but that it cannot be. The appetite (not as a specific appetite, but as a condition of appetite in general) is a first-order object to his reflection, but the object of the appetite cannot be identified by reflection; the work of identifying it is complicated and difficult, and one in which people constantly make mistakes.

11.34. This is true of all propositional thinking. *The 'subject' of a proposition or 'what the proposition is about' is never a first-order object.* When it is mistaken for one, that may be because it is a selection from one (e.g. in the proposition: 'This patch is blue'), or because the abstract concept of a first-order object is mistaken for a first-order object (e.g. 'a first-order object is extended' may be taken for a singular proposition when it is really an induction).

11.35. The 'predicate' of a proposition, likewise, is never a first-order object but always a concept. That is why logic applies to propositions; in the first instance it applies only to concepts. That is also why any proposition may theoretically involve a mistake, though it is reasonable enough to say that there are mistakes people don't make.

11.36. The importance of the distinction between true desires and false desires becomes evident as soon as one reflects on the importance for all practical life of 'knowing what you want'. Someone completely in the grip of confusion might say: 'Important no doubt, but childishly easy: all you need is introspection (meaning reflection), and that gives you infallibly the right answer.' But reflection does not give you any answer at all, let alone an infallible one.

11.37. The 'Vanity of Human Wishes' does not lie in men's desiring what is not to be had or what, if obtainable, is unobtainable by themselves. It lies in their being mistaken as to what they want. In the first instance (afterwards the accumulation of experience enables a man to guess at what he wants with a better chance of being right) the only way of finding out what one wants is by trial and error: trying various things and seeing whether the discomfort of unsatisfied appetite yields or persists.

11.38. Thomas Carlyle, posing as the sage he never was, suggested that the impossible maxim 'know thyself' should be 'translated' into the partially possible one 'know what thou canst work at'. A wiser man would have seen that the Delphic maxim is not so much impossible as inexhaustible.

11.39. Part, indeed the first part, of knowing yourself is knowing what you want. This is not only the first thing a man can know about himself, it is the first thing he knows at all. It is not impossible, though it is very difficult. But a man who does not know what he wants will never know what he can work at. The Carlylese gospel of work is no substitute for the Delphic gospel of self-knowledge. Either work is based on self-knowledge or it is a form of self-intoxication, and the gospel of work a recommendation to pointless, purposeless activity for men who lack the courage to think and can only dissipate their energies in a blind fury of self-deception.

11.4. 'Whatever', says Hobbes,[1] 'is the object of any man's Appetite or Desire; that it is, which he for his part calleth *Good*; and the object of his Hate, and Aversion, Evill.' And Spinoza:[2] 'it is clear that we do not strive after, will, have an appetite for, or desire a thing because we judge it to be good; but that on the contrary we judge a thing to be good because we strive after it, will it, have an appetite for it, and desire it.'

11.41. I make bold to say that each is setting out to express the doctrine which I take to be true, that the word *good* with its equivalents in various languages means *object of desire*, but that in each of them this doctrine is obscured by certain confusions of thought and never quite clearly expressed.

11.42. First, Hobbes fails to *distinguish between appetite and desire*. Spinoza goes further and identifies not two but four very different things: conation, volition, appetite, and desire. Unless these false identifications are cleared up the statements I have quoted mean nothing.

[1] *Leviathan*, p. 24.
[2] *Ethics*, iii, prop. 9, *schol.* 'Constat . . . nihil nos conari, velle, appetere neque cupere quia id bonum esse iudicamus; sed contra nos propterea aliquid bonum esse iudicare quia id conamur, volumus, appetimus atque cupimus'.

11.43. Secondly, does Hobbes think that calling a thing good is the same as calling it an object of appetite or desire, or are they two different things with some kind of 'because-therefore' relation between them? And what does Spinoza think about the same question?

11.44. I think that the first alternative is what they both mean. But I will not spend on that question the space that would be necessary to explain my reasons for thinking so.

11.45. Thirdly, is Hobbes in earnest about the *individualistic tone of his statement*? If so, he is in error; for the word 'good', or any equivalent in any language, is used in common by numbers of men; and if every man used it in a sense peculiar to himself, to signify the object of his own desire and nobody else's, there would be (so far as that word is concerned) not a language but a babel.

11.46. Men are very much alike in their desires; they wish for the same kinds of things on the same kinds of occasions; on any given occasion they are apt to desire a given thing, not as being that thing and no other, but as being a thing of that kind, food for example or drink.

11.47. Being thus in agreement as to certain kinds of things they habitually desire on recurrent types of occasion, they are in agreement about *calling* (as Hobbes says or as Spinoza says *judging*) anything that belongs to one of these kinds *good*, even when they are not at the moment in the state of desiring anything of that kind. A man must be terribly surfeited if he cannot call food good in abstraction from his actually desiring it; though to call it good means only that he does (habitually or recurrently) desire it.

11.48. Fourthly, and arising out of this, the possibility that because any two men are very much alike at bottom, or live in the same world (two expressions that mean pretty much the same thing), they have the same sort of desires *becomes a certainty* when they so far share a common language as to talk intelligibly to each other about these desires.

11.49. Talking intelligibly to a man means using sounds or the like which he is accustomed to making and hearing, and also meaning by these sounds things that he is accustomed to mean by them. If you try to tell a man about a kind of desire that he has never had, it is not so much that he will not believe you; he will not understand you.

11. 5. *'Good' means 'desired'*; or, what is not easily to be distinguished from this, *desirable*, meaning 'worthy to be desired', not (as Mill interprets it in a famous passage) 'able to be desired'. In the same way 'beautiful' means 'loved' and also 'lovable' or 'worthy to be loved', for the same act of loving which finds its object beautiful makes its object beautiful, or justifies itself by making for itself an object towards which that practical attitude is the only one possible (8. 43–45).

11. 51. With the conversion of appetite into desire, beauty is converted into goodness. The difference is that desire may be true or false (11. 3).

11. 52. Whereas you cannot be mistaken in thinking what you love to be beautiful ('is' and 'seems' are not here distinguishable), you may very easily be mistaken in thinking what you desire to be good, that is to say you may be mistaken in desiring it or thinking you want it.

11. 53. There are two different kinds of motives which the reader may have for repudiating, with that indignation which betrays the substitution of heat for light in a man's mind, the doctrine that 'good' means 'desired'.

11. 54. One arises from the fact of *abstraction*. The object of desire is an abstraction from the act of desiring: and to be good is to be an object of desire and hence an abstraction. Now abstractions are always indeterminate; and hence, as Plato has eloquently reminded us, what is good is only good in some specific way: good 'as this' or good 'for that', never just good or wholly good or 'good in itself'.

11. 55. In other words, an object of desire is never utterly desired, it is always desired conditionally or qualifiedly: desired 'since I can't get anything better' or desired 'since I must have a thing of that kind'. What is desired and hence desirable or good is only desired, desirable, good, in certain ways: in others it may be (if we are clear-sighted enough, always is) loathed, loathsome, bad.

11. 56. This reflection (disconcerting except to one who has learned the lesson of Christian love, ἀγάπη, 'overlooking the faults' of what you love) drove Plato into a wild-goose chase after some object that should be absolutely good, 'good in itself';

where I respectfully decline to follow him; because I do not think that the kind of thing which he was searching for is to be found.

11. 57. The second motive arises from *hypocrisy*. Being ashamed to let people know that we desire what in fact we do desire and hence in our hearts think good, we pretend not to desire anything so low; or at any rate to know, while desiring it, that it is not really good; that is, that we do not really desire it.

11. 58. So we run in a circle, each pretending to conform in his opinion of what is good to the imaginary opinions of his fellow men, and each professing to abhor himself as wicked because he desires what other men loathe.

11. 59. These difficulties vanish when you recollect that being good is being good in certain ways, and is quite compatible with being bad in others; and when, recollecting this, you take courage to confess your desires and your opinion, inseparable from them, that in desiring a thing you think it good.

11. 6. Tam O'Shanter wished to get drunk. If he had reflected on this desire he would have formed the proposition that getting drunk was a good thing. We are not told that he did; but Burns reflected on it when he wrote the poem, and you and I reflect on it when we read the poem: it was a type of desire Burns had shared and did not mind admitting it.

11. 61. Burns says quite candidly that getting drunk is a good thing: not only a thing the drunkard thought good, but a thing the poet knows to be good, and expects his readers to agree. So stern a moralist as Wordsworth did agree, and praised the poem for its moral truth.

11. 62. 'Care, mad to see a man sae happy, e'en drown'd himself amang the nappy . . . kings may be blest, but Tam was glorious, o'er all the ills of life victorious.' That care should be drowned is not the only good thing in the world; in some ways it is a bad thing; but is anybody prepared to deny that in some ways (unimportant ways let him call them who does not know what care can be) it is a good thing? Is anybody prepared to deny that a victory over all the ills of life, however precarious and temporary, is a good thing?

11. 63. Getting drunk is, of course, giving way to a deadly sin. But let us give even sin its due. Men are led

into it (not into all sins, but into some, this among them)
by desire. So far as any act is conceived as gratifying a
specific desire it is conceived as in some specific way good,
not only by the sinner but by virtuous people who share the
desire but do not yield to it.

11. 64. In giving sin its due we need not give it
more. A simple act is good, but only good in certain ways.
In certain other ways, where desire is not concerned, it is
neither good nor bad; in others definitely bad. Tam achieved
his good at a price which only a fool would pay.

11. 65. 'But is the object of a man's desire really good or
only apparently good? We have admitted that here, in
desire, we come for the first time across the distinction
between truth and error; must we not add that although to a
man in a state of desire what he desires necessarily seems
good that is an illusion incidental to desire, and that the same
man "in a cool hour" can often see that what he once thought
good is not good at all?'

11. 66. I reply: There are cool hours and cool hours. A
man who turns cool about one thing (ceases to desire it)
ceases, I admit, to think it good. But unless he has lost all
interest in life his ceasing to desire that thing accompanies
beginning to desire something else; and on reflection he
finds that he now thinks the second thing good.

11. 67. You can say, if you like, that desire makes men
see goodness where in fact there is none. But the facts by
which you would prove it equally tend to prove that desire
alone opens men's eyes to whatever goodness there is.

11. 68. Properly considered, what they prove is that
goodness is a thing of the mind; a thing *bestowed* upon
whatever possesses it by mind's practical activity in the
form of desire; and then discovered, wherever it is discovered, by mind's reflective activity which now for the
first time assumes the form of knowledge.

11. 69. So far is it from being true that desire makes us
fancy good where in fact there is none, that desire first
makes us able to know (knowledge being the theoretical
function of which desire is the practical counterpart); and
good is the first thing we come to know.

XII

HAPPINESS

12. 1. Is there any general name that men give to the things they desire or think good?

12. 11. So far as we know, the question was first asked by Aristotle; in any case he was certainly the man who discovered the right answer: 'Happiness'.

12. 12. The only thing that has led anyone to cavil at this answer is failure to understand it.

12. 13. Some people have found themselves uninterested in the question; and very naturally; there are other practical functions beside desire, and other questions to answer about the practical life of men beside the question: 'What do they wish for?'

12. 14. Others have thought (it is hard to say why) that by 'happiness' Aristotle meant pleasure or a collection of pleasures; or in some other way have misunderstood his answer to the question.

12. 15. Since my own argument has here debouched into the well-trodden path of Aristotle's, I will summarize in my own words, allowing myself a certain freedom of interpretation, the gist of what Aristotle has said on the matter.

12. 2. Happiness or well-being is a combination of internal well-being and external well-being.

12. 21. Internal well-being or well-being in relation to oneself is *virtue*.

12. 22. External well-being, or well-being in relation to what is other than oneself is *power*.

12. 23. Virtue and power, which together make up happiness, are so far from being incompatible that it may be doubted whether they are separable.

12. 24. Perhaps any defect in virtue goes with a defect in power and vice versa.

12. 25. We get the ideas of virtue and power by reflection on desire.

12. 26. Desire, unlike appetite, distinguishes the self from the not-self; hence the good and the bad (the objects of desire and aversion) are always twofold.

12. 27. Primarily the good is a desirable condition of the self as such; secondarily it is a desirable condition of the self in its relation to the not-self. And so with the bad.

12. 28. Now desire as such is a practical process whose starting-point is passion. What we desire, whatever else it may or may not involve, is always to be rid of passion.

12. 29. The bad self is the self *liable to passion*: liable to become frightened or angry in response to what is inflicted on it by the not-self.

12. 3. In relation to the not-self the bad self is the self *at the mercy of the not-self*; liable to be helplessly acted upon by the not-self.

12. 31. To be a self of such a kind as to be frightened or annoyed by the action of other things upon it is to have the *vice* of cowardice or irascibility; the opposite is to have the *virtue* of courage or temperance.

12. 32. To be a self of such a kind that the not-self can frighten or annoy it is to be at the mercy of the not-self: to lack *power* in relation to the not-self.

12. 33. Liability to passions is one form of *unhappiness*. But essentially to be unhappy is to be in the power of circumstances, things other than oneself standing round oneself, constricting one's movements by their presence, forbidding one to do anything except what they permit.

12. 34. Happiness and unhappiness are not the consciousness of freedom from passion or the force of circumstances, and of subjection to these things, respectively; they are that freedom itself and that subjection itself. As we shall see, so far from being states of consciousness they are not even first-order objects of consciousness: they are second-order objects, the terminal and initial points of desire, abstractly considered.

12. 35. The fundamental form of unhappiness is not being forced by circumstances to behave viciously, it is being forced by circumstances at all. Happiness is a condition in which the self not only rises superior to the passions which are provoked in it by circumstances, but to force of circumstances as such. The happy self is *master of circumstances*.

12. 36. This is the meaning of Aristotle's doctrine that a man cannot be happy without a certain provision of 'external' goods: not things he is, like temperate and brave and wise and just, 'virtues', but things he has, like land and friends and children.

12. 37. John Stuart Mill tried to define happiness in terms of pleasure. 'By happiness', he says,[1] 'is intended pleasure, and the absence of pain; by unhappiness, pain and the privation of pleasure.'

12. 38. The wording is odd. 'Intended' by whom? As the context shows, not by English-speakers but by the sect maintaining the 'creed' and talking the esoteric jargon of Benthamite utilitarianism.

12. 39. Mill was not describing what the words in correct English actually mean; he was stating a theory in which that idea was reduced, careless of what was lost in the process, to terms of feeling.

12. 4. Nietzsche, Germanically confusing a question of moral science with one of national hatred, expressed his opinion of utilitarianism by saying that no man wants to be happy; only Englishmen want to be happy; what a man wants is not happiness but power.

12. 41. At Trafalgar and Waterloo Englishmen replied to the taunt 'nation of shopkeepers' by destroying the worshipper of force who had flung it in their teeth.

12. 42. They may yet live down the more pitiful taunt of what his schoolfellows called 'The Little Parson'.

12. 43. Our word 'happy' is intentionally equivalent to εὐδαίμων in Greek and to *felix* in Latin. Εὐδαιμονία is Aristotle's name for 'the human good', and *felix* was a title assumed as a matter of course by about a hundred Roman emperors.

12. 44. Pending the obliteration of Nietzsche's force-worshipping supermen, we need not blush to confess that, at a rather low level of consciousness, what was good enough for Greek philosophers and Roman emperors is good enough for us.

12. 45. As for Nietzsche's antithesis of happiness and power, the less said about that the better for Nietzsche's memory.

[1] *Utilitarianism*, ch. ii, *ad init.*

12. 46. If Aristotle's distinction between happiness and pleasure was denied by Benthamite utilitarians, his doctrine of external goods was denied by the Stoics, who argued that a good man could be happy even upon the rack.

12. 47. This was no answer to Aristotle. A man who dominated circumstances would not be on the rack. The Stoics erred in considering only that aspect of happiness which concerns a man's relation to himself.

12. 5. The happy self, virtuous and powerful, is what we all desire to be. Is the desire ever realized?

12. 51. People have been known to say that it is; but the state which they call happiness is notoriously unstable, and Aristotle is surely right to protest that a happy man would be no chameleon.

12. 52. The truth is that happiness is not a first-order object but an abstraction from desire. It is essentially an ideal, not a fact; though an approximation to it is a fact, and may be thought a close enough approximation to usurp the name.

12. 53. *In relation to himself*, happiness for a given man means *goodness*: freedom from every state of himself from which he wishes to be free; these being passions.

12. 54. He is free from them not through the mercy of circumstances but through his power to defy circumstances: his 'virtues'; these, as Spinoza[1] memorably says, being not means to the condition of happiness but elements in it.

12. 55. *In relation to what is not himself*, it means *power*: the power to prevent the not-self from doing to him anything at all; not by a stoical indifference to its onslaughts but by a triumphant counter-attack, putting it where he wanted it to be, like a Roman emperor with his enemies round him, each with hands tied behind his back. That picture is what 'felix' meant.

12. 6. *Unhappiness* is a *negative ideal*; not an actual experience, nor the name for what we desire to obtain; but the name for *what we desire to get rid of*. We can never wholly get rid of it, but we are never wholly possessed by it. Hegel has a famous passage on what he calls 'The Unhappy

[1] *Ethics*, v, prop. 42: 'Beatitudo non est virtutis praemium, sed ipsa virtus.'

Consciousness'. There is no such thing. Unhappiness is not a form of consciousness, it is an abstraction from the consciousness of desire.

12. 61. In relation to *a man's self*: unhappiness is *badness*, it is being at the mercy of his passions, being unable to be the self he wishes to be.

12. 62. In relation to *what is not himself*, unhappiness is *weakness*; the condition in which he cannot do anything but everything is done to him by circumstances.

12. 63. In face of this *tyranny of circumstances* it is no use being frightened; it is no use being angry; the only thing left is to be miserable.

12. 64. That is no actual use, either; but then it is a response to a situation that never actually arises. An occasion for unhappiness is never an occasion for being merely unhappy; it is always an occasion for a mixed emotion of happiness and unhappiness.

12. 65. The more we feel it as an occasion of sheer unhappiness, the more we can be certain that there are in it occasions of happiness which we have overlooked: that in fact we are happier than we know.

12. 66. Unhappiness is a familiar element in the consciousness of our relations with God, nature, and man. I shall say a word about each of these singly.

12. 67. In every case we have to do with something not ourselves, and the occasion for unhappiness is our weakness as compared with something that has power over us.

12. 68. In relation to God *the notion of unhappiness is the notion of sin*; where (as usual) being 'sinful' does not mean being morally bad, doing what is wrong, neglecting one's duty, or the like, but being feeble, being weak in relation to God, being unable to stand up to Him or face a comparison with Him; unable to walk with Him or to call Him friend.

12. 71. The thought that I am 'sinful' lives, as it were, parasitically upon the thought that my desire for what has been called 'justification', ability to stand up to God, is partially at least gratified.

12. 72. It is only in retrospect that a St. Paul or a St. Augustine can tell us how unhappy he is What he tells us is how unhappy he was (he did not know it at the time, but he knows it now by the force of contrast) before the hand of God was stretched out to save him from his sins.

12.8. The same thing in relation to the world of nature is a phenomenon that strikes us very forcibly in the documents of nineteenth-century thought.

12.81. 'Nature' appears as an *immensely powerful soulless machine*; man as one of the things it has made, gifted unlike itself with sentience and intellect, but doomed to destruction when the law of averages or the Second Law of Thermodynamics shall decree that the thing which made him in the course of its random movements shall, in the course of the same random movements, crush him.

12.82. It is characteristic that people were far more sure this was going to happen than able to explain why it must happen. Their certainty that it was going to happen was in fact emotional; it was a product of unhappiness.

12.83. It was not an idea clearly worked out, nor one capable of being clearly worked out.

12.84. It was a form of unhappiness parasitic upon the corresponding form of happiness, namely the emotion generated by the fact that, just then, man was proving with unexampled rapidity and in unexampled variety his power over the natural world.

12.85. And even the terminology of the unhappiness betrayed this happiness, though unintentionally.

12.86. A machine is something made by man for the execution of his own purposes; a soulless machine is one which, not being alive, cannot rebel against its maker; an immensely powerful machine is one which puts immense power into its maker's hands.

12.9. Our favourite nightmare in the twentieth century is about our powerlessness in the giant grip of economic and social and political structures; the nightmare which Professor Arnold Toynbee[1] calls '*The Intractableness of Institutions*'.

12.91. The founders of modern political science made it clear once for all that these Leviathans are 'Artificial Animals', creatures formed by the art of man, 'for whose protection and defence' they were intended.[2]

[1] *A Study of History*, vol. iv.   [2] *Leviathan*, p. 1.

12. 92. This is the ground of the nightmare. Oppression and exploitation, persecution and war, the torturing to death of human beings in vast helpless masses, are not new things on the face of the earth, and nobody thinks they are; nor are they done in the world on a greater scale or with more refinement of cruelty than they have been done in the past; nor have we grown more sensitive, to shrink, as men once did not, from blood.

12. 93. But Hobbes (and others, but especially Hobbes) has for the first time in history held up a hope that there would be 'protection and defence' against these things; and by now the hope has sunk into our common consciousness; so that when we find it to be precisely the agents of this longed-for safety that are the chief authors of the evils for whose ending we have made them, hope turns to despair and we are ridden by another Frankenstein-nightmare, like Samuel Butler's nightmare of humanity enslaved to its own machines, only worse.

12. 94. But the despair, once more, is parasitic upon the hope.

12. 95. If the hope went, the despair would go too. If we believed Marx's monstrous lie that all States have always been organs for the oppression of one class by another, there would be nothing to make all this fuss about.

12. 96. To strengthen the hope until it overcomes the nightmare, what must be done is to carry on the work, sadly neglected since Hobbes and a handful of successors began it, of constructing a science of politics appropriate for the modern world.

12. 97. Towards such a science this book is offered as a contribution.

XIII

CHOICE

13. 1. A MAN about to choose finds himself aware of a situation in which alternative courses of action are open to him. It is between these that he chooses.

13. 11. I distinguish choice from decision only as two words which mean nearly enough the same thing to be left here undistinguished.

13. 12. The kind of choice with which I am concerned in this chapter is only one kind: the simplest; mere choice or mere decision, uncomplicated by any reason why it should be made in this way and not that; in fact, *caprice*.

13. 13. If the reader thinks that caprice is a subject unworthy of his attention, let him skip the chapter.

13. 14. Choice is not *preference*, though the words are sometimes used as synonyms. *Preference is desire as involving alternatives.* A man who 'prefers' *a* to *b* does not choose at all; he suffers desire for *a* and aversion towards *b*, and goes where desire leads him.

13. 15. Preference involves a situation where there are alternatives, but *closed alternatives*. There are alternatives, for a man who cannot control his fear of bulls, between walking calmly past this one's nose and running away; but preference closes the alternative and forces him to run away.

13. 16. Choice presupposes that the alternatives are open. A man in a position to choose whether he shall walk calmly in front of the bull's nose has open alternatives to choose from (13. 1).

13. 17. This leads us to the *problem of free will*. There are many pseudo-problems of free will. There is the question: 'Are we free?' Clever men have invented arguments to prove that 'we' are not. Thus arose the controversy in which Dr. Johnson (creditably, for a man so addicted to argument) refused to take part, with the memorable pronouncement, 'Sir, we know that we are free, and there's an end on't'.

13. 18. Johnson was pointing out (correctly) that freedom is a first-order object of consciousness to every man whose mental development has reached the ability to choose. In choosing, every man is immediately conscious of being free; free, that is, to choose between alternatives. Arguments as to whether this immediate consciousness is to be trusted are futile, as involving the Fallacy of Misplaced Argument (4. 73).

13. 2. The problem of free will is not whether men are free (for every one is free who has reached the level of development that enables him to choose) but, how does a man become free? For he must be free before he can make a choice; consequently *no man can become free by choosing*.

13. 21. The act of becoming free cannot be done to a man by anything other than himself. Let us call it, then, an act of *self-liberation*. This act cannot be voluntary.

13. 22. 'Liberation from what?' From the dominance of desire. 'Liberation to do what?' To make decisions.

13. 23. There are innumerable kinds of freedom, differing from each other in either of two ways or both. Every kind has a positive aspect and a negative aspect. Positively it is freedom to do something of a special kind. Negatively it is freedom from a special kind of compulsion. If anyone uses the word 'freedom' to me I expect him to answer the questions: 'Freedom to do what?' 'Freedom from what?' Not to parade the answers all the time, because that would be boring; but to have them up his sleeve if they are wanted.

13. 24. Failing this, either the 'freedom' of which he speaks means nothing; or at any rate he does not know what it means.

13. 25. The freedom of the will is, positively, *freedom to choose*; freedom to exercise a will; and, negatively, freedom *from desire*; not the condition of having no desires, but the condition of not being at their mercy.

13. 26. This state of freedom is achieved by an act of which we know that it is (i) involuntary, (ii) done by the same person whom it liberates (13. 21). What else do we know about it?

13. 27. Negatively, it is the act of refusing to let oneself be dictated to by desire. We hear of a man 'controlling his appetites'; but under what circumstances can this really be done?

13. 28. The process that is nipped in the bud is strictly speaking not the process from unsatisfied appetite to satisfaction, but the process from the unhappiness of ungratified desire to the happiness of gratified desire. A little thought will show the reader why this must be so.

13. 29. Positively, this act is the *acceptance of unhappiness*; the acceptance of badness in oneself and weakness in relation to other things; the renunciation. of virtue and power as things one no longer cares to pursue.

13. 3. Since the desiring self simply consists of the practical 'urge' from unhappiness to happiness, this act is a cutting off of all that is going on in the life of the man who does it; as a kind of suicide, it goes by a name intolerably debased in the passage from mouth to mouth: *self-denial*.

13. 31. The acceptance of unhappiness by a man who wishes for nothing but happiness, and *is* nothing but the act of wishing, is certainly a strange and improbable thing to happen, though not an impossible one; it is the only way by which a man attains a more valuable thing than happiness, freedom; and the consciousness of being free, *self-respect*.

13. 32. The man who denies himself and gains self-respect is richly rewarded; but *that is not why he does it*. His act of self-denial, not being a voluntary act (13. 21), cannot be a utilitarian act, the exchange of one thing for something more valuable.

13. 33. And if he knew what he stands to gain, he would not value it. What charm has self-respect for a man whose desires are concentrated on happiness?

13. 34. Can such an act be explained by appeal to something like what Freud calls the 'death-instinct'?

13. 35. Not unless the sleep-producing property of opium can be explained by reference to a *vertus dormitiva*.

13. 36. If anyone wants to multiply occult entities, let him go ahead, say I; but let him remember that, when he has fabricated one, he will do himself no good by inventing a second whose only function is to undo the work of the first.

13. 37. Let us by all means invent psychological forces called *instincts*, to explain why men pursue their own happiness and do what they want to do. More often than not, this is the way in which they do behave.

13. 38. Only you cannot have it both ways. It is a good rule that most men, most of the time, pursue happiness; so good, indeed, that it is worth betting on. But the rule cannot be stated in such a way as to explain the exceptions to itself, and make you win the bets you have lost.

13. 39. In defiance of psychological probability, men do sometimes neglect or defy what is called their 'duty to themselves', and in consequence make the strange discovery of freedom. Whether any non-human animal has ever done this I do not know; among human animals more, perhaps, have been credited with doing it than have actually done it.

13. 4. There is no sense in asking, when a man is found behaving in this way, 'why' he does it. The word 'why' has many well-established senses; none is appropriate here.

13. 41. But there is much sense in asking 'how' he does it; and the answer is: *'By the use of speech'*.

13. 42. A man liberates himself from a particular desire *by naming it*; not giving it any name that comes at haphazard into his head, but giving it its right name, the name it really has in the language he really talks.

13. 43. Once he has done this he can do it again; most easily for another desire of the same kind; but in principle, with more or less difficulty, for any desire whatever.

13. 44. Such at least is the doctrine common to Spinoza, the authors and divulgators of fairy-tales, and psycho-analysts.

13. 45. What liberates a man from his *passiones*, says Spinoza (the 'things that happen to a man', in fact his desires), is 'the strength of the intellect'; which by 'forming the idea' of a given *passio* converts the *passio* into an *actio*. Forming an idea is thinking, and thinking is done in words.

13. 46. There is a type of fairy-tale in which a human being gets into the power of a demon, and escapes by learning the demon's name and pronouncing it when challenged (Edward Clodd, *Tom Tit Tot*, is a comparative study of the type).

13. 47. 'The aim of psycho-analysis', says Freud (*Jenseits des Lustprinzips*, 1920; Rickman's *Selections*, p. 171), is 'the bringing into consciousness of the unconscious.' How can the patient be liberated from the 'compulsions' to which he is subject? By being brought to recognize the repressed elements in his experience from which they proceed.

13. 48. So much for the technique of self-liberation. As for its consequences, the doctrine that a man acquires free will by conquering his passions is fundamental to at least three, if not four, major religions: Confucianism, Buddhism, and Christianity, with its offshoot Mohammedanism.

13. 49. The pre-Christian thinkers of Europe, unlike those of Asia, did not realize this. They knew that there was such a thing as choice, and they described it with care; but they did not know that it lay on the other side of a door which could only be opened 'in defiance of psychological probability' (13. 39).

13. 5. The care with which they described it, therefore, was to a great extent thrown away; their whole system of thought was moribund before Christianity began to correct its errors.

13. 51. In modern Europe the doctrine that freedom results from the conquest of passion is popularly associated with Christianity, and the denial of that doctrine (a denial in many ways tempting) is popularly called 'paganism'.

13. 52. But a modern European 'pagan' is not maintaining any view that was maintained before the coming of Christianity. What he is maintaining is an escapist fantasy, or a group of escapist fantasies.

13. 53. Its essence is a proposal to abandon freedom, both practical, in the shape of an organized life, and theoretical, in the shape of a scientific life; and to do so deliberately, by a voluntary exchange of this contemptible Christian world for a better pagan world.

13. 54. An inconsistent proposal, because the act of abandoning freedom is to be a free act, and the act of choosing the world which you think better is to be an act of choice. In brief: the proposal is to decide on a life from which decision shall be excluded.

13. 55. Such a deliberate jettison of deliberation itself is impossible; what is possible is one that shall not be deliberate, but due to psychological causes.

13. 56. The possession of free will is achieved (13. 21) by an act of self-liberation, done involuntarily by every 'normal' man when his mental powers have reached a certain stage of development.

13. 57. This achievement of free will marks the stage at which, in modern Europe, a man is supposed to reach intellectual maturity.

13. 58. If anything interferes with the course of his mental development, this step may never happen; he will then become a man who is incapable of growing up; perhaps a man who hates[1] the thing (mental maturity) he does not possess.

13. 59. A further complication is possible. He may not entirely lack the condition of mental maturity, and none the less he may be entirely ignorant of possessing it and regard those who do possess it as his enemies.

13. 6. The act of self-liberation begins by being preconscious, and a long time may elapse between its being done and its being reflected upon.

13. 61. The present case (13. 59) is that of a man who has achieved the state of mental maturity but, for one reason or another, is not aware of having done so.

13. 62. As opposed to the man who never grows up, we have here a man who cannot or will not admit that he has grown up.

13. 63. Where the act of self-liberation is preconscious a man's will is, so to speak, asleep; latent, waiting to be aroused into activity by what is called 'arousing his self-respect', that is, making him conscious that he is free without being aware of it.

13. 64. This arousing of self-respect is extremely important in the practice of government and education. Persons thus engaged constantly find themselves meeting men who are incapable of decision. The rule for overcoming this state is: 'Arouse his self-respect.'

13. 65. There is also the converse rule for depriving a man of the ability to make a decision: 'Undermine his self-respect.'

13. 66. But this is a rule for devils. If you are a man, never act on it. There are no circumstances in which it can

---

[1] For the meaning of this term see 10. 35–7. I use it here deliberately for a confused state of mind.

be to any man's advantage that another man should become incapable of decision. It is very tempting to fancy that there are; but there are not.

13. 67. There is a stage of mental growth at which self-respect is precarious. The conquest of desire is achieved, but there is, or is fancied to be, a danger that some desire more powerful than the rest may break loose and *take charge*.[1]

13. 68. Fear of this is a motive for the *asceticism* which is common at this stage, when men try to bolster up their self-respect by deliberately doing things they would rather not. The impulse dies away at mental maturity.

13. 7. The last topic with which I shall deal in this chapter is the distinction between '*the will*' and '*the deed*'.

13. 71. 'The will' is making up your mind, or deciding, to do something; 'the deed' is carrying out that decision.

13. 72. When I am conscious of deciding, the deciding is the first-order object of my consciousness; what I decide to do is a second-order object, an abstraction from that.

13.'73. Like all abstractions, it is not quite determinate. To a man making a decision the deed which he is deciding to do is never completely definite. He thinks of it as having certain characteristics; the rest he leaves to be settled when it comes to carrying out the decision.

13. 74. However hard he tries to think out in every detail what he intends to do, he cannot. The will is always a blank cheque on the deed.

13. 75. It is better not to try very hard. An over-detailed plan is an impediment to its own execution. The most successful men of action prefer, while planning the main lines of what they intend, to leave the details for extemporary decision; a man incapable of even thus much improvisation is no man of action, and cannot make himself one by meticulous planning.

13. 8. A voluntary act is not *preceded by* a decision to do it; it *begins with* a decision to do it.

---

[1] 'To get out of control and act automatically esp. with disastrous or destructive effect' (*O.E.D.*, Supplement, art. 'Charge', § 13). Sailor's language. A heavy cask e.g. 'takes charge' when it breaks loose in a seaway and rushes from side to side of the ship, defeating efforts to secure it.

13.81. But the process from the will to the deed is at every stage under the control of will; the will is not content to initiate the process, leaving the details to be completed by another hand; it fills in the details itself as it goes on.

13.82. A will, as distinct from the corresponding deed, is an example of *practical thinking*. So far as it is thinking, it expresses itself (like all thinking) in words; thus the intention to shut the door is expressed as a thought by saying 'I will shut the door'.

13.83. But in addition to being a thought, it is also practical; and as practical it expresses itself by the initial stage of the action of shutting the door; for example, lifting my hand in the appropriate way.

13.84. What do I do, at this incipient stage, with the rest of the action, the part that I leave unperformed? I do not simply ignore it; I 'intend' it, which is a way of thinking about it and, like all thinking, is accompanied by speech—an appropriate form of speech.

13.85. The development of the process from the will to the deed involves the progressive conversion of intention or decision into performance. There are perhaps occasions on which thought turns wholly and without residue into deed; more often the process is incomplete, and some of what began as intention ends as—what shall we say?—frustrated intention.

13.86. Thought, I say, turns into *deed*, not into *act* or action; for these words, which are sometimes used for the deed as opposed to the will, are often by ancient and respectable usage employed for the will as opposed to the deed.

13.87. The 'acts' of parliament, the 'acta' of any committee or deliberative body, are decisions or choices as yet unexecuted; wills, not deeds. The same use of the word 'act' is very common in devotional literature.

13.88. The same usage is found in Shakespeare:

> Betweene the acting of a dreadfull thing,
> And the first motion, all the *Interim* is
> Like a *Phantasma*, or a hideous *Dreame*

says Brutus; where 'acting' is the decision, the will, as opposed to what he calls 'motion', the execution, the deed.

13.89. And the things which Hamlet says 'lose the name

of Action' cannot be deeds, for the things he is talking
about never culminate in deeds, so the name of deeds was a
name they never had.

13. 9. They are decisions that come unstuck. When
their author's mind was made up they had the name of
action; but he has changed his mind; so they have lost it.

XIV

REASON

14. 1. 'REASON' as the name of a mental function or form of consciousness, rational thinking, is thinking one thing, *x*, because you think another thing, *y*; where *y* is your 'reason' or, as it is sometimes called, your 'ground' for thinking *x*.

14. 11. Like every mental function, this is preconscious until a man reflects on it. He then becomes aware of thinking *x* because he thinks something else, he knows not what; further reflection identifies his reason for thinking *x* as a second proposition, *y*; still further reflection convinces him either that *y* is his *ratio cognoscendi* for *x*, and *x*'s *ratio essendi*, or else that it is neither.

14. 12. A piece of rational thinking involves at least two propositions standing to each other as ground and consequent. Let us call them as before (14. 1), *x* and *y*; and let the whole be symbolized: $y \rightarrow x$, read: 'somebody thinks *x* because he thinks *y*.'

14. 2. Rational thinking begins when a man accustomed to propositional thinking (11. 22) starts making a distinction not made in propositional thinking as such: the distinction between 'the that' and 'the why'.

14. 21. A man who reflects upon a piece of propositional thinking and asks himself whether he has really done it, and answers in the affirmative, is said to 'know' the proposition concerned.

14. 22. This is the simplest form of knowledge,[1] knowledge of 'the that'. Knowledge is the conviction or assurance with which a man reaffirms a proposition he has already made after reflecting on the process of making it and satisfying himself that it is well and truly made.

14. 23. 'Then this conviction may be misplaced, in which case knowledge is fallible?' That is so. Men are always trying to escape from so precarious a position; but in vain.

14. 24. Meanwhile they have what, as a matter of fact,

---

[1] Cf. 11. 11, where I have allowed myself to use the term *knowledge* for what turns out, on further reflection, to be merely *propositional thinking*.

they call knowledge; and this, as a matter of fact, is fallible.
A man may amuse himself by saying: 'If it is fallible, you
ought not to call it knowledge'; but whom is he in that case
addressing? There is nobody whose withers will be wrung
by his reproof. You cannot fight the dictionary.

14. 25. Men reflecting on the knowledge they possess
soon realize that it is fallible. However much they try to
drug themselves by reiterating the fact that they are convinced of a given proposition, the thought of its fallibility
teases them. What they get by this reiteration is only a
repetition of 'the that'; by inventing a 'why' they alleviate
their distress by obtaining a new kind of reassurance.

14. 26. A ground or reason for a given proposition is
what provides this new kind of reassurance.

14. 27. It is in fact a second proposition, y, standing to the
first, x, in the relation $y \rightarrow x$.

14. 28. This is how men come to search for reasons; a
reason being anything which can give me the (temporary)
assurance that my knowledge is trustworthy.

14. 29. It is this practical act of trying to alleviate the
distress caused me by the untrustworthiness of my knowledge
that gives rise to the distinction between 'the that' and
'the why'.

14. 3. Reason is distinguished into *theoretical reason* and
practical reason: i.e. reason for 'making up your mind *that*'
(reason for what logicians call a proposition) and reason for
'making up your mind *to*' (reason for what moralists call
an intention). We shall see that, of these two, practical
reason is the prior: it is the original form of reason, theoretical reason being a modification of it; and by the Law of
Primitive Survivals a practical element is always present in
a case of theoretical reason.

14. 31. After all, reason is always essentially practical;
because to be reasonable means to be interested in questions
beginning with 'why'; and this happens because people
crave for reassurance against the fallibility of their knowledge.

14. 32. *Practical reason* comes into existence when a man
forms an intention, reflects on it, and asks himself whether he
really means it. His intention threatens to come unstuck and
'lose the name of action' (13. 9). He seeks for a y which may

confirm this x; something from which the x may follow as a necessary consequence.

14.33. Nothing can confirm the resolution with which a man regards his intention except the discovery that another intention, upon which he is fully resolved, stands to it in the relation of ground to consequent. He will ask, for example, 'Need I get out of bed and hammer in that peg?' 'I must' (comes the answer), 'if I do not want the whole tent to blow down.'

14.34. This is a case of practical reason, where the strong resolution not to let the tent blow down acts as a ground of the weaker resolution to get out of bed at once.

14.35. *Theoretical reason* comes into existence when a man first, by propositional thinking, makes up his mind that something is so; and then, seeking to confirm this piece of propositional thinking, looks for a reason why he should think so.

14.36. A man who asks for such a reason is presupposing that he is free to think the thing or not, according as he finds reason for thinking it or not.

14.37. Theoretical reason, therefore, is based on the presupposition that a certain kind of propositional thinking, viz. that about which questions beginning 'why' can be legitimately asked, is a matter of free will; is not the mere acceptance of something 'given', but is a voluntary decision to think *this* and not *that*.

14.38. This is why theoretical reason always contains a primitive survival of practical reason (9.5).

14.39. The warning already given (4.73) against the Fallacy of Misplaced Argument has made it clear that first-order objects are things about which questions beginning 'why?' must not be asked. Such questions are legitimately asked only about objects of the second and higher orders (abstractions).

14.4. If x is an intention, any ground for it, y, must be another intention (14.34). One intention supporting another both form part of the same intention, which includes them both and perhaps other things. Let us call this larger intention I.

14. 41. If *x* is a proposition about whose truth someone desires reassurance, it follows that *y*, the ground of that reassurance, must be a proposition of whose truth he is satisfied; *x* and *y* are here abstractions from a first-order proposition (P) which includes them both and perhaps other things as well.

14. 42. As long as I and P are first-order objects, they are matters of immediate conviction or resolution (14. 32) as the case may be; to offer reason for either would involve the Fallacy of Misplaced Argument.

14. 43. To demand confirmation for either would be to place it in a context of other intentions or other propositions that might afford grounds for it; that is, to reduce it to the level of an abstraction. Not to think *that it is* an abstraction, but by a practical act (at first, no doubt, preconscious) *to make it* an abstraction.

14. 44. An intention is made into an abstraction by surrounding it with a context of other intentions; a proposition, by surrounding it with a context of other propositions.

14. 5. Practical reason is prior to theoretical reason, which is a modification of it (14. 3).

14. 51. Were it not so, there would be no accounting for a tendency which, everyone knows, besets the work of theoretical reason: the tendency to *anthropomorphism*.

14. 52. We reason anthropomorphically when we seek reasons for the behaviour of things other than ourselves on the analogy of the reasons we have already found for our own behaviour.

14. 53. Thus when a fly-rod hooks me in the ear, a hammer hits me on the thumb, or a bicycle throws me into the ditch, I think of them as maliciously thwarting my endeavours to control them. In myself, malice of this kind is a familiar object; I cannot help ascribing it to these non-human agents.

14. 54. The existence in me of a tendency to think in this way is not a thing I am proud of. I try to laugh myself out of it or, if I cannot get rid of it, to think of it as a mere example of the way in which thought exhibits vices which need not be taken seriously

14. 55. Why should there be such a tendency? It is *a*

*trace of practical reason surviving into the theoretical reason that
has developed out of it.*

14. 6. Theoretical reason, by the Law of Primitive
Survivals (9. 5), inherits the tendency to anthropomorphism,
as an innate tendency which can be conquered (that is,
rendered harmless) but not abolished, from its parent,
practical reason.

14. 61. We cannot help thinking anthropomorphically;
but we are provided with a remedy: our own laughter at
the ridiculous figure we cut, incorrigibly anthropomorphic
thinkers inhabiting a world where anthropomorphic thinking
is a misfit.

14. 62. Knowing as we now do that the first kind of reason
to come into operation is practical reason, we shall next
proceed to study its various types.

14. 63. For us, committed to the plain historical method,
that means cataloguing the various types of practical reason
ordinarily spoken of by modern Europeans when they talk
about the subject.

14. 64. I find that there are three of these. Why three I
neither know nor ask. It is not because three is in my eyes a
magical number; but I find that people talking about practical reason distinguish various types of it, and that these
types, under inspection, resolve themselves into three falling
in a certain order.

14. 65. There are certain missing words (three missing
words, when I make allowance for synonyms), one of which
is used on any one occasion when a modern European
answers the question: 'Why did you do that?' He will
answer:

14. 66. (1) 'Because it is useful.'

14. 67. (2) 'Because it is right.'

14. 68. (3) 'Because it is my duty.'

14. 69. In the following chapters I shall explain what
these answers mean.

XV

UTILITY

15. 1. THE first answer to the question: 'Why do I choose (or, did I choose) this course of conduct which I call *x*?' was: 'Because it is useful' (14. 66).

15. 11. To call a thing useful is to call it useful *for* something. Useful for what? For a purpose or intention, co-existing as a practical thought in my mind with the other purpose which, relatively to it, I call useful.

15. 12. Here, then, are two purposes with a relation between them; each is, therefore, a second-order purpose; we will call them *x* and *y*, *y* being the reason for *x*.

15. 13. As an element in this complex, *y* is called 'end' and *x* is called 'means'. To say 'I do this because it is useful' is to say 'I do *x* as means to *y*', often not explaining what *y* is.

15. 14. For 'useful' we sometimes say 'expedient'; sometimes 'good', or 'good for something', namely the end; sometimes 'necessary', or (once more) 'necessary for something'; or any one of many possible alternatives.

15. 15. A purpose explained as useful I call a 'utilitarian' purpose, and action consisting in the formation and execution of such a purpose 'utilitarian action'.

15. 16. Croce, who has done much for the theory of utilitarian action, calls it 'economic action'. In deference to current usage, I prefer to keep the word 'economic' for a special case of utilitarian action, namely a case involving more than one agent standing in *social relations*.

15. 17. Thus when I visit my tobacconist and give him a sum of money, receiving a pound of tobacco in exchange, I prefer to say that there is only one economic action, our joint action, the exchange of money for tobacco; but two utilitarian actions, one on my part, giving up money for the sake of getting tobacco, and one on the tobacconist's part, giving up tobacco as means to getting money.

15. 18. Where the reason for *x* is a utilitarian reason the formula $y \rightarrow x$ takes the special form $y\,(U)\,x$, to be read: '*y* is the utilitarian reason for *x*; in other words *x* is means to the end *y*'.

15. 2. What is the essence of the means-end relation? I shall divide my answer into two parts, one positive, the other negative.

15. 21. The positive part will consist in describing the rational elements in that relation.

15. 22. For it is in part a rational relation; to say: 'I choose *x* as means to *y*' does go some way towards explaining why I choose *x*.

15. 23. But it is only a partial explanation. Even at best it leaves much unexplained.

15. 24. Its negative side, its non-explanation of certain things, is as much part of its essence as its positive side, its explanation of others. This negative side, therefore, must not be neglected (cf. 15. 5).

15. 3. What constitutes the positive or explanatory element in utility? It is *not a time-relation*. Time-relations often appear as elements in a means-end relation; but they are never of its essence.

15. 31. A man plants apple-trees for a utilitarian reason: he wants apples. In this case years may elapse between planting the trees and gathering the first crop.

15. 32. A man turning on the electric light has much less time to wait between pressing the switch and finding the room illuminated. Generalizing from these and similar examples, one might be tempted to say that the means precede the end in time in the order of execution; and that in planning the end precedes the means in time.

15. 33. On this view, you begin by planning the means; for example to grow apples on your own trees. Then you choose places for the trees, then set about buying them, and so forth. You conclude that utility is in essence a reciprocal time-relation such that in planning the end comes before the means, while in execution the means come before the end.

15. 34. But neither sequence is universal, nor even common enough to be very probable next time.

15. 35. In the order of execution, means and end are often simultaneous. A man who gets rid of weeds by pulling them up has no time to wait between the two operations; for there are not two operations, there is only one. So with a man who clears his path of a rival by murder.

15. 36. In planning, the end does not always come before the means; sometimes they are planned simultaneously, sometimes the means are planned first.

15. 37. Proverbial wisdom favours the last alternative. 'Cut your coat according to your cloth' means, if I understand it aright, 'plan your means before proceeding to plan your ends.'

15. 38. What is essential in the relation between means and end, however, is not that there should be any special time-sequence but that there should be a *logical interrelation* such that each plan, the means-plan and the end-plan alike. is checked and corrected by reference to the other.

15. 39. These time-sequences, therefore, which sometimes occur in means-end relations and sometimes do not, so far from constituting the essence of such a relation, are not even always present where there is such a relation.

15. 4. Time-relations, however, are very often used as *symbols for logical relations*. People often say that one thing 'precedes' another in time when they mean that it precedes it in logic; and one kind of logical priority is the priority of ground to consequent. That is the kind which is in question here.

15. 41. We have already taken x to symbolize the means and y the end. Interpreted on the above method, the suggestion before us is that, in planning, y implies x (that is, y is ground and x consequent); in execution, or as deed, x implies y. There is a relation at the will-stage which is reversed at the deed-stage; but it is not (as was suggested) a relation of time; it was an implication.

15. 42. In planning, x is decided upon because y is decided upon. It makes no difference to the pattern y (U) x whether y is decided upon capriciously or for a reason; and if the latter, it makes no difference what the reason is. All that is essential to the pattern is that y should be chosen, and that the choice of y should logically necessitate the choice of x.

15. 43. A man plans to do y; he finds that he cannot think that plan out unless he thinks it out as the plan of doing y by doing x. The word 'cannot' refers to a logical necessity. The y-plan logically necessitates the x-plan.

15. 44. In carrying out these plans *the necessitation works* *the opposite way.* It is x which, as deed, necessitates y as deed. The man planning to get rid of his rival was logically driven into planning his murder because he could not think how otherwise to do it; when he comes to carrying out the plan, all he does is to murder him; the fact of his murdering his rival logically entails getting rid of him.

15. 45. The reader may perhaps be willing to agree that the necessitation of the x-plan by the y-plan is a logical necessitation, because plans are thoughts, and the relation of one thought to another may be a logical relation; but he may object to my saying that the necessitation of the y-deed by the x-deed is a logical necessitation, because these are not *'thoughts'* but *'deeds'*, and the connexion between them is consequently not a 'logical' connexion but a 'real' connexion: perhaps a case of physical causation: anyhow, not a case of implication.

15. 46. I reply: it is a case of implication. There are not two deeds: there is one deed with two interrelated 'aspects', or 'characteristics', or 'predicates', or whatever name you wish to use for what I call 'abstractions' from the deed. It is one of these abstractions that necessitates the other; and a relation between two abstractions whereby one necessitates the other is a logical relation.

15. 5. So much for the positive element in utility. It comes to this. Utility, on its positive side, is a relation between one second-order choice x and another y, such that a man making up his mind to do y is logically constrained to make up his mind to do x as well; and a man carrying out a decision to do x is logically constrained thereby to do y. To say that x is useful is to say that this rather complicated situation is the situation in which x is involved.

15. 51. If this were all utility meant, there would be no difference between saying that x is useful, that x is right, and that x is somebody's duty. In respect of its positive element utility is identical with rightness and duty. The implication of x by y in planning, and the converse implication of y by x in execution, is the general characteristic of practical reason as such, and is found in every form of practical reason.

15. 52. What distinguishes utility from rightness and duty is not any positive characteristic but a *negative charac-*

teristic. It is because utility stops short where it does, explains only so much and no more, that utility is only utility and not rightness or duty. Its *differentia* is the peculiar limit of its rationality. I hasten to explain.

15. 6. Let us return to the case of buying tobacco. The business of utilitarian thinking is to explain such an act as going into a shop and giving a certain sum of money to the person serving there. But how much of this act does it explain; how much does it leave unexplained?

15. 61. It only professes to explain so much of the act as is done from free choice. If I found the shop in occupation of the police carrying out an order against the sale of tobacco, or of the tobacco I wanted, a utilitarian would no longer think of my purchase of tobacco, or my non-purchase of tobacco, as a thing it was his business to explain.

15. 62. Even within the limits of free choice, there may still be much which it is not for utilitarian thinking to explain. Suppose the tobacconist told me a hard-luck story about the rent, and suppose this induced me to pay his rent for him. Paying my tobacconist's rent for him is, from my point of view, perhaps a duty; perhaps a right act; it is not a utilitarian act; and utilitarian thinking cannot explain it.

15. 63. It hardly professes to. But there are other things about the act in question which one might have expected it to explain; which, surprisingly perhaps, it does not. My end, getting a pound of tobacco, explains why I pay the tobacconist a certain sum of money. But the cash in my pocket, not to mention the credit at my disposal, allows me to make up that sum in several different ways; as between these various ways my plan leaves the choice entirely open. The choice has to be made before the plan can be carried out; but how is it made? It cannot be made by reference to the end; it can only be made by what, from a utilitarian point of view, is caprice; in other words, something that a utilitarian point of view leaves unexplained.

15. 64. This is only one of several irrationalities about utilitarian action; in other words, limitations in the utilitarian explanation of action. Here is another; like the last, concerned with the indeterminacy of means.

15. 65. The plan is to make payment to the tobacconist.

But who is the tobacconist? He is a legal personality which covers, for example, the proprietor of the business, or his wife, or his child, or his hired assistant. As between these possible recipients of the cash, the plan leaves me with an open choice. I do not know how many persons are authorized to take my money; far less know them all by sight. But I have to make up my mind to whom I shall tender payment. It is a question on which utilitarian thinking throws no light.

15. 66. The y-plan or end is equally indeterminate. It is to buy a pound of tobacco. What pound of tobacco? The tobacconist may have before him a new crate holding six dozen pounds. Which of them is it my plan to buy? The answer is not to be found by any inspection of the plan. In fact, it is not provided by any sort of utilitarian thinking. This is another point at which utilitarian action is based on caprice.

15. 7. The openness of these various options, however, is not a deliberate feature of utilitarian action. If it had been, the specifications involved by the x-plan and the y-plan would have been what logicians call, or called, 'universals'; generalizations to which it is essential that they should admit of many different individual realizations.

15. 71. But this does not happen. It makes no difference, so long as I have enough money to pay for one pound of tobacco, whether I could produce the sum in other ways. So long as the tobacconist has one pound of my tobacco in stock, it makes no difference whether he has others or not.

15. 72. The plans which are an essential feature of utilitarian action are indifferent to the distinction between a plan that can only be realized in one way and one that can be realized in several. Utilitarian action deals with individuals, not universals; but none of these is an individual proper, *individuum omnimodo determinatum*; each is an indefinite individual, required to satisfy certain specifications but free to vary so long as those specifications are satisfied.

15. 73. An indefinite individual, such as those which occur in utilitarian thinking, may be planned, for the plan may be left vague; but the plan cannot be carried out, for in the process of execution the points left vague must be somehow settled.

15.74. There is, accordingly, an inevitable discrepancy between what can be explained on utilitarian principles and what happens in the world.

15.8. This is the negative characteristic of utility. It explains nothing except the abstract conformity of the means-plan with the abstract specifications of the end-plan. Each of these plans is an indefinite individual. Everything except the conformity of these indefinite individuals to one another is, from the utilitarian point of view, irrational. What is irrational means what my principles of explanation do not explain. An irrational element in the self is called 'caprice'; one in the not-self is called 'accident'.

XVI

RIGHT

16. 1. THERE are, or were, people calling themselves utilitarians, and adopting what they called the 'creed' that utility is the only form of practical reason.

16. 11. Their self-chosen title betrays them. Words having terminations like 'utilitarian', 'utilitarianism', are properly *sectarian* titles referring to beliefs, or rather practical programmes, adopted not for scientific reasons but for motives of sectarian loyalty. Words of this type are some-times used, without understanding their implications, with respect either to themselves, or others, by persons who fancy that they are conferring a scientific title (see further, 41. 13).

16. 12. The belief that utility is the only form of practical reason, when the so-called utilitarians adopted it, was a deliberate challenge to the established doctrine that there is another form, namely *right*; for its upholders justified it (or tried to) by arguing that right is only utility under another name.

16. 13. This was an allegation about the facts of linguistic usage. 'Right' and 'useful' are well-established words in English, to say nothing of other languages. The utilitarian position was that they meant the same thing. The appeal was to the facts of language. To the facts, then, let us go.

16. 14. The adjective 'right' has in English a continuous literary history from the ninth century onwards. In the course of time it has developed a great variety of meanings. It is remarkable how little they vary. The *Oxford English Dictionary* lists over fifty; but all are differentiations of a single original meaning, namely 'straight'.

16. 15. This fact did not wait to be discovered by the authors of *O.E.D.* F. H. Bradley called attention to it in 1876 (*Ethical Studies*, p. 187; ed. 2, 1927, p. 207): 'Right is the rule, and what is conformable to the rule, whether the rule be physical or mental: e.g. a right line, a "right English bulldog" (Swift), a right conclusion, a right action.' It does not speak well for English philosophy since then that the meaning of the word has been repeatedly discussed as if the fact were still unknown.

16. 2. A straight line is called 'right' because the act of drawing it is controlled by the geometrical instrument called a 'rule' or 'ruler'. An angle of 90 degrees is called a 'right' angle with similar reference to a carpenter's or draughtsman's square.

16. 21. That is one sort of 'rule', a material rule made of wood or metal. A rule of another kind (in fact an inductive proposition telling you what to expect) is that one of a man's hands, generally the same hand, is stronger and more skilful than the other. The hand which 'as a rule' is the stronger and more skilful is called, by reference to that rule, the 'right' hand.

16. 22. We now come to a third type of rule; the type that here especially concerns us. The 'right' key for a given lock is any key (not one key, but any one of a *set of right keys*) which in the case of that lock obeys the rules, which a locksmith has to know, governing the relations between lock-form and key-form. The 'right' drug for a disease is a drug which conforms with the rules, which physicians have to know, correlating diseases with drugs. The 'right' time is time kept by a timepiece whose movements conform with a rule correlating them with the movements of the standard clock at Greenwich Observatory.

16. 23. I spare the reader further examples. He understands by now, I hope, why the utilitarian appeal fails; why 'right' as a matter of fact *never* means 'useful'. A thing is useful, or the opposite, in relation to the end it achieves; it is right, or the opposite, in relation to the rule it obeys. What is right may be *also* useful, and what is wrong may be also useless; but not always; and even when these coincide the coincidence is not an identity.

16. 24. The wrong key, or even a bent wire, may sometimes serve to work a lock; for a man who knows how to use it, it would be as useful as the right key for that occasion, though not for others when his skill deserted him; but that does not make it the right key. Perhaps it is *de fide* for a utilitarian that no one ever opened a lock except with the right key; but not for the rest of us.

16. 3. Right may be symbolized by a special case of the

formula $y \rightarrow x$, namely $y(R)x$, read 'x is chosen because it is right, i.e. because it conforms with the rule y.' In every case of $y \rightarrow x$ we know that y and x are two second-order purposes, distinguishable parts of one and the same complex purpose. A rule, then, is a kind of purpose. What kind?

16. 31. It is a *generalized purpose*: not the purpose to do one thing on one occasion, which (as we saw in the case of utility) may be a vaguely defined thing done on a vaguely defined occasion, but a purpose to do things of a certain kind on all occasions of a certain kind.

16. 32. This is a *regularian principle* or *rule*. To act on a regularian principle is to decide upon a general way of behaving, defined as involving some act of a specified kind if and when some occasion of a specified kind arises.

16. 33. This only defines the rule; and a rule is only one part of a regularian action. There is also the decision to obey the rule, or to disobey it: to do one act of the specified kind now, an occasion of the kind specified in the rule having arisen; or, alternatively, to do something else. The x-element which the y-element serves to explain is the first alternative; it is the act in which you do the thing you decided to do; deciding when you made the rule, carrying out your decision when you obey it.

16. 34. It is sometimes believed (first) that rules are functions of social activity; that a rule is normally, if not invariably, made by one person and obeyed by another; and (secondly) that making a rule is a complete act, done on one occasion and that obeying it (or breaking it) is a second complete act done on another occasion. Both beliefs are false.

16. 35. Rules are an important feature of social life, but they are not peculiar to social life. A man may, and often does, make rules solely for himself: this, indeed, is regularian action in its simplest form, and unless we understand this we shall never understand the complex case in which one man makes a rule for another to obey.

16. 36. Making and obeying a rule are sometimes separated in time, just as they are sometimes divided between agents. But this again is a complication of the simplest case, where the y-resolution to have such and such a rule is simultaneous with the x-resolution to obey it.

16. 37. Regularian action in its essential form is the making and obeying of a single rule by a single agent at a single time. The x-element and the y-element are unseparated parts of a single, though complex, decision; the decision y (R) x, the decision a man may express by saying 'this is what I decide to do as a general thing, if and when the present conditions recur; and I begin by doing it now.'

16. 4. Now for the complications. They are intelligible only if we remember that the characteristics of the simplest case are likely to reappear, by the Law of Primitive Survivals (9. 5) in the more complex cases.

16. 41. Social activity (19. 57) is a sharing of activity between different agents, the activity shared still figuring in the consciousness of those agents as a single, undivided activity; not a case of 'I do this and you do that', but a case of 'we do *this*', a '*this*' which comprises both the 'this' and the 'that'.

16. 42. Each thinks of himself both as doing his own share of what they agree to call '*this*', and as 'authorizing' the other to do his share; where 'authorizing a man to do an act' means 'willing' or 'deciding' that he shall do it.

16. 43. An action in the form $y \rightarrow x$ can be in this sense shared between two partners, X and Y, if X does x and authorizes Y to do y and vice versa.

16. 44. A utilitarian action y (U) x, where x is e.g. fetching a draught of water and y is drinking it, may be thus shared between X the fetcher and Y the drinker, if each authorizes what the other does. X not only fetches water, he fetches it for Y to drink; he authorizes a drinking of it; in particular a drinking by Y. And Y must authorize X to bring him a drink of water; Y's plan to drink it must include a plan that someone, in particular X, shall fetch it.

16. 45. A regularian action y (R) x may be shared in the same way. Each partner, in planning his share of the action, plans the whole action; the plan being so organized that it specifies X's share as the carrying out of the x-element and Y's share as the carrying out of the y-element. In this sense X authorizes Y to make a rule and Y authorizes X to obey it.

16. 5. Regularian action may be distributed over agents; it may also be distributed over times. A rule is often made on the occasion of first obeying it; it may be made without an occasion for obeying it having yet arisen. As in the case of a utilitarian action the unity of the entire action must be consciously recognized. At the first time, t_1, a mere rule is made, but by somebody who thinks that occasions will arise for obeying it; he thinks that there will be a future time, t_2, for obeying the rule he is now making. At this future time, t_2, he is obeying or disobeying a rule he is conscious of having made.

16. 51. Regularian action not only admits, but ordinarily at least implies, a different sort of time-distribution, namely the application of the rule to different occasions arising at different times. The y-purpose, or rule, in this case explicitly refers to a plurality of cases on which it is to be obeyed. Even if it is not known that any such occasions will actually arise, the rule provides for them if they do.

16. 6. It was pointed out above (15. 8) that a utilitarian ground never fully explains why just this action and no other is done. The same is true of regularian grounds, though in a different way.

16. 61. This is because the regularian ground is a generalization, expressly admitting of alternative realizations. I recognize a rule to tell the truth; I recognize that I, Panurge, have been asked by this man, Pantagruel, to tell him who I am and what I want; what exactly does the rule require me to do? Panurge gave Pantagruel the required information in fourteen different languages, of which it transpired that Pantagruel knew only one. Suppose Pantagruel had known all fourteen, did the rule bid Panurge use them all?

16. 62. A rule only specifies *some* act of a certain kind. The application of it to a given occasion bids me perform one, and only one, of the acts which would conform to its specification. The acts which so conform may be many or few; which they are, depends not on the rule but on the circumstances; if they are many, I have got to choose between them, but the rule cannot tell me how. From the regularian point of view my choice between the alternatives is a matter of caprice.

16. 63. Regularian explanations, like utilitarian explanations, are at best partial explanations. *They never explain why*

a man does this act; they only explain why he does *an act of this kind*, one of the alternative actions specified by the rule. If, like Kant, you call a rule 'an imperative', you must add that there can be no such thing as a 'categorical imperative'. Rules as such are disjunctive. No rule ever bids you 'do this and nothing else.' Any rule bids you, if and when certain conditions arise, 'do this or this or this' ... any act, no matter what, conforming with the general type laid down by the terms of the rule.

16. 64. But we need not make things out worse than they are. A good deal of fuss has been made over the fact that one rule may conflict with another. If 'right' means 'according to rule', as it does (16. 15), the same action may be both right and wrong, according as it is judged by different rules; and, since it is thought (I do not know why) that the same action cannot really be both right and wrong, either right action is impossible or else 'right' cannot mean 'according to rule'.

16. 7. If there is a rule to tell the truth and also a rule to save human life, what are you to do when an intending murderer asks you where his intended victim is hidden? If you deceive him you tell a lie, which is wrong; if you do not, you become accessory before the fact to a murder, and that is wrong too.

16. 71. This is a famous brain-twister planted upon the world by Kant and Fichte. I will begin by offering a straight answer.

16. 72. 'It depends upon what kind of a man you intend to be. A rule is a generalized purpose defining a certain type of conduct or way of life as the one you mean to adopt. If your rule is to tell the truth at all costs, which is what Kant and Fichte think it ought to be, you will tell the truth at the cost of human life, which in their opinion is of value only as providing a vehicle for "the moral law". If your rule is to save human life, tell a lie. Kant and Fichte will be very shocked; but need you care?'

16. 73. But a sensible man does not go bald-headed into a brain-twister. He wants to know which end to take it by. Let us try asking what is meant by the formula 'there is a rule to tell the truth'.

16. 74. A rule is a generalized intention. 'There is a rule' means: somebody (unspecified) has a certain generalized intention. It may provide him with a reason for acting in a certain kind of way; but it will do so only if he is what we call a reasonable man, that is, a man in the habit of abiding by his generalized intentions. Whether it will provide anybody else with a reason for acting in that sort of way is another question. If a hook which is right for trout-fishing is wrong for salmon-fishing, make up your mind what fish you are after. Is anybody so fanatical a Kantian as to think that every man must live by the same rules, whether he lives in a monastery or in 'the world', whether he is a minister of religion or an officer in the army, whether he is an ancient heathen Greek or a modern European Christian?

16. 75. Further, it is essential to a rule that it should be as accurately defined as may be. How exactly shall we define this alleged rule to tell the truth? Does it mean: tell everything you know or believe, for twenty-four hours a day without stopping, to everyone within earshot? If it does, it is a rule which no one but a fool will for a moment imagine himself to recognize. I do not know what it does mean. There are many rules of truthfulness, specifying different kinds of truth which it is right to tell different kinds of people on different kinds of occasion. There is none that tells me to point out his victim's hiding-place to a murderer. Why Kant thought there was, I will not spend time here asking.[1]

16. 76. It would be a serious matter if there were a conflict between two rules each meant to provide a partial definition for one and the same way of life. It would prove that the idea of that way of life was a hopelessly confused idea. Its victims should give up trying to live with their heads in a muddle; unmake the rules they have been so foolish as to make; and think out a way of life in which it is possible to live.

16. 77. But regularian thinking has its limitations. Even the best-thought-out rules leave much to caprice and accident (15. 8). I have not tried to mention all their short-

---

[1] Briefly, his error on this point was due to herd-marching (33. 35), characteristic of the German he was.

comings. What I have tried to convince the reader of, probably in vain if he has been brought up on German philosophy, is that for any man who tries to live rationally there are always conflicts between one way of life and another. The same thing happens in utilitarian action. What conduces to one end often frustrates another. Never mind; be content if your means conduce to the ends you are actually pursuing. In the same way the rules you are trying to obey are hard enough to obey as it is; do not make them harder by attaching to them a degree of importance which no rule can ever have.

XVII

DUTY

17. 1. THE third type of reason for a choice was: 'because it is my duty' (14. 68). We have now to think what people mean by this expression: and the first step is to look at the history of the word.

17. 11. It is formed by adding a common Romance suffix to 'due', which represents the Latin *debitum*, 'owed'. 'Duty' in the abstract is the state of something's being owed: 'a duty' is a thing owed.

17. 12. 'Due' and 'duty' first appear in English in the late thirteenth and early fourteenth centuries to describe various aspects of the state of indebtedness. They always contain a reference to the past, *debitum* being a past participle; a past act of incurring the debt; logically past; it need not be also temporally past (17. 21).

17. 13. They are medieval words, and in the Middle Ages the idea of debt was associated less with the expectation of a money payment than with that of a payment in kind; or, still oftener, that of rendering to a 'lord' a 'service' not necessarily conceived as having a monetary equivalent.

17. 14. The idea of a debt[1] incurred by one act and discharged by another had already found a vernacular English expression in a new sense of the Germanic verb 'owe'. Originally this meant 'own', but from the tenth century onwards it is the current English translation for *debere*.

17. 15. When 'due' and 'duty' first appeared in English, therefore, they found Germanic synonyms derived from the verb 'owe' already established; in particular the past tense 'ought', where the same reference to a logically past act of incurring debt is implied.

17. 16. Etymologically, then, 'it is my duty to do this' and 'I ought to do this' mean the same; viz. that I am conscious of an obligation or debt incurred in the past by an act that generated the obligation, and to be discharged in the future by the act referred to as 'this'.

---

[1] In Roman law an obligation always arises *vel ex contractu vel ex delicto*: Gaius iii. 88.

17. 17. In modern English, consciousness of obligation is distinguished from other forms of consciousness by the name 'conscience'. 'Conscience' has a first-order object, viz. the obligation itself. From this various abstractions are made, as usual, in pairs. I will mention two such pairs.

17. 18. First, myself as under obligation, and being under obligation as the state in which I am. Secondly, the obligation's initial and terminal points: the act of incurring it and the act of discharging it.

17. 19. 'Obligation' is a Roman law term which, like 'society', keeps its meaning substantially (not absolutely) unchanged in modern languages. In English we have another Germanic equivalent, whereby 'to be under an an obligation' is 'to be bound'. A third doublet, simplest of all expressions for sheer consciousness of obligation, because it contains no reference to the act of incurring, is the word 'necessary' or 'must'; or in older English (and still in some other Germanic languages) 'shall'.

17. 2. In the simplest or essential case the acts of incurring and discharging the obligation are acts of *the same person*. I am immediately conscious of an obligation. Reflecting, I conceive it as my obligation: I regard both the initial act of incurring it and the terminal act of discharging it as acts which are (were, are to be) acts of mine.

17. 21. The words 'initial' and 'terminal' refer essentially not to temporal priority but to logical priority. There need not be a time-series in which the existence of an obligation is subsequent to its being incurred.

17. 22. If there is such a series it is a complication, as in the cases of utility and right (16. 5). The condition of its arising is that the agent's consciousness of himself as agent, and his consciousness of the action's identity, are preserved throughout.

17. 3. Let us consider the complication. Suppose the agent to be aware of the obligation at the time t_2; let him have incurred it at an earlier time t_1; and let him discharge it at a later time t_3. At t_2 and t_3 he must be conscious of having incurred the obligation at t_1; but at t_1 he need not be conscious that there will ever be a time t_2 when he will be under an obligation as a result of what he is now doing.

17. 31. An obligation may be incurred unawares. This is

generally, but not always, where it *nascitur ex delicto*; through ignorance of the law, which excuses no man, the agent does not know what he is letting himself in for.

17. 32. Or an obligation may be distributed over various agents. B may 'hold himself responsible' for a debt incurred by A. This is not legal fiction, nor indeed a fiction at all; it is a fact of consciousness that B may thus hold himself responsible for A's action without either believing or pretending that he did it.

17. 33. A still further complication is possible. B finds himself under an obligation; he ascribes its origin to an act on the part of A; he regards it as discharged by a third person C who by taking the responsibility for it releases both A, who incurred it, and B, who found himself saddled with it.

17. 34. The importance of this case in the history of the European conception of duty will appear if we call A Adam, B the believer, and C Christ. The believer thinks of himself as saddled with responsibility for Adam's sin, and as freed from it through assumption of it by God Himself in the person of Christ.

17. 35. This is the idea of the Atonement, which has sometimes been denounced as a legal quibble forced upon an alien and inappropriate context. Nothing could be farther from the truth. The idea is an integral part of the ordinary moral consciousness, at least in Christendom; it is perplexing only to a man who is too weak in the head to follow the logic of a case where an obligation is distributed over three agents.

17. 4. The formula for an act of duty is y (D) x, read: 'I choose to do x because it is my duty.' As before, there are two decisions, a y-decision and an x-decision, the former the ground of the latter.

17. 41. In this special case of the general formula $y \rightarrow x$, I will not waste time over general features. The reader can without difficulty work them out for himself. I will attend to the special characteristics that distinguish this case from those of right and utility.

17. 5. The special characteristics of duty are (1) determinacy and (2) possibility.

17. 51. Duty admits of no alternatives. Whatever is my duty is an *individuum omnimodo determinatum*. There is only one of it; it is not one of a set of alternatives; there is nothing that will do as well.

17. 52. In the first place it is *my* duty and nobody else's. There is only one agent, an agent having free will; viz. myself, who am called upon to do it. (This is not inconsistent with the doctrine of the Atonement; the literature of that conception everywhere insists that Christ frees sinners from obligation by doing what he is in no sense bound to do.)

17. 53. Secondly, any duty is a duty to do 'this' act and only 'this', not 'an act of this kind'. The relation between *x* and *y* is a one-one relation.

17. 54. Here duty differs both from right and from utility, each of which is what is called a many-one relation; the ground fits so loosely on the consequent that it fits a number of different alternatives equally well (or equally badly) and never allows you to say about any 'That and no other is the foot that the shoe fits.'

17. 55. Hence dutiful action, among these three kinds of rational action, is the only one that is completely rational in principle; the only one whose explanations really explain; the only one whose answer to the question: 'Why did I do that action?' (namely, 'because it was my duty') answers precisely that question and not one more or less like it.

17. 56. But the idea of duty is, after all, an abstraction, not a first-order object; and, like all abstractions, incompletely determinate. If you say to yourself: 'I will do my duty' you are saying that there is one thing, and only one, which you have in mind to do; but *you do not say what it is*.

17. 57. Like every form of immediate consciousness (and every form of consciousness is immediate in relation to its first-order object) 'conscience' is as nearly infallible as a reasonable man will expect; but what is the business it 'infallibly' carries out?

17. 58. To tell me that I am under an obligation; *not to tell me what the obligation is*. To answer that question demands a process of logical thinking, over and above the intuitive or immediate process which answers the question: 'Have I got any obligations, never mind what?'

17. 59. If that question is answered in the affirmative, I have next to find out what it is that I am under obligation to do, asking and answering successive questions in the form: 'Is it this?' 'Is it this?' 'Is it this?'

17.6. The second characteristic of duty is *possibility*. Whatever a man is under obligation to do is an act which that man is here and now able to do.

17.61. It does not follow (as the faint-hearted are accustomed to think) that a man is released from a duty to do something because he *supposes* it impossible to him. Perhaps he was wrong in thinking he could not do it; nobody knows what he can do until he tries, and tries hard.

17.62. Kant saw this and said it with admirable brevity that *'ought' implies 'can'*. Unhappily Kant made nonsense of it by embedding it in a regularian theory of duty: I mean a theory which denied the very existence of duty, as the utilitarian theory does but in a different way, by alleging that 'duty' is only another word for 'right'.

17.63. Duty, said Kant, is 'the necessity of acting according to the law'. If it were, then 'ought' would not always imply 'can'; it would, for example, never imply 'can' when[1] the act in question meant acting in accordance (as it often does) with rules involving contradictions.

17.7. That is why Kant's moral theory, as Cicero said of Cato, inhabits a world that is not a world of facts: it lives 'in Plato's Republic', not 'in the sewage of Romulus'.

17.71. That is why Bradley,[2] after a long trial, dropped it and called on 'religion' to make good the fatal defects which he could not but see in 'morality'; the Kantian, regularian morality which he called 'my station and its duties'.

17.72. That is why Sir David Ross[3] in the long run drops it, and calls upon 'moral goodness' to make good the fatal defects of the 'rightness' which he identifies, in spite of misgiving, with 'duty'.

17.8. When a man says that such and such an act is his duty, or says that it is not, or wonders if it is, what does he

---

[1] Looked at more closely, never at all; since (as Kant failed to see) no rule can enable me to decide between the alternatives of which it bids me do one (16.61). In this passage I waive that point.

[2] See *Ethical Studies*, Essay vi.

[3] See *The Right and the Good*, for 'Moral goodness', ch. vii; for the 'misgiving', pp. 3–4.

mean by the phrase: 'his duty'? *A man's duty on a given occasion is the act which for him is both possible and necessary: the act which at that moment character and circumstance combine to make it inevitable, if he has a free will, that he should freely will to do.*

17. 81. Conscience tells him that there is something he ought to do. It does not tell him what. The question what it is, to the distress of academic moralists, does not admit of an answer either conclusive or unequivocal; only an answer of the kind we call '*morally* certain'; an answer, roughly, in the form: 'I have considered x, y, and z as claimants for the title of my present duty: x is a better answer than y, and y than z; but there may be a better answer than any, which I have overlooked.'

17. 82. Of the many questions that I can fancy the reader asking I will permit myself to mention one. 'How, if the idea of duty is an abstract and therefore to some extent ambiguous or indeterminate idea, can my duty be an *individuum omnimodo determinatum*? Must it not be a mere specification, like utility or right, realized in alternative ways?'

17. 83. Duty in general is such a specification. But my present duty is not. 'My present duty', like 'the present king of England', is a phrase which at any given time applies to only one thing or person, although many different persons have been kings of England at different times, and many different acts have been at different times my present duty.

XVIII

THEORETICAL REASON

18. 1. In all forms of rational thinking a distinction is made between the self and the not-self. Such thinking is primarily practical; its first function is to ask and answer the question: 'Why am I doing this?' It has, however, a secondary function, to ask and answer questions about what is not myself.

18. 11. These may be called 'theoretical' questions; but they are never purely theoretical (1. 63). They arise out of practical problems concerning the relations between the self and other things; their answers are obtained by doing something to things and watching the result; and these answers are always in effect solutions for the practical problems out of which they arise.

18. 12. Consider the place of experiment in natural science. An experiment means an interference by a natural scientist with some process of nature. The 'experimental method' in natural science is the method wherein a scientist comes to understand a natural process by interfering with it. Where this method is used there is no purely theoretical thinking; theory goes hand in hand with practice.

18. 13. Is there nowhere such a thing as 'purely theoretical thinking'? There is; but it is not real thinking, and it does not lead to real knowing. It is the thing called academic thinking or make-believe thinking, to which reference has already been made. Real thinking is always to some extent experimental in its method; it always starts from practice and returns to practice; for it is based on 'interest' in the thing thought about; that is, on a practical concern with it.

18. 2. The questions about a thing wherein the thinker has an interest will be different kinds of questions according to differences in this interest. A man will have a different theoretical attitude towards things other than himself according as his practical attitude towards them is different; and his practical attitude towards them will be different according to differences in his attitude towards his own actions.

18. 21. The main difference there can be in his attitude towards his own actions is whether the reasons he gives himself for these actions are habitually given in terms of utility, right, or duty. These three ways of explaining my own actions to myself entail respectively three forms of theoretical reason, or three ways of explaining to myself the world around me.

18. 3. To a man whose attempt to explain his own actions has got as far as the principle of utility and no farther, it is self-evident that rationality and utility are the same. To understand a thing is to think of it in terms of ends and means. In the question: 'Why does this thing do what we find it doing?' the word 'Why?' always means 'to what end?'

18. 31. This habit of thought existed among the ancient Greeks, and is freely documented by their literature. They thought of their own practical life in utilitarian terms; they consequently thought of their relations with the world about them in utilitarian terms; and therefore they thought of that world itself in utilitarian terms. Nature, they thought, had her ends; and devised means to those ends. That is the first axiom of Greek science.

18. 32. It was still the first axiom of science in the Middle Ages, whose forgetfulness of Greek ideas has been grossly exaggerated, and the Renaissance. It was hardly questioned until the sixteenth century, and its abandonment was still a debated question in the eighteenth.

18. 33. The 'teleological' view of Nature has often been called irrational. It is not wholly rational, for the utilitarian explanations which are the only ones it can give make large drafts on the irrational, on the world of caprice; but it has a rational basis; it follows inevitably from a teleological or utilitarian view of human action: and its merits or defects as a view of man's environment exactly correspond with its merits and defects as a view of man himself.

18. 34. Derived as it was from a utilitarian consciousness in man, it could only be abandoned when displaced by another view of Nature similarly derived from a form of practical consciousness, not utilitarian, that had replaced the utilitarian consciousness of the ancient Greeks. This event, the origin of the modern European mind, may be dated to the middle of the sixteenth century.

18. 4. European man had long ago become rule-conscious. The process of becoming so had extended over several thousands of years. The beginning of such a process can never be dated; the historian can first detect it at work when it has been going on for a long time. The early civilizations of the Near East display a regularian consciousness which is their chief legacy to their Mediterranean successors.

18. 41. The Greeks sat light to this ancient tradition; the Romans re-established connexion with it; that is why the social and political experiments of the Greeks perished for lack of root, while the Romans created a legal fabric that is still alive.

18. 42. The regularian tradition of the ancient East survived into modern Europe chiefly through the work of Roman law and Jewish religion. To the man of the Middle Ages, trained in a Christian school where those two lessons had been thoroughly assimilated, it was a commonplace that right took precedence of utility; the business of man was not to achieve ends but to obey laws.

18. 43. It is idle to ask: 'Whose ends? Whose laws?' An end that I achieve is my end, and a law that I obey is my law; none the less mine for being someone else's too, as indeed they must be if I live in a society. In this regularian consciousness, which had become what I call a commonplace in the Middle Ages, the Law of Primitive Survivals (9. 5) was at work, and an element of utility was alive; an act which was essentially recommended on regularian grounds, as conforming with law, was also recommended on utilitarian grounds, by reference to divine or human rewards and punishments; but everybody knew that utilitarian motives were subsidiary to the regularian motive, respect for law as such.

18. 44. Modern science arose when men began to think of the world around them as they had already grown accustomed to thinking of themselves: in terms of law and obedience to law. Modern science is a structure of thought whose armature is the idea of a 'Law of Nature'.

18. 45. Like Greco-Medieval science, it is not wholly rational; its explanations always make considerable demands on irrationality or caprice, which it calls 'brute fact', a conception whose position in modern science is due to the imperfectly rational character of its regularian explanations; but is rational in the sense that it is logically derived from a regularian or legalistic view of human life; whatever defects it may have as a view of the natural world are inevitable, incorrigible under terms of its foundation charter, arising from and corresponding to similar defects in the regularian conception of human activity, the form of practical reason from which it is derived.

18. 5. The idea of obligation or duty, as we have seen, had its practical origin in the time, let us say, of Hammurabi; ground to a finer edge, it was the work of the Roman jurists. To an impatient eye, obsessed by the slower tempo of events nearer in time to ourselves, its history since then may seem to consist mainly in confusion with the ideas of utility and right. But a process of disentanglement has been at work. To follow this process is to follow the rise of history.

18. 51. For history is to duty what modern science is to right, and what Greco-Medieval science was to utility: a picture of the outer world, painted in colours that the painter has already learned to use for his self-portrait.

18. 52. The consciousness of duty means thinking of myself as an individual or unique agent, in an individual or unique situation, doing the individual or unique action which I have to do because it is the only one I can. To think historically is to explore a world consisting of things other than myself, each of them an individual or unique agent, in an individual or unique situation, doing an individual or unique action which he has to do because, charactered and circumstanced as he is, he can do no other.

18. 6. In the consciousness of duty there survive traces of right and even of utility. So the historical consciousness does not abolish with a clean sweep the 'scientific' consciousness, the consciousness of man as confronted by an alien world of Nature; nor even what we nowadays lightly condemn as the unscientific consciousness of man confronted by a world subject to the very imperfectly rational reason of utility.

18. 7. To the historical consciousness these worlds are not illusions; they are not (of course) first-order objects given immediately to consciousness; no world can ever be that; it is always a not-self as opposed to a self, one of a pair of abstractions, either of which is thinkable only as correlative with the other.

18. 8. The Nature of modern science and the Nature of Greco-Medieval science, from the point of view of the historical consciousness which is up to now the limit of European man's theoretical development as the consciousness of duty is the limit of his practical development, are thus just as much abstractions as they always were; but not on that account either unreal or problematically real. Argument is needed in order to discover their features, just as it always was; but not in order to assure ourselves of their existence.

18. 9. What is new about the situation of Nature relatively to our twentieth-century consciousness is not that it is an abstraction, an object of scientific study as abstractions have to be and not of immediate awareness, but that it is an abstraction one order higher than it was. It is not the primary object of scientific study; that description for us applies only to the world of human affairs.

18. 91. The object of scientific study, for a man who has taken his part in the progress of human thought down to the present time, is history. The world of Nature, first the law-abiding Nature of modern science and secondly the end-seeking Nature of Greco-Medieval science, is as real as you will; but it is not history, it is the background of history.

18. 92. It is in the world of history, not in the world of Nature, that man finds the central problems he has to solve. For twentieth-century thought the problems of history are the central problems: those of Nature, however interesting they may be, are only peripheral.

PART II

SOCIETY

XIX

TWO SENSES OF THE WORD 'SOCIETY'

19. 1. In modern European languages the word 'society' has two senses, which for the purposes of political study must be distinguished: confusion is fatal. From the formal logician's point of view the one which I shall enclose in quotation marks (thus: 'society') is wider and stands for a genus; from the historical point of view the one which I shall print unadorned (thus: society) is the older, and the other an extension of it.

19. 11. It is only in the present chapter that I shall need to distinguish them typographically. Thereafter I shall not use the word except in what I take to be its true and proper sense.

19. 12. Before considering what these senses are, I crave the reader's patience for a few preliminary observations (19.2–44).

19. 2. Societies and 'societies' are kinds of *wholes*: they are made up, like all wholes, of *parts*.

19. 21. A society or 'society', however, is not the only kind of thing that is a whole or is made up of parts.

19. 22. There is a kind of thing called a *class*. A class is a whole whose parts are *members*; which does not tell us much, because *member* is only the Latin for part; originally, it is said, part of a human or animal body.

19. 23. The distinguishing mark of a class is that it is a whole whose parts, its 'members', are mutually related by way of *resemblance*.

19. 24. But most things have some resemblance to each other, without necessarily being on that account members of the same class. Membership of a given class demands a certain *kind* and *degree* of resemblance.

19. 25. In order that any group of things should constitute a class, there must be somebody who settles what the kind and degree of resemblance is. This is a practical act: it is called *classifying* the things which, by virtue of it, become members of a class.

19. 3. There is a book-case in front of me. As containing a number of books, it constitutes a whole of which those books are parts.

19. 31. Some of these books have red bindings.

19. 32. Red shades off by degrees into brown, purple, orange, and so forth; before I can speak of 'red books' as a class, I must settle what constitutes red.

19. 33. Let us suppose that by simply looking at the books I could know what the colour of each is; still this would not involve the classification of the colours I see into, for example, red and some other colour.

19. 34. There is a practical act whereby I decide at what point in the gradation from red to purple (or what not) I shall stop calling the colour I see 'red' and shall begin calling it 'purple'.

19. 35. This 'drawing the line' between red and other colours is the act of classifying. On acts like this classes depend for their existence; all classes (the reader will find) being *artifacts*, depending on practical activities for their existence and depending for their *publicity* as between various persons on these persons performing practical activities of similar kinds; for many classes are *private* to the persons who made them.

19. 36. To say that various persons draw the line between red and other colours in such a way that each understands what the other says about these colours, is to say that these persons stand to one another in a social relation; the relation of a *society or 'society'* (I do not distinguish until 19. 8).

19. 37. *A class and a society are different things,* a society (or 'society') being an activity which gives rise to a sort of analogue of itself in the shape of a class; a society (or 'society') being the combination of many agents into a single complex agent, and a class being a collection of many things into one, in virtue of their resemblance.

19. 4. The distinction between the idea of a society or 'society', and the idea of a class, is one which I must be content with here very briefly indicating. It cannot be properly expressed until the distinction between a society and a 'society' has been made clear; that is why the statement of it by Whitehead, who is interested in the fallacious attempt of modern logic *to reduce the idea of a society or 'society' to the idea of a class*, lacks perfect clarity.

19. 41. Once there is a society, *belonging to it* is a point of resemblance among its members: there is a *class* consisting of all the members of the society.

19. 42. Not, you will observe, 'consisting of the things *commonly said to be* members of that society'. The question is not whether they are commonly said to be but whether they really are. If yes, their genuine membership of the society constitutes them genuine members of the class; if no, their alleged membership of the society makes them only allegedly members of the class.

19. 43. You cannot reduce a thing we will call A, namely membership of the society, into a thing we will call B, namely membership of the class of members of that society; for unless there really were the thing called A, there would not be the thing called B, which there is because there is, antecedently, A. A class and a society or 'society' are different things, and of the two the society or 'society' comes first.

19. 44. I have here followed Whitehead in attacking a widespread error of modern logic. What leads to a certain lack of clearness in his attack is that he concerns himself with two terms only when in fact there are three: he is anxious to show that neither a society nor a 'society' can be reduced to a class of its own members, but not in the relation between a society and a 'society'. It is as if he were anxious to conceal one confusion while recovering another.

19. 5. The word 'society' in modern European languages is borrowed from the vocabulary of Roman law.

19. 51. *Societas* is a relation between *personae* (that is, human beings capable of sueing and being sued, who must be free men and not slaves, Roman citizens and not foreigners, male and adult, not in the *manus* or *patria potestas* of another but heads of families) whereby they join together of their own free will in joint action.

19. 52. Such a relation comes into existence by what is

called a 'social contract' or 'contract of society', a contract to become *socii*, partners.

19. 53. A '*social contract*' is a 'consensual' contract, like purchase-and-sale; its essence is simple agreement of will, which is valid at law even though unaccompanied by the ritual formalities which Roman law required as a condition of legal validity in some other contracts.

19. 54. The *indispensable elements* of any social contract, according to Roman law, are three: (1) reciprocal agreement; (2) common interest (both parties must stand to gain under the terms of partnership: a 'leonine society', like that of the lion and the ass in the fable, where one party is excluded from benefit, is legally invalid); and (3) *affectus societatis*, a bona fide intention to form a partnership.

19. 55. The *obligations* to which a social contract gives rise, again, are three: (1) to make your own contribution to the expenses of the partnership; (2) to promote the interests of the partnership with the same care which you would devote to your private interests; (3) to share profit and loss with the other partners.

19. 56. This is the sense the word originally bore, and (taking it by and large) the sense it still bears to-day in some, though not all, its usages in the European languages. By 'taking it by and large' I mean to allow for certain modifications which have affected the implication of the word since the Romans.

19. 57. Thus, the Roman idea of a *persona* excluded the possibility that a contract could be formed by anyone not male, not adult, not a Roman citizen. These were safeguards, so to speak, of the idea that no one could legally be a party to a contract unless he was capable of making up his mind for himself and explaining it, if need be, in court. The idea which the Roman formula tried to safeguard was the idea that a contract must be a *joint activity of free agents*; their free participation in a joint enterprise.

19. 58. This is the idea which the modern use of the word society, when used in its proper sense (which it sometimes is not), tries after its own fashion to safeguard. Think of such phrases as 'the Co-operative Wholesale Society', 'the Royal Society', 'County Society'. In every case there is an intention to describe a joint activity shared by free agents, though these are never Roman citizens and may not be male nor adult.

19. 59. A quite different type of change in the meaning of the word, affecting not its *inessentials* but its *essentials*, began in the late seventeenth century where we find people beginning to write about 'societies' of plants, without believing or implying that plants are free agents. In 1878 when Monsieur Espinas wrote his famous book *Les Sociétés animales* it was quite in order for him to describe various non-human gregarious animals as forming 'societies' in a sense which would have outraged a Roman lawyer, not so much because it involved speaking of an ant or bee as if it were a Roman citizen but because it involved speaking of it as if it were possessed of free will. (For these modern changes in the meaning of the word society, see further, 20. 6 seqq.)

19. 6. Lately Professor A. N. Whitehead has taken a further step: he has applied the term 'society' for the electrons which go to make up an atom.

19. 61. Whitehead is emphatic that a 'society' in this sense is not a class, and that it would be a blunder in logic to confuse the two things. The difference is that a class consists of members related by *resemblance*, a 'society' of one related by *participation*.

19. 62. Wherever there is a 'society' there is something shared among the members of that 'society': something divided into as many parts as there are members in the 'society', and assigned in a one-one relation to the members.

19. 63. Each book, taking up a certain amount of shelf-space on a shelf divided among them, would thus afford an example of 'participation', and be a member of a 'society'; so would each ant having its place in the nest; and so would each electron occupying its own constantly changing position in the pattern of the dance which, according to modern physics, is an atom. Of these things, each has the share which belongs to it of a divided whole.

19. 64. The English language has not chosen to provide for itself a word to fit this idea; why not? Never mind, suppose we decide to have one, and let it be 'society'. All that the word 'society', thus used, implies is the fact which

I call a *suum cuique*, that is, a one-one relation between sharers or participants and shares.

19.65. Where there are sharers and shares there is an act of sharing or division; and an act implies an agent.

19.66. 'Let us be careful. There is a distinction, is there not, between owning in severalty, where that which is owned is divided into shares, and owning jointly, where there is no such division? It is true that persons sharing an apple commonly divide it; but what about persons sharing a horse, or a friend, or an umbrella? Here to divide would be to destroy; and a kind of sharing is devised, to meet the case, where there is no division.'

19.67. What is it that is shared in cases like that of an umbrella? There is a 'thing', a contraption of silk and metal or what not, which shelters a certain space from the rain, the space in question moving as the thing that shelters it is carried forward. Two persons are said to share the umbrella; but that is only a short way of saying that they share the benefit of the umbrella, the shelter from the rain which the umbrella provides; this 'shelter' means the sheltered space, divisible into various parts and actually, perhaps, so divided by voluntary agreement between participants.

19.68. And so with a horse or a friend. In each case there is something which is divisible without detriment, such as the time spent riding the horse or talking to the friend; and in each case this is what is divided into shares

19.7. I have called the reader's attention to a false reduction of 'societies' to classes (19.4). It is made because the modern logicians who make it are 'class-minded', that is, inclined to accept any sort of nonsense if it is couched in terms of classes; none the less, it is nonsense.

19.71. It is the converse of an old error. Certain Greek logicians tried to carry out the opposite error, and reduce the idea of a class to the idea of a 'society'.

19.72. We do not know who they were; but we are reasonably well informed about their doctrine. They maintained that the resemblance between, for example, red things was really a case of participation; that each of them shared in something called redness. On examination this was found untenable because the implications of calling something a case of resemblance contradicted the implication of calling it a case of participation.

19.73. It was believed at one time that the doctrine in question was Plato's; and the belief that the resemblance between two good things (for example) consisted in their having a 'share' in something called 'goodness' (something independent, of course, of the participants that share it; something existing 'itself by itself' as an undivided whole, the undivided shelf-space or umbrella) was known as 'Plato's theory of Ideas'.

19.74. It is a fact, however, that Plato nowhere writes like a man setting out to expound that theory, though he does in several of his earlier dialogues write like a man accepting it. In one dialogue at least (the *Parmenides*) he writes like a man setting out to criticize it, and criticizing it, in fact, conclusively.

19.75. His criticisms are based on the recognition that since sharing implies division, and since resemblance implies the undivided unity of that with regard to which there is resemblance, resemblance cannot either be or involve sharing; the idea of a class, constituted by resemblance among its members, is one thing, and the idea of a 'society', constituted by the sharing of something among its members, is a different thing.

19.8. The difference between a 'society' and a society is this: each of them has a *suum cuique* (19.64); in each of them the members have a share in something that is divided among them; but in a society proper the establishment and maintenance of the *suum cuique* is effected by *their joint activity as free agents* (19.57).

19.81. A society is a 'society' constituted by free activity on the part of its members.

19.82. A person who disbelieves in free activity disbelieves in the existence of societies, but he may still believe in the existence of 'societies'.

19.83. Karl Marx was such a person; and this was why, denying as he did the existence of societies, he spared himself the pains of solving social and political problems by simply denying that they existed.

19.9. 'It is not men's consciousness that determines their

existence; on the contrary, it is their social existence that determines their consciousness.'[1]

19.91. 'In the present-day world', I venture to paraphrase Marx, 'there is a certain economic order. The position of this or that man in the economic order does not, as the classical economists say, depend on what he thinks about that order and what portion he therefore undertakes to discharge. It is imposed upon him by brute force; and more than that, when once imposed it determines the way in which he thinks both about it and about everything else.'

19.92. Marx is contending that the early nineteenth-century world of economic relations, what he called the capitalist system, *was not in the proper sense of the word a society*. The classical economists talked about it as if it were one; as if it were a world of partnership in which men engaged of their own free will. If this had been so, then 'the consciousness of men' would have 'determined their social existence'.

19.93. But it was not. It was a world of slaves. A man born into it could no more accept or reject what it offered him than a man born into an ancient Roman *familia* of slaves could accept or reject a contract of labour offered him by his employer.

19.94. The proposition quoted from Marx, therefore, so far from being fundamental to the essence of society, tells you nothing about society except that in the modern world there isn't any. If you squeeze it, you will get an error. Says Marx: 'It is their *social* being that determines their consciousness' (*gesellschaftliches Sein*), when in fact he is denying that they have any social being. The German word, unlike the English, is not derived from the Latin and is not an equivalent for the Latin. The words *society, social,* contain a reference to free will; even if only, in the form I print as 'society', to free will as excluded; the words *Gesellschaft, gesellschaftlich* do not.

[1] 'Es ist nicht das Bewusstsein der Menschen, das ihr Sein, sondern umgekehrt ihr gesellschaftliches Sein, das ihr Bewusstsein bestimmt' (Karl Marx, *Kritik der Politischen Ökonomie*, ed. 5, Stuttgart, 1910, p. lix; being no. 4 of the 'propositions' set forth in the *Introduction*).

XX

SOCIETY AND COMMUNITY

20. 1. WE are concerned not with relations between stars or electrons or books or bees, but with relations between men.

20. 11. In the future, therefore, I shall replace the distinction made in the last chapter, between a society proper, and the same word used in a vaguer sense and distinguished by inverted commas, by a distinction intended to apply only to human relations: *community* and *society*.

20. 12. By a community I shall mean a state of affairs in which something is divided or shared by a number of human beings.

20. 13. This state of affairs I called the *suum cuique* of the community (19. 64).

20. 14. What matters to the existence of a community is that it should have a *suum cuique*. Its taking one particular form and not another makes no difference to the thing's being a community; though much to what kind of community it is.

20. 15. The coming into existence of a given *suum cuique* I may, perhaps, call its *establishment*, in the passive sense of coming to be established.

20. 16. Let there be children and apples; and let the apples be divided somehow among the children. The children are a community; in particular, a community of apple-eaters. They do not plan their lives so as to make them include, from time to time, whatever seems to them especially important; on the contrary, they mostly do whatever they especially want to do, unless there is anything against which they are specially warned by someone whose warnings they take seriously.

20. 17. In some way as this, with or without the intervention of what is called 'will', or the making up of some person's mind to some course of action, a community gets established, and communal habits of acting (which is the same thing) are established among certain groups of human beings.

20. 18. There is another thing to be said about the *suum cuique* of any given community. It may have to do with anything on earth, such as the distribution of apples; but there are some things which it must have to do with and cannot neglect, whatever kind of community it may happen to be. Thus, any community must have a home or place in which corporately it lives.

20. 2. What, then, do I call a society? It is a kind of community; but what kind? Every community is a community because there is something that its members share; what the members of a society share is *social consciousness*. If men are the only animals that can be, strictly speaking, members of a society, that is because they are the only animals which have and can therefore share a social consciousness, or, which comes to the same thing (for you can have neither without having the other), a *will*.

20.21. Social consciousness, like all forms of consciousness, is primarily a practical consciousness; not a 'making up your mind *that*' but a 'making up your mind *to*'. It is primarily not an awareness of being a member in a society, but an act of deciding to become a member and to go on being a member: a will to assume the function of partnership with others in a common undertaking, and a will to carry out that function.

20. 22. People become partners by deciding to behave like partners. A society or partnership is constituted by the social will of the partners, an act of free will whereby the person who thereby becomes a partner decides to take upon himself a share in a joint enterprise.

20. 23. Social consciousness involves the consciousness of freedom. A society consists of persons who are free and know themselves to be free. Each knows the others to be free as well as himself. If consciousness of freedom is a mark of being mentally adult, a society can consist only of mentally adult persons.

20. 3. Whatever is a society must be a community, because a society is a kind of community, a society being a community and something more (20. 16).

20. 31. It must be a community before it is a society, where 'before' carries a logical sense, the sense indicated by the 'pre' in the statement that its being a community is a 'presupposition' of its being a society.

20. 32. The logical sense of priority may or may not be

accompanied by a temporal sense. If it is, a particular society may have been a community during a time when it had not yet become a society. During that time it was what I shall call a *non-social community*.

20. 33. Later on I shall explain (21. 5) that there is always a process in the life of a society by which it becomes a society from being a non-social community, and that its emergence from the state of a non-social community into that of a society is never complete.

20. 34. A community depends for its existence upon something that makes it a community and keeps it a community; that is, allots to its members their respective shares in whatever is divided between them, and causes them to remain faithful to this allotment; maintains the *suum cuique* which is the essence of its communal character.

20. 35. The establishment and maintenance of the *suum cuique* is called *ruling*.

20. 36. A society rules itself by the activity of its members' social will; a society is a *self-ruling* community. A non-social community needs for its existence to be ruled by something other than itself.

20. 37. Ruling is either *immanent* or *transeunt*.

20. 38. It is *immanent* when that which rules rules itself, the same thing being both agent and patient in respect of the same activity.

20. 39. It is *transeunt* when that which rules rules something other than itself: when in respect of one and the same activity of ruling there is one thing which is agent, the ruler, and another thing which is patient, the ruled.

20. 4. Theoretically, or in terms of the abstract logical relation between the two, there is no reason why a self-ruler should be involved at all in transeunt ruling, either as agent or patient, and no reason why an agent or patient in transeunt ruling should either be or not be also a self-ruler.

20. 41. But in practice (that is, when the implications of the two are taken into account) immanent rule is a presupposition of being an agent in transeunt rule.

20. 42. A community must be ruled if it is to exist (20. 34). If it is a society it has a will, namely the joint will of its members, and rules itself.

20. 43. In ruling itself it is *self-originating* and *self-maintaining*; it comes into existence by the act of this joint will, and is kept in existence by the same joint will.

20. 44. The same will which originates and maintains it can also originate and maintain a non-social community of what are called its *dependents*. A non-social community must depend on something (20. 36); what it depends on, or is ruled by, may be a society.

20. 45. Something capable of ruling itself sometimes appears to be (but is not in fact) ruled by something else. I refer to the case in which one thing is said to have *authority* over another.

20. 46. Authority is the name of a relation between B who 'has authority' to do something and A who '*authorizes*' him or 'gives him authority' to do it. Where 'it' is a transeunt action there is a third party C to whom A authorizes B to do it. In that case B's relation to C may involve the use of force (20. 5; see further, 21. 72).

20. 47. For example B is a surgeon who undertakes to remove C's appendix. The removal involves the use of an anaesthetic; and this, as rendering C's will inoperative for a time, amounts to force. If B knows his business, he will insist on receiving authority; because if C should die under the anaesthetic the coroner's court will ask for evidence that authority was given. The giver is called A, who at first sight appears to be the same as C; but looking closer you find that the decision to have the appendix out was a *joint decision* on the part of surgeon and patient (where the patient is adult and of sound mind). There is a *society*, A, of which the surgeon B and the patient C are members, each of his own free will, and whose joint enterprise is the removal of C's appendix by B. It is this society as a whole that authorizes B to take out C's appendix.

20. 48. *Authority is a relation between a society and a part of that society to which the society assigns the execution of a part of its joint enterprise.* This may involve the use of force by one part upon another part of the society. As thus exercising force upon C, B is not ruling the society; the society, as always, is ruling itself; B is a part of itself which it is using in the course of its rule over itself to exercise force on another part of itself.

This force is exercised by authority of the society; and therefore according to the free will of every member of the society, including C.

20.49. The patient may be a child; in which case the decision to remove its appendix will be jointly made not by surgeon and patient but by surgeon and patient's parent. The child is not a party to that decision. From the child's point of view the removal of its appendix is an act of *force* jointly exercised upon it by parent and surgeon. The child as undergoing this joint or social force is a *dependent* (20.44) upon the society.

20.5. The word 'force' in political contexts never means 'physical force', as when a stronger man 'forces' open a weaker man's fingers and 'makes' him let go what he is holding. It always means 'moral force' or mental strength.

20.51. Moreover it is a relative term. It signifies not mental strength as such but one man's superiority in mental strength to another. When A is said to exercise force upon B, what is meant is that A is strong relatively to B, and uses this superiority to make B do what he wants.

20.52. The mental powers of A and B respectively may be roughly gauged by the scale of mental development sketched in Part I of this work. A's mental strength is superior to B's if A's mental development has gone as far as will and B's no farther than passion or any stage below it; if A's has gone as far as passion and B's no farther than desire or any stage below it; and so on.

20.53. But A and B may both have reached the same stage, yet in terms of that stage A may be stronger than B. It may be a question of will, and A's will may be stronger than B's; it may be a question of passion, and A's passions may be stronger than B's; it may be a question of desire, and A's desires may be stronger than B's.

20.54. Secondly, the development from any stage to the next above it is conditional on a certain *quiescence* in the activities of the lower and is impeded by any violence on their part; and the maintenance of the higher-level activity is imperilled, even when once it has been achieved, by increased violence on the part of the lower-level activity.

20.55. The law that a higher-level activity is easiest to establish and easiest to maintain when lower-level activities are relatively quiescent (that is, the reverse of violent) I call the *Law of Quiescence*. For brevity's sake I will spare the reader explanations, illustrations, and references to other statements of the law.

20. 56. If B is a member of a non-social community he has no will of his own. His orderly life as a member of a community cannot be based upon his own will, for he has none; it must be based on what from his point of view is force. Force may be here only a name for the mental superiority of someone else to himself. This other person (or society) will be the person or society upon which he is dependent.

20. 57. This mental superiority of A to B may consist in A's having a will when B has none. But it need not. It may (by the Law of Quiescence) consist in A's having no will when B has one; granted that A has such violent emotions (passions, desires, and the like) that, infecting B's emotions with a like violence, they break the power of B's will and render it inoperative.

20. 58. Suppose B is frightened, but has just enough strength of will to control his fear and behave courageously. Now suppose that A also is frightened and utterly unable to control his fear. By giving way to his own fear he may so infect B that B becomes unable to control his own. B's will to behave courageously breaks down; and thus A, who has no will at all, is stronger than B, who has a will but one not strong enough to maintain itself under the strain of his own fear *plus* the fear with which A has infected him. By thus infecting B, A forces him to be a coward; forces him unintentionally, but forces him none the less.

20. 59. When a man suffers force *the origin of the force is always something within himself*, some irresistible emotion which makes him do something he does not intend to do; either intending something else but having his intention swept away by the force of the emotion, or having no intention whatever. If B suffers force at the hands of A, it is A who excites in B this irresistible emotion; perhaps intentionally, perhaps unintentionally; perhaps only because he too suffers an irresistible emotion of the same kind.

20. 6. After this digression on force, let us return to society. I have said that we inherit both the name 'society' and the idea for which it stands from Roman law. I have enumerated the main points of the Roman idea (19. 51–5); I will now make the necessary modifications to bring it into harmony with the correct or precise modern European use of the word. All I need say about the history of these modifications is that they represent the experience of social life as it reshaped itself during the first fifteen centuries of the Christian era, by which time the modern usage had been established.

20. 61. For the Roman doctrine that a society or partnership is possible only as between *personae* (19. 51) I substitute the modern doctrine that it is possible only as between *persons*, where a person means an agent possessed of, and exercising, free will.

20. 62. Free will is a matter of degree (21. 54); so we must qualify this by saying that a given society, being formed for the prosecution of a given joint enterprise, is possible only as between agents having the strength of will which that enterprise demands. Modern Europeans expect a woman of a certain age, not being mentally deficient, to have the degree and kind of free will which are needed for her consent to her marriage, and think that consent indispensable to the marriage; but do not expect a boy of seven or eight to have the degree and kind of free will which would be needed for his consent to joining a school. They do not, therefore, think this consent necessary for his becoming a member of the school. The marriage is not thought valid unless the woman consents to it; there is no such condition when a boy goes to school.

20. 63. For the doctrine that a society is initiated by a 'social contract' which belongs to the type of contract called 'consensual' (19. 53) I substitute the doctrine that it is initiated by the act of declaring a decision to initiate it; this declaration to be made or subscribed to by every party in joining the society, in any terms that make his decision clear to the other or others.

20. 64. For the triple doctrine of reciprocal agreement, common interest, and *affectus societatis* (19. 54) I substitute this same double doctrine of decision to initiate a partnership in a given enterprise and intelligible expression of this decision by every party to every other. Nothing else is needed in order that a society may come into existence. Nothing but the abiding by these decisions is needed in order that it may continue to exist.

20. 65. For the triple doctrine concerning the obligations to which a social contract gives rise (19. 55) I substitute the simple doctrine that every party, by making the contract, declares his will to pursue the common aim of the society. What he contracts to do (what Roman law calls the 'obligation' to which his participation in the contract subjects him) is solely to pursue the common aim: the detail of this 'obligation' will depend on the detail of the aim. By what I call the *Principle of Limited Liability* his 'obligation' is limited to this aim and all it implies, the latter often including much not specified in any description of the aim.

20. 66. No society has a claim on its members involving more than this. It is in the nature of a society that the obligations of membership should be limited to obligations involved in the pursuit of the common aim. There is no kind of obligation that may not be thus involved. So simple and commonplace a joint enterprise as going for a walk together may commit one partner to risking his life in defence of the other; so simple a joint enterprise as playing a game of chess may commit him to keeping his temper when he is beaten; and keeping your temper is harder for most men than risking your life.

20. 67. The more clearly these implications are understood, the more men's eyes are open when they incur such liabilities.

20. 68. When they are realized after being blindly incurred a man may accept them, which is the courageous and loyal thing to do; or he may denounce the contract, which he can do unblamed if the liability has been deliberately concealed from him or is one which he could not be reasonably expected to foresee; or, thirdly, he may be psychologically unable (through cowardice or the like) to 'rise to the occasion' by facing it, in which case he ceases to be a partner in that society because his will is not strong enough to face the problems involved in membership (20. 62).

20.7. In studying the nature of a society we are not studying an hypothetical or imaginary entity. We are studying a thing with which those of us who are grown men are very familiar.

20.71. Examples have already been given, where two men decide to go for a walk together or to play chess together (20. 66).

20.72. I take a society of two because it is the simplest type in which all the features of social activity are present: free will on the part of all members and a joint enterprise freely engaged in by each and recognized by each as freely engaged in by the other.

20.8. I have deliberately chosen examples involving no economic issue, no corporate *lucrum* or *damnum*, because I wish the reader to understand that society or voluntary partnership as such does not involve the economic issues attached to it by Roman lawyers.

20.81. Roman lawyers were interested in partnership chiefly because of the economic issues it sometimes involves. But in itself it involves no such issues, and in fact the Roman civilians have left us a theory of partnership which holds good with very slight and obvious modifications where none are involved.

20.82. The reader who studies these modifications (20. 61–5) will see that the idea of society contains none of the economic suggestions read into it by modern thinkers who have swallowed whole what they have found in text-books of Roman law instead of looking at the facts for themselves.

20.9. He will see that the essence of partnership is that men voluntarily behave as partners, which they can do only so far as each, in virtue of his free will and his recognition of free will in the rest, joins with them in a common enterprise like going for a walk together or sailing a boat together.

20.91. Society is the sharing of certain persons in a practical social consciousness verbally expressed in a formula like: 'We will go for this walk' or: 'We will sail this boat'.

20.92. In this formula the word 'we' expresses the social character of the consciousness: the word 'will' its practical character. The concluding words are a definition of the common enterprise.

20. 93. The social consciousness is the consciousness of myself together with certain others all deciding to do a particular thing, to divide that thing into various parts, and to distribute these parts, which together make up the enter-prise, among the persons who together make up the society.

20. 94. Without this consciousness of joint free decision to undertake and share a certain action there might be membership of a non-social community, but there could be no membership of a society.

XXI

SOCIETY AS JOINT WILL

21. 1. How does a man become possessed of a social consciousness? How does he become able to think: 'We will'?

21. 11. By the same process which enables him to think: 'I will'. That process has been described in Part I; culminating phase in chapter xiii.

21. 12. A man who has got as far as this has been long accustomed to distinguish between himself and something not himself. It is from experience of making this distinction, without which he cannot think of himself at all, that he comes to reflect on his own act of decision, in other words, to think: 'I will'.

21. 13. The idea of oneself is always correlative to the idea of something not oneself. The idea of oneself as a self of a particular kind is correlative to the idea of a not-self of the same kind.

21. 14. The idea of oneself as having a will is correlative, therefore, to the idea of something other than oneself as having a will.

21. 15. When a child first discovers that free action is going on, it does not yet know how far the freedom of which it is aware belongs to itself or to things other than itself.

21. 16. But it knows that such freedom does not belong exclusively to itself. It has a vague idea of things other than itself which are free agents, and identifies them at random with the cat, the rain, the dark, the doll, and so forth.

21. 17. These it regards as things that might be free agents with whom social relations might be established. And so far it is guilty of no mistake.

21. 18. But when it thinks of itself as actually a free agent, free in some actual decision actually made, it misinterprets the behaviour of the cat and so forth as evidence that they too have had a hand in these decisions. It thinks that there is social activity where in fact there is none.

21. 19. No man has any idea of himself as a free agent, without an idea of free agents other than himself and of social relations between them. No man has an accurate idea of himself as a free agent without an accurate idea of free agents other than himself and of social relations between them.

21. 2. A man engaged in a joint enterprise has a general idea of the enterprise as a whole and a special idea of the part in it allotted to himself. Unless he has both these ideas he has no social consciousness, and without social consciousness there is no society.

21. 21. But they are not equally precise. Of the enterprise as a whole he has only a general' (relatively vague or indeterminate) idea; of his own share he has a 'special' (relatively precise or determinate) idea.

21. 22. He has to know the nature of his own share accurately enough to do it. Beyond this his knowledge of the enterprise as a whole need only be very vague. He must know that there is a whole; but he need not know what it is, except that it is the whole to which his own share belongs.

21. 23. Similarly, he must know that there are other agents who are partners with himself in this undertaking. But he need not know exactly who they are. Just as it is enough that he should know there is a whole enterprise, so it is enough that he should know there is a whole of members, and that each member has his share.

21. 24. For vague knowledge, belief may be a substitute. To believe a statement is to accept the authority of the man who makes it: and what authority is we already know (20. 45–9).

21. 25. Granted that a society exists, it may authorize one of its members to assign their tasks to each, and without knowing in detail what he has done accept on his authority his report that he has done it.

21. 26. In that case a given member does not know, he only believes, that the members have received each his own task. If the belief is unfounded, there is still a society; there is a society of fools, combining to believe the word of a knave. But there is not the society of which the fools believe themselves to be members.

21. 27. If a society consists in the practical social consciousness of its members (20. 22) it follows that a society is nothing over and above its members. It has no will but the will of its members; no activity but the activity of its members; no responsibility but the responsibility of its members.

21.28. If it authorizes some member to do something, that member is responsible for it to the society, and the society is responsible not only for the project it authorizes him to execute, but for seeing that he carries it out.

21.29. The activity of ruling, whether immanent or transeunt (20. 37), is among the activities of a society; perhaps, together with all it implies, the only activity of a society. The ruling whether of itself or its dependents which a society does is wholly done by its members as their joint work, and the responsibility for it rests wholly on its members' shoulders.

21.3. The members of a non-social community are faithful, not of their own free will but in virtue of some force (20. 5) brought to bear upon them, to a communal order or way of life originated and maintained in them by something that is not their will but, for example, the will of a society upon which they are dependent (20. 44).

21.31. What they do as members of the non-social community, not being done of their own free will, is in that case done jointly by the members of the society upon which they are dependent, and they are not responsible for it. Those are responsible who force them to do it.

21.4. All social consciousness involves a distinction between the idea of a *particular society* and the idea of a *universal society*.

21.41. The idea of a *particular society* is the idea of a society distinguished from other societies not by having different members but by having a different aim.

21.42. The idea of a *universal society* is the idea of a society having no special aim which might distinguish it from any other; the idea of a society whose only aim is to be a society; one, therefore, which has for members all such agents as, being conscious of free will in themselves and each other, are able to be members of any society at all.

21.43. The idea of a universal society is implied in the idea of a particular society. For the aim of a particular society is always twofold. First, it aims at establishing social relations between agents capable of social action; secondly, it aims at devoting this social activity to a particular enterprise.

21. 44. The universal society can never be realized as an actual society having its own membership, its own organization, its own executive, and so forth. Attempts have been made over and over again so to realize it. In politics we have the Roman Empire with its claim to world-wide domination, a claim which has been repeated by innumerable aspirants to world-conquest, some pinning their faith to force and conquest by military means, others trusting in consent and believing that the world could be reduced, if only men of good will got together, to a single federation.

21. 45. The futility of these claims, and the folly of the dreams to which they have given rise, have been proved by innumerable facts. I will mention only one.

21. 46. The League of Nations was originally designed to consist of all such political communities as would declare themselves peacefully disposed towards each other. What broke the League of Nations was not the fact that a group of Powers arose pledged to aggression, a group of wolf-minded 'have-nots' regarding the League members as sheep-minded 'haves': but the fact that the League (having been conceived by a man too incompetent in politics to recommend his own conception to the country of which he was President) was run by men too ignorant of politics to see that this result was inevitable.

21. 47. They thought of the League as a kind of heaven on earth. They ought to have known that if you aim at a heaven on earth you are certain of getting a hell on earth.

21. 5. The reason why no actual society can be the universal society is that no actual society can ever lose all trace of the non-social community out of which it has emerged. To be a universal society is the same as to be a society; to exist only because its members, by freely embarking on a joint enterprise, constitute it a society. But every society that actually exists comes into existence because its members do partly achieve this social consciousness.

21. 51. Every society that actually exists is a partly non-social community whose members, awakening to conscious-

ness of their own and each other's freedom, have begun to
convert it into a society and have carried the process of conversion up to a certain point, but have left it unfinished. If
the process had been brought to completion everything that
distinguishes the particular society from any other particular
society would have vanished; the society would have become
completely social; it would have become the universal society,
which it never does.

21.52. For example, any society formed by myself will be
subject to the same non-social conditions to which I am subject: it may be a society for the study of mathematics, but it
will consist in the first instance of Englishmen and others
with whom I find it easiest to converse. There will be a barrier,
more or less impenetrable, against Russians and others whose
language I do not know.

21.53. I did not set out to form a society limited to
English-speakers; but that is in effect more or less what I do.
What I set out to create is a universal society: what I find
myself forced to create is a society of English-speakers.

21.54. There is always a discrepancy between the social
will and its products. The social will always aims at the
universal society; what it produces is always some particular
society which is half-way between the universal society and
a non-social community.

21.55. The reason why such discrepancy exists is that no
one can even try to abolish it. What even the most energetic
and enlightened reformers of society aim at doing is not to
abolish the non-social community, but to *transform* it: to
transform it into a society, but not to transform it out of
sight; to transform it so that the continuity of the initial state
with the final state remains visible. If he could produce a
final state which was no longer visibly continuous with the
initial state, nothing would have been transformed; no
problem would have been solved.

21.6. Persons joining a society must be *free* before they
join it; they must be *equal* in the sense that each is possessed
of that degree of freedom which the decision to join that
society demands.

21.61. After joining it they are still free and equal not only
in these senses but in the further sense that they now equally

possess the status of membership. But this equality presupposes a certain *inequality*; and it also generates inequalities of other kinds. These inequalities are not hostile to equality. Equalities in certain respects between members of the same society are quite compatible with inequalities in other respects; their coexistence being in fact essential to the structure of a society.

21.62. Some inequalities between members of a society are *compensated* so as not to interfere with the smooth working of the society. The stronger of two walkers carries the knapsack on this principle; the better chess-player gives the other a pawn.

21.63. Other inequalities are, by the society that recognizes them, *turned into assets*; used in such a way as to improve its chance of success in pursuing its common end. It is an asset to the walking-party as a whole that its best map-reader should carry the maps.

21.64. A third way of treating inequalities found to exist 'by nature' in a society is merely to recognize and build on them. An example of inequality so treated is *initiative*, which is a mental inequality, natural (i.e. not due to the action of the society itself), and indispensable to the society.

21.65. Whenever two parties come to an agreement to pursue a common end, one must say: 'Let us do so and so', and the other must say: 'Yes, let us'. The first has what I call initiative, and without initiative no society can be formed.

21.66. To possess it is a mental endowment; it is ability to plan a course of action to which the others will agree, and power to state one's invention convincingly. These abilities are '*natural*', that is, not originated by the action of the society itself but taken into account, as things already existing, in the formation of a society. It does not follow that they are *innate*; like much else, including freedom itself, they are products of pre-social experience.

21.67. Another kind of inequality is not 'natural', but is created by society itself. This is *authority* (20.45). This is the fact that one member of a society, A, gives orders which B obeys.

21.68. Command and obedience are found, not in all societies, but in all where the nature of the common task is such as to require them. Watch two men moving a piano; at a certain moment one says 'lift', and the other lifts.

21. 69. The authority whereby one is empowered to give this order is not based on one man's superior skill in furniture-moving, nor on his superior rank in a feudal hierarchy, nor on his superior literacy or greater age or ability to hold more beer; cases might be found in which any one of these or a hundred other conditions were taken into account, but none is relevant: *the decision who shall give advice is part of the structure of the society* and exists, like every part, by an act of joint free will.

21. 7. Each partner agrees to the formation of the society, and hence agrees to give such orders as it is his business to give and obey those which it is his business to obey. And reciprocally, each authorizes the other to do the share that falls to him.

21. 71. This is the theory of command-and-obedience (or, in one word, authority) as a feature of social life. As a feature of non-social life it is an utterly different thing. In a society a command is given because the partners have agreed that in certain circumstances it shall be given. It is obeyed because they have agreed that it shall be obeyed. Giving the order and obeying it are social functions, allotted by common agreement to certain members of the society. In commanding and obeying each is doing what he has decided to do with the authorization (20. 46) of his fellow members, and doing it because, being a man of free will, he is a man whose decisions stand firm.

21. 72. What is called authority in a non-social community is an entirely different thing. It is not authority, it is force. The so-called command of A over B is A's exercise of force upon B. The so-called obedience of B to A is B's enforcement by A.

21. 73. A may force B to do something by promise of *reward* or threat of *punishment*. By the first A excites in B an irresistible desire; by the second an irresistible fear. These are irresistible only if B is slavish enough for the promised reward or the threatened penalty to overwhelm any will he may happen to possess. If his will is strong enough he will laugh at them.

21.74. Reward and punishment have no weight with free men, and the theory of them has no place in the theory of society. It belongs to the theory of the non-social community to which it is essential. It is by such methods that non-social communities are established and maintained. Moreover, so long as the men thus controlled are sufficiently foolish, they can be just as easily controlled by an insincere or impossible promise as by a truthful one; just as easily by an empty bluff as by an honest threat. In that case they are controlled by *fraud*, which is not a different thing from force but a special form of force specially adapted for use against fools.

21.75. We have already seen (20. 59) that the exercise of force is either *voluntary* or *involuntary*. Let us reflect on this distinction. Where it is voluntary, either a real command (an explicit statement of what is to be done) is given and also reinforced by exciting in the recipient emotions which will compel him to do what he is told; or else the real command remains unexpressed, the man who gives it knowing exactly in his own mind what he intends the recipient to do but not troubling to explain it to him because he could not understand it; all he can do is to suffer enforcement by cajolery, threats, or the like.

21.76. If it is involuntary, not only is no real command given, none is even conceived. The slave-driver sinks to the mental level of the slaves he drives. His rages or the like are not mere enforcements of a clearly conceived intention, they are substitutes for it. Napoleon, by his own account, guarded against this danger; his outbursts of passion, said he, were not allowed to 'rise higher than this' (pointing to his chin): he kept his head clear, or said he did; he retained in spite of them, or claimed to retain, that coolness of mind which is freedom. How is this done? To perform an act of free will a man must not only be free, he must know himself to be free (13. 11). But the idea of myself as a free agent is inseparable from its correlative, the idea of free agents other than myself (21. 13). No man can think himself free except as integrated in a context of other free men constituting with himself a society (21.19). Slave-driving is compatible with freedom only if the slave-driver retains the conviction of his own freedom by consorting with other men whom he recognizes as free.

21. 77. The 'corrupting influence of power' is a commonplace. Power means the exercise of force; it corrupts by undermining a man's will and reducing him to the level of his own slaves. A slave-driver, getting out of the habit of explaining to his slaves what he means them to do, gets out of the habit of formulating his intentions even to himself. He can retain that habit only by discussing them on equal terms with his equals.

21. 78. Plato knew this. He has left us a psychological study of the political slave-driver (in Greek 'tyrant') and a psychological study of the slave, the 'tyrant's' subject. The results are the same. The lack of free will, the inability to resist the pressure of emotional forces, which makes the slave a slave, is also what makes the 'tyrant' a 'tyrant'.

21. 79. To narrate the genesis and career of the 'tyrant' (for us to-day, as it was for Plato or the Hellenistic period, an absorbing task) is not exactly the business of political science, because the field of activity in which the 'tyrant' distinguishes himself is not, strictly speaking, political. For the time being, let us call it pseudo-political. Of course, the phrase pseudo-political does not tell us anything; it only describes what a thing is not, not what it is. That is why it is only a stopgap.

21. 8. *Freedom*, as I have reminded the reader (20. 62), *is a matter of degree*. On certain questions and in certain circumstances an agent may be capable of decision, or free; on other questions or in other circumstances the same agent may be utterly unable to prevent a certain passion or a certain desire from taking charge. It is always possible that a given society may break down into the non-social community out of which it has arisen, and cease to exist as a society (21. 5), because it is confronted by a certain kind of question or practical problem.

21. 81. This happens when the agents of whom that society is composed degenerate from a condition in which they are capable of free decision into one in which their will may be said to *crack*; and for any man, I suppose, there are conditions under which a crack of the will would happen.

21. 82. Persons who constitute themselves a society may foresee the possibility of its breaking down into a non-social community, and provide against this in two ways: first by so organizing the society that the duty of giving orders is assigned to those of themselves whom they judge best able to resist the strains to which the society is likely to be exposed.

21.83. The second method, in case the first should prove insufficient, is a kind of machinery whereby any one of themselves whose will may happen to crack may be forcibly prevented from impeding the rest in their work of living politically.

21.84. This machinery is called *criminal law*. It is not for everyday use; it is meant to come into operation only if and when the society to whom it serves as a life-saver shows signs, in spite of all other precautions, of breaking down into a non-social community.

21.85. Criminal law is not a universal feature of social life. Most societies have nothing of the kind. Two men going for a walk make no provision for the contingency that one of them might through deliberate malice lead the whole party astray. A dozen sailing a schooner make no provision for the contingency that one during his trick at the wheel might, to serve his private ends, deliberately wreck the ship. The Society of Antiquaries make no provision for the contingency that one of its Fellows, reading a paper to the rest, might hoax them with a spoof discovery.

21.86. Crime is an action by one member of a society prejudicial not to the rights of another member but to the pursuit of its self-appointed task by the society as a whole. This is a somewhat lately invented idea in the history of law; among the ancient Greeks and many so-called primitive peoples it is unknown; even among the Romans it exists only in an incipient form.[1]

21.87. Not only is the idea of providing against crime, as distinct from tort, unknown in most societies, but where it does occur it rests on the assumption that crime will be committed only when the society has to some extent broken down into a non-social community by the cracking of some member's will and the member's ceasing in consequence to function as a member of that society; though he may perfectly well continue to be a member of the non-social community from which it was derived.

---

[1] I am content here to agree with the late Sir Henry Maine.

21.88. Crime and society are incompatible. Not that, when once a society has been formed, its members are protected by some magic against lapsing into criminality; but that, if and when they do lapse into criminality, they have already (before joining the body of criminals) ceased to function as members of society.

21.9. To conclude this chapter, I distinguish between a *temporary society* and a *permanent society*.

21.91. I do not mean that some societies last only for a time, while others last for ever. No society lasts for ever, because nothing human does that. There remains a distinction which is worth noticing.

21.92. This is a distinction between two kinds of enterprise, one intended to terminate within a length of time, planned to reach a conclusion at some definite period in the future; this I call a *temporary enterprise*; the other intended, in Stevenson's words, to 'travel hopefully' but not 'to arrive': no time of termination being either stated or implied; this I call a *permanent enterprise*.

21.93. Examples of a temporary enterprise are going for an hour's walk, or digging this flower-bed until it is dug; in the second case the event is placed at a given time in the future relatively to certain other events though not to the clock. Or getting married for 'so long as ye both shall live'; you do not know when the first of you will die, but you know that it will happen. Every marriage is a temporary enterprise; death inevitably dissolves it.

21.94. Examples of a permanent enterprise are the advancement of science or the prevention of cruelty to animals. They may be divided into two kinds. In one, the raw material of the enterprise (for example, cases of cruelty to animals) is constantly being supplied by some inexhaustible source (for example, human depravity); in the other the enterprise is such that by its very success it provides a supply of raw material for itself. The advancement of science is conceived as leading to a point from which further advancement is always possible and is indeed required by the terms of the enterprise.

21.95. Every society is formed for the joint prosecution of some enterprise. Where it is a temporary enterprise, I call the society a temporary society; where permanent, a permanent society.

21. 96. A society of two persons joining in a walk intended to last for x hours or y miles is a temporary society; it is intended to be dissolved when that number of hours or miles of walking have come to an end.

21. 97. A society for studying the antiquities of a given district is a permanent society; for its promoters expect that any advancement in the study will reveal new objects and attract new students. These expectations may be falsified, and the society may perish from lack of interest; but it is the expectations, not their fulfilment or non-fulfilment, that make the society permanent or temporary.

XXII

THE FAMILY AS A MIXED COMMUNITY

22. 1. A FAMILY is what I call a *mixed community*; that is to say, one part of it is a *society* (I shall call this the family-society): the other part, which I call the nursery, is a *non-social community*.

22. 11. Most communities, if not all, are mixed communities; as the reader will see if he thinks for himself.

22. 12. The nursery consists of children.

22. 13. It is a non-social community because the children do not join it of their own free will; they are drafted into it when they are too young to consent; and any community whose members become members without their consent and remain members without their consent is a non-social community (20. 32).

22. 14. For the same reason, the nursery is not run by the children.

22. 15. But if there are to be children there must be nurseries; children need care, and the nursery is an institution for looking after children who are too young to look after themselves.

22. 16. If nurseries are to exist, there must be two kinds of persons not constituents (or members or inmates) of the nursery.

22. 17. There must be *parents* who replenish it, and there must be *nurses* who run it.

22. 18. In the simplest possible case the same persons discharge both functions, parents acting as nurses and nurses as parents.

22. 19. Not only is this logically the simplest case, it is historically by far the commonest, and not among human animals only; without prejudice to the claims of other conceivable families, therefore, I call this the *typical family*.

22. 2. The typical family consists of a nursery together with a society having the double function, relatively to the nursery, of replenishing it and running it.

22. 21. I assume that the typical nursery is not self-filling or capable of replenishing itself, because any human being young enough to need the care that a nursery provides will normally be too young to have children; but that it is self-emptying, because every child in time grows up, becomes able to fend for itself, and automatically leaves the nursery.

22. 22. These assumptions are near enough to the truth to justify us in making them.

22. 23. The traditional European nursery is not in fact self-emptying; in so calling it I am ignoring facts which I shall have to emphasize in the very next chapter (23. 62); to emphasize them before that time has arrived, however, would be wantonly to confuse my exposition.

22. 24. I will make another assumption: that human beings fall into two classes, the childish and the adult or grown-up.

22. 25. The childish, I will assume, are drafted into nurseries where their parents look after them as they must be looked after if they are to survive. Slowness in arriving at maturity is characteristic of the human young, and entails not only slowness in learning to find their own food, but also slowness in learning to refrain from acts dangerous to their own and other children's life.

22. 26. Suppose I have exaggerated these dangers; suppose human children do better than we think uncared-for; still there are dangers that a parent fears and has to guard against.

22. 27. Human beings, I will assume, commonly reach physical maturity and mental maturity at about the same time of life; an assumption, once more, not so wildly remote from the truth that we need hesitate to make it.

22. 28. As physically mature, they become able to have children; as mentally mature, they become able to fend for themselves and also to organize their own children into a nursery.

22. 29. On these assumptions puberty not only liberates a child from the conditions of nursery tutelage, but also enables him to set up a nursery of his own; and the human race, freaks apart, is divisible into those young enough to need the tutelage of a nursery themselves, and those old enough to provide it for others.

22. 3. This fancy picture is not very distant from the facts of traditional European life.

M

22. 31. It is still closer to the facts of savage life, where puberty marks at once emergence from the state of childhood and initiation into the adults of the tribe, and the signal for marriage.

22. 32. If that is not the case among Europeans the reason is that European life is a more complicated and more dangerous thing, one harder to find your way about in; and demands a correspondingly longer educational preparation.

22. 33. We pay for these complications and dangers by interpolating between (say) 14 and 24 ten years spent in education which prolong the work of the nursery.

22. 34. European marriage is the normal preliminary to the procreation of children. According to European ideas it is a *social contract* (19. 53) whereby a man and a woman become partners in the enterprise of producing children.

22. 4. The parents, in virtue of that contract, constitute the family-society (22. 1). To conceive marriage as a society and the act by which it is initiated as a contract is the modern European conception; but it was not the early Republican conception at Rome (23. 33); and there are customs, even in modern Europe, suggesting a certain hesitation about it (23. 39).

22. 41. As a society, marriage is conceived as a self-originating status; freely originating itself through the joint act of getting married, and freely maintaining itself through the joint act of living in matrimony.

22. 42. Children are a product of these acts, jointly produced by the two parents.

22. 43. Once children are born they have to be looked after. They need an ordered or regular life, and cannot of their own initiative either provide or demand it.

22. 44. To do either, they would have to have a will, and a child needs a regular life long before it has a will.

22. 45. The need becomes perceptible to an attentive parent in two ways, physiologically and psychologically, without any free will on the child's part.

22. 46. A child visibly thrives when a regular life is provided for it and imposed upon it; and visibly pines when that provision is lacking.

22. 47. A child noticeably craves order and regularity in everything to do with its life; enjoys it when it is forthcoming, and clamours for it when it is not.

22. 5. Parents who wish their children to thrive and enjoy such health as they may (that the average parent is thus disposed is an assumption, once more, not too remote from the facts) have a motive for providing them with an orderly life. Granted these assumptions the nursery will be a normal, even if unintentional, consequence of marriage.

22. 6. The typical or simplest family (22. 18) may be complicated in various ways. I will mention a few.

22. 61. I will begin with the Platonic case (not that it is a relatively simple one; quite the reverse) where the family suffers interference, and (as examination shows) destructive interference at the hands of the body politic. The family is here divided into three parts instead of two; we have the parents, who, instead of the richly diversified functions attached to parenthood in a tradition that was already old when Plato wrote, have in his family only the function of producing offspring; we have the children; and we have the nurses or educators provided by the body politic. Why Plato propounded so odd a scheme I will not pause to explain.

22. 62. Another is the Roman case where the family is extended to embrace a second non-social community of slaves; slaves being, like children, looked after and ordered about partly, though not exclusively, for their own good, because they are not mentally adult and therefore cannot fend for themselves.

22. 63. Among the richer classes in modern Europe there is a type of family like the Roman, with 'servants' instead of slaves; the difference being that a 'servant' is treated at law as capable of owning property and making contracts; whereas a slave has in the eyes of the law no rights whatever as against the 'master' who owns both him and everything he produces.

22. 64. Another type of what may be called an extended family consists of human beings interrelated, whether by agnation or by cognation, otherwise than parents and children. Thus, in the extended patriarchal family, married sons continue to live in their father's house and under his authority.

22. 65. Another is the polygamous family, where the

nursery is recruited by the children of a group containing more than one woman, or more than one man, or both.

22. 66. I am not at all certain where this list ought to end, or on what principles we should be justified in extending it or curtailing it.

22. 67. For example, is a family extended (as I have called it) by conferring a regular status upon non-human members or, as we call them, pets?

22. 68. And what about even human members who enjoy a merely adoptive relation with the main stem of the family?

22. 69. These complications need not be here further discussed or even enumerated. For our present purpose they can all be subsumed under our simplest case.

22. 7. For scientific purposes we are safe from all criticism if we flourish our typical case beneath the reader's nose, and refer all questions about the rigid definition of the family, as such, to that.

22. 8. And, let us remember, without rigid definition there is no science; and the aim of this treatise is to be scientific.

22. 9. In brief: a family consists of parents and children; whatever, over and above that, claims to be recognized as belonging to it has no scientific title to membership.

XXIII

THE FAMILY AS A SOCIETY

23. 1. THE society which forms the nucleus of any given family is a temporary society (21. 9).

23. 11. It consists of a man and a woman (normally, these two and no more) who by mutual agreement, that is by marriage, constitute themselves a society.

23. 12. This society is called a married couple; the male member is called husband, the female member wife.

23. 13. According to custom, which varies, the joint will invests these positions with varying degrees and kinds of authority (20. 45).

23. 14. It is not essential to a marriage that there should be an intention of jointly producing children; but I shall argue (23. 5) that this intention is normal in modern Europe.

23. 15. If there is no such intention the joint enterprise at which the society aims is companionship.

23. 16. In that case it is a temporary society whose joint aim expires when one partner dies.

23. 17. Christians live in hope of a resurrection to eternal life; but the articles of their faith instruct them that 'when they rise they neither marry nor are given in marriage'; and that marriages contracted during earthly life no longer hold good.

23. 18. If some Christians hope for a reunion of married couples beyond the grave, it is a hope against which they have been warned.

23. 19. If there is intention of producing children, the society is still a temporary one, due to expire at least on the death of the first partner.

23. 2. Where marriage entails the intention of producing children, and where that intention is fulfilled, I call it a *normal marriage*.

23. 21. A normal marriage passes through a life-cycle in which it will be useful to distinguish three phases.

23. 22. The first is before any children have been born; or rather, since *nasciturus pro nato habetur*, before any have been conceived.

23. 23. The second is when the children are still too young to help the parents with the work of providing house and home, food, and so forth.

23. 24. The third is when the children are becoming by degrees old enough to take this work off the parents' shoulders.

23. 25. In the first phase the family is merely a particular society; though one formed, as any particular society must be, out of a non-social community (20. 32), namely that in which the married persons have grown up.

23. 26. It is also a society which by the joint will of its members is working at turning itself into something more than a society, namely a mixed community (22. 1).

23. 27. In the second phase the family has thus transformed itself. It is now a mixed community consisting of a social nucleus of parents and a non-social community of children; the children are engaged in growing up, and the parents, partly, in helping them do so.

23. 28. In the third phase the children, having grown up to the point of possessing free will, and being thus eligible for membership in the family-society, are incorporated in that society.

23. 29. How this incorporation happens we shall have to consider (23. 62). For the present let us examine the structure of the normal family as it exists in the second phase.

23. 3. It is a community which as a whole is non-social, though it contains a social nucleus. Free will is not indispensable to membership. It is not by the baby's free will that it becomes, as it certainly does become, a member of the family.

23. 31. I have described the parents as a social nucleus of this community. This implies that marriage is a social contract between a man and a woman. This again implies that the man and woman must be both physically and mentally adult, or capable of having children and also capable of entering into a contract.

23. 32. These implications of calling a husband and wife a society are regarded by modern Europeans as conforming with the facts. Modern Europeans believe that both a man and a woman, when physically adult, are normally adult in mind as well; that each has attained freedom of will to that degree and in that kind (21. 8) which is required in the ordinary circumstances of modern life by the decision to marry, and to marry a certain person.

23. 33. The earliest documents of Roman law reveal a society in which no such belief was held. At the time whose customs are recorded by the Twelve Tables a woman had always to be in somebody's *manus*. By marriage she normally passed from her father's *manus* into that of her husband; or, if her husband had a father living, into that of her father-in-law. The marriage was not a contract between man and woman, for a woman was not regarded as capable of contract; nor indeed was a man, unless he was a *paterfamilias*; it was a contract either between the bridegroom and the bride's father, or else between the two fathers.

23. 34. At a later date, when the idea of *manus* was becoming obsolete, and when marriage was beginning to be looked upon in the modern way as a contract between bridegroom and bride, the earlier customs were neither condemned as barbaric, or contemptuous towards woman, nor were they forgotten. They were regretted as symptoms of a vanished virtue.

23. 35. The days of Roman respect for women, the days of the honoured and virtuous Roman matron, were days when a woman at marriage passed from one man's hand to another, her own consent being no more necessary to the transaction than a cow's consent is necessary to the transaction whereby one man sells her to another.

23. 36. Or so it was thought by the Romans of the late Republic and early Empire. The reader may call this a characteristic piece of sentimentality on their part; a glorification of a past that when it existed was barbarous; but that does not dispose of the problem.

23. 37. The problem is not whether women are capable of contract, in other words possessed of free will, but how far certain kinds of women in certain kinds of circumstances can reasonably be counted upon to possess it. Different answers will have to be given to this question according as it is asked about the women of early Republican Rome or the women of modern England. It makes a difference how women are brought up, and to what kinds of strain their wills are exposed in the daily life of the world they live in.

23. 38. There need not be any contradiction between the various beliefs current about female psychology at various times. Each may have been sound, granted the conditions of the time. The fact that a woman was expected in ancient Rome to be incapable of arranging her own marriage, and in modern England to be capable of it, does not prove that the same causes produced different effects, still less that the old fools in Rome or England, whichever you like, did not understand their own daughters; what it most likely proves is that the conditions of female education were different in the two places, and that the products of that education differed correspondingly.

23. 39. The modern marriage customs of European peoples preserve an interesting 'survival' of early Roman practice. It is still usual, at least in the religious ceremony, for a bride to be 'given away' by her father or someone acting for him, as if the act in which she is concerned were not a contract between her husband and herself but, as the Twelve Tables conceive it, the passive transference of a woman from one man's 'hand' to another's. The practice is a fragment of Roman law, and pretty ancient Roman law at that, embedded in the customs of the Christian Church. Now if, in these days, Europeans think that women are capable of contract, and that the ancient belief that they can be bought and sold like cows is obsolete, why does the ritual expressing it survive? 'Survivals of this kind are common', say (or used to say) the followers of the late Sir Edward Tylor. But are they common? If a ritual practised by certain persons expresses a certain belief, it is evidence that the belief is alive. A second belief inconsistent with it may be alive too; why not? Many people hold beliefs which are inconsistent; and in Tylor's day (*Primitive Culture* was published in 1871) it was not known that repressed beliefs found an outlet in ritual acts; but everyone knows it now.

23. 4. Modern Europeans, with the top of their minds, conceive a marriage as a contract between a man and a woman; but at the bottom of their minds they are not so sure; they are haunted by an idea which in their saner moments they know to be savage, the idea that it is the transference of a chattel from one owner to another.

23. 41. A certain doubt whether a marriage is based on free consent or imposed on the principals by *force majeure* is not really so alarming as at first it may seem to be.

23. 42. This is because 'every particular society has about it a trace of the non-social community out of which it has emerged' (21. 5).

23. 43. If every particular society represents no more than a partial emergence of this or that human aggregate from the non-social condition which is, as Hobbes would say, 'the natural condition of Mankind', why boggle at the discovery that the customary ritual of Christian marriage contains more than a suggestion of being derived from non-social conditions?

23. 44. Had it not been so, that ritual would have failed to express an integral part of what modern Europeans feel on entering upon matrimony: that the spouses they choose are only in part chosen by themselves, and that the other part represents a choice bequeathed to them, so to speak, by their parents and relatives.

23. 45. It is the positive part, the element of freedom, to which we call attention when we describe marriage as a contract. We do not deny the negative part, the fact that there is also an element of unfreedom. There is a negative element in a marriage as in any other particular society.

23. 46. Freedom is always a matter of degree (21. 8). A man can only progress in freedom by gradual stages; converting into objects of choice things he began by accepting at the hands of *force majeure*.

23. 47. Because a marriage was partly due to the force which marks the traces of a non-social community, it does not follow that these traces cannot be progressively eliminated by the growth of freedom. A marriage that is at first something less than a contract becomes more and more of a contract as the husband and wife, leaving behind them the partly childish frame of mind in which they originally embarked upon it, face its responsibilities in a spirit of progressive freedom. That is what we call making a success of the marriage.

23.48. With that qualification I repeat that modern Europeans think of marriage as a contract between husband and wife.

23.5. What do they regard as the joint aim of the society it initiates? I reply, the propagation of children. That is the joint purpose to which, in proportion as they think of their marriage as an act of free will, they regard themselves as devoted.

23.51. It is the widespread knowledge of contraceptives that has made this statement possible. Before the use of contraceptives was generally understood in Europe, the counter-proposition could be maintained (as, *mutatis mutandis*, it can still be maintained now in respect of persons ignorant of contraceptives) that the normal aim of marriage was the gratification of sexual desire, and that the procreation of children was normally an accidental by-product of this.

23.52. Nowadays, owing to the knowledge of contraceptives, there is a large body of persons who only have children when they do so by their own free will; and anyone acquainted with such persons distinguishes among them couples who regard marriage as an occasion for the procreation of children from couples who regard it as a licence for sexual gratification.

23.53. Any observer will agree that among inhabitants of this country the former attitude is normal to the marrying or recently married sort, the latter exceptional.

23.54. It is not only the observer whom reference to the knowledge of contraceptives enables to clear up his mind on the question how marriage is normally regarded by married persons whose confidence he enjoys. Reference to the same fact enables or rather compels married persons to make up their minds on the question of their own practical attitude towards marriage.

23.55. When contraceptives were unknown, married people did not have to make up their minds whether they thought of marriage as an opportunity for sexual indulgence, with children as a possible by-product, or as primarily a partnership in the procreation of children. About the beginning of the present century, when my elders began discussing this question with me, it was plain that in general they had not made up their minds between the two views, but were inclined towards the first. Now people have to make up their minds.

23. 56. This is the result of widespread knowledge concerning contraception. It has produced in my lifetime, within social strata well known to myself, a virtual abolition of what in my youth was the standard or ordinary attitude towards marriage and a substitution of the opposite attitude.

23. 6. The non-social family community consists primarily of children whom the parents hope to bring to a condition of physical and mental maturity. When that hope is fulfilled as regards any given child, the child emerges from the non-social community and, being now possessed of free will, becomes capable of social life. It may now undergo incorporation into the family-society, or it may help to form a new society, for example, by marrying in its turn. Because a single person may be a member of different societies, these alternatives are not mutually exclusive.

23. 61. But some children die young; others are mentally deficient. This subdivides the non-social part of the family into two: members capable of ultimate incorporation into the family-society and members not so capable.

23. 62. What does incorporation mean? I spoke above (22. 21) as if a child grew up by its own efforts alone to the point of automatically leaving the nursery; but I warned the reader that this assumption neglected the work done by the parents and perhaps others in educating the child.

23. 63. The process of education is partly carried out by the child upon itself; partly by others upon it. The first part is blind, because the child is working at it knows not what; but efficacious, as all self-education is efficacious. The other part is less efficacious because the adult educator is working to produce a condition in something other than himself; but it is not blind, because the adult educator has at any rate some idea of what he wants to produce.

23. 64. But this is not all. The child, on attaining a certain degree of maturity, does not automatically leave the nursery and take a place in the family-society. His incorporation requires an act on the part of those who already constitute that society. This act develops through many phases.

The parents' readiness to welcome him as an equal must be made clear to him from an early stage in his life as a promise which, as he grows up, they must be prepared to redeem by degrees. Like the commencement of his babyhood, the commencement of the child's adult life is an event he cannot bring about solely by his own efforts; it is partly that, but partly it is something done to him by the existing family-society. Unless the parents do their share it will never happen; and the child, its desire to grow up frustrated, will remain indefinitely in the psychological condition of child-hood. And, unlike some parts of the child's education, this is a part which the parents cannot delegate. They must do it themselves.

23.65. Let us go back to the distinction (23.61) between children expected and not expected to grow up. If the first alone were in question the family might be defined as a de-vice whereby adult human beings produce other adult human beings. The rest would then be failures or breakages in this attempt.

23.66. But parents not only sometimes show themselves backward to incorporate a growing child in their own society as soon as he is capable of it, and anxious to keep him a child; they even sometimes deliberately enlarge the class of depen-dants not expected to grow up by adding to it *non-human pets* which can be trusted never to grow up. The non-human pet is essentially a mental defective valued and cherished in the household precisely for its mental deficiency.

23.67. The *idiot child* is in the same position. Parents who have idiot children and cherish them, and those who adopt non-human pets as substitutes for children, prove that they have a need which idiot children or non-human pets can satisfy. This is a different need from that which is satisfied only by producing children and educating them to the point of mental maturity.

23.7. The need on the part of human beings to have children has already been distinguished from sexual desire (23.5 seqq.). If the first is called the reproductive instinct and the second the sexual instinct, they are two 'instincts', not one. Let us consider the first by itself. First, is it a 're-productive' instinct? Secondly, is it an 'instinct'?

23. 71. If it is a 'reproductive' instinct it should drive men to produce not babies unlike themselves but grown men like themselves: at least, if reproduction means what it says. But the need to produce adult children is only one of three distinct needs which are confused by lumping them all under the head of a reproductive or parental instinct.

23. 72. First, there is the fact that adult persons want babies. This is popularly supposed peculiar to women; but it is shared by men. It is closely connected with sexual desire, but not impossible to dissociate from it, still less distinguish from it. In its normal shape, as associated with sexual desire, it is the fact that a man not only wants a baby but wants to have it by a certain woman, and that a woman not only wants a baby but wants to have it by a certain man.

23. 73. Secondly, there is the fact that both men and women want not only babies but children. A man or woman wants to have something which occupies the position of his child; something to look after and care for, something whose development he not only watches with interest but actively promotes; something (I will add) to bully and browbeat without a chance of its hitting back, something absolutely dependent upon him, looking up to him with adoration as its only benefactor and trembling before him as its all-powerful despot.

23. 74. This need to have a child is quite distinct from the need to have a baby; each can be satisfied when the other is not; one by having a baby that dies, the other by adopting a child of someone else's. Of the various elements which I have mentioned in the preceding paragraph there are some which do not square with a sentimental view of 'human nature'. They consist of desires which a reader who shares that view will protest that he does not entertain. He does not want to bully and browbeat and tyrannize over his children or the dogs which take their place. I congratulate him.

23. 75. Thirdly, there is the fact that both men and women, especially men, want not only children but grown-up children: children who have arrived with one's own watchful help at intellectual maturity. This alone should be called, if you call it an instinct, the 'reproductive' instinct (23. 71).

23. 76. The 'instinct' which consists in wanting a baby is satisfied by having a baby that dies in infancy; an event which, however distressing to the parent, does not leave him with his 'parental instinct' entirely unsatisfied. The one which consists in wanting a child can be satisfied by having an idiot child or a non-human pet (which is to all intents and purposes an idiot child), a creature that was never my baby and will never be my grown-up son or daughter.

23. 77. It is a fact easy to verify that the parents of an idiot child do not regard it as a 'breakage' (23. 65); they take great delight in it, especially the mother, who is more apt than the father to regret and sometimes even impede a child's growing up. The 'instinct' to have a grown-up child can be satisfied by acting as teacher to other people's nearly grown-up children: standing *in loco parentis* to them and (to be frank) stealing for oneself what their parents ought by rights to have.

23. 78. There is something distasteful about that, sweet though the stolen waters are; just as there is something distasteful about lavishing one's 'parental instincts' upon a dog or an idiot child or even an adopted child; and for that matter something distasteful about gratifying one's sexual desire for a woman without becoming the father of her children. Sex and the three forms of paternity are all linked together in a man's consciousness in such a way that to separate any one from the rest offends him.

23. 79. But what is a man to do? The best life, and what every sound man wants, is to be a complete man, *teres atque rotundus*: but if he cannot warm both hands before the fire of life is he not to warm the one there is room for? Half a loaf is better than no bread; and the loaf of parenthood is divisible into many slices.

23. 8. There is no such thing as a 'parental instinct'. What vulgarly goes by that name is not the same as the sexual 'instinct'; it is not even one thing. It is a confused mixture of three different 'instincts', separate and capable of separate satisfaction. I have now to ask (23. 7) whether these three things are rightly called 'instincts'.

23. 81. The word 'instinct', though often used by persons who think they are using it scientifically, is not a scientific term. It properly means anything that is implanted in a man; properly, therefore, it is a wholly unscientific omnibus-word for any element in 'human nature'.

23.82. But as popularly used it refers to an appetite (7. 1 seqq.) or desire (11. 1 seqq.), the two things not being distinguished. I have spoken of 'wanting' babies (23. 72), children (23. 73), and grown-up children (23. 75). Is 'wanting' or even 'wishing' the right word?

23.83. There is certainly sexual appetite, developing with the development of consciousness into sexual desire. But I have distinguished, as I am led to do when I reflect on the significance of contraceptives (23. 52–5), between this and 'wanting' children; and even a reader who refuses to follow me will have to do so if and when those who threaten us with ectogenesis have made good their threats.

23.84. Is there an appetite for parenthood, developing with the development of consciousness into a desire for parenthood?

23.85. There is not. Parenthood is not an object of appetite or even desire. It is an object of will. There is no appetite for parenthood; there is no desire for parenthood; there is only a purpose or intention of parenthood.

23.86. Parenthood is often achieved without any such intention. But when that happens it comes about not through the operation of any parental 'instinct' but as a by-product of the sexual 'instinct'.

23.87. That parenthood in any one of its three separate forms is an object of will and not of 'instinct' is a fact revealed, and (since the fact in question is a fact of consciousness) established as well as revealed for modern Europeans by the practice of contraception. This practice has made modern Europeans conscious of a freedom of which they were hitherto not conscious: it has enlarged their freedom as well as their consciousness of freedom.

23.88. If the practice has enemies—enemies in principle, objecting not to this or that contraceptive method but to contraception as such—it is for that reason. They are persons who aim at circumscribing human freedom. They would like men not to be free at all; if that is impossible, they will fight every advance of freedom step by step. They are enemies of free will.

23. 9. 'Man is born free', says Rousseau, 'and everywhere he is in chains.'

23. 91. I do not doubt that truths, and important truths, can be told in Rousseau's language, where the word 'born' is intended to make you think not about the facts of human infancy but about a mysterious, half-divine, and altogether imaginary thing called Human Nature, as remote from the world of fact as those equally mysterious and no less imaginary Rights of Man which were connected with it by the American and French revolutionaries.

23. 92. The facts of human infancy are dirtier and less picturesque, perhaps, than the fancies of Rousseau; but they are a safer foundation on which to build a science of the relations linking a man to his fellow men.

23. 93. In human infancy the fact, as known to me at least, is that a man is born neither free nor in chains.

23. 94. To be free is to have a will unhampered by external force, and a baby has none.

23. 95. To be in chains is to have a will hampered by something which prevents it from expressing itself in action; and a baby has none.

23. 96. A man is born a red and wrinkled lump of flesh having no will of its own at all, absolutely at the mercy of the parents by whose conspiracy he has been brought into existence.

23. 97. That is what no science of human community, social or non-social, must ever forget.

XXIV

THE BODY POLITIC, SOCIAL AND NON-SOCIAL

24. 1. THERE is a kind of community of which political theory hopes to offer a scientific account. Let us call it the body politic.

24. 11. Is a body politic a society or a non-social community? And let us remember to use the words accurately.

24. 12. The Greeks and Romans thought it was a society.

24. 13. Modern thinkers regard it as a non-social community in process of turning into a society, a process never completed.

24. 14. Let us begin with the ancients. They thought of a body politic as a number of free agents united to pursue a common enterprise.

24. 15. Such a whole was, for example, Athens. Athens was a πόλις, a 'city', and 'cities' are what the science of 'politics' sets itself to study.

24. 16. But what is a city? What is it made of? You and I might think it was made of houses: but no ancient Greek would have dreamt of suggesting that answer; for him it was obvious that a city was made of citizens.

24. 17. Then what was a citizen? A kind of human being; one that is male, and grown up, and free, and . . . well, that is enough to start with and more; it is too much to allow you or me to think ancient politics an easy game.

24. 18. Not that modern politics is any easier; it is, in fact, harder. Let us go back to the ancients. A citizen of Athens, according to them, was someone who possessed various rights in the corporation called Athens.

24. 19. Never mind what these rights were in detail; it is not important to remember. What is most worth your while to remember is that citizens of Athens are one thing; inhabitants of Athens quite another.

24. 2. The inhabitants of Athens, or its population, included, beside citizens, (1) women, (2) children, (3) slaves, and (4) foreigners. Of these non-citizens some were privately dependent on individual citizens; others publicly dependent upon groups of citizens.

24. 21. The business with which the science of politics was concerned fell into two parts, public and private. Whatever was public business was concerned with carrying on the joint enterprise for which the society existed or some part of it, for example working a mine which was public property. Whatever was private business was concerned, for example, with a man's management of his own land or his own slaves.

24. 22. Although the body politic was a society, certain elements in it, as I have shown in 23.42, may have been non-social in their nature.

24. 23. Such was the mutual exclusiveness by which a member of one body politic was automatically debarred from belonging to another body politic.

24. 24. This was an element of non-sociality in the tiny Greek bodies politic.

24. 25. It may be compared with the element of non-contractuality which survives in Christian marriage, the ritual of giving away the bride (23. 39).

24. 26. In cases of this kind an institution has been handed down, with regard to most of its details, in what I may be permitted to call a 'dominant' form; but one of these details (and perhaps others) has taken what may be called the opposite or 'recessive' form.

24. 27. There is no reason why this should not sometimes happen; but there seems to be a reason why it should not happen very often; as there seems to be a reason why the same sequence of numbers should not turn up very often in a game of chance; not that the reasons are the same.

24. 28. Ancient political life is the life, and ancient political theory the theory, of the city (πόλις), which was a society made up of citizens upon whom non-citizens were dependent.

24. 3. Medieval political life is the life, and medieval political theory the theory, of the 'state' (*l'état*, *lo stato*), a term belonging to the international European language of the later Middle Ages and derived from the Latin *status*, used as a legal term for a man's status with regard to rights.

24. 31. In the Middle Ages a very remarkable change of opinion had come about as to what the body politic was.

24. 32. People had come to think of the body politic no longer as a society, a community of free and adult men collectively managing their own affairs; they had come to think of it more as a collection of human animals, not necessarily free and not necessarily male, but just human.

24. 33. Hence in the Middle Ages a body politic was conceived as a non-social community; not a self-ruling body of adult Englishmen or what not, but simply a collective name for people born in a certain place.

24. 34. But this non-social mass was conceived as permeated by infections, so to speak, of sociality; and these increased in vigour as the Middle Ages went on.

24. 35. It was conceived as splitting itself up into various groups called 'estates', each with rights and duties of its own.[1]

24. 36. Rights and duties were assigned to these 'estates' in the early Middle Ages by the customary law of the community with irruptions of imperial or quasi-imperial power; in the later Middle Ages by legislation (28. 63).

24. 37. One such estate normally came to be regarded as ruling over the rest; this estate was 'supreme' over the rest, or, as the Middle Ages called it, the 'sovereign' of the rest.

24. 38. By the late Middle Ages the conception of the body politic has taken a new shape. There are no more 'citizens' collectively attending to the 'res publica' and individually looking after their wives, children, slaves, cattle, and so forth.

24. 39. At first sight you might think that there are just two things, both of them new things: sovereigns and subjects; and that the new pattern of politics is the pattern of the relations between them.

24. 4. It is more complex than that. Medieval writers call the relation between husband and wife a case of sovereignty; so that the same person might be both sovereign and subject.

24. 41. Moreover, there was another new thing, liberties. Liberties, as understood in the Middle Ages, were what a sovereign gives a subject; for example, in a feudal country, the tenure of certain land on condition of military service.

24. 42. Liberties, enjoyed by individuals or corporations,

---

[1] There were not three of these 'estates', but a vague indefinite number; cf. A. F. Pollard, *The Evolution of Parliament*.

are the most important elements in the new political pattern
of the later Middle Ages.

24. 43. When we emerge from the Middle Ages into the
daylight of the Renaissance with Machiavelli (*The Prince*
belongs to the year 1512) we find this pattern beginning to
break down.

24. 44. 'The State' rules over a body of subjects on whom
it has bestowed, as the price of its allegiance, numerous
liberties; but where is this process to end?

24. 45. It can only end in the bankruptcy of the Prince
and the taking over of his business by his creditors, the
grantees of feudal and other liberties. But will they run the
business? Are they fitted for it?

24. 46. Machiavelli showed that the subjects' will is,
negatively, the rock on which the prince's power, unless he
steers wisely, will be shipwrecked. He did not also show that,
positively, it is the rock on which that power can be built.

24. 47. The medieval pattern has for him broken down
because those who hold liberties by princely gift are not sure
to honour the obligations arising out of them. They are not
conscious of any obligations; only of liberties.

24. 48. What Hobbes discovered was that 'the state' or
'the sovereign' does not rule by force at all, but it still rules;
it rules by authority (20. 45). It rules because its constituent
subjects, who are (some of them; not all) across the boundary
which divides man as a social being from man in a state of
nature, have achieved social life and are therefore able to
confer authority.

24. 49. This is the great discovery of Hobbes in political
science; a greater discovery than any other made in that
science since perhaps the time of Aristotle.

24. 5. What is a body politic? Is it, as the Greeks believed, a society of citizens corporately ruling themselves and
having non-citizen dependants, wives, children, and so forth?
Or is it, as the Middle Ages thought, a non-social community, a human herd which strong men rule and good men
would wish to rule well?

24. 51. Hobbes said: 'It is both. It changes out of one
thing into the other. The medieval account of it represents
the starting-point of the change, the Greek account of it the

finishing-point. Between these two points it is always moving, and the movement is what constitutes the life of a body politic.'

24. 52. Looking back from the time of Hobbes, one sees a process whereby a Greek or social body politic has turned into a modern or non-social body politic, and that again into a new kind of body politic, a new social kind, in what is called the 'bourgeois' life of the medieval and post-medieval age; in this set of changes you see changes not in political theory but in political fact.

24. 53. But there is also a change taking place in political theory. The Greek theory of political life as the theory of a social body politic has turned into the medieval theory of a non-social body politic, and that again into the conception of the 'bourgeoisie' as the root of all princely authority.

24. 54. The reader may object to our having the argument in both ways at once. A body politic, he may say, must be either a society or a non-social community; it cannot be both at once. Choose which you like, but abide by your choice.

24. 55. The answer is: '*Must be*, say you, but when? We are in a world where nothing stays put, but everything moves; the things we say must move, too, in the same rhythm as the things we are talking about.'

24. 56. This answer was worked out by Plato, who did a good deal of the pioneer work out of which Aristotle systematized what we call 'logic'.

24. 57. All logic is concerned with discussions; but Plato distinguished two kinds of discussions, 'eristical' and 'dialectical' (*Meno*, 75 *c–d*).

24. 58. What Plato calls an eristic discussion is one in which each party tries to prove that he was right and the other wrong.

24. 59. In a dialectical discussion you aim at showing that your own view is one with which your opponent really agrees, even if at one time he denied it; or conversely that it was yourself and not your opponent who began by denying a view with which you really agree.

24. 6. The essence of dialectical discussion is to discuss in the hope of finding that both parties to the discussion are right, and that this discovery puts an end to the debate. Where they 'agree to differ', as the saying is, there is nothing on which they have really agreed.

24. 61. Plato's belief that dialectical discussion was scientifically superior to eristical discussion (that is, superior as a means of reaching, not mere agreement, but the truth) rested on the assumption that there was what I will call a 'dialectic in things', which the 'dialectic in words' of a dialectical disputant would somehow reproduce or follow in the rhythm (24. 55) of his argument.

24. 62. This assumption was one that Plato's compatriots had lately learned to make. Heraclitus, one of whose pupils had been an early teacher of Plato's, had laid it down that *everything moves and nothing stays still*. This opinion was sadly disconcerting to the general run of Greek thinkers, to whom it followed that nothing could be known; for how could anything be known unless it stayed still?

24. 63. Plato's discovery was *how the intellect could find its way about in a Heraclitean world*. The answer is: *think dialectically*.

24. 64. A Heraclitean world is not a world of compromise; there might be compromises in a non-Heraclitean world; it is a world of *change*. Change implies a pair of contradictories (call them *x* and not-*x*) so related that the positive term is gradually gaining on the negative term: there is something that *was* not-*x*, but whatever was not-*x* is turning into *x*. Think of a pot of paint in which you are mixing more and more white with some other colour, say black. The paint was never either pure black or pure white; it is always turning into a paler and paler grey.

24. 65. And if you settle upon any standard of light-greyness with which at any moment it conforms, you must be ready to give that up as a standard which by now has been left behind. This readiness to give up something which at a certain time you settled upon as true is dialectical thinking.

24. 66. I spoke of paint, mixed of white and black (24. 64). The same thing would apply to a community, mixed of social and non-social elements.

24. 67. Such a community might be described, by attending to the positive element, as a society; by attending to the

negative element, as a non-social community. Yet it might be one community that was being so described; the difference being only a difference in 'point of view', a *dialectical* difference.

24. 68. According to Hobbes (though Hobbes seems hardly to have recognized Plato's work on the subject) *a body politic is a dialectical thing*, a Heraclitean world in which at any given time there is a negative element, an element of non-sociality which is going to disappear, or at least is threatened with abolition by the growth of the positive element; and a positive element, an element of sociality.

24. 69. No one, of course, after identifying a certain negative element in an actual political situation, would prophesy its disappearance, unless he were a fool; a sensible man knows that on such occasions threatened men live long.

24. 7. Political science can only identify the threat to its continued existence; cannot predict its downfall.

24. 71. The world of politics is a dialectical world in which non-social communities (communities of men in what Hobbes called the *state of nature*) turn into societies.

24. 72. Such communities are called *families*; they come into existence because men are born babies and have to be looked after; not inexorably, there is nothing to prevent the opposite from happening; but the psychological tendency by which parents are drawn to look after their children (22. 5) is generally efficacious, and so the nursery generally comes into existence.

24. 73. The parents are able to exercise *transeunt rule* over their children because they are capable of *immanent rule* over themselves.

24. 74. And so there is a self-ruling community, or society, upon which the children are dependent; and into this society the children are drawn as they grow up: not inexorably, again, because something may go wrong with them, we will not ask what; but that incorporation of the now adult child into the family-society is what generally happens.

24. 75. By a dialectic of the same kind the *subjects* in a body politic grow up into sharing the work of rule.

XXV

THE THREE LAWS OF POLITICS

25. 1. POLITICAL life is the life characteristic of a body politic.

25. 11. A body politic is a non-social community which, by a dialectical process also present in the family, changes into a society.

25. 12. At a relatively early stage in this process (there is no stage at which it has not yet begun to operate) the body politic is a mixed community (22. 1) consisting of a social nucleus and a non-social circumnuclear body. The first are called the rulers; the second the ruled.

25. 13. The first class is a society and rules itself.

25. 14. Its members are 'persons' or agents possessed of free will.

25. 15. It also rules the second class, which is a community only because it is ruled.

25. 16. Members of the second class are devoid of free will.

25. 17. Let us call the first class the 'council' of the body politic; the second its 'nursery'.

25. 18. The body politic, as consisting of council and nursery, has to provide for the recruitment of each.

25. 19. It recruits the council by promotion from the nursery; it recruits the nursery by breeding babies, and taking the consequences.

25. 2. In this recapitulation I have stated the simplest possible case with regard to the body politic, as I previously (22. 4) stated the simplest possible case with regard to the family.

25. 21. The simplest body politic differs from the simplest family only at one point.

25. 22. Each is divided into a social part and a non-social part; but whereas the family-society is a temporary society (23. 1) the political society is a permanent society.

25. 23. The council or 'state' or 'sovereign' (24. 3 seqq.) is a permanent society because its work is never done.

25. 24. In a body politic new babies are always being born; the nursery is always being replenished and the work of imposing order upon it is never concluded.

25. 25. Equally, the work of establishing relations between it and the council is never concluded, nor the work of ordering the council itself, for that, too, is constantly being recruited.

25. 26. These three problems (the problem of determining a way of life for the council; of determining a way of life for the nursery; and of determining the relation between the two) have all to be solved by the council, and are the main part of what is called the *constitutional* problem.

25. 27. The constitutional problem also includes problems with regard to the subdivision of these two classes, to which I shall come later on (25. 46).

25. 28. Because the composition of a body politic is always changing the constitutional problem can never be solved once for all; there must always be a 'state' ready to solve it. The 'state', therefore, is a permanent society.

25. 3. When historical studies were in their infancy this difference between the family-society as a temporary society and the 'state' as a permanent society was often overlooked.

25. 31. Bacon was repeating a commonplace of the time when he wrote that 'In the youth of a state, arms do flourish; in the middle age of a state, learning; and then both of them together for a time; in the declining age of a state, mechanical arts and merchandize' (Essay lvii, *Of the Vicissitude of Things*).

25. 32. No one who takes the trouble to verify his assertion by appeal to historical facts now universally accessible will say, as Bacon here does, that one and the same 'state' has different excellences according to the different lengths of time since its foundation.

25. 33. A later form of the same error is Marx's prediction that the 'state' would 'wither away'; one of the many symptoms that Marx, the enemy of Utopian dreams, was himself addicted to them in the special form of millennial dreams. A Utopia is a wish-fulfilment fantasy, inherently unrealizable; a millennium is a Utopia dated in the future.

25. 34. As long as there is a body politic there must be

a 'state'. It cannot 'wither away', though it may so change
as to be unrecognized by short-sighted observers; because
there will always be work for it to do. The birth of new
babies into the body politic, and the time-lag between their
birth and the attainment of mental maturity which releases
them from the necessity of being ruled by others and others
from the necessity of ruling them, forbid a final solution of
the constitutional problem.

25. 35. The error was already ancient when Bacon repeated it. In our own time it has been revived, like many
other long-exploded errors, by those specialists in obsolete
ideas, the Fascists of Italy and the Nazis of Germany.

25. 36. Mistakenly thinking that the histories of Italy
and Germany begin respectively with Cavour and Bismarck
or thereabouts, or even later, they boast of their own political
youth and declare France or England, whose history is
notoriously longer than that, to be senile.

25. 37. This is nonsense, and nonsense many centuries
out of date. However, to do them justice, they do not mean it
for sense. They mean it for a threat, and their meaning is well
enough understood: 'Thinking you richer and weaker than
ourselves, we propose to attack you and steal your wealth.'

25. 38. The belief that a 'state' in its lifetime exhibits
something like the melancholy Jaques's 'seven ages of man'
disappears as soon as it is realized that a 'state' is a permanent
society. The belief only arises from a false analogy between
the 'state' and the family-society, which because it is a temporary society does pass through phases of that kind (23. 21).

25. 39. The simplest analysis of a body politic (25. 2)
rests on the fact that any body politic consists in part of
rulers, in part of ruled.

25. 4. This again rests on the fact that it includes some
members who, having reached the necessary point in mental
development, have a will; and others who, not having
reached that point, have none.

25. 41. Will depends on freedom; and freedom is a matter
of degree (21. 8). This complicates our simplest possible
analysis of the body politic without, however, falsifying it.

25. 42. The simplest possible analysis is into those who,
having reached mental maturity, are capable of free action

and those who are not. The second class are only fit to be ruled; the first are fit to rule.

25. 43. But the minimum qualification for fitness to be a member of the ruling class is a very low one.

25. 44. People having that qualification and no more are capable of free action only when the problem to be solved is the easiest possible kind of problem and the circumstances in which they have to solve it are the easiest possible kind of circumstances.

25. 45. Where the strains are greater, greater strength of will is needed to resist them and to make a free decision.

25. 46. The ruling class may, therefore, be subdivided into a multiplicity of graded subclasses demanding as their qualification for membership strength of will in different degrees.

25. 47. The highest subclass will consist of those members who are able to resist the severest emotional strains and make a free decision about the hardest political problems in the hardest circumstances.

25. 48. Lower subclasses will find places for persons who can only solve easier problems or solve them in easier circumstances.

25. 49. Thus the ruling class as a whole becomes a hierarchy of ruling subclasses, differently endowed with strength of will.

25. 5. Something of the same kind happens in the ruled class. Here, however, the subdivision rests not on differential strength of will, whether innate or produced by some kind of education; but on what I will call, borrowing a word from the theory of magnetism and electricity, 'induction'.

25. 51. Induction is something whereby a body not charged with electricity or magnetism behaves as if it were so charged, owing to the proximity of a charged body.

25. 52. The 'induction' of which I speak is something whereby a human being incapable of will (or capable only in a low degree) behaves as if he were capable (or capable in a higher degree) owing to the proximity of a being thus capable.

25. 53. A decision that is really free is one which a man makes for himself. His resolution is his own and nobody else's.

25. 54. If he has not the strength of will to make a decision, or if the circumstances are such that he cannot make one, he may still outwardly behave as if he had made it because he is subjected to force; for example his officer's revolver may drive him against the enemy. He is now a slave, but a slave outwardly behaving like a brave man.

25. 55. But there is a third alternative. Between the condition of a free agent who has a will of his own and the condition of a servile agent who is forced by another to behave outwardly as if he had one, there is the condition of an agent who has a will but a weak one; serviceable enough when led by a stronger will, but incapable of standing alone. To continue the example of the preceding paragraph, he does not need to be driven against the enemy by his officer's revolver; he can be led against the enemy by his officer's example.

25. 56. This inspiration of a weak will by a stronger is what I call (25. 5) 'induction'. It happens not only where a man of weaker will is in contact with a man of stronger but where a man almost but not quite capable of voluntary action is in contact with a man who is so capable.

25. 57. It thus enables men not quite fit for membership of a ruling class in right of their own mental powers to become fit for it when they are well led by their mental superiors. It does not enable them to do everything their superiors could do; it only narrows the gap between them without abolishing it; but it does at least bring into existence a class, recruited from those members of the ruled who, being by mental development most near to being fit for the life of ruling, are rendered fit for that life when they are inspired by wise and vigorous leadership from above.

25. 58. Subdivisions thus appear in the ruled class, based on the varying wisdom and vigour with which 'induction' is administered from above, and the varying capacity to welcome it below. The better the rulers, and the better the ruled, the more this process will elevate sections of the ruled to temporary and induced membership of the rulers.

25. 59. This 'induction' is not radically different from education. The inductive process often repeated is an important part of all education. Response to good leadership is part of becoming a good leader. And conversely a good leader is always teaching his followers to become leaders in their turn.

25. 6. I will now summarize what has been already said in three propositions which I will call the THREE LAWS OF POLITICS.

25. 61. They are meant to hold good of every body politic without exception, irrespective of all differences between one kind and another.

25. 62. All good political practice is based on grasping them, and most bad political practice is based on failing to grasp them, as rules of political activity.

25. 63. All good political theory is based on stating them, and most bad political theory is based on denying them, as truths that hold good of every body politic.

25. 7. The FIRST LAW OF POLITICS is that *a body politic is divided into a ruling class and a ruled class.*

25. 71. Human beings are born babies; and babies, or even children some years old, must be looked after if they are to survive. They can survive only in nurseries which they cannot rule. They cannot even authorize the rule of others, for they neither enter these nurseries nor remain in them of their own free will.

25. 72. No one denies this or ever has denied it. The only question is whether children are members of the body politic or no. For the Greeks they were not (24. 17). For modern Europeans they are (24. 33). Concerned as we are with the modern European mind (9. 3) we accept the modern European answer.

25. 73. That answer commits us to holding that every body politic, whatever else it contains, contains at least a *nursery*, that is, a ruled class or the nucleus of one; and a ruling class.

25. 8. The SECOND LAW OF POLITICS is that *the barrier between the two classes is permeable in an upward sense.*

25. 81. That is, members of the ruled class must be susceptible of promotion into the ruling class.

25. 82. For the ruling class must not be allowed to die out; it always has work to do, and must always be fit to do it; for it constitutes a permanent society (25. 23).

25. 83. It is assumed here that membership of the ruling class is conditional on passing some kind of judgement as to suitability for ruling, and that this judgement cannot be passed on a new-born baby; though when it takes place, who carries it out, and what are the qualities he looks for, are questions I do not undertake to answer.

25. 84. All I imply is that *there is some quality which is held to make a man fit to be a ruler*; and that by some kind of test the presence of this quality can be recognized.

25. 85. Let us call this quality *rule-worthiness*. It is obvious, I think, that rule-worthiness will not in all cases be the same thing; it will differ with the characteristics of the ruled.

25. 9. This brings us to the THIRD LAW OF POLITICS: namely that *there is a correspondence between the ruler and the ruled*, whereby the former become adapted to ruling these as distinct from other persons, and the latter to being ruled by these as distinct from other persons.

25. 91. Working *directly*, or from the ruling class downwards, the ruler sets the fashion, and the ruled fall in with his lead.

25. 92. But the Third Law also works *inversely*, from the ruled class upwards, and determines that whoever is to rule a certain people must rule them in the way in which they will let themselves be ruled.

25. 93. Both setting the fashion and following it may be done either consciously or unconsciously; but the process is most likely to take the inverse form when it originates unconsciously in the mere, blind, unpolitical stupidity of the ruled, imposing limits on what their rulers can do with them.

25. 94. An example of this law occurs when vigorous rulers teach the ruled to co-operate with them and to develop, under their tuition, a vigorous political life, a similarity in political enterprise and resource, like their own. In this way that portion of the ruled class which is more closely in contact with the ruling class receive a training for political action which enables them to succeed, in time, their rulers. Here the *freedom* whereby the rulers rule percolates, owing simply to the process of ruling, without any intention that it shall do so, downwards through the strata of the body politic.

25. 95. But this only happens when the rulers are vigorous. Let the rulers be of a slavish sort, and what will percolate is slavishness.

25. 96. When that happens in a body politic, it is hard to say whether the percolation is downward or upward; and the inquiry has little importance.

25. 97. What is important is to know whether the process to which the body politic is subject is increasing or diminishing. Here is a ruling class, of one or more: to what does its rule tend? To the advancement of freedom, and therefore the ability to cope with political problems, or to its diminution? It is no use raising the question whether freedom is a good thing or not: freedom in the ruling class is nothing else than the fact that the ruling class rules, and the cry against freedom which accompanies the rise of Fascism and Nazism is a confused propaganda for the abolition of one thing (freedom for *the ruled*) where the distinction between that and another thing (freedom for *the ruler*) is overlooked. Of course no Fascist or Nazi protests against freedom for the ruler!

25. 98. In Plato's *Republic* the 'tyrant' is not a skilful and determined politician who seizes power for himself, but a piece of flotsam floating on the political waves he pretends to control, shoved passively into power by the sheer lowness of its own specific gravity. This is quite possible by the inverse working of the Third Law of Politics. Hitler, referring to Plato's sense of the word 'democracy', claims to be a democratic ruler. He claims that he has been, so to speak, *ejected* by the automatic working of a mob, which elevates to a position of supremacy over itself whatever is most devoid of free will, whatever can be entirely trusted to do what is dictated by the desires which the mob feels.

XXVI

DEMOCRACY AND ARISTOCRACY

26. 1. THERE might be a man who denied the First Law of Politics on the ground that he was thinking of a body politic in which every member should rule, and none be ruled. I call him a *doctrinaire democrat*.

26. 11. There is also an opposite error, the error of forgetting that the function of ruling, in any body politic, must be a function of that body itself, so that where a 'self' is *a body politic* all rule is self-rule. One who forgets that I call a *doctrinaire aristocrat*.

26. 12. These are hostile to each other. But democracy and aristocracy, properly understood, are not hostile to each other. They are mutually complementary.

26. 13. Each of them gives a partial answer to the question: 'How shall we make the ruling class as strong as possible?'

26. 14. Democracy answers: '*By enlarging it so far as is possible.* By recruiting into it, to discharge one or other function, every member of the ruled class who may constitute an addition to its strength.'

26. 15. Aristocracy answers: '*By restricting it so far as is needful.* By excluding from its membership everyone who does not or would not increase its strength.'

26. 16. There is no quarrel between these answers. The inevitable recruitment of a ruling class from its correlative ruled class is a dialectical process, part of the process which is the life of the body politic. Democracy and aristocracy are *positive and negative elements in that process*.

26. 17. The rise of doctrinaire democracy or doctrinaire aristocracy happens when these elements are considered in *false abstraction* from the process to which they belong, and then considered *eristically* as competing for the politician's loyalty. One must be the better worth following: which?

26. 18. Abstraction is a necessary part of thought. In thinking of a process of change you must think of its positive and negative elements in abstraction from the process.

26. 19. False abstraction is the same thing complicated by a falsehood: the falsehood, namely, that these two opposite elements are mutually independent and hostile entities.

26. 2. Thus democracy and aristocracy, which are really correlative rules for the process of drafting members from the ruled class into the ruling class (the rule 'go as far as you can' and 'don't go farther'), are misconceived as two independent and hostile rules: the rule 'recruit them all' and 'don't recruit any'.

26. 21. It is between fictitious entities like this that 'eristic' discussion (24. 58) most loves to get up a dog-fight. The best kind of dog-fight; one in which the combatants, being fictitious, can never be killed and, being tied together by a dialectical bond, can never run away.

26. 22. A fight of this kind is the best example of those make-believe discussions which are called 'academic discussions' (2. 55).

26. 23. Except in the make-believe of academic debate no one has ever attacked or defended either the idea of pure democracy or the idea of pure aristocracy; nor has there ever been in real life such a thing as a pure democracy or a pure aristocracy.

26. 24. Everyone, except where the positions feigned to be maintained or attacked are false abstractions, maintains and always has maintained the view I am here advocating: that every democracy is in part an aristocracy and every aristocracy in part a democracy; that every body politic consists of two parts, a politically active or ruling class and a politically passive or ruled class, the first consisting essentially of persons who are mentally adult and so able to rule themselves and others, the second consisting essentially of persons who are not mentally adult and so have to be ruled by the rest; and that of these 'positive' and 'negative' classes members must always be passing from the second to the first. What is important is that the right ones should pass.

26. 25. Each part may contain 'passengers'.

26. 26. The ruling class may contain persons not capable of ruling, granted the political problems calling for solution and the circumstances in which they have to be solved.

26. 27. The ruled class may contain persons capable of

ruling but debarred from it on frivolous grounds (in some cases it is easy to decide that grounds are frivolous, in others not so easy) or unwilling to do it.

26. 28. The problem of getting the best available rulers (and, what is included in this, the problem of sacking any who can be replaced by better men) is so important for the welfare of a body politic that no pains should be spared to find and enlist them. What is difficult is to keep the issue clearly before your mind: to recollect that the only admissible ground of inclusion in the ruling class is ability to do the required work; the only admissible ground of exclusion is inability to do it.

26. 3. Here we part company with Plato and the ancients generally. What they demanded of a ruler was ability to do any kind of political work that might turn up. What we demand is ability to do the work that has now to be done. This is the great difference between the pagan outlook and the modern or Christian outlook. It is because Christendom takes time seriously (31. 68) that it refuses to join in the Greco-Roman quest for a superman-ruler, able to solve any kind of problem and resist any sort of emotional pressure, the ideally wise man of Plato and the Stoics, the divine king of Hellenistic thought, the god-emperor of the Romans.

26. 31. Christendom (which elsewhere I have called modern Europe) has renounced the quest for supermen not because it would not be nice to have one but because they are not here and now to be had, and we can here and now do without them.

26. 32. Sad experience, not least in the twentieth century, but not a novelty of that century (Aesop stated it in the fable of King Log and King Stork), shows that when people want them here and now they are apt to get what the Greeks called a tyrant (25. 98).

26. 33. If there is one thing characteristic of the Christian world it is the habit (which the ancients never acquired) of doing now, whether in politics or in science (31. 68), what has to be done now, and leaving other things for another time.

26. 34. A Christian body politic wants a ruling class good enough to get along; capable to-day of doing to-day's job; constantly reinforced and constantly purged, as the work it has to do changes, by recruitment of whatever competents may be found among the ruled and by removal of whatever incompetents may be found among the rulers.

26. 4. Throughout the history of Europe the democratic principle and the aristocratic principle have always been the positive and negative halves of a single idea: the idea that since, by the First Law of Politics, every body politic contains a ruling class and a ruled class, and since by the Second Law there is always a passage between the two, corporately controlled by the rulers themselves as if they were a society of Clerk Maxwell demons, the rulers must see to it, positively or democratically that every member of the ruled class able to do the work that now has to be done should enter the ruling class, and negatively or aristocratically that every member of the ruling class not up to that work should find his level and sink into the ruled.

26. 41. To an ancient Greek, democracy meant the rule of a city by a class of citizens distinguished for their numbers but undistinguished either for noble birth or exceptional wealth.

26. 42. The political machinery which was called democratic consisted in appointment to most offices, though not all, by lot as opposed to election on the principle that any citizen (and all citizens were automatically members of the sovereign assembly) was competent, though chosen at random, to discharge these duties in the city to which he belonged.

26. 43. This was not a doctrinaire democracy. An ancient Greek, to whatever school of politics he belonged, would agree that obviously none but an adult free male native of a city could take part in ruling it. The entire female sex, the entire body of immature manhood, the entire slave population, and all resident foreigners were automatically excluded from the citizen body.

26. 44. Even the extremest republican democrats of whom we are told never held out to these four classes a hope of taking part in the public affairs of the body politic whose dependants they were.

26. 45. So aristocratic an element in even the most democratic Greek political thought and practice never seems to have evoked a protest from a Greek politician or a Greek philosopher.

26. 46. Rome shows the same mixture of aristocratic and democratic elements. Every schoolboy knows about the struggle between the patricians and plebeians, and knows how decisively it ended in the plebeians' favour. Was the result a democracy? The result was certainly the sovereignty of the Roman People; but what was the Roman People?

26. 47. As in a Greek city, it consisted in the first instance of adult, male, free natives of Rome. I say 'in the first instance', because one secret of Rome's political greatness was her lavish extension of citizenship to persons who were not natives of Rome. But even in legal theory or speculative thought there was never a hint of extending it to women, children, or slaves.

26. 48. The Roman People was at first much smaller than the population of Rome. By degrees it became much larger. But it never coincided with it, and at no time did it include every part of it. 'Populus' in Latin, like 'demos' in Greek and 'people' in English when correctly used, which sometimes it is not, is a word with a certain aristocratic flavour.

26. 49. It never means a mere mass of population, a totality of inhabitants, a crowd. It always means those of the population who are able to discipline themselves, and not only can do so but have done so; who being endowed with free will have organized themselves in a definite pattern according to definite rules corporately made by them for themselves and corporately imposed on them by themselves: a society.

26. 5. Democracy and aristocracy being thus mingled in Roman political life from at least the early Republic, it is not surprising to find them still mingled in the Empire.

26. 51. 'A decision of the Emperor', say the jurists, 'has the force of law'; but why? Because, they tell us, the sovereign people without losing any part of its sovereign power has authorized its first magistrate the Emperor to discharge certain functions which form part of that sovereign power.

26. 52. If the Principate was *de facto* not only an aristocracy but an *autocracy* or *despotism* (that is, an aristocracy of one) its powers rested *de jure*, according to legal theory, upon a democratic basis, the sovereignty of the people; the idea of 'the people' being one in which democracy was strongly coloured with aristocracy.

26. 53. It is hardly surprising that well-informed writers under the Empire, when they raised the test question: 'Is the Emperor subject to the law or supreme over it?' should disagree as to the answer. Pliny in his Panegyric to Trajan says that the Emperor is not above the law, he is subject to it. Seneca in his treatise *Of Clemency* tells us that the Emperor is not bound by the law, only by his mercy.

26. 54. This mingling of democratic and aristocratic elements long survived the Roman Empire. It survives to-day in all European or Europeanized countries.

26. 55. After the fall of the Western Empire, when its place was taken on the one hand by the Papacy and the Holy Roman Empire and on the other by a number of 'barbarian' successor states, the Papacy and Empire agreed with the 'barbarian' successor states in showing both democratic and autocratic elements; but comparatively speaking the Papacy and Empire leant more to autocracy, the 'barbarian' successor states more to democracy.

26. 56. Feudalism played here an important part. Wherever feudalism was strong it prevented monarchies from developing into autocracies. Feudalism is a form of land tenure; the tenant holds land of the king in return for military service; under such a lease the landlord has certain rights and no more. Any feudal monarch who wished to copy emperors or popes and become an autocrat would find his ambitions baulked by the whole strength of the feudal system under which he held his royal position.

26. 57. Richard II of England, imitating Boniface VIII, claimed to be supreme over the law. His laws, said he, were in his mouth and sometimes in his breast, and he by himself could change and originate the laws of his realm. For that absolutist claim, among other things, he lost his crown.

26. 58. Popes and Holy Roman Emperors, more directly inheriting the autocratic practice of the Roman Emperors, tended (as well-advised feudal monarchs did not) to magnify their office into an autocracy.

26. 59. As the Middle Ages drew to a close a conflict set in between two schools of political thought, one relatively autocratic and one relatively democratic; the democratic wing basing itself on the common law, the autocratic on the Roman law; whose revival, even in the countries where it was not 'received', led everywhere to an accentuation of the aristocratic or autocratic element in the mixed tradition, and was fostered on that account by would-be autocrats.[1]

26. 6. It was no novelty, therefore, when autocracy triumphed in the French monarchy of the sixteenth century; or when Hobbes, seconding with his pen the Stuart design of carrying on the work of the Tudors and making the government of England an autocracy on the French model, argued that autocracy was not the antithesis of democracy but democracy itself pushed to a logical conclusion.

26. 61. The argument is by no means paradoxical to a reader who knows something of Roman law and European political history; but it has driven many readers brought up in the unreal atmosphere of an academic dispute between doctrinaire democracy and doctrinaire aristocracy to wonder helplessly whether Hobbes was an autocrat posing as a democrat or a democrat posing as an autocrat.

26. 62. It was no novelty, again, when the French Revolution, commonly to this day misrepresented as the revolt of an oppressed multitude against their oppressors, swept away the privileges of the nobility not because they ruled harshly but because they did not rule; and substituted a government that did.

26. 63. Was the French Revolution a democratic movement or an aristocratic movement?

26. 64. Democratic, says common opinion, and in many ways it was. But it was also aristocratic. 'Aux armes, citoyens' was a call not to the population but to the people (26. 48).

26. 65. The 'people' on which the Revolution aimed at bestowing power was not the population as a whole.

[1] That is why the modern countries which have learned most from feudalism, through the channel of common law, call themselves, and are called by others, *'democracies'*.

26. 66. It was not a rabble; it was the *bourgeoisie*; and the *bourgeoisie* was already an organized body corporately possessed of economic power. The problem of the revolutionaries was to bestow political power where economic power already lay.

26. 7. Political thought in the nineteenth century for the most part allowed itself to be dazzled partly by the French Revolution itself and partly by a misunderstanding of its nature; failed in particular to apprehend its continuity with the long historical process out of which it had grown; failed to see it as the legitimate offspring of that process, a development of tendencies long visibly at work, predictable long beforehand by any intelligent observer and predicted by many; in fact, if 'revolution' means an essentially surprising thing in which something essentially new comes into existence, not a revolution at all.

26. 71. The word 'revolution' was borrowed towards the end of the seventeenth century by the vocabulary of politics from the vocabulary of literary criticism. In literary criticism it meant what Aristotle in his *Poetics* had called a 'peripety', of which word 'révolution' was a literal translation. The idea was that a play or novel or the like contained one character with which the reader or spectator (as psychologists say) '*identified*' himself, technically called 'the hero', who to begin with is either a happy and prosperous man or a wretched and miserable man.

26. 72. Well, the story goes jogging along like that, rubbing in the hero's happiness or unhappiness as the case may be, and then suddenly a surprising thing happens. By a '*reversal of fortune*' for which the reader is unprepared (though the author may have thrown out warnings which, if he is very sharp, were not wasted upon him) the 'hero' is plunged from happiness into unhappiness, in which case the story is a 'tragedy', or raised from unhappiness into happiness, in which case it is a 'comedy'.

26. 73. The reader, because he identifies himself with the hero, is saddened by a tragic peripety and gladdened by a comic one. In *Othello*, for example, he is saddened (because he identifies himself with Othello) at the change whereby the hero, from being gloriously happy in his love, is ruined by jealousy. In *Tom Jones* he is gladdened at the change whereby the hero, from being persecuted and discredited in the eyes of his benefactor by a number of 'villains', is cleared of all accusations and restored to Squire Allworthy's favour.

26. 74. This is all right so far as it goes, but it is superficial. In the first place, there are many good plays and many good novels without any peripety. There is none in *Hamlet*; there is none in *Don Quixote*; and these works have always been greatly admired. In the second place, there can be no peripety without a 'hero'; and there are many fine works of literature in which there is no one character with which the reader is invited to identify himself; for example *Julius Caesar*. In the third place, even where the peripety is important, the writer's skill and the reader's intelligence combine to eliminate from it the element of surprise and present it as inevitable granted the characters and circumstances of the story. It is a weakness in *Tom Jones* that Squire Allworthy (a sensible man, we are told) should so long and so readily believe the calumnies brought against the hero. It is a weakness in *Oedipus Tyrannus* that coincidence should play so large a part in the causation of the peripety.

26. 75. Even in its proper literary sphere, then, the idea of 'revolution' was overworked by the French and other critics of the seventeenth century. The transference of that idea to political history, which first happened when people spoke of 'the glorious Revolution' of 1688, began by indicating and went on by perpetuating a superficial conception of history.

26. 76. Historians to-day know that all history consists of changes, and that all these changes involve 'reversals of fortune'. But the historical idea of a revolution implies that normally the course of history flows, as if by the Newtonian First Law of Motion, uniformly in a straight line: then it waggles, and you are surprised. This is how people really did think about history in the seventeenth and eighteenth centuries; it is one of the many signs that they did not know very much history.

26. 77. 'What do you call it the second time round?' said an eighteenth-century squire to a landscape-gardener who walked him round the garden he had laid out and called his attention to a certain feature with the words: 'This is what

we call the Element of Surprise.' If a twentieth-century reader of history came to an incident that surprised him, he would know what to call it. He would call it a piece of bad history: something his author had failed to explain.

26. 78. The second element in the historical (or, let me say, pseudo-historical) idea of revolution is the element of self-identification. You must identify yourself, as you read, with the character who succeeds after temporary failure or fails after temporary success. You must think of historical characters as 'heroes' and 'villains'. It is easy to do this, and idle or frivolous readers and even writers of history habitually do it and find it very amusing. But if you write or read history to get at the truth you must not do it. This again is a thing they did not know in the seventeenth and eighteenth centuries; but everyone knows it to-day.

26. 79. To stop being surprised when the course of history waggles, and to think of it as waggling all the time; to stop taking sides, and to think of 'heroes' and 'villains' alike as human beings, partly good and partly bad, whose actions it is your business to understand; this is to be an historian.

26. 8. That is why, except in a purely conventional sense, as a legacy from a less historically minded past, the word 'revolution' has fallen out of use among historians much as the word 'chance' has fallen out of use among physicists.

26. 81. Each is a pseudo-scientific term whereby one's own ignorance of why an event happens is offered as an answer to the question why it happens. If a physicist said 'that happened by chance' he would be saying 'I don't know why it happened and it surprised me'. So if an historian said 'that was a revolution'.

26. 82. The word is still current in the vocabulary of politics; but not with any scientific significance; only an emotional one. It means an event whereby the mighty are put down from their seat and the humble and meek exalted. It is uttered, if you are one of the mighty, with intent to freeze your blood; if you are one of the humble and meek, to give you opium-dreams of coming felicity.

26. 9. With too few honourable exceptions the nineteenth-century politicians, dazed by their false view of the French Revolution and the mirage of 'Revolution' as such, thought that recent events in France and America had once for all exploded the pretensions of autocracy and had once for all established democracy as the only political system rational in theory and tolerable in practice.

26. 91. That would indeed have been surprising if it had happened; for it would have meant the end of an academic debate between two false abstractions; an end reached not in the schools but in the tougher world of political facts.

26. 92. But it had not happened. The dialectical process of political life had not come to an end. Both elements in it, as a closer study of the French or American Revolution would have shown, were very much alive.

26. 93. But wish-fulfilment fantasies in the special shape of millennial fantasies (25. 33) were often mistaken in the late eighteenth and early nineteenth centuries for facts; and this was an error of the same kind.

26. 94. For that error we are now paying in the feats of a new autocracy, the millennial dreams of its dupes, and the Messianic pretensions of its leaders, the arch-Fascists and arch-Nazis of to-day.

26. 95. The movement which they lead, like the movement which led to the French Revolution, is partly democratic, as all constitutional changes are, in the sense that it gives political power to men who have not previously possessed it.

26. 96. Partly, like all constitutional changes, it is aristocratic, in the sense that it began with a driving from power of some who previously held it; who lost it through their own fault because they did not hold it firmly enough to retain it. They found their level.

XXVII

FORCE IN POLITICS

27. 1. POLITICAL life contains an indispensable element of force. This marks off the life of a body politic from the life of a society, which is like it in many respects; and assimilates it to the life of a family.

27. 11. Family life, too, is in part a matter of force, because family life involves looking after children, and children have to be looked after without their consent.

27. 12. The body politic, like the family, contains a nursery; in this case a ruled class which is a nursery of rulers as containing human beings in process of education for the business of rule.

27. 13. So far as the ruled are not yet capable of ruling and therefore not yet able to rule themselves they must be ruled without their consent by those who are capable of it.

27. 14. 'Why must they?' For many reasons. First because they like it and, if it is not done, crave for it. Conversely, because the rulers like it. For a man of weak or undeveloped will nothing is so pleasant as being ordered about; for a man of strong will, as ordering others about.

27. 15. Secondly for their own good. Children have to be looked after, not only because they like it, but because being looked after is to be protected from self-inflicted and mutually inflicted injury and death (22. 25).

27. 16. Thirdly for the good of the rulers. The good of the rulers is to rule; first immanently, to rule themselves, and then transeuntly, to rule others, namely those members of the same body politic who are incapable of rule.

27. 17. Fourthly for the good of the entire body politic. For what is to the good both of the rulers and of the ruled is to the good of the body politic as a whole.

27. 18. If it is the rulers' duty to pursue the good of the body politic as a whole, it is part of their duty to rule those members of it who cannot rule themselves.

27.2. They must be ruled by force, for they cannot be ruled otherwise. What 'force' means we already know (20. 5 seqq.).

27.21. Force includes fraud (21. 74). Neither the rule of a family over its own children nor the rule of a body politic over its own subjects can dispense with the use of deceit.

27.22. Those who are sentimental about family life dislike this, but those who have experience of family life know it. The same is true of political life.

27.23. But the use of fraud, like the use of force, whether in family life or in political life, has its limits.

27.24. The hedonistic principle (27. 14) will not provide such a limit. In general, it is true, children like being ordered about; but in particular they often dislike this or that order. No good parent allows it on that account to be disobeyed.

27.25. The utilitarian principle (27. 15–18) does provide a limit. If an order is for the good of the family as a whole it is justified even though it may be unpleasant to give and unpleasant to obey. If it is not for the good of the family as a whole, it is not justified. And so with the duty-principle (27. 18–19).

27.26. So with fraud. To deceive a child for its own good is justified by the utilitarian principle. So is to deceive it for the good of the parent as such; not for the good of the parent as an individual but for the sake of the parent's efficiency as ruler of the family; in order that the rule of the family may be carried on.

27.27. Deceit of these kinds (to which only a person who takes a sentimental view of parental ethics will object) is not only justified, it is a parent's duty.

27.28. Show me a parent who will not deceive his child for its own good or to facilitate the difficult work of ruling the nursery, and I will show you a bad parent.

27.29. The same is true of political life. The ruled class proverbially *vult decipi*; deceit on the part of rulers if it is for the good of the ruled or for the facilitation of ruling is not only justified; it is, whatever sentimentalists may say, a duty.

27.3. There is, however, a limitation of another kind. This arises from the dialectical character both of family life and of political life.

27.31. What I have said about ruling children by force and fraud is true only so far as the child is only a child.

27.32. What I have said about force and fraud in political life is true only so far as the ruled are not yet capable of ruling (27. 13).

27.33. In a well-ruled family the parents never forget that the child is a man in the making, and always treat it not only as the child it is but as potentially the man it is going to be.

27.34. In a well-ruled body politic the rulers never forget that the ruled are (by the Second Law of Politics) in training to become rulers; and in the meantime (by the Third Law of Politics) must be treated as partaking, in their degree, of the moral freedom or will-power (an intellectual thing) which in an eminent degree is peculiar, by the First Law of Politics, to the rulers.

27.35. What does this limitation mean in practice?

27.36. A wise parent knows he must often rule by force; but he knows that he must never bluff. He must never promise a reward he cannot or will not give; he must never threaten a punishment he cannot or will not inflict.

27.37. He knows he must often lie; but he knows he must never tell a lie he cannot 'get away with'. Relatively to the child's critical powers as now existing, or to be developed in the near future, and the child's sources of information as now available or shortly to be available, the lie must hold water.

27.38. The same is true of political life. Force and fraud are used by a capable ruler only upon those of his subjects most backward in political education. For the less childish they are differentially replaced by 'induction' (25. 5) and other forms of partial and progressive sharing in the liberty of the ruler.

27.39. And if 'never bluff' is a good rule in family life it is good in political life. If a wise parent never bluffs, and never tells a lie he cannot get away with, it is because he cannot afford to lose face. His statements, his promises, his threats must be credited if they are to be efficacious. Any falling off in their credit is a falling off in his power.

27.4. A ruler who comes to his work convinced that the

ruled have a taste for being bullied and deceived will not fear such loss of face because he will never risk it.

27. 41. He will only bully those of his subjects who are childish enough to need it, and so with deceit; he will only deceive so far as deceit is called for.

27. 42. A ruler who values his power and is anxious not to lose face remembering that his subjects include people of all kinds from the intelligent to the foolish, from those who almost call out to be bullied to those who rebel at the slightest suggestion of force, will choose the lesser evil: *not to be found out.*

27. 43. If you tell the same lie to fifty thousand people, and one of them sees through it, you have backed the wrong horse: you had better not have told that lie.

27. 44. Run the risk of being found out only when you can turn that event into a victory for yourself; which can sometimes be done.

27. 45. The contrast between Hitler and Mussolini in this question is very instructive. Both are professed liars, religious in it: but Mussolini, with Latin logic, thought that any lie would do, whereas Hitler knew that your lies must have a basis.

27. 46. In the result, Mussolini in 1941 threw away I will not try to say how many empires, which Hitler had to win back; Mussolini revealing himself as the merest puppet whose strings Hitler pulled.

27. 47. Reverting to the distinction between aristocracy and democracy, we observe that the principle of *aristocracy* is the principle of *force*, whereby the more powerful rules the less powerful in virtue of his superior power; the principle of *democracy* is the principle of *self-government*, whereby a society rules itself.

27. 5. Throughout European history, from at least the times of ancient Greece, democracy and aristocracy (of which autocracy, 26. 52, is a variant) have gone hand in hand as the positive and negative elements of a dialectical development, democracy always promoting the inclusion of competent recruits from the ruled class into the ruling class, aristocracy always checking that process when the candidates were thought unsuitable.

27. 51. In the nineteenth century the idea grew up that there was no dialectic in the case; the relation between these opposing principles was not *dialectical* but *eristical*; constitutional history had been an age-long battle between the two, and the French Revolution had settled it in favour of democracy.

27. 52. Such a replacement of dialectical process by eristical process is always illusory and always dangerous.

27. 53. The supposed victory in an imaginary eristic of one false abstraction over its opposite means the replacement of a dialectical process in which the two co-operate by a continuation of the imaginary eristic; the thing supposed to be vanquished (it is not really vanquished) engages in a war of revenge and tries, or rather its partisans try, to inflict a crushing blow on the thing falsely supposed to be victorious.

27. 54. The eristical movement is imagined to proceed pendulum-wise. In the cockpit of make-believe disputation where false abstractions are set to fight, each instead of being put out of action by defeat (which cannot happen because the fancied combatants are really united by a dialectical bond, 26. 21) draws strength from it and comes back reinvigorated to the imaginary fight, with improved prospect of victory in the next round.

27. 55. The real dialectic of harmonious co-operation between contradictory principles, theoretical and practical at once, which is the spectacle history presents to those who take part in it intelligently, is thus imagined as being replaced by a false dialectic of oscillating conflict between false abstractions.

27. 56. This is the spectacle history presents to those who take part in it uncomprehendingly. It is not a thing that really happens, it is a mistake people make about what happens.

27. 57. But they really make it, and though this be madness yet there is method in it; the whole mistake is the logical consequence of making false abstractions (26. 17).

27. 58. 'If it is not real, how can it be dangerous?'

27. 59. It is dangerous in the sense in which the snakes of delirium are dangerous: not that their bite is to be dreaded, but that they are symptoms of a dangerous condition.

27. 6. The illusion that in the late eighteenth century democracy triumphed over aristocracy generated the opposite illusion that a reassertion of aristocracy was imminent; and as the nineteenth century went on and the dialectic of constitutional development proceeded, always with democracy taking the positive part, the two illusions were intensified together.

27. 61. That is why a recrudescence of Platonic 'tyranny' on a large scale has now taken place.

27. 62. That is why it has been especially successful where, as in Germany and Italy, a supposedly democratic form of government had been introduced in a doctrinaire spirit, imposed under the strain of defeat on the Germany of the Weimar Republic and in uneasy imitation of other countries on nineteenth-century Italy, into a country inadequately grounded in the tradition of political dialectic.

27. 63. That is why, as an anti-dialectical system of politics, it has succeeded in overwhelming France, where the dialectic of political life has never been well understood; for the defeat of France in 1940 was not a strictly military defeat but a defeat in the realm of political ideas.

27. 64. That is why it has hitherto failed to conquer England. Whether the failure will be permanent depends not on strictly military issues but on whether the English retain the mental vigour to hold on to the lesson that political life is essentially dialectical.

27. 7. Let me illustrate the way in which the English held on to this lesson in the nineteenth century from the history of English politics during that century.

27. 71. For most of the century English political life was dominated by two parties, Liberal and Conservative.

27. 72. By the First Law of Politics, freedom of will in a body politic of the modern European type is in the first instance peculiar to the ruling class.

27. 73. By the Third Law of Politics it percolates differentially throughout the whole body politic; more vigorously according as the work of ruling is more efficiently done.

27. 74. By the operation of this law the ruled are progressively, but differentially, assimilated in psychological character to their rulers.

27.75. The process works without being consciously promoted by human effort, and similarly cannot be impeded by human effort. It is an automatic consequence of the act of ruling.

27.76. But this process, like other processes in a body politic not capable of promotion or arrest by human will (a change in the birth-rate is an example), may become first an object of reflection and then of regulation to the ruling class.

27.77. Conscious regulation polarizes itself into two conscious efforts, one positive and the other negative.

27.78. The positive effort is an effort to hasten it; the negative is an effort to retard it.

27.79. To hasten the percolation of liberty throughout every part of the body politic was the avowed aim of the Liberal party; to retard it was the avowed aim of the Conservative party.

27.8. The relation between them was consciously dialectical. They were not fundamentally in disagreement. Both held it as an axiom that the process of percolation must go on. Both held that given certain circumstances, which might very well change from time to time, there was an optimum rate for it, discoverable within a reasonable margin of error by experiment.

27.81. Both knew that it must be watched and kept under control. Both knew that if it went too fast, and equally if it went too slow, the whole political life of the country would suffer.

27.82. The work of watching and controlling this process was shared by the two parties in an entirely dialectical spirit; a spirit of agreement to find and maintain the optimum rate for the time being.

27.83. So complete was the agreement that on occasion one party could steal the other's thunder. Disraeli crowed over the Reform Bill of 1867 that he had 'dished the Whigs', meaning that under his leadership the Conservative party, by extending the franchise, was adopting the traditional Liberal policy.

27.84. Another Conservative once explained that he was 'a brake' on the vehicle of progress; and, he continued, it was necessary for a vehicle to have a brake. He meant that the Conservative policy was not to stop the vehicle but to slow it down when it seemed likely to go too fast. Nothing could be a plainer statement of the Conservative's essentially dialectical function.

27. 85. From the point of view of one who does not understand that political life is dialectical, it is easy to bring two opposite criticisms against the two-party system. Each criticism conceals a desire for tyranny.

27. 86. First, that the parties are rivals, wasting in friction energy that would be more usefully spent in getting ahead with the work.

27. 87. But the two parties were not rivals. They were agreed in fundamentals. They were united, and consciously united, in work which everyone in those days considered important: controlling the rate at which freedom percolated through the body politic. What the partisan of tyranny objects to is that freedom should percolate at all; he wants the body politic to be saturated with servility.

27. 88. Secondly, that the parties were not rivals; that they merely posed as rivals, wasting energy in a pretence at rivalry. They were combining, says one, to exploit the proletariat. They were combining, says another (or perhaps the same), to bolster up a cretinous parliamentary system; when a party with the courage of its convictions would have defined its policy and carried it out through thick and thin.

27. 89. But the two parties, though agreed on fundamentals, differed in function. One was charged by common consent with seeing that the process did not fall below the optimum velocity; the other that it did not exceed it. So two barristers may agree in resolving that justice shall be done; but they are charged with seeing that the court shall know what there is to be said for the plaintiff and for the defendant respectively.

27. 9. Though the opposition of Liberalism and Conservatism was a dialectical opposition, it is doubtful whether both parties were equally aware of this.

27. 91. The most remarkable event in our political history during the twentieth century has been the eclipse of the Liberal party. Why did it happen?

27.92. In a dialectical system it is essential that the representatives of each opposing view should understand why the other view must be represented. If one fails to understand this, it ceases to be a party and becomes a *faction*, that is, a combatant in an eristical process instead of a partner in a dialectical process.

27.93. The Conservative who described his party as a brake on the vehicle of progress understood that the vehicle must be propelled. Did any Liberal understand that it must have a brake?

27.94. I speak under correction, but I think not. From what I remember of Liberals, and from what I know of the literature of Liberalism, I think they pictured themselves as dragging the vehicle of progress against the dead weight of human stupidity; and I think they believed Conservatives to be a part of that dead weight.

27.95. Conservatives understood that there must be a party of progress. Liberals, I think, never understood that there must be a party of reaction.

27.96. This was a serious matter for the Liberals, who always prided themselves on 'having a philosophy' and in particular a philosophy of politics. If the Conservatives understood the Liberals, and the Liberals did not understand the Conservatives, this was a self-deception.

27.97. That, I suggest, was why the Liberal party disappeared. It was not because the Labour party arose and by degrees took its place as the party of progress; if the Liberal party had known its business it would have absorbed the Labour party instead of being replaced by it. It was because the Liberals did not understand the dialectic of English politics.

XXVIII

THE FORMS OF POLITICAL ACTION

28. 1. POLITICAL action pure and simple is will pure and simple; but differs from will as such in being, first, the joint will of a society, the rulers of a body politic; secondly, that will exercised immanently upon those who exercise it as the self-rule of that society; and thirdly, the same will exercised as force in transeunt rule over a non-social community, the ruled class of the body politic.

28. 11. Failing this there is no political life. Granted its presence there is at any rate the first and central manifestation of political life: there is rule; both immanent rule and transeunt rule.

28. 12. It is not essential to political life that this will should be a rational will.

28. 13. It is a rational will if it elaborates itself into a complex decision where one part of what is decided is the ground upon which another is willed as consequent. But it need not be thus elaborated.

28. 14. What is essential is that there should be a joint will imposed by certain agents upon others.

28. 15. This will must be expressed intelligibly, if not to the ruled (who need not be mentally developed enough to understand it), at least to the rulers; for the rulers have to will jointly, and this they cannot do unless they understand one another, that is to say, discuss their purposes in a way intelligible to all.

28. 16. Without language there is no thought. Without thought, and thought of a somewhat highly developed kind, expressible only in a somewhat highly developed form of language, there is no will. Without joint language or discussion, again of a highly developed kind, there is no joint will.

28. 17. An 'eristic' (24. 58) political process can go on without discussion. Aiming as they do at victory, the parties to it may very well use force (20. 5) or attempts at force; for each tries to crush the rest, and this is best done not by discussion but by violence: that is, by civil war among the rulers.

28. 18. A 'dialectical' (24. 59) political process, aiming not at victory but at agreement, might certainly go on without discussion in words, if a language of gesture or other non-verbal language was once fairly established; but, as it is, verbal discussion is the only kind which men can extensively use for political purposes.

28. 19. Parliaments are not an end in themselves, they are means to the end of dialectical politics. Their function is to establish agreement of will among rulers on political questions.

28. 2. Contemptuous language about the 'talking-shop at Westminster', expressing not a desire for better talk, but a discontent with talk as such, are consciously or unconsciously due to dislike of dialectical politics and desire for its replacement by some kind of civil war; a 'class war' not between rulers and ruled but among the rulers themselves.

28. 21. This again is due to dislike of will or practical intelligence as the active force in political life and a desire to replace it by tyranny.

28. 22. Granted that the rulers discuss their various views, and arrive at a joint decision, this decision will next be issued as a joint command to the non-social community of their dependants, the ruled.

28. 23. A command issued by a society to a non-social community is not an act of authority (20. 48) but an act of force (20. 5). It is an act whereby the ruled are compelled to do what the rulers tell them to do by means of such things as rewards and punishments (21. 73).

28. 24. They need not know with any precision, in their capacity as merely subject to rule, what it is that the rulers mean them to do. There is no political will unless the rulers know; but this knowledge need not be shared by the ruled.

28. 25. The more it is shared by the ruled according to their varying abilities, however, the more completely the whole body politic will share in its rulers' will and in the freedom on which it depends.

28. 26. And the more this happens the stronger the body politic will be, and the more able to stand up to the rough-and-tumble of political life.

28. 27. For unless Schiller is right to describe stupidity as the strongest thing there is (the thing against which even the Gods fight in vain), we are justified in thinking that as in other cases an intelligent body politic is likely to be stronger than an unintelligent; one ruled by will, with will diffused throughout it as widely as possible, than one ruled by desire-ridden or passion-ridden stupidity.

28. 28. In the traditional terminology of politics a single command issued by the rulers to the ruled (28. 23) is called a *decree*.

28. 29. A decree is an executive act, not a legislative act. It is political action in its first, most primitive or rudimentary, form, a joint act of the rulers psychologically enforced by them upon the ruled.

28. 3. The decree is the simplest form of political action because it represents the simplest form of will, namely caprice, transposed into the key of politics.

28. 31. If there is a form of political action corresponding to caprice we shall expect to find another form corresponding to reason; in fact three such forms, corresponding to the three forms of reason: utility, rightness, and duty.

28. 4. Political *utility* means the distinction in political action between end and means.

28. 41. A *political end* is something jointly willed by a ruling class for its entire body politic and imposed by force upon the ruled class which is not immediately expressed as the object of a decree: either because it cannot be thus immediately expressed, since the state of things aimed at can be immediately realized only by the act of a person or persons not belonging to that body politic; or because, though it could be thus immediately expressed, it is for some reason better not thus expressed.

28. 42. An example of the first case is Napoleon's intention of starving England. Because the English were not his subjects he could not give effect to this intention immediately by a decree ordering them to go without their dinner.

28. 43. Since it could not be an immediate object of political action, therefore, it had to become an end of policy, indirectly aimed at by decrees so framed as to realize, not it, but means to it.

28. 44. An example of the second case is the conversion of sumptuary laws into taxes on luxuries. It may be desirable on occasion to lower your body politic's standard of living.

28. 45. It could be done directly by forbidding expenditure on things of certain kinds. If you are afraid of doing this directly because you fear that your fellow rulers will not agree to give such a command, you can do it indirectly by taxing expenditure of that kind.

28. 5. Political action in its utilitarian form is called *policy*. A policy is a political end pursued by political means, or political means used in pursuit of a political end. The end is an object of will pursued by a ruling class: the means is an object of will pursued by a ruling class in order thereby to realize the end.

28. 51. Each is corporately and deliberately pursued by the ruling class and imposed by it upon the ruled: but, since achievement of the means automatically entails achievement of the end, the ruling class need not explain the end to the ruled. It need only explain (where the ruled are intelligent enough to have anything explained to them) the means. The end may be concealed.

28. 52. The utilitarian form of political action, therefore, is one which facilitates the concealment of a ruler's purposes from the ruled.

28. 53. Such concealment is commonly called Machiavellian; a name originating no doubt from a vulgar inappreciation of the moral earnestness of that very great man Niccolo Machiavelli, but expressing a sound enough criticism both of Machiavelli and of the Renaissance political life whose spokesman he was.

28. 54. Machiavelli, like a true son of the Renaissance, inherited from the ancients a utilitarian view of action.

28. 55. He inherited from the Middle Ages not only a Christian morality but the doctrine that the Church was the final authority on morals. It was a burning question for him how the idea of the Church's moral supremacy could be adjusted to the exigencies of political life. An unanswerable question; inevitably the answer given by Machiavelli was no answer.

28. 56. The moral authority of the Church was a ruin,

but an imposing ruin. You had to ignore it in practice; but you had to be polite to it in theory. The exigencies of political life were pressing and had to be recognized.

28. 57. Under the influence of the ancients it was the fashion to see in political life only that part which was utilitarian. So Machiavelli decided that the authority of the Church covered only moral questions: political questions, being essentially utilitarian questions, were outside it.

28. 58. It was a sham answer because it gave all control of men's actions to the 'state' and instructed them to ignore the moral authority of the Church. It divided power over human actions between Church and State by the simple method of giving one claimant all the substance and the other all the shadow.

28. 59. The vulgar judgement is right to think that Machiavelli saw in political action only its utilitarian form; and right to think this an error. But it was not a private error, it was an endemic error. The word 'policy', which by etymology means the same as political action and by custom means only its utilitarian form, is more in evidence. The custom can only have grown up among men who saw nothing in political action except its utilitarian form. Such were the men of the Renaissance.

28. 6. The second rational form of political action, the third form altogether, is *law*. Law is the political form of right; it is *regularian action in its political form*.

28. 61. We know that regularian action in general involves two 'actions' or decisions (16. 33), distinguishable parts of a single complex action (16. 3), one a generalized decision to do many things of a specific kind on occasions of a specific kind (16. 32), the other an individualized decision to do one act of the specified kind now, an occasion of the specified kind having arisen. The first decision is called making a rule, the second is called obeying it.

28. 62. In the political form of regularian action the rule is called a law. The act of making a law is called *legislation*. The act of legislation is corporately done by the joint will of the ruling class. In so far as the ruling is immanent, the act of obeying is done by some member of the ruling class in the carrying out of an intention which he formed when he joined in making the law. In so far as the ruling is transeunt, the act of obeying is done (under compulsion by the ruling class) by some member of the ruled class. This compulsion is called *administering* the law.

28.63. In modern Europe the fact of legislation as a normal political activity begins to appear in the thirteenth century; its theory (first so far as I know with Marsilius of Padua) in the fourteenth. Until the thirteenth century there were only preconditions out of which legislation was to grow. There was unmade customary law existing in communities as a way in which the community habitually acted, often administered by properly constituted courts and enforced by means of standardized rewards and punishments; and there were decrees of executive officers which might be interpreted (as the rescripts of Roman emperors were) as constituting additions to the body of customary law.

28.64. The very elaborate medieval Icelandic law, of which we have an account in the sagas, was a customary law. It was not positive law because it involved no legislation. The same is true of the equally elaborate law of the Roman Republic and of the Greek cities. It is difficult for us, familiar as we are with the idea of legislation as a normal form of political activity, and taught as we have been to think of the Middle Ages (quite falsely) as a time of intellectual stagnation, to realize that this is an idea we owe to the Middle Ages and one not possessed by the ancients.

28.65. It is curious to see how narrowly the ancients missed it: avoiding it by a number of devices almost as if they were dodging it on purpose.

28.66. First, although the word 'legislation' is one we owe to the Romans, the Romans did not clearly distinguish in their own minds between what we call legislation and the enactment of an executive decree.

28.67. Secondly, both they and the Greeks regarded it not as a normal political activity but as something exceptional.[1]

---

[1] Any text-book of Roman Law will be found to emphasize this. For example: 'Many *leges* were enacted during the existence of the assemblies' (which, however, 'had not a free hand in legislation'), 'but, the XII Tables apart' (which, of course, were never enacted, only promulgated), 'they were never a main source of private law'(Buckland, *Manual of Roman Private Law*, 1928, p. 5).

28. 68. Thirdly, it was regarded as an activity which did not quite belong to the human sphere but called for a divine, or at any rate superhuman, agent.

28. 69. For example, Pericles (of whom perhaps Aristophanes was not merely joking when he endowed him with attributes proper to Zeus) is said to have given the Athenians a new 'law' determining the necessary qualifications for citizenship. The word translated 'law' means indifferently 'custom', a fact symptomatic of a time and place when law was customary law, and legislation unknown. The philosophers who worked out the theory of the Greek city have nothing to say about legislation. The historians tell us that, when a law of some Greek community could be traced to its origin, in an historical event, the event was commonly not an act of legislation but an act of 'law-giving'; and that 'law-givers' were commonly worshipped after their death as half-divine.

28. 7. The 'formal' essence of a law, what makes it a law and is common to all laws as such, is (i) that it should be an act of will on the part of the rulers, (ii) that it should be obeyed by the rulers themselves in the process of carrying out their own joint decision, (iii) that it should be obeyed by members of the non-social community of the ruled because they are forced by the rulers as providing for its administration.

28. 71. The 'material' essence of a law, what makes it this law and not another law, is the rule or mode of life which it specifies.

28. 72. *Promulgation* is not of the essence of a law, though it is desirable so far as, by the Third Law of Politics, members of the ruled class become able to obey it intelligently. Even without it the rulers can know what the law is, because they have decided to make it; so they can obey it freely. The ruled can obey it unconsciously, by becoming accustomed through rewards and punishments to adopt a mode of life which they need not be able to formulate to themselves.

28. 73. Promulgation becomes possible so far as the ruled become capable of co-operating with their rulers. When possible it is desirable; for it is better politics to let people know what they are to be rewarded for doing or punished for not doing, instead of habituating them to obey a law unconsciously by simply enforcing it without telling them what it is.

28. 74. Laws can be enforced in this way, without promulgation; but at huge expense of labour on both sides and with incalculable loss of political efficiency.

28. 75. A body politic which includes a large number of members among the ruled who are intellectually capable of understanding a promulgated law will *ceteris paribus* be enormously stronger than one which does not. Promulgating a law in that case is a step towards training the ruled to co-operate with the rulers, and is therefore an article of political wisdom.

28. 76. Before leaving the subject of law I must say a word about *international law* with special reference to the present day.

28. 77. 'How can there be a genuine international law', people say, 'without a properly constituted legislature to enact it and a properly constituted executive to enforce it? No wonder, lacking these things, the state of international law is pitiable. Let us see to their provision; then we shall have a proper international law.'

28. 78. This is folly, and wicked folly. It is because people talk like this that the condition of international law is so pitiable. They are 'sabotaging' international law under the pretence of succouring it. They are like a householder who should have said, some time under the Heptarchy, 'I won't keep the peace in my own house. The police ought to do it.' If people had talked that way every man's house would have been a bear-garden and there would never have been any police.

28. 79. International law in the modern European world is the customary law of a very ancient, international, non-social community. Its condition resembles the condition of law in the Iceland of the sagas, where men were to be found who knew, and would tell an inquirer, what the law was, but where there was no person or class of persons professionally charged with the business of enforcing it: where most men for the most part obeyed it, and thought the worse of the bad men (most of whom, according to the sagas, seem to have been women) who habitually broke it; but where the only way of enforcing it was for men who wanted it obeyed to get together and smash a man notoriously given to breaking it. All these conditions are fulfilled (some more than fulfilled) in the twentieth century with regard to international law except the last. We seem to prefer that international law should not be respected rather than that we should do anything so crude as to smash notorious offenders against it.

28. 8. The third form of rational action is *duty*.

28. 81. Doing your duty (17. 8) means doing (i.e. deciding by an act of free will) the only thing you can do (decide by an act of free will).

28. 82. A man's duty is a thing which for him in his present position, both internally or with respect to his 'character' and externally or with respect to his 'circumstances', is both possible and necessary: something he can freely decide to do, and the only thing he can freely decide to do.

28. 83. Duty as a form of political action is the case where a decision made by a ruling class and enforced by them upon the corresponding ruled class is made because no alternative is possible.

28. 84. This must not be confused with the case where a 'decision' falsely so called is made under the psychological constraint of passion or desire as the only one these forces allow: as when the Germans in 1914 pleaded that they 'had' to violate the neutrality of Belgium because otherwise they could not have invaded France with any prospect of success. Such a thing is not a decision. The necessity which makes it inevitable is not the intelligible necessity to which a free man bows, and in bowing shows himself free; it is 'the tyrant's plea', the excuse of an unfree agent for doing what he was driven to do by psychological forces he was too weak to resist.

28. 85. Political duty is political action done by one who recognizes that the element of caprice involved in policy and in law has disappeared. The element of caprice in policy is the ruler's freedom to adopt either of different conceivable ends for the body politic. He may direct it this way or that; he is able to direct it whichever way he chooses.

28. 86. The element of caprice in law is that one law defines one way of life for a body politic and a different law a different way of life; a body politic is capable of living in either way; the ruler, choosing one and rejecting the other, chooses capriciously.

28. 87. In political duty these choices disappear. The ruling class may still invent means to a given end, but the policy (or combination of means and end) at which they arrive is not one policy out of several alternative possible policies between which they have to choose but the only policy they regard as open to them.

28. 88. Alternatives which might be thought open are closed, either because the ruling class knows that the body politic cannot, being the kind of body politic it is, adopt that policy (it may, for example, be a courageous policy; and the body politic may consist of irredeemable cowards) or because the circumstances are such that a given policy is judged incapable of succeeding (for example, the policy may involve a war against a power judged greatly superior).

28. 89. The choice between different ways of life each thought possible for the body politic disappears in the same way either for internal reasons or for external reasons. The alternatives may be reduced to one because, the body politic having the traditions it has, it would repudiate all but one as ways of life in which it will not acquiesce; or because, living in the conditions in which it does live, all but one are ways it would be chimerical to pursue.

28. 9. The idea of action as duty, as we have seen, is inevitable to a person who considers it historically. History is the science of the individual; the individual is the unique; the unique is the only one of its kind, the possible which is also necessary. The more a man accustoms himself to thinking historically, the more he will accustom himself to thinking what course of action it is his duty to do, as distinct from asking what it is expedient for him to do and what it is right for him to do; and the more he will accustom himself to thinking in the same way of other people's actions explaining them to himself not by saying 'this person did this action in pursuit of such and such an end' or 'in obedience to such and such a rule' but 'because it was his duty'.

28. 91. Thinking historically about politics will produce the same results. A man who accustoms himself to think historically about political questions that confront him in the present will ask, not how he and others can attain certain ends or obey certain rules, but how they can do the one thing which is open to them as self-respecting men, conscious of their several freedom and each other's, agreeing upon a joint action in doing which each will be doing his duty.

28. 92. Thinking historically about past political actions (for history is not, as an historian once said, 'past politics': past politics only becomes history when it is thought about historically, not as an expression of human caprice, not as an illustration of man's pursuit of his ends, or obedience to his laws or laws not his own, but as an expression of the idea of duty) he will seek to explain this or that past political action as proceeding from the agent's idea of duty.

28. 93. The doctrine that duty is a form of political action, indeed the only form, has been energetically expressed by Treitschke in his lectures on politics; whose merit it is to repudiate with some violence the doctrine that political action is essentially utilitarian and to assert that it is 'subject to the universal moral law'.

28. 94. Political utilitarianism was a doctrine inevitable in the ancients, and equally so in the medieval and Renaissance thinkers whose repertory of ideas was drawn in the main from Greco-Roman sources. It was lamentable in nineteenth-century liberals; who nevertheless, formally at least, did for the most part adopt it as a concession to their industrial and commercial orientation. When we leave words behind and think what they stand for, we get a very different picture.

28. 95. The ostensibly utilitarian view of the nineteenth-century liberals covers a profoundly moral conception of political activity; the noisily moralistic language of Treitschke veils a doctrine which is squalidly utilitarian.

28. 96. Outraged by the way in which liberals, especially in England (a country for which he is never tired of displaying his contempt and of whose history, I will add, he is never tired of displaying his ignorance), take an ostensibly utilitarian view of political action, and anxious, it would seem, to emulate his Prussian predecessor Frederick the Great in re-nouncing whatever resembles Machiavellianism, Treitschke comes forward to support the doctrine that political action is essentially moral. Defending that doctrine in words, however, he is led by his eloquence to overlook the fact that the view he is actually maintaining is purely utili-tarian.

28. 97. 'We must then admit the validity of the moral law in relation to the State and that it cannot be correct to speak of collisions between the two' (*Politics*, E.T. (1916), 2 vols.; vol. i, p. 92). But: 'When we apply this standard of deeper and truly Christian ethics to the State, and remember that its very personality is power, we see its highest moral duty is to uphold that power. The individual must sacrifice him-self for the community of which he is a member, but the State is the highest community existing in exterior human life, and therefore the duty of self-effacement cannot apply to it' (ibid., p. 94).

28. 98. Transeunt ruling may be called power; and trans-eunt ruling is certainly the function of a 'state' or ruling class in its relation to the ruled class. But if a society is to rule a non-social community of dependants it must first rule itself, immanent rule being a presupposition of transeunt rule (20. 41). Now Treitschke does not deign to tell us what he means by 'self-effacement', so whether he is right to say that a 'state' has no such duty I have no way of knowing. But if by 'self-effacement' he meant self-discipline, self-control, self-denial (13. 32) he is completely wrong. He is denying to the 'state' what is in fact its first and most important function, immanent rule; denying to it a function without which it can never be a 'state' at all but only a non-social community; joining (and this is why I suspect that such an interpretation, discreditable though it is, involves no in-justice to so incorrigible a worshipper of the German people) in a long-standing German propaganda against will as such in which the word 'will' is used, first perhaps by Schopen-hauer, to mean something that is not will at all, but only passion or desire or something even lower.

28. 99. Behind the Tartuffe-snivel about 'deeper and truly Christian ethics' lies a lust for power (not power to do this or power to do that, but power in the abstract) which is as nakedly utilitarian, in the lowest and most contemptible sense of the word, as a miser's lust for money. To say that the state's 'highest moral duty' is to uphold its power is, *ceteris paribus*, the same as saying that a firm's 'highest moral duty' is to get richer than its rivals. Such was the doctrine on which the Professor of History at Berlin was feeding the mind of young Germany towards the close of the nineteenth century.

XXIX

EXTERNAL POLITICS

29. 1. THERE are three stages in political life. They are not temporally distinct, they are logically distinct. In time they proceed (for each of them is essentially a process, or rather a complex of processes, some of them temporal) concurrently; but although they go on at the same time they are logically related as prior and posterior: the first is a presupposition of the second and the second of the third.

29. 11. The first stage is *society.* Society is the joint activity of various wills in which a number of persons immanently (20. 38) rule themselves.

29. 12. The second stage is *transeunt rule,* the relation between a society as jointly ruling a non-social community, and the non-social community that it rules. As thus related, the society becomes a ruling class (in a body politic, if it is a permanent society; in a family, if it is a temporary society) and the non-social community a ruled class.

29. 13. The third stage is the activity whereby the body politic attends to problems arising out of its relations with other bodies politic. This activity is called *external politics.*

29. 14. These stages form a logical series in the sense that, though temporally they all coexist, logically each presupposes what goes before; could not exist unless that existed simultaneously to generate it: as in a machine where one shaft drives a second and that a third all the shafts rotate at once; but the rotation of the first causes rotation in the second, and that rotation in the third.

29. 15. Problems connected with the transeunt rule of one class in a body politic over another are problems of *internal politics* in so far as the rulers envisage them as problems confronting their joint social consciousness for solution by their joint social will.

29. 16. This implies that the rulers have a social consciousness and a social will: form a community whose members organize themselves as a society of their own free will. Internal politics presupposes social life or immanent rule.

29. 17. Similarly external politics presupposes internal politics.

29. 2. Each of these three stages has a dialectic of its own. Each is a Heraclitean world in which everything moves and nothing rests (24. 64). Each involves constant change from a 'not-*x*' into an '*x*'; but the values of '*x*' and 'not-*x*' are different in each case.

29. 3. The *dialectic of society* is the conversion of what begins as a non-social community into a social community. The agents who at first merely find themselves related in certain ways owing to circumstances over which they have no control construct for themselves a system of relations for which their wills are jointly responsible: voluntarily converting the non-social community of which they merely find themselves members into a society of which they are members in so far as they resolve to be members.

29. 31. This conversion of a non-social community into a society can never eliminate all traces of the non-social community from which it began (21. 5).

29. 32. The problem of immanent rule is not how to eliminate these traces, but how to prevent them from impeding the particular form of social life which it is proposed to realize.

29. 33. To eliminate the traces themselves would be a task, not for a dialectic, but for an eristic.

29. 34. It would mean working not for an agreement with 'the forces of reaction' (as the engine called the brake, 27. 93) but for their annihilation.

29. 35. The dialectic of society operates consciously. It works only because the people in whom it works intend that it should work. Men do not become members of a society in a fit of absence of mind. They only convert themselves from involuntary members of a non-social community into voluntary members of a society by deciding to do it.

29. 4. The *dialectic of internal politics* is the conversion of a ruled class into collaborators in the act of ruling: the percolation of freedom throughout the body politic (25. 94).

29. 41. This dialectic can operate unconsciously. It is a mere consequence of ruling that the ruled should become by degrees collaborators with the rulers. Even if the rulers do not mean this to happen, even if they try to stop it, their own act of ruling will bring it about, so long as that act is an act of free will.

29. 42. But if the act of ruling is not an act of will but an involuntary act due to irresistible passion or desire, what percolates through the body politic will be not freedom but servility; the Third Law of Politics will operate negatively (25. 95).

29. 43. The dialectic of internal politics is consequential upon the dialectic of society in the ruling class. If the ruling class could become entirely a society the dialectic of internal politics would eliminate from the life of the body politic every element of force. The reason why that can never happen is that the ruling class can never wholly become a society (29. 31).

29. 44. In proportion as the ruling class makes itself a society it begins to make its own subjects into co-operators with itself. In proportion as it fails to banish non-social elements from itself it cannot, however hard it tries, lift its subjects to the level of co-operators. Suppose the ruling class of a certain country were so deficient in harmony among themselves that the predominant group in it could only prevail by massacre or repression of its rivals. Suppose that predominant group wanted, like an early nineteenth-century autocrat, to raise the servile masses from their state of servitude by granting them a constitution. Anyone who understood politics could predict that the constitution would be a failure; not because the rulers were making a purposely deceptive promise, but because they were promising what was not theirs to give.

29. 45. The elements of force in the internal politics of a given community, then (not arbitrary or unneeded force, but force absolutely necessitated by the impossibility of ruling without it), are due to two causes neither of which is removable. First, political immaturity on the part of the ruled; that is, the incompleteness of the process which, if complete, would entirely convert the ruled into co-operators with their rulers. Secondly, social immaturity on the part of the rulers; that is, the incompleteness of the process which, if complete, would entirely convert the rulers from a non-social community of involuntary members into a society of voluntary agents joining, each by his own free will, in a common course of action.

29. 5. The *dialectic of external politics* is a process whereby problems arising out of relations between different bodies politic, about which they do not agree at first, are converted from matters of non-agreement into matters of agreement.

29. 51. This process is partly dependent on conscious efforts in the right direction, namely efforts on the part of the ruling classes; partly it is independent of such efforts; the ruled, namely, have not to promote it but only to accept it.

29. 52. Dialectic is not between contraries but between contradictories (24. 68). The process leading to agreement begins not from disagreement but from non-agreement.

29. 53. Non-agreement may be hardened into disagreement; in that case the stage is set for an eristic in which each party tries to vanquish the other; or, remaining mere non-agreement, it may set the stage for a dialectic in which each party tries to discover that the difference of view between them conceals a fundamental agreement.

29. 54. There must always be a certain non-agreement between the foreign policies of any two bodies politic.

29. 55. The cause of this non-agreement is irremovable; it is simply *the difference between the bodies politic.*

29. 56. The foreign policy of each towards the other is just its practical attitude towards a problem arising out of the relation between them; the mere fact that they are different bodies politic makes it inevitable that they should have different practical attitudes towards any such problem.

29. 57. It is sheer Utopianism to think that any expedient whatever could remove the causes of such disagreement. To think, for example, that it would disappear if the ruling classes or their diplomatic representatives were drawn from similar strata of the population, such as feudal aristocrats or large-scale manufacturers or working men or wearers of the same old school tie or party uniform, is to display political imbecility in its most exaggerated form.

29. 58. Such a difference in external policy is called a *conflict of interests* if political life is conceived in terms of utility; a *conflict of rights* if it is conceived in terms of (international) law; a *conflict of duties* if it is conceived in terms of duty.

29. 59. Actually all three phrases are appropriate.

29. 6. Granted that these 'conflicts' (non-agreements, not disagreements) are inevitable, how are they to be dealt with?

29. 61. There are two possibilities. They may be dealt with *dialectically*: that is by a process leading from non-agreement to agreement; or they may be dealt with *eristically*, that is, by hardening non-agreement into disagreement and settling the disagreement by a victory of one party over the other.

29. 62. To adopt the second alternative is to make *war*. To regard the second alternative as the only one available in such cases is to think of war as the only possible relation between bodies politic; to think that every body politic is permanently at war with every other.

29. 63. *War is a state of mind.* It does not consist in the actual employment of military force. It consists in believing that differences between bodies politic have to be settled by one giving way to the other and the second triumphing over the first.

29. 64. War is *the eristic of external politics*: the practical attitude towards a problem in external politics which consists in assuming that it cannot be settled dialectically by agreement but must be settled eristically by the victory of one party over the other.

29. 65. Victory and defeat are likewise states of mind. To be victorious is to think yourself victorious; to be defeated is to think yourself defeated.

29. 66. It is equally war if the two parties engage in armed conflict until one comes to think itself victorious and the other defeated, or if there is only a threat of armed conflict. Yielding to a threat is yielding to fear, and that is yielding to force (20. 59).

29. 67. It is equally war if the threat is sincere or a bluff. The force to which the defeated party yields is the same. Fraud, we know (21. 74), is force.

29. 68. It is equally war whether the threat is explicit or implicit. A hectoring diplomat who never actually threatens war is making war.

29. 69. It is equally war whether the force used or threatened or hinted at is force of arms or force of (for example) economic or religious sanctions. To propose the supersession of war by economic sanctions was one of the most transparent insincerities of the League of Nations. Those who made the proposal never troubled to think what war meant.

29. 7. War is a *reversal of the dialectical methods hitherto employed* in the two previous stages of political life to constitute the rulers a society and them and the ruled together a body politic.

29. 71. There would be no external politics unless there were already the internal politics it presupposes and the social life which this presupposes in its turn.

29. 72. Social life is consciously dialectical. It goes on only because the persons engaged in it deliberately aim at agreeing together (29. 35).

29. 73. The life of internal politics, presupposing this conscious dialectic, is dialectical too, but unconsciously (29. 41).

29. 74. Unless these two dialectics went on there would be no external politics of any kind whatever, and consequently no war.

29. 75. To wage war, therefore, is to reverse a policy on which the belligerents depend for their very existence.

29. 8. It is sometimes said that war is the effect of a *psychological cause*, which may be called, for example, the *pugnacious instinct of mankind*.

29. 81. If it were it could never happen. The same cause would already have reduced the belligerent bodies politic to non-existence; and if there were no bodies politic there could be no war.

21. 82. If there is a pugnacious instinct, and if there are any bodies politic, they exist only because that instinct has been not once but twice overcome; once by a dialectic whereby a ruling class has formed itself, however incompletely, into a society, and once by a dialectic whereby different classes have formed themselves, however incompletely, into a body politic.

29. 83. Men who make war are already accustomed to handle the problems of their social life and the problems of their internal politics in a dialectical spirit. Making war or acquiescing in war means departing from that dialectical spirit and replacing it by an eristical spirit when it comes to a problem of external politics.

29. 84. Acquiescing in war, or allowing it to be forced upon one, no less than making it, or forcing it upon others.

29. 85. A war is not, like a nursery quarrel, a disaster whose fault can be laid entirely at the door of the party which 'began it'. The proposal to punish 'the aggressor' was another of the many blunders made by the League of Nations (29. 69).

29. 86. Any aggressor in any modern war, if he knew his business, could put up a convincing case, before any tribunal capable of listening to him, to prove that he only fights because he has to fight; and that unless he strikes first, at a time of his own choosing, he risks being struck when his chance of success is smaller.

29. 87. At least, he could argue not only sincerely but convincingly that this was true to the best of his knowledge and belief. The Germans undoubtedly planned the war of 1914; but in their own view it was forced upon them by the 'encirclement' to which (they believed) they had been subjected.

29. 88. If A attacks B because he is afraid of B and is convinced that he must hit first, the blame is shared. A is acting, admittedly, like a criminal lunatic; but B is to blame for having been so foolish as to frighten him into a fit of aggressiveness.

29. 9. Does it follow that B, admitting that the blame falls partly on himself, ought not to hit back but to adopt a policy of non-resistance?

29. 91. That is a doctrine which has been preached under the name of *'pacifism'*, an ungrammatical name for an illogical idea.

29. 92. Two of those who lately preached it in this country, Lord Russell and Mr. Joad, publicly recanted in the summer of 1941.

29. 93. They are to be praised for having owned up to a mistake which must for the rest of their lives discredit everything they say or have said about ethical or political questions; but our business is neither to bury nor to praise them but to see what the mistake was.

29. 94. It was *to think that 'pacifism' means being against war*. To be a 'pacifist' is not to be anti-war, it is *to be pro-war*.

29. 95. It is to acquiesce in the findings of war as the only valid solution for differences between bodies politic as regards their external relations, and to cast yourself, or rather the body politic to which you happen to belong, in the role of defeated party.

29. 96. The 'pacifist' does nothing to decrease war. On the contrary, he promotes it to the utmost of his power by ensuring, so far as in him lies, that the war-makers shall have their reward.

29. 97. Not realizing that modern war is a neurotic thing, an effect of terror where there is nothing to fear and of hunger where the stomach is already full, he proposes to deal with it by throwing away his arms so that the war-makers shall not be afraid of him, and giving up what they would snatch (from him or others) so that their hunger shall be appeased.

29. 98. *'Pacifism' is war-mongery complicated by defeatism.* The 'pacifist' is not interested in politics. He is interested only in his own 'clear conscience'. Let the world be given over to the sword, his conscience is clear so long as he was not the first to draw it. That he forced others to draw it is nothing to him.

XXX

WAR AS THE BREAKDOWN OF POLICY

30. 1. WHY do wars happen in the modern world? Because the modern world handles its external politics in an eristic spirit. The evidence of prehistory suggests that it was perhaps not always so. The earliest human communities of which we know seem not to have waged war. This seems to indicate that at some time something went wrong with the tradition of political life. What can it have been?

30. 11. It was a breach of continuity between social life and the life of internal politics on the one hand, and external politics on the other. Cases of non-agreement as between members of a society or between classes of a body politic must have gone on, after that event, being handled dialectically, as they must have been handled before it; and as they still traditionally are.

30. 12. But cases of non-agreement in external politics must have begun to be handled eristically; a tradition we still inherit.

30. 13. No one can know why the tradition came so long ago into existence; but it ought to be possible to tell what force still keeps it alive.

30. 14. War has been called a *continuation of policy.*

30. 15. The phrase may mean any one of several different things.

30. 16. In one sense to-day's smooth running of a machine or floating of a ship is a continuation of its running smoothly or floating yesterday. In a different sense the continuation of that is the machine's breaking down or the ship's sinking. In the first sense the continuation of life is more life; in the second sense it is death.

30. 17. To remove the ambiguity I will call the first kind of continuation an *extension*, the second kind a *breakdown*.

30. 18. If policy implies the voluntary act of choice by which a society rules a non-social community, is war an extension of policy or a breakdown of policy?

30. 19. If it is an extension of policy no special explanation of its occurrence is needed; if a breakdown of policy, we need an explanation.

30. 2. There is always an element of force even in the life of a society, so far as the society contains in itself traces of the non-social community out of which it has grown.

30. 21. But so far as the society is a going concern these traces of non-sociality are not allowed to interfere with the pursuit of its joint aim.

30. 22. Its policy is to pursue that aim. Its policy, therefore, involves a dialectic which, as need arises, converts a state of non-agreement into one of agreement.

30. 23. The positive element in the dialectic of society is called *harmony*; that is, agreement between its members as to a joint aim; and harmony is an object they consciously pursue.

30. 24. They never achieve it entirely. But so far as the society is a going concern they achieve from time to time as much of it as they need.

30. 25. In a body politic the element of force is more conspicuous. So far as the ruled class are merely ruled and not yet co-operators in the work of ruling they must be ruled by force; but the very act of ruling establishes something called *law and order*, by whose operation they gradually exchange the sheer passivity of being ruled for a share in the activity of ruling (24. 75).

30. 26. To *establish law and order* and thus, even unconsciously, to set this dialectic working is the first article of any policy for their rulers.

30. 27. Since policy in social life and policy in internal politics agree in being dialectical, an extension of policy in the external sphere would be dialectical too. It would aim at the thing which in external politics is parallel to law and order in internal politics and to harmony in social life. This is called *peace*.

30. 28. Where policy has hitherto been dialectical, war is a continuation of policy only in the sense in which death is a continuation of life, or a breakdown in a machine a continuation of its smooth running (30. 16). *War is the breakdown of policy* (30. 17).

30. 3. Why does such a breakdown occur? For any one

of three reasons, which I will enumerate; but the first reason throws us back on the second, and that on the third.

30. 31. The first reason is: *because men charged with the conduct of external politics are confronted by a problem they cannot solve.* To solve it would be to solve it peaceably, that is dialectically. They would solve it in that way if they could; but they fail.

30. 32. But why do they fail? Not because the problem is insoluble in itself; no problem is; but because they have approached it in the wrong way.

30. 33. What is it in them that makes them approach the problem in the wrong way and so render it, as thus approached, insoluble? It cannot be an instinct of pugnacity or the like (29. 82), because if there is such a thing it has been defeated time and time again.

30. 34. But it may be (here we come to the second reason) *because the internal condition of the body politic is unsound*; because law and order have not been well enough established.

30. 35. Every student of politics knows that this is a frequent cause of war. Rulers often make war because their subjects are recalcitrant to their rule; which is a way of saying, because they rule their subjects unskilfully and therefore unsuccessfully. The fact of war both increases their loyalty (thus making rule easier for an incompetent ruler) and justifies the enforcement of more rigorous demands upon it (thus making rule easier for an exacting and heavy-handed ruler).

30. 36. Ill governed bodies politic tend to be warlike; the ill government is a cause in their internal politics of a tendency to war in external politics. The force by which rule has to be maintained within them extrapolates itself in force exercised upon their neighbours. If you can't keep your subjects quiet, says the Tyrant's Handbook, make war.

30. 37. But why should you be such a fool at your job that you can't keep your subjects quiet? once more, a further explanation is needed. So we come to the third: *because the rulers are at loggerheads.* If one section of the rulers pulls one way and one another, especially if this inner disharmony goes so far that one faction massacres or otherwise forcibly suppresses the other, such disharmony seriously diminishes their ability to rule.

30. 38. If ill governed bodies politic are warlike (30. 36) bodies politic that suffer from disharmony among their rulers are ill governed and therefore warlike. The resulting wars do not cure the inward corruption; they intensify it; but they mask it, because no one suspects a people at war to be so 'moral', so well governed, so attentive to law and order, as the same people at peace.

30. 39. *The ultimate cause of war is disharmony among the rulers.* Wars happen because traces of non-sociality are not completely overcome by the 'dialectic of society' whereby a ruling class harmonizes itself. This is the permanent and irremovable (29. 45) cause of ill government within a body politic, and that is the proximate cause of war without. Political visionaries propose from time to time that 'the causes of war' should be removed. It cannot be done. They can only be counteracted by incessant efforts to promote a dialectic of external politics.

30. 4. Recent English politics contains an interesting example of a Government forced into war by disharmony among the rulers; interesting because the policy whereby war was rendered inevitable was a 'pacifist' policy, so that the example also provides an example of the truth that 'pacifism' is a form of war-mongery (29. 98).

30. 41. Herr Hitler's rise to power in 1933 was at once followed by German rearmament. On 12 November 1936 the Prime Minister Mr. Baldwin defended himself in the House of Commons for not having long ago informed the House of this fact, explained the threat which it involved, and called for counter-rearmament.

30. 42. Such a warning, he said, would have involved him in defeat at the polls.

30. 43. 'I cannot', said he, 'think of anything that would have made the loss of the [future general] election from my own point of view more certain.'

30. 44. To paraphrase: Mr. Baldwin would have liked to ensure peace for his country by making it too strong to be attacked by a declared enemy which, he knew, was preparing for war.

30. 45. He could not do that because he was politically too weak: so he steered the country into a war which he rightly regarded as the inevitable outcome of his action, a war to be fought under grave disadvantages against a well prepared enemy: because what he called 'this pacific democracy' would have it so.

30. 46. A body politic which knows that its very existence depends on a policy whereby law and order is established within itself, and that on a policy whereby harmony is established as between its rulers (and a body politic which does not know this is one which does not know enough about politics to come in out of the rain) knows that the direct continuation or extension of these policies in the external sphere is a peaceful policy whereby non-agreements are replaced wherever possible by agreements. Not war, but peace, is the extension of policy; war is not the extension of policy but its breakdown.

30. 47. War is due, not to political strength, but to political weakness. It happens because men encounter problems in external politics which they have not the political ability to solve; that is because they have failed to solve the antecedent problems of internal politics; that again is because they have failed to solve the problems of social life.

30. 48. Plato was right in thinking that all political problems, external as well as internal, would prove soluble if once the problem of providing a satisfactory ruling class were solved. Where he went wrong was in thinking that to solve this problem meant providing an ideally perfect ruling class. That is neither possible nor necessary. What is needed is to provide at any given time a ruling class good enough for the work which at that time is required of it (26. 34).

30. 49. We have seen how in the traditional pattern of European political life this is effected by a dialectical process of constitutional change in which democracy is the positive element and aristocracy the negative (26. 4).

30. 5. There are theoretical conditions, however, in which war might be called not a breakdown of policy but an extension of policy.

30. 51. Let us try to reconstruct them, beginning at the beginning.

30. 52. Let there be what we will call a *Yahoo herd*: a

community whose members are hardly, if at all, distinguishable in bodily structure from human beings, at any rate to
the superficial glance of the observer whose anatomical and
physiological knowledge is small; but let them lack the
intelligence we are accustomed to expect in human beings.
To be precise, let their mental development have been
arrested at the point marked by the close of the twelfth
chapter of this work, just short of free will.

30. 53. This herd might have a sort of leader, dominant
over the rest in virtue of his strength, his cunning, and the
violence of his emotions.

30. 54. He would in a sense know what he was doing; he
would be conscious of the situation in which he was acting,
and his actions would be to him second-order objects of
consciousness; but they could not be objects of his will, for
he would have no will. Purpose would be impossible to him.
But he would exercise, though not voluntarily, a certain
control over the rest of the herd; biting and beating them or
making as if to bite and beat them whenever they did anything he disliked, and so forcing them into the mould of
a communal life pleasing to himself.

30. 55. There might be a second herd consisting of this
herd's dependants or slaves, related to them somewhat as
aphides are related to ants, but installed in this relation and
maintained in it by violence on the part of the first herd
towards the second. This second herd would superficially
resemble a ruled class.

30. 56. Such a herd would enjoy on the whole a happy
life. Those who bullied the rest would not only obtain by
doing so various gratifications for their various passions and
desires; they would also, and chiefly, get gratification from
the mere act of bullying. Those who were bullied would not
only find happiness in the communal prosperity won for
them by the strength and cunning of their leader; they would
also, and chiefly, find happiness in simply being bullied;
worshipping their leader with a dog-like devotion and revel-
ling in the delightful feeling of herd solidarity with their
fellows.

30. 6. Of such a 'natural' (that is, non-social) condition of
mankind Hobbes wrote that it would afford 'no place for

Industry; because the fruit thereof is uncertain: and consequently no Culture of the Earth; no Navigation, nor the use of the commodities that may be imported by Sea; no commodious Building; no Instruments of moving, and removing such things as require much force; no knowledge of the face of the Earth; no account of Time; no Arts; no Letters; no Society; and which is worst of all, continuall feare, and danger of violent death; And the life of man, solitary, poore, nasty, brutish, and short' (*Leviathan*, p. 62).

30. 61. Hobbes's picture calls for at least one correction.

30. 62. The Yahoos would not be solitary. They would not, of course, be social, not having free wills; but they would be *gregarious*. They would find pleasure in each other's company. They would crowd together with animal delight in propinquity. They would join together gleefully in hymns of corporate self-praise and praise of their adored leader.

30. 63. They would quarrel, no doubt, and enjoy quarrelling; but only within limits. If their quarrels went so far as to endanger the corporate strength of the herd, which the leader, thinking in terms of enmity towards other such herds, would conceive as his own strength and cherish accordingly, the leader would check it.

30. 64. Further, the Yahoo is more *imitative* than Hobbes knew.

30. 65. There is a kind of imitation quite independent of any intelligent appreciation of the action imitated; and the Yahoo herd would be as imitative as a herd of monkeys.

30. 66. If the Yahoo herd was surrounded by intelligent human societies it would certainly imitate their ways, though without sharing the intelligence on which these were based. If they cultivated the earth, sailed the sea, and the like, it would do the same; not because its members had the intelligence to invent these and other arts for themselves but because they imitated the actions of those who could.

30. 67. It would always be at war with them; but this war would only be a violent form of parasitism (already in essence forcible so far as it was fraudulent) which began by imitating its neighbours' behaviour or stealing their tricks and ended by appropriating the fruits of their behaviour or stealing their goods.

30. 68. Let us dignify the acts by which our Yahoo leader imposes order on the Yahoo herd (30. 54) with the name of a 'policy'. It would not be a policy because it would not be deliberately or freely decided upon; but let us call it one.

30. 69. *Of that 'policy' war is an extension.* The Yahoo policy is a systematic appeal to force within the Yahoo herd; not force dialectically conceived as preparing the way for agreement (30. 99), but force eristically conceived as operating by itself in a world of competing forces where the possibility of agreement is ruled out. Let policy be a name for the internal organization of the Yahoo herd, and Clausewitz is right: war is 'a continuation of policy'.

30. 7. In the foregoing paragraphs I have outlined a picture of the Yahoo herd. From what sources have I drawn it? Partly from Hobbes; partly from Swift; partly from Dr. Trotter's *Instincts of the Herd in Peace and War*; partly from Tarde's *Les Lois de l'imitation*; partly from other books. But that is not the point. There is a thing which each of these authors has described in his way and I have tried to describe in mine. What is that thing?

30. 71. The Yahoo herd is not a fact. It is not a state of human life known to historians by interpretation of evidence as having existed at some time in the remote past, like the Beaker Civilization. It is not a state of human life discovered by anthropologists as existing in their own time among members of some outlandish tribe like the Arunta.

30. 72. *The Yahoo herd is an abstraction.*[1] In painting a picture of it we have been trying to describe what human life would be like if men were not social.

30. 73. Strip off in thought, from human life as it is, the features belonging to sociality and to the free will which (in its communal aspect) is identical with sociality, remem-

---

[1] Swift himself says this plainly in a letter of 29 September 1725 to Pope: 'I have ever hated all Nations, Professions, and Communities; and all my love is towards Individuals: for instance, I hate the Tribe of Lawyers, but I love Counsellor such a one, and Judge such a one: 'Tis so with Physicians (I will not speak of my own trade) Soldiers, English, Scotch, French, and the rest. But principally I hate and detest that animal called Man, though I heartily love John, Peter, Thomas, and so forth.' He is explaining to Pope the design of *Gulliver's Travels*, so the reference to Yahoos is explicit. (*Works of Alexander Pope*, 1770, vol. vi, p. 137).

bering that apart from that communal aspect its individual aspect cannot exist (21. 14); and the remainder is the Yahoo herd.

30.74. 'If the thing is an abstraction, if it never exists and never can exist as a fact, why trouble to paint a picture of it?'

30.75. Because, if we are trying to control a process of change, as in the world of politics we are always doing, we have to know what the changing thing is changing into, and what it is changing out of; or what we are trying to change it into and what we are trying to change it out of.

30.76. The initial and terminal points of change are not facts (only phases of the change are facts); they are abstractions from the fact of change; but anyone who means to control the change must have clear ideas of them.

30.77. Where a change is reversible, it is especially important to have ideas of both; for people often confuse symptoms of progress with symptoms of degeneration, symptoms of growing better with symptoms of growing worse.

30.78. As long as people believed in a law of progress this was not thought to matter; there could not be degeneration; any change must be for the better.

30.79. We of the twentieth century do not believe in a law of progress. We believe that a thing may and sometimes does change for the worse. It matters to us, therefore, to know which end of the process is the right end and which the wrong; so that, granted we need not hope ever to reach the one or fear ever to reach the other, we can tell which is being brought nearer by a certain change.

30.8. The Yahoo is always with us; that is why hopes for the abolition of war are vain.

30.81. No society is altogether a society (21. 5). Every society, so called, is partly the society into which it is trying to turn itself, and partly the Yahoo herd it is trying to leave behind.

30.82. These defects in sociality are the source of war. They vitiate the life of every ruling class; they vitiate the relation between rulers and ruled in every body politic; they vitiate the relation between every body politic and every other.

30. 83. In the first case they impair the harmony which is essential to a ruling class; in the second they impair the law and order which is essential to a body politic; in the third they impair the peace which is essential to the relations between one body politic and another.

30. 84. Any individual case of such defect is removable and will yield, not to some new remedy hitherto unknown, but to the remedies that have been familiar and successfully tried for thousands of years: the various forms of technique for coming to an agreement which I call dialectic.

30. 85. But with the curing of one defect another will come into existence. Defect as such is not curable; it is only infinitely changeable. There will always be war, but it will always be turning into a new kind of war.

30. 86. The neurotic or terrified wars of the twentieth century differ in kind from the democratic, hopeful, expansive wars of the nineteenth, and those from the mercenary dynastic wars of the eighteenth, fought under sporting rules like the royal sport they were. The world is always breeding new types of Yahoo.

30. 87. In order to deal with them as they appear, the political consciousness of mankind must be infinitely adaptable.

30. 88. To create a tolerable system of relations between bodies politic, not a perfect system nor a permanent system, for that is impossible, but a system adapted to the needs which it finds pressing at the time, it must always be ready to use force, and always a new kind of force, against criminals within a body politic and enemies outside it who would forcibly destroy what has been already achieved without replacing it with anything better.

30. 89. All political life involves change, and all change involves destruction. But a change may be dialectical, orientated away from the Yahoo towards the society of free men, or it may be anti-dialectical, orientated away from the society of free men towards the Yahoo.

30. 9. It is a commonplace that a good cause justifies war.

30. 91. *A good cause is the cause of peace.* One body politic would be justified in making war upon another if, being itself bent upon peace, that is to say bent upon the advance-

ment of human intelligence, human will, and human reason
not only in its own subjects but in the world at large, it should
find itself attacked or threatened by another which had
already reduced itself by corporate stupidity and corporate
servility as far as possible to the level of a Yahoo herd, and
was bent upon reducing the rest of mankind to match.

30. 92. The second, by its very existence, would constitute
a threat to the existence of the first; and the first is bound
to take up the challenge, not only for the sake of its own
self-preservation (a powerful motive, but not by itself a valid
one; there are men who, whatever they think about it themselves, would be better dead; and there are bodies politic, so
to call them, which are so useless to the world in their
parasitic imbecility and so dangerous to their more intelligent
neighbours that they would be better destroyed) but for the
sake of the world at large.

30. 93. In this case a war waged by the first against the
second, and conducted vigorously, ruthlessly, and conclusively to the destruction of the second (its destruction as a
body politic, not the destruction of all its members, many
of whom in spite of their political incompetence might prove
capable of a useful life under the shelter of men more intelligent than themselves) would be justified as serving the cause
of intelligence, the cause of will, the cause of political vigour,
scientific efficiency, and everything else that is included in
the one word 'peace'.

30. 94. I will not stay to insist upon the gravity of what
Burke called 'bringing an indictment against a nation'.
Charges of the kind which the first body politic in any
instance will bring against the second are not unlike those
which, more or less frivolously, any belligerent will bring
against any other. A wise man will never bring them unless
he can support them by the clearest evidence.

30. 95. For any given case this will consist of two parts,
one concerned with general principles and one with details
varying from one case to another according to the special
variety of Yahoo that the world is at the moment producing
(30. 86). The first part a reader who has studied this chapter
and the one next before it knows already; the second part
it is not yet our business to consider.

30. 96. It would be more appropriate to raise a question of a general kind. It has been said (30. 9–93) that in certain circumstances war may serve the cause of peace. 'How can this be? The process toward peace is dialectical, and war is the negative element of the dialectic. War is what the dialectic, so far as it succeeds, abolishes and replaces by peace. Surely war can never bring peace nearer.' That is an important 'pacifist' argument; at bottom the only 'pacifist' argument.[1]

30. 97. It is false. Peace and war are not contradictories like white and not white; they are contraries like white and black. Now dialectic is not between contraries, it is between contradictories (24. 68). There is no dialectic, therefore, between peace and war. Peace is a special kind of agreement; war a special kind of disagreement. There is no dialectic for converting disagreement into agreement. What is converted into agreement is not disagreement but non-agreement (29. 52).

30. 98. Non-agreement is inevitable where each party takes his own view of a problem arising out of the relation between them (29. 55). This non-agreement is 'hardened into disagreement' (29. 53) by being treated in an eristic spirit. Disagreement cannot be directly reduced to agreement; for where there is real disagreement, though one party is prepared to argue the disagreement away, the trouble consists in the fact that the other will not argue. He will not listen to reason. He must be reduced to the state of a man ready to listen to reason before the dialectic can begin.

30. 99. War serves the cause of peace, and is therefore politically justified, when it is the only available method of

[1] For I take exception to the arguments derived from pacific maxims in the recorded teaching of Christ; not because I disregard that teaching, but because I believe it directed not to problems of external politics but to problems of private conduct. I do not think so ill of Christ's human intelligence as to believe Him unaware of the fact that, teaching as He did under the Roman Empire, problems of external politics were for Him and His contemporaries in the hands of the Emperor; and I make bold to say that when He bade men 'render unto Cæsar the things that are Cæsar's' (Mark xii. 17; Luke xx. 25) He made it known for His will that His disciples should leave them there.

discouraging a people who are individually the victims of their own emotions, and collectively a prey to the tyrannous but popular 'rule' of a sub-man whom they hail as a super-man, from pursuing abroad an aggressively belligerent policy, the natural extension of the tyranny to which they are accustomed at home, and forcing them to realize that the only way to prosperity at home is through peace abroad.

XXXI
CLASSICAL PHYSICS AND CLASSICAL POLITICS

31. 1. 'THE *classical physics*' is the current name for a theory of the natural world which we owe chiefly to Galileo in the late sixteenth and early seventeenth centuries and to Newton in the late seventeenth.

31. 11. This theory held the field until the late nineteenth century, when small, but to a scrupulous thinker fatal, defects in it began to be recognized by every serious student.

31. 12. Even to-day, obsolete though it is, it remains classical in the sense in which Homer and Virgil are classical poets: not that we hold them models for every poet's imitation, but that we hold them especially deserving of study by everyone who wishes to master the art of poetry.

31. 13. We do not think that Galileo and Newton have said the last word about physics; we think that they have said something from which every student of the subject must begin, though he must not hope to find it entirely acceptable.

31. 14. What he must learn by studying their work, even at second or third hand in popular manuals and text-books for the young, is to accept the principle on which it rests.

31. 15. It is a double principle. It is that inquiries of this kind must be based on an empirically accurate study of facts, and on a logically accurate study of implications. The facts must be right and the logic must be right. No amount of rightness in logic will compensate for even the smallest error in fact; no amount of rightness in fact for even the smallest error in logic.

31. 16. Let us put this by saying that facts are the 'matter' of such an inquiry and logic its 'form'. It must be materially sound, that is, its facts must be right; and formally sound, that is, its logic must be right.

31. 17. The logic, or formal part, of an inquiry concerning the natural world is mathematical. Galileo said that the book of nature is written by the hand of God in the language of mathematics: Newton called his chief work 'The Mathematical Principles of Natural Philosophy'.

31.18. They were saying the same thing: that the logic of physics is mathematics. They did not call their science 'physics'; for them that was a term of abuse, the name of an Aristotelian-medieval pseudo-science; what we call physics they called natural philosophy or experimental philosophy.

31.19. Neither (need I say?) fell into the error of identifying logic in general with mathematics. That error has been preached of late, but it has no warrant in the classical physics.

31.2. There is a theory, worked out by Hobbes in the middle of the seventeenth century and restated with minor differences by Locke at the end of that century and Rousseau in the eighteenth,[1] which I call the *classical politics*.

31.21. It is an attempt at a science of human life in one special form, namely political life.

31.22. Like the classical physics it can no longer be regarded as containing the last word about its subject. Not having found its Einstein it cannot be regarded as definitely superseded. What we have is not a successor for it but a rather vague agreement as to where it needs correction.

31.23. But it is still classical in the sense that every beginner in the subject, on pain of going ill-grounded, must start with it. It may not have said the last word, but it has said a first word which no one who takes the subject seriously can afford to forget.

31.24. It is a product of the same seventeenth-century notion of scientific method as the classical physics. Like that (and indeed like every 'modern science', every science that obeys the rules laid down early in the seventeenth century by the two great fathers of modern scientific theory, Bacon and Descartes) it stands on two legs.

31.25. One leg consists of facts ascertained either by observation or experiment. The other consists of abstractions.

31.26. If these are the legs of the science, what is its body? The dual nature of the legs reappears in the body. The symbiosis of factual thinking with abstract thinking which I have metaphorically described by saying that the science rests on two legs might be alternatively described by

[1] I omit Spinoza from this list only because his *Tractatus Politicus* was left a fragment at his death.

saying that its body consists of two parts: an armature of abstractions reinforcing a concrete whose aggregate consists of facts.

31. 27. A still better metaphor is one of Bacon's. The scientist is neither an 'ant', storing what it finds lying about ready-made, nor a 'spider', spinning a web out of what its entrails secrete. He is a bee, visiting innumerable flowers and collecting the nectar it finds in them; but storing not this nectar in its crude state but the honey into which it turns it (*Novum Organum*, I. xcv).

31. 28. The scientist collects crude facts, but he stores only what he has converted them into: *laws*. Laws are the body of a science. Laws are what it is a scientist's business to come at. Laws are what a master-scientist has to teach. Laws are what a pupil-scientist has to learn.

31. 29. A law is neither a crude fact nor (as some ant-logicians pretend) a collection of crude facts. It cannot be established by an observation or an experiment, or many of them. Nor is it a theorem in pure mathematics, to be established by a mathematical operation. It is midway between the two: a hybrid. It is what the scientist can breed from facts by crossing them with pure abstractions, which is another way of saying what Bacon said. It is what he can breed from pure abstractions by crossing them with facts. If any reader knows too little of scientific work to understand the metaphor, I willingly apologize for its obscurity.

31. 3. Modern science needs two different kinds of raw material: crude facts and pure abstractions. To combine these into science is called 'interpreting' the crude facts and 'applying' the abstractions.

31. 31. To interpret a set of crude facts is to get at what is called their 'law'. To apply a pure abstraction is to think of it as the law of a set of crude facts.

31. 32. Modern science (31. 24) is two different processes arriving at the same result. One process is *interpreting facts*; a conversion of crude facts into laws by mixing the nectar you get from flowers with the acid you secrete in your own inside and thus turning it into honey.

31. 33. The other is *applying abstractions*: starting with pure abstractions and converting these into laws by bringing them into relation with the facts whose laws they henceforth are. 'Are', I say, not 'are thought to be'; the Newtonian law of gravitation is (not 'is thought to be') the law of direct variation as the product of the masses and inverse variation as the square of the distance between the centres. In formulating this law Newton was applying ideas in pure mathematics that had long been familiar.

31. 34. Interpreting facts and applying abstractions are really not two processes but one. If you keep your eye on the factual element you think of this process as a process which the facts undergo by having abstractions mixed with them.

31. 35. If you keep your eye on the abstractions you think of it as a process which the abstractions undergo by having facts mixed with them.

31. 36. These fixations of the eye have their uses; but they must not become obsessions. You can fix your eye on the bicarbonate of soda and think of baking-powder as made by adding to it double its amount in cream of tartar: or you can fix your eye on the cream of tartar and think of yourself as adding half its amount in bicarbonate of soda.

31. 37. Only a very cretinous pupil will fancy these rival methods of making the powder, or the 'rationalism' and 'empiricism' ascribed to seventeenth-century thinkers, rival theories of scientific method.

31. 38. Double or single, the process is richly illustrated by Galileo and Newton and the many physicists who were working about the same time (to mention physicists only); and theoretically expounded partly by Galileo himself, less so by Newton; whose theoretical exposition interested himself but little and, to tell the truth, interests his readers even less.

31. 39. If Galileo's practical work awaited completion by Newton, his theoretical work awaited completion by Bacon and Descartes.

31. 4. The classical politics can be described in the same metaphorical ways as resting on one leg of factual thinking and one leg of abstract thinking (31. 25) or as having a body whose armature, made of abstractions, reinforces a concrete whose aggregate consists of facts (31. 26), or of laws arrived at by a double process of 'interpreting' facts and 'applying' abstractions (31. 31–3).

31.41. What matters is not that the reader should choose among these or other metaphors, but that he should understand what they mean to describe.

31.42. However the classical politics is described the description will involve reference to three different things.

31.43. First, a reference to facts, the *explicanda* of the science.

31.44. Second, a reference to pure abstractions, its *applicanda*.

31.45. Third, a reference to laws which it is the aim of the science to determine. These will be related to the facts as the explanation of them; to the pure abstractions as the application of them.

31.46. The facts are facts of political life, as the facts to be explained by the classical physics are facts of the natural world. Like them, they are ascertained by observation and experiment: it is important that observations and experiments alike should be skilfully planned in order that the facts thereby ascertained should be worth ascertaining, and accurately made in order that they should be securely ascertained.

31.47. The facts in which either science is interested may be ascertained either by observation or by experiment. Different kinds of facts, having different degrees of scientific value, are ascertainable in these two ways. Facts ascertainable by mere observation are what are called common-sense facts, i.e. facts accessible to a commonplace mind on occasions frequent enough to be rather often perceived and of such a kind that their characteristics can be adequately perceived without trouble: so that the facts concerning them can be familiar to persons not especially gifted and not especially alert.

31.48. Experimental facts are facts ascertainable only when the events (physical or political) which they concern are purposely staged by means of human interference with the course of physical or political events; such interference being planned to show a peculiarly alert observer what happens in circumstances specially controlled and specially favourable to observation.

31.49. Experimental facts are harder to ascertain than

common-sense facts; the ascertaining of them calls for a greater understanding of what the science needs and a greater control over the facts it has to explain; experimental facts are thus more valuable than common-sense facts, more instructive to the scientist.

31. 5. Most sciences begin by studying common-sense facts and pass on to experimental facts when their technique is sufficiently advanced. There are no lessons which a science can learn by observation that it could not learn equally well (and more easily) by experiment, given the technique to make the experiments. To use common-sense facts is characteristic of a science whose technique of research is not sufficiently advanced to replace them by experimental facts; to prefer common sense to experiment is characteristic of a man who, being too clumsy or too stupid for advanced methods, wants his scientific technique to be clumsy and stupid like himself.

31. 51. The abstractions brought with them by the classical physicists to the work of interpreting the facts of nature, so far as these are revealed to man (very incompletely, no doubt; nor will any man seriously think the part so revealed a fair sample of the whole) by the double method of observation and experiment, were the abstractions of *pure mathematics*.

31. 52. Like the facts to which the classical physicists applied them, these were of two kinds, elementary and advanced. Elementary facts were the common-sense facts ascertained by mere observation; advanced facts were those which could only be ascertained by experiment.

31. 53. *Elementary* mathematics comprised those operations in pure mathematics which the sixteenth- and seventeenth-century natural scientists inherited from the ancients. We still give this repertory the distinguishing epithet of 'elementary' arithmetic and the like.

31. 54. *Advanced* mathematics comprised operations invented by mathematicians in modern times, and added to the repertory they inherited from the ancients, such as the Cartesian analytical geometry and Newton's method of fluxions or (if you prefer) the Leibnitian differential calculus.

31. 55. The classical politics, like the classical physics,

dealt with two kinds of facts; and dealt with them by applying to them two kinds of abstractions. All the facts were facts of political life, and in order that these should become *explicanda* for a political scientist the scientist must have encountered them in his experience of political life; he must therefore be a man of political experience, a man who knew his way about political life and knew what one was apt to find going on there.

31.56. But these facts were of two kinds, elementary and advanced.

31.57. The elementary facts were familiar to every man who had lived in a body politic and watched its life going on round him; or even to men who had not lived in a body politic but had taken stock of their goings-on from the point of view of a detached observer. The detached observer, hermit on a mountain-top or the like, is a favourite character in romantic fiction. If he really exists, the facts he can know about the life in which he does not mingle are just the elementary ones; the obvious ones; the sort of facts you can know about a shoe without knowing where it pinches.

31.58. The advanced facts can only be ascertained by a man who, being no longer content with the superficial knowledge of a detached observer, feeds his craving for a deeper insight by staging experiments and noting the results. Such a man must be a more alert observer than the detached spectator. Moreover, he must be in a position which enables him to try his experiments: he must be in a *position of rule*.

31.59. The *abstractions* which the classical politics brought to the work of interpreting its facts were the abstractions of *law*. As mathematics is the logic of physics, so law is the logic of politics.

31.6. These again were of two kinds, elementary and advanced. Elementary law, for the authors of the classical politics, was Roman law; which they knew as well as the classical physicists knew Euclid and the multiplication table, and for the same reason. Advanced law meant the revision, partly expansive and partly corrective, which Roman law had received in the legal institutions of medieval and modern Europe; and not only in the countries which 'received' Roman law: on the contrary, especially in those which did not; whose lawyers by no means neglected the study of Roman law, and owed a great deal to it in the formulation of their own. This revision of Roman law was as important for the classical politics as the revision of Greek mathematics by the invention of analytical geometry and the differential calculus for the classical physics.

31.61. All modern science recognizes what I will call *the principle of the limited objective*. That is the most fundamental difference between the modern sciences and the sciences of ancient Greece.

31.62. Ancient sciences aimed at an unlimited objective. They defined their aims by asking questions like: 'What is Nature?' 'What is Man?' 'What is Justice?' 'What is Virtue?' A question of this sort was to be answered by a *definition* of the thing. From this definition, which had to state the 'essence' of the thing defined, implications could be derived, each implication being the statement of some 'property'.

31.63. For example the geometry of the triangle had to begin with a definition of the triangle. It is a 'property' of the triangle that its angles are together equal to $180°$; you 'prove' that 'property' by showing that it is logically implied in the definition of the triangle.

31.64. The form of question: 'What is x?' demands an answer telling you the essence of x; telling you everything you need know about x in order to work out a complete science of it. The idea of a science, for an ancient Greek, was not only the idea of a science of x but the idea of the complete science of x. There could be only one science of a given thing: for unless it grasped the essence of the thing it was not a science of it, and one thing had only one essence. When that was discovered, all the 'properties' of the thing could be deduced.

21.65. By 'a given thing' I mean, not a given material body (the pen with which I am writing, or the like), but whatever kind of thing it is that constitutes the object of a science. The Greeks very early discovered that this could not be a material body, and this discovery has never been seriously challenged.

31.66. To seek for x a single essence from which all the 'properties' of x are logically deducible is to propose a science of x with an unlimited objective. That is implied in any question of the form: 'What is x?'

31.67. To a question in this form, for example: 'What is Nature?' modern science answers: 'I do not know. What the essence of nature is nobody knows, and nobody need care. When they asked that question the Greeks were asking a question too vague to be precisely answered.'

31.68. Limit your objective. Take time seriously. Aim at interpreting not, as the Greeks did, any and every fact in the natural world, but only those which you think need be interpreted, or can be interpreted (the two things are not, after all, so very different); now, choose where to begin your attack. Select the problems that call for immediate attention. Resolve to let the rest wait.

31.7. The classical physics obeyed the principle of the limited objective, limiting its explanatory efforts to such facts as *admitted of mathematical treatment*. The unlimited objective, the hope of understanding Nature at large, was abandoned. In its place was put the limited objective, understanding so much of Nature as could be measured, weighed, or in some other way treated mathematically.

31.71. The principle of limited objective, applied to physics with memorable results by Galileo, was not first laid down by Galileo. It was first expounded by those too little known writers (if they were better known the main lines of European history would be better understood) whom we call the Christian Fathers. The sciences with unlimited objectives went bankrupt with what is called the collapse of ancient paganism. The Christian sciences (*nostra philosophia*, one of the Fathers calls them) are sciences with limited objectives.

31.8. The authors of the classical politics did not aim at explaining all political facts whatever; if they had, the masters of modern scientific theory (not to mention the Fathers) would have written, so far as they were concerned, in vain.

31.81. Their aim was a science of politics which should explain a certain class of political facts by reference to the idea of society.

31.82. No one doubted that some at least of the facts

presented by the natural world were partly at least susceptible of mathematical treatment; so that the classical physics would for some time at any rate not be gravelled for lack of matter in pursuing its limited objective of reducing to applied mathematics whatever in nature was so reducible.

31.83. No one doubted that some elements in that admittedly complex thing we call political life were homogeneous with the facts of social life or partnership; and that the project of limiting our objective to the study of these elements in political life would give results; limited, but worth having.

31.84. Granted the principle of limited objective, the decision to explain one class of facts necessarily involved a decision to renounce, at any rate for the present, all attempt at explaining other facts, perhaps equally numerous, perhaps equally important, no doubt equally real. The classical physics gave up, at any rate for the present, all attempt at explaining the so-called 'secondary qualities'. That did not matter. You judge a science by its success in doing what it aims at doing, not by its failure to do what it never set out to do. Later, perhaps, some part of what is now jettisoned may be reclaimed; Newton's *optics* is a case in point. If some part cannot be, it will remain unexplained; which need worry nobody, because no modern scientist ever thought that any group of facts could be completely explained.

31.9. The principle of explanation from which the classical politics began was the idea of society. As the classical physicists drew their geometry in the first instance from Euclid, so the classical politicians drew their idea of partnership, its origin in a 'social contract', the obligations to which that contract gave rise, and the *conditio sine qua non* of its being made, namely the 'personality' or free will of the parties, in the first instance from the Roman civilians.

31.91. But it was not legal antiquaries, interested in Roman law as a bygone system of ideas and practices, who created the classical politics. The inventors of the classical politics were not a set of men who dug up the theory of *societas* from Roman text-books and travestied modern problems by dressing them up in this borrowed vesture, as a Félicien David might travesty Napoleon by dressing him up in a toga.

31.92. Just as the mathematics inherited from ancient Greece formed part of the armature of the classical physics only because it still lived as an integral part of modern mathematics together with new developments of it like analytical geometry and the differential calculus, so the Roman law of society formed part of the armature of the classical politics only because partnership was a thing with which, in various forms, the people who created and accepted the classical politics were very familiar, a thing whose working they knew by personal experience: not only out of Roman law books, but out of the 'bourgeois' life of medieval and post-medieval Europe.

31.93. This experience, partly reinforcing and partly correcting what those books told them, was derived from the partnerships of medieval and modern economic life (land-tenure, industry, finance, and so forth), the partnerships of medieval and modern craft and education (universities and other guilds), the partnerships of modern religion (especially the sects of nonconformist christianity), and the partnerships of modern political life (political 'parties'). It is by correcting the ideas of the Roman civilians in the light of this long medieval and modern experience of partnership in many different forms that I have been able (20.6 *seqq.*) so to modify those ideas as to bring the central notion they express into harmony with the modern European use of words.

XXXII

SOCIETY AND NATURE IN THE CLASSICAL POLITICS

32. 1. WE are now ready to state the problem of the classical politics.

32. 11. 'The facts of political life are not well understood; we do not mean theoretically understood by practitioners of a fugitive and cloistered virtue peeping out of their hermitage windows to spy on the body politic; that is inevitable and does not matter; we mean practically understood by men who, being engaged in politics, will do their work amiss to the detriment of the whole body politic unless they understand what they are doing.

32. 12. 'It is to the interest of the whole body politic, and of every body politic, that they should be better understood. The indispensable preliminary to this is that they should be correctly ascertained: and in this connexion we recall with gratitude the work of Machiavelli, whom (as against his many detractors) we praise for having opened an unflinching eye to these facts.

32. 13. 'But with Machiavelli the work of political science has not yet begun. His work, admirable though it was, was not political science itself but only preliminary to political science. A science begins when someone chooses (out of a collection of facts relative to a certain subject) some of a special kind which he thinks he can here and now explain.

32. 14. 'Some of the facts relative to political life are of a kind with which we are familiar in another and a simpler context. These are *social* facts. The nature of social life is well known to us partly from Roman private law and partly from our own experience of joint activity.

32. 15. 'Facts of the kind which constitute social life occur in political life, though mixed with others. Political life is partly, though not entirely, social in character.

32. 16. 'Here, then, we have a limited objective for a science of politics: *to study the social elements in political life.*

32. 17. 'The non-social elements which, together with these social elements, make up political life as a whole we

s

know to exist; but we do not propose to offer a scientific account of them. We not only know them to exist; we know that they must exist; for social life means partnership, and partnership means joint action by mentally adult agents; and these must be human beings who have lived a certain number of years before attaining that condition.

32. 18. 'The infancy and youth of a human being who is going to become capable of social life must be lived under non-social conditions. The assertion that political life is partly social implies that it is also partly non-social; since human beings are already members of a body politic during their infancy and youth.

32. 19. 'Political life combines a social element and a non-social element. Our aim is to give an account of the social element. As to the non-social element, we assert that it exists, but for the present we give no account of it, just as contemporary physics, giving an account only of the quantitative element in the world of Nature, asserts that there is also a qualitative element but does not offer an account of it. The element we do not profess to explain we will call "nature": the state of nature, the natural condition of mankind: where the word "nature" stands, as it usually does, for the negative partner in a pair of correlative terms, the positive partner here being "society", and "society" being understood as a state into which men put themselves by doing something to themselves which the civilians call entering into a social contract.'

32. 2. Thus defined, the method of the classical politics is justified by the principle of limited objective. Political life presents facts of many different kinds: that method gives you, in effect, the rule to begin somewhere: the classical politicians did begin somewhere.

32. 21. More than that, they began at the right end. It is the most weighty of all testimonies to the merit of the classical politics that it recognizes in the facts of political life not only a complex that must be attacked somewhere, if any scientific treatment of it is to be attempted, but a polarized complex, a thing with two ends: a dialectic.

32. 22. These two ends are 'society' and 'nature'; 'society' meaning that part of political life which consists in agree-

ment between mentally adult persons for the purposes of joint action, 'nature' meaning the rest.

32. 23. What that 'rest' consists of the classical politics does not say, or rather it does not say in positive terms. It tells us what it is not; it does not tells us what it is. All it has to say about the natural condition of mankind is that it is a condition of human life not due to agreement among the human beings who share that condition. The classical politics gives a positive, detailed, and adequate account of 'society'. All it says about 'nature' is that it is that element in political life which is not society.

32. 24. If we are asked to describe in positive terms that element in political life which is not society, we can refer to the somewhat elaborate account, given piecemeal in this Part, of the non-social community.

32. 25. We know how its membership is constituted; what place it has in the family and in the body politic; and how its existence in these complex communities confers on the activity of the community the attribute of force.

32. 26. We have described positively, if only in outline, that end of the polarized complex of political fact which the classical politics described negatively by calling it the state of nature, meaning the state of human life which is not social.

32. 27. When I said (32. 21) that the classical politics began at the right end, I implied that political life is dynamic. It has not only two ends like a bit of string, it has two ends like a mill-race, one where the water goes in and one where the water comes out.

32. 28. Politics is a process whereby one condition of human life is converted into another. A process whereby A is converted into B has a positive end B (the end where the process is complete) and a negative end A (the end where the process has not yet begun).

32. 3. The great merit of the classical politics is that it knows political life to be dynamic or dialectical. It teaches that, of the two ends between which political life is polarized, one is positive and the other negative. It teaches that the positive end is social in character: that is, consists of relations between human beings established by their free adoption of a joint purpose.

32. 31. It teaches that this can only be done by converting into a society what was not a society; and that, again by bringing about a capacity for free will in human beings which hitherto did not possess it, in other words educating them up to mental maturity.

32. 32. The classical politicians described this as bringing men out of the 'state of nature' into the 'state of civil society'. They understood that such a process could not happen of itself; it had to be brought about by hard work; and the hard work had to be done by persons who were already mature in mind, already possessed of free will, already members of a society.

32. 33. They looked upon the process as one whereby a centre already infected with freedom, existing in an uninfected environment consisting of human beings in the 'state of nature', gradually infects the environment and brings it into a condition of homogeneity with itself: brings it out of the 'state of nature' into the 'condition of civil society'.

32. 34. It was Rousseau who said this more clearly, and perhaps saw it more clearly, than the other classical politicians. But it was implied in the view of political life common to them all from the start that political life involves the conversion of human beings fit as yet only for membership of the nursery into human beings fit for membership of the council chamber: that the work done in the council chamber is to recruit itself, with all that this implies. The life of politics is the life of political education.

32. 35. In conducting a process what you have to understand is its terminal point. You have to know what you are aiming at. If you are trying to teach a child Latin you have to know not child psychology but Latin; as much Latin as you want to teach the child, which may be extremely little.

32. 36. To this indispensable knowledge of Latin you may have to add knowledge of child psychology if the child is very unmanageable. But even so the main thing is to know Latin. The main thing is to know what you are aiming at. To know where you started from is secondary; and is important only when you are not sure whether you are going forwards or backwards.

32. 37. If political life is dynamic, what is absolutely needed for its successful prosecution is understanding of its positive end: understanding of the condition which you are working to introduce into the body politic.

32.38. Who needs this understanding? Obviously the ruling class: the ruled class does not need it in so far as it is merely passive to the act of ruling, and a mere spectator does not need it at all.

32.39. By the Third Law of Politics, so far as the ruling class does its work successfully the freedom or will-power characteristic of it percolates throughout the body politic and is thus constantly tending to convert the ruled or non-social element into part of the ruling or social element. So far as this process actually takes place there is no need to describe the non-social element. If all the water that goes in at one end comes out at the other, we need not bother to measure it at both ends. If the non-social element is an evanescent element wholly eliminated as the political process goes on by the conversion of involuntary members of the original non-social community into voluntary members of a social community, the social end of the process is not only the right one to begin at, it is the only one that need be thought about.

32.4. If the classical politicians had argued thus they would have been logically justified in postponing inquiry into the positive characteristics of the 'state of nature' not only for the present, but for ever. There is no evidence that they did postpone it for ever; only that they postponed it. Nor is there evidence that they expected the 'state of nature' to vanish and be wholly superseded by a social condition.

32.41. Rather the opposite. The question is actually raised in three different forms by Hobbes, who is by far the toughest and most resourceful, as well as the most original, of the thinkers I have named. He answers it every time in the negative.

32.42. In the first place, Hobbes tells us that in certain respects people remain in the state of nature, though in others they have emerged from it into the state of civil society.

32.43. In the second place, he says that some people never emerge from it at all, though if this passage is rightly understood I think it will be found to be only a variant of the first.

32. 44. In the third place, he says that even when the negative conditions characteristic of the state of nature have been surmounted through the creation of a civil society they are only suspended, not abolished. The process of political life is reversible. If there is sometimes a progress whereby the freedom and sociality of the ruling class diffuses itself throughout the non-social community of the ruled, there may equally well be a regress whereby a freedom and sociality once achieved may be lost and a society break down into a non-social community. We who no longer believe in a law of progress find it delightful, after wading back through the bog of nineteenth-century wish-fulfilment fantasies, that Hobbes did not believe in it either.

32. 5. I will remind the reader of three passages. First comes his chapter on the 'NATURAL CONDITION *of Mankind*' (*Leviathan*, chap. xiii).

32. 51. 'The savage people in many places of America, except the government of small Families, the concord whereof dependeth on naturall lust, have no government at all' (ibid., p. 63).

32. 52. Clearly implying that in other parts of the world as well there is a kind of family government (to call it government) quite different in character from that of a civil society: a non-social state of human life in which the order necessary for the existence of a 'small Family' (surely not only a family of savages) is imposed by the will of the strongest upon those who are less strong; by the parents upon the mentally immature children; and the mentally immature love to have it so.

32. 53. So long as there are children, I suppose him to mean, the non-social community never comes to an end. It is not by strength of will, it is by what Hobbes calls a 'naturall lust', a non-voluntary or 'instinctive' (to use modern jargon) subservience of the mentally weak to the mentally strong, that a child so loyally supports in every detail the *suum cuique* of the nursery.

32. 54. Secondly, particular ruling classes, each keeping order within the limits of its own body politic, keep no order among themselves; but are to one another in a state of nature, 'having their weapons pointing, and their eyes fixed upon one another; that is, their Forts, Garrisons, and Guns upon the Frontiers of their kingdoms; and continuall Spyes upon their neighbours; which is a gesture of War' (ibid.).

32.55. If ruling classes are one-man autocracies, these absolute monarchs are a kind of person who never emerge from a state of nature. If (which is Hobbes's explicit doctrine) they may consist either of one man or of many, Hobbes is here telling us that each member of a ruling class is in a state of nature relatively to any member of a different ruling class but in a state of civil society relatively to another member of his own.

32.56. Thirdly, even where the state of nature has been suspended as between one man and another, by their agreeing to constitute a society and thus entering mutually upon a civil life, strains are at work tending to make the agreement break down.

32.57. Hobbes enumerates the chief strains as Competition, Diffidence, and Glory: 'the first [maketh man] use Violence, to make themselves Masters of other mens persons, wives, children, and cattell; the second, to defend them; the third, for trifles, as a word, a smile, a different opinion, and any other sign of undervalue, either direct in their Persons, or by reflexion in their Kindred, their Friends, their Nation, their Profession, or their Name' (*Leviathan*, p. 62).

32.6. These are cited, not as three causes why there should be a state of nature; but as three causes why attempts to get out of a state of nature by mutual agreement should fail. There can be no 'cause' why a state of nature should exist.

32.61. To understand that is merely to understand the vocabulary of seventeenth-century science. The state of nature in political theory is like the state of rest in physical theory. It does not need a cause to bring it about. It needs a cause to cancel it. There are causes of motion. There are no causes of rest.

32.62. But there may be causes of stoppage. A cause of stoppage, for a seventeenth-century physicist, is a cause counteracting an already caused motion and re-establishing a state of rest. So, for a seventeenth-century politician, there cannot be causes why a state of nature should exist: there can only be causes why it should be replaced by a state of civil society; causes of which the classical politics has given us an account in the exaggeratedly utilitarian style of the age; and counteracting causes (Competition, Diffidence, and Glory, as aforesaid) whereby these motives to the creation and maintenance of civil society are overridden and the civil society breaks down into a state of nature re-established.

32. 63. Is the state of nature, as such, a state of war? The reader will remember that Hobbes says yes: Locke says no.

32. 64. 'For WARRE', says Hobbes (*Leviathan*, p. 62), 'consisteth not in Battell only, or in the act of fighting; but in a tract of time, wherein the Will to contend by Battell is sufficiently known . . . the nature of War, consisteth not in actuall fighting but in the known disposition thereto, during all the time there is no assurance to the contrary. All other time is PEACE.' And he argues that according to this definition the 'naturall condition of mankind' is one of war all against all, abrogated only by a mutual agreement among certain men to keep the peace; an agreement implemented by the creation of an executive to see that it is kept.

32. 65. For Locke there is a 'plain *Difference between the State of Nature, and the State of War* . . . which . . . are as far distant as a State of Peace, good Will, mutual Assistance and Preservation, and a State of Enmity, Malice, Violence and mutual Destruction, are from one another. Men living together according to Reason, without a common superior on Earth, with Authority to judge between them, is *properly the State of Nature.* But Force, or a declared Design of Force upon the Person of another, where there is no common Superior on Earth to appeal to for Relief, *is the State of War*; and 'tis the Want of such an Appeal gives a Man the Right of War even against an *Aggressor,* tho' he be in Society and a Fellow-Subject' (*Treatise of Civil Government,* § 19).

32. 66. Neither is simply right. The issue is not a straight one. Hobbes, as usual, is truer to the terms of the theory they both accepted. If you agree in postulating a state of nature defined merely negatively as a state of non-sociality, you cannot distinguish the state of nature from the state of war, and Hobbes was right not to distinguish. But if you think of political life dynamically you ought to think of the state of nature dynamically. To think of it positively will, in fact, imply thinking of it dynamically.

32. 67. When the situation is seen from this point of view, one realizes not only that Locke is closer to the facts than Hobbes, but that Hobbes goes far towards anticipating Locke's criticism of himself. To return to our parallel from physics (32. 61), war is to the state of nature as the stopping of a clock is to its being at rest.

32. 68. If political life involves, by the mere establishment of law and order, the progressive establishment of sociality where there was once non-sociality, war is not the mere absence of sociality in these parts of the body politic; it is a catabolic process in the opposite sense, a politically wasteful or destructive activity, an activity involving the breakdown even of such degree of sociality as has been already achieved by an inward corruption of the body politic waging it, an increase of crime, immorality, and whatever things the establishment of law and order tends to diminish (30. 39) as well as a cessation of the attempt, by the further advancement of law and order, to diminish them still more.

32. 69. 'Competition, Diffidence, and Glory' are causes, not of the state of nature, but of war; the state of nature catabolically re-establishing itself on the ruins of a civil society. They are motives (as we now commonly say; the word 'cause' having been arbitrarily limited of late to physical 'causes') inducing men to stop acting in concert and begin acting as members of a non-social community: psychological forces beneath which their social will cracks and lets in the flood of war.

32. 7. The men who created the classical politics were not professors. They were men of the world and they lived among men of the world.

31. 71. Their interest in political life was not formed by reading academic treatises. It was formed by taking part in politics and in conversation with men whose part in it was a main concern of their lives; men who were able to discuss it intelligently not simply because they were intelligent men but because they knew what they were talking about.

32. 72. The classical politics, as an attempt to explain political life (so much of it as should prove susceptible of such explanation) in terms of social life, required of its readers two qualifications.

32. 73. First, it called for experience of political life, so that they should know for themselves the problems it attempted to solve.

32. 74. Secondly, it called for experience of social life, so that they should know for themselves the idea by whose application it attempted to solve them: the idea of partnership and the ideas connected with it.

32. 75. These works demanded in their readers a familiarity with the facts of political life and also a familiarity with the facts of partnership, not only as set forth by the Roman civilians, but as existing in the economic life, the life of learning and education, the religious life, and the political life of the modern world.

32. 8. The classical politics, created by that most English of Englishmen Thomas Hobbes, is redolent of English life in both respects.

32. 81. It is characteristic of a people trained for centuries in experience of political life (when the *Leviathan* was written parliament had taken shape[1] three and a half centuries ago) and for centuries in experience of social life.

32. 82. This double experience was general throughout the civilized world, in spite of the campaign, conducted by the new monarchical absolutism of the 'State' in France and Spain and the 'Church' in Tridentine Romanism, to obliterate that experience.

32. 83. This campaign had raised not one ghost alone of the Roman imperial absolutism, but several, 'sitting crowned upon the grave thereof'[2]; for the whole earth, said Pericles,[3] is the grave of famous men, and it is not in Rome alone that the Roman Empire lies buried, and not in Rome alone that its ghost has started up from its ruins.

32. 9. Such was the condition of the world in the middle and late seventeenth century that the *Leviathan* could be understood without a commentary not only by another Englishman like John Locke but by a Portuguese Jew living in Holland, heir to the Jewish tradition of social life in

---

[1] By 1295 'there is, we may say definitely, a parliament; the great outlines have been drawn once for all' (Maitland, *Constitutional History of England* (1909), p. 69).

[2] *Leviathan*, p. 386 (part 4, chap. xlvii).   [3] Thucydides, ii. 43.

economics and religion and the Dutch tradition of republican politics; a 'citoyen de Genève' (as Rousseau called himself on the title-page of the *Contrat social*) brought up in an essentially similar atmosphere of political republicanism and economico-religious social life; and in fact by almost anyone accustomed to breathe the air of western Europe.

XXXIII

DECLINE OF THE CLASSICAL POLITICS

33. 1. From Rousseau the classical politics overleapt the western and southern parts of Germany, whose hesitant and late-flowering[1] intellectual life had perished in the Thirty Years' War, to find rest for the sole of its foot in Königsberg.

33. 11. Prussia belonged neither to the Byzantine East, like Russia and the Balkan lands, nor to the Latin West, the countries whose loyalty and aversion were focused on Rome.

33. 12. It was a march fortified, rather than civilized, by the Teutonic knights against the Slavdom that supplied the bulk of its own population. The Prussian royalty and nobility owed a sort of homage to the West; they had little contact with the West.

33. 13. Frederick the Great, an absolute monarch more or less after the French model, made it his aim to reinforce that contact and thereby civilize his subjects.

33. 14. But his French literary lapdog turned homesick; his Thuringian musical lapdog turned insolent and said plainly in what he called (tongue in cheek) the *Musikalisches Opfer* that his *roi soleil* was a very poor hand at inventing a fugal subject; and odd things happened when his profes-

---

[1] Rashdall (*The Universities of Europe in the Middle Ages*) speaks of scholastic guilds or universities springing into existence 'without any express authorization of king, pope, prince,' or prelate', and as 'spontaneous products of that instinct of association which swept like a great wave over the towns of Europe in the eleventh and twelfth centuries' (ed. 2, 1936, vol. i, p. 15). He adds a quotation from Mosheim (*Ecclesiastical History*, E.T., 1826, vol. iii, p. 137) that educators were herein copying the social life of 'illiterate tradesmen', where the epithet of disparagement is typically German.

In Germany this associative movement nowhere led to the spontaneous formation of even a single university. The spontaneous formation of universities went briskly forward from the beginning of the thirteenth century in France, Italy, England, Spain, Portugal, and even Bohemia and Poland; but no universities at all were founded in Germany until near the close of the fourteenth. The very few which arose in that century were all due to papal or princely action or the two combined, except Cologne (1388), which was founded by the municipality. During the fifteenth and sixteenth centuries many universities arose in Germany (only in the west and south) but none by spontaneous association; all by papal or princely action.

sorial lapdogs began introducing the Prussian intelligentsia to the political ideas of the West.

33. 15. We are told (and there is evidence for it) that the reading of Rousseau provoked the thoughts set forth in Kant's ethical writings.

33. 16. The curious thing is that the unsolved problem of giving a positive instead of a merely negative meaning to the phrase 'state of nature' aroused no echo in Kant's mind nor in the minds of his readers, as it must have done in the mind of anyone who followed the thread of Rousseau's argument.

33. 17. 'Man is born free,' says Rousseau in the first words of the *Contrat social*, 'and everywhere he is in chains. How did this happen? I do not know,' he goes on, and bursts into tears.

33. 18. What is worrying him is his failure to attach any positive meaning to the phrase 'state of nature', the name given by the classical politics to the non-social community into which babies are born and hence not born free (23. 93): his failure, and that of the whole classical politics, to achieve a *theory of the non-social community*.

33. 19. We, who know this, are inclined to pat him consolingly on the back like his friend David Hume on a famous occasion[1] and murmur: 'My dear sir! my dear sir!'

33. 2. Rousseau's German readers were so far from understanding what his difficulty was that they agreed to mean by 'the natural condition of mankind' not the nursery, but the cave; not the opposite of society, but the opposite of civilization. *Naturmensch* is the German for 'savage'.

33. 21. The qualifications for understanding the classical politics were knowing your way about the political world and knowing your way about the social world (32. 73–4).

33. 22. It is no wonder that Rousseau's tragic first paragraph should have been left uncomprehended not only by Kant but by all the brilliantly gifted men whose work, with Kant's, makes up the history of Germany's brief but splendid golden age.

33. 23. Eighteenth-century Prussia had nothing to com-

---

[1] *Philosophical Works of David Hume*, 4 vols., Edinburgh, 1826; vol. i, p. lxxxiii.

pare with Jacobean England's three-and-a-half centuries'
experience (32. 81) of political life; far less, even, than
absolutist France.

33. 24. France had gone absolutist after a long medieval
experience of political life; Prussian absolutism had no such
background; untempered even by epigrams, it was a far more
absolute absolutism than the model it imitated.

33. 25. Nor had Germany (where universities were
founded by royal command for the enhancement of royal
glory; where religion, as an Erastian apanage of politics,
gave rise to no free association; where even business, that
fertile source of partnerships, was a despised activity characteristic of the persecuted Jews) anything to compare with the
vigorous growth of social life in Western countries.

33. 26. To an eighteenth-century German, therefore, the
problem of classical politics was no problem: because owing
to the social backwardness of German life the phenomenon
by observing which Machiavelli had set the ball rolling had
never occurred in the German consciousness: I mean the
spontaneous creation by subjects of a social order capable of
protecting their rights against a prince inclined to override
them (24. 46).

33. 27. For the same reason the classical solution of that
problem by reference to the idea of society was no solution.

33. 28. It was as if Newton's comparison of the moon's
orbit to the fall of an apple had been expounded to an audience
that had never heard of the Copernican solar system and had
never seen an apple; or as if some Italian Renaissance treatise
on the theory of love, like Nifo's *De Amore*, had met with an
audience of eunuchs.

33. 29. Given the facts, what is surprising is not that the
Germans made such nonsense of the classical politics but that
some of them, notably Hegel when he wrote the *Rechtsphilo-
sophie*, came so near to making sense of it.

33. 3. What the Germans in general did with the classical
politics was to misunderstand it as a confused exposition of
two sciences: *Sittenlehre*, the theory of customary or conventional morals, and *Rechtslehre*, the theory of law.

33. 31. The law and morals in question were the law and
morals of a German principality as seen by a subject who

never dreamed of doing anything except either what was prescribed by convention or what was ordered by the prince and his servants.

33. 32. The subject lived, moved, and had his being in a non-social community ordered and maintained partly by what passed (when the question was raised, as it was late in the eighteenth century) for the immemorial tradition of the German people; partly for the docilely accepted despotism of this or that princeling and his still more despotic officials.

33. 33. These two sources of law and order were not clearly distinguished. Men ill supplied with historical knowledge cannot tell whether a habit they possess was imposed upon them lately by a divine autocrat or long ago by a divine ancestor in whom the wisdom of the tribe was incarnate.

33. 34. The second alternative is the more flattering, at any rate the flattery is more fulsome.

33. 35. Ancestor-worship and autocrat-worship are both forms of communal self-adoration or what I will call *herd-worship*; but the first is a more explicit form of it than the second; that is why it was so eagerly snatched at when the German romanticists offered it to their compatriots about the end of the eighteenth century.

33. 36. Herd-worship is a very ancient and widespread religion. It expresses a man's feeling of powerlessness in the grip of a non-social community of which he is a member but not a willing member, though certainly (so far as the thing is really a religion) an enthusiastic and on the whole a happy member; a community he did not help to create and cannot, however slightly, alter by deliberate or voluntary action.

33. 37. The community is to him a sheer fact. Its customs are peremptory commands which he must obey or suffer destruction at its divine but merciless hands.

33. 38. In the terminology of the seventeenth century a community of that kind exists not 'by art' but 'by nature'; and the religious attitude towards such a thing is warranted by another seventeenth-century formula, the Spinozistic identification of Nature with God.

33. 39. And pat came the rediscovery, due in great part to the Germans of this period, especially Hegel himself, of Plato and Aristotle; who had said as against the Sophists that

the city existed not 'by convention' but 'by nature'. The revival of Greek philosophy by the German romanticists was in one thing at least a disaster: it gave the Germans (and their followers) what they mistakenly thought good authority for rejecting the classical politics; which in fact they rejected because, owing to their country's social and political backwardness, they could not understand it.

33. 4. Hobbes had inaugurated the classical politics by asserting that 'that great LEVIATHAN called a COMMONWEALTH, . . . is but an artificiall Man; though of greater stature and strength than the Naturall, for whose protection and defence it was intended' (*Leviathan*, p. 1).

33. 41. The making of such an 'artificiall Man' is of course a function, indeed the essential function, of social life: for the 'artificiall Man' is only Hobbes's vivid name for the joint social will.

33. 42. Kant and his successors, if they had known this passage, would have thought it nonsense and blasphemous nonsense; first because there cannot be an 'artificiall Man', since there cannot be free social activity; secondly because 'the state' (they revived the Renaissance word as if to emphasize their inability to grasp any more modern point of view) is for them neither artificial in its origin nor human in its essence, but natural in its origin (33. 38) and divine in its essence; though, as Hegel scrupulously says, it is not God but only an avatar of God, *der Gang Gottes in der Welt*.

33. 43. The Germans who insisted with Hegel on the 'objective' character of the social and political 'spirit', or with Màrx on the indifference of the economic order to the consciousness of those involved in it, were offering their disciples what professed to be a criticism of the classical politics but was in fact only a statement of their inability to understand it.

33. 44. For the classical politicians had already insisted, even to damnable iteration, on this same idea; the idea of a non-social community or what they called a 'state of nature'; whose existence, they added, did not prevent the men engaged in it from collaborating in the creation of a social life.

33. 45. The Hegelian and Marxian 'criticism' of the classical politics was a reiteration of the first clause in the

belief (incredible as it must appear) that it was a novelty, complicated by a denial of the second.

33. 46. Why did they deny the existence, even the possibility, of free joint activity? Partly, no doubt, because they lacked experience of it.

33. 47. The Germans had lived from time immemorial *procul negotiis, ut prisca gens mortalium*, in the state of nature itself; lapped in the bosom of an all-embracing non-social community where the relations between man and man were as independent of their will as the relations between child and child in a nursery are independent of the children's will.

33. 48. This independence of the communal order upon the members' wills could be indifferently expressed by ascribing the origin of that order to the immemorial wisdom of the tribe or to the inspired will of the autocrat who rules the tribe or ruled it yesterday.

33. 49. But that is not a complete explanation. 'Surely', the reader will object, 'no set of human beings can be so utterly innocent of social experience as all that. The Germans must have had *some* social experience. They must have repressed it instead of reflecting on it.'

33. 5. This is in fact what happened. There is evidence that as early as the fifteenth century there were Germans who looked upon social experience and the freedom it implies with horror, and clung with passionate zeal to the servitude of a non-social community. The *Imitation of Christ*, by a Rhineland author, Thomas Haemmerlein (1380–1471), contains a whole chapter (i. ix) in dispraise of freedom, beginning: 'It is a great matter to live in obedience; to be under a superior and not to be at our own disposal. It is much safer to obey than to command.' So long has herd-worship been a part of the German tradition.

33. 51. If 'Thomas à Kempis' is here expressing an idea long familiar to his countrymen as a principle of daily life, their own non-participation in the spontaneous 'wave of association' which swept over other European countries three or four centuries earlier (33. 1, note) was deliberate. The movement passed them by because they thrust it from them. When at last they became involved in an echo of it, their horror of freedom twisted it into a new kind of servility.

T

Their universities had to be imposed upon them by popes and princes. Their Reformation exchanged the yoke of Rome for the yoke of princelings of whom it was to be said, in a truly Lutheran spirit, 'cuius regio eius religio'.

33. 52. I said (33. 28) that the introduction of the classical politics into Germany fell as flat as the introduction of a treatise of love into an audience of eunuchs. I withdraw. The case resembled not so much one of impotence as one of fanatical hostility towards sex. The Germans made nonsense of the classical politics because they feared and hated the freedom of social life.

33. 53. No people which had lived so long and so loyally under the conditions of a non-social community could fill up the fatal lacuna in the classical politics by adding to it the one thing it needed, a theory of the non-social community.

33. 54. Living permanently in a non-social community does not enable a man to construct a theory of the non-social community, any more than living permanently in a state of unconsciousness enables a man to construct a theory of un-consciousness.

33. 55. A theory is a product of rational thinking; rational thinking presupposes freedom of the will; and a man who lives at a level below freedom of the will is not in a position to construct a theory of anything whatever.

33. 56. He may, with that imitativeness which so often characterizes low mental development (30. 64), go through the motions of constructing a theory; and to men who can-not or will not think rationally such a mock-theory is just as good as a real theory; probably better, because designed to flatter and please them, and hence greatly superior in their eyes to the truth, which is often neither flattering nor pleasant.

33. 57. The reason why Germans could not construct a theory of the non-social community and thus make good the crying defect of the classical politics is not, however, that they lived in a non-social community, at a level of mental development (therefore) below the level at which theories can be produced. It is not quite so simple as that.

33. 58. It is not that they lacked experience of free will; it is that they had repressed that experience ever since at

least the fifteenth century at the bidding of their most popular leaders.

33. 59. What made Luther the idol of the German people was not his rebellion against the Papacy: it was his fidelity to the German tradition of herd-worship.

33. 6. The German hatred of freedom, reinforced as it was by Luther, did not make Germans incapable of thinking rationally, but it tended to distort their idea of what thinking rationally is.

33. 61. The stronger the hold this tradition has on a German the more powerfully he is driven by a kind of fanatical piety if not to abstain from rational thinking altogether, at least to practise it only with the proviso that it shall redound to the greater glory of the German people.

33. 62. When at length the Western European tradition of scientific thought found a foothold in Germany, the strain arising from the coexistence of these two traditions very soon made itself felt.

33. 63. Strictly speaking, the two are incompatible; but compromises of various sorts can be arranged.

33. 64. The compromise is easiest in natural science, which is perhaps the reason why natural science has been more successful than any other kind in Germany.

33. 65. The German herd-worship need not interfere with natural science at all, provided it is so far relaxed as to permit the worship of truth as well as the worship of the German people.

33. 66. It has, of course, always led German scientists to overestimate the value of their own scientific work and that of other Germans; but this is an error in the history of natural science, not necessarily involving error in natural science itself.

33. 67. In historical studies compromise is harder. Where the German people comes as a character on the stage of history, the quest of truth gives way to quest for the glory of the German people; where it does not, the pious German either loses interest in the story or comforts himself with a substitute: treating ancient Greeks or the like as honorary Germans.

33. 68. Even in the most favourable case, where the conclusions of honest research are flattering to German vanity,

there is no real compromise; there is only a fortunate co-incidence between the claims of truth and the claims of herd-worship.

33. 69. Herd-worship can be indulged, therefore, with no outrage to the claims of truth; for truth now claims nothing that her most implacable enemy, prejudice, need fear to grant.

33. 7. In the political and social sciences herd-worship is fatal. The difficulty of being loyal simultaneously to the German tradition and to the Western European scientific tradition is here at its maximum.

33. 71. The Western European scientific tradition here means approaching the problems of political life by con-centrated reflection on social experience; the German tradi-tion regards social experience, the experience of free men in free partnership, as abominable, and reflection upon it as obscene.

33. 72. The fact that to be a German with intellectual in-terests is to suffer from a divided consciousness, wherein the German tradition of herd-worship is at grips with the Western European tradition of scientific thought, was per-ceived by Nietzsche; who warned his countrymen against the nationalism which, in his own lifetime, was deliberately em-phasizing all that was anti-rational in the German tradition, and exhorted them to be 'good Europeans'.

33. 73. Yet Nietzsche, who died insane, was himself a victim of the disease he diagnosed.

33. 74. It is in his writings that we find the most servile documents of German herd-worship; the self-adoration of the 'blond beast', the *te Deum* of the 'will to power'.

33. 75. The 'State-worship', as it has been called, which is endemic among Germans who have written on politics, is not a genuine State-worship, for it lacks the notion of a state. It is herd-worship.

33. 76. The clearest proof of this is to be found in Marx.

33. 77. At first sight Marx appears to be a very bad case of state-worship. His chief task, according to himself, was to serve as herald for a peculiar kind of revolution: not a 'bourgeois' revolution in which property was to be divided up among small owners, but a 'socialist' revolution in which property was to be transferred to 'the state'.

33. 78. Why it should be taken out of the hands of the 'bourgeoisie' Marx told his disciples at enormous length. But his attack on the 'bourgeoisie' nowhere contains any attempt to state a case against the 'bourgeoisie'. There is demonstration that the 'bourgeoisie' had done pretty badly as owners of property; there is no attempt to show that any alternative owners had done, or would have done, or would do, any better. His diatribes are in fact a rationalization of that purely emotional attitude which a contemporary has described by telling us of the disgust with which, in speaking, he would spit out the word 'bourgeois'.

33. 79. His doctrine that 'the state' was destined to 'wither away' (25. 33) proves that he had no conception of a ruling class, the thing which Machiavelli called a 'state'. When Marx says 'state' he means 'non-social community'. His socialism, based negatively on the traditional German hatred of freedom and hence of the 'capitalists' who are, for him, the chief representatives of freedom in European history, is based positively on the traditional German worship of the herd, and culminates in an act whereby the believer offers himself and everything he has in sacrifice to the adored object. The God of Marxism is a jealous God, and will have no rivals.

33. 8. The same obsession with herd-worship explains the oddest freak of Marx's intellect, his so-called *dialectical materialism*.

33. 81. 'Dialectic', we have seen, is Plato's name for a peaceful, friendly discussion in which the disputants aim at agreement, as opposed to a discussion embittered or rendered warlike by their aiming at victory (24. 61–5).

33. 82. In addition to the psychological value of arriving at agreement a dialectical discussion has the scientific value of arriving at truth when what is discussed is a 'Heraclitean world' in which there is a 'dialectic of things': where 'everything moves and nothing rests' (24. 71–6).

33. 83. Hegel, who did more than any other man to revive the study of Plato and Aristotle in the modern world, not an unmixed blessing (33. 39), reintroduced the Platonic word 'dialectic' in its Platonic sense.

33. 84. In doing so he made at least one very bad mistake. Recognizing that a 'dialectic of words' to be scientifically

valuable must be accompanied by a 'dialectic of things', he inferred that these two dialectics must be processes of the same kind; each must proceed from abstraction, through synthesis with its opposite abstraction, towards the concrete.

33. 85. Hegel thought that a dialectical world is a world where everything *argued itself into existence*.

33. 86. He thought that a Platonic 'dialectic in words' set the standard of a dialectical pattern to which the 'dialectic of things' must conform.

33. 87. This was theology, and anthropomorphic theology of a quite low type. 'In the beginning was the word, and the word was with God, and the word was God.'

33. 88. Hegel says outright that his dialectical logic is an exposition of the nature of God; and that the transition from God to Nature in his *Encyclopaedia* is an exposition of the process whereby God creates Nature.

33. 89. The mistake is the Fallacy of Misplaced Argument. Hegel aims at building up the concrete out of abstractions; not realizing that, unless the concrete is given from the start, the abstractions out of which it is to be built up are not forthcoming (6. 58–9).

33. 9. Now why (I ask) did Marx, instead of eradicating Hegel's mistake, think it enough to '*stand the dialectic on its head*' and make it a 'materialistic' dialectic instead of an 'idealistic' dialectic?

33. 91. It was not because the fallacy is any less fallacious that way up. Either way up, the dialectic deals with abstractions. Either way up, it pretends to extract a concrete rabbit from an abstract hat. Either way up, it fails.

33. 92. No student of history is in doubt as to the bankruptcy of the Hegelian dialectic regarded as an historical method. The fashion of taking it seriously has been dead, even in Germany, for close on a hundred years.

33. 93. The fashion of taking its Marxian inversion seriously still flourishes, but is no better based. It is even worse based; because neo-Marxism has blown the gaff by declaring that 'truth is a bourgeois illusion': where 'truth' means historical truth, and 'bourgeois', as usual in Marxist terminology, is merely an expression of disgust (33. 78); and the whole declaration means: 'dialectical materialism does not lead to historical knowledge; but who wants historical knowledge? it leads to the kind of flapdoodle pious Marxists like to be told.'

33. 94. Why (I ask) did Marx perform this unprofitable operation? 'Because he was stupid enough to think that it would cure the faults of the Hegelian dialectic'? Stupidity, I reply, is not a *vera causa*. If he thought that, I want to know why; and to say 'because he was stupid' is not an answer.

33. 95. 'Because he was comforted by the blessed word materialism'? If so, wherein lay its power to comfort him?

33. 96. Marx came dangerously near confessing the truth when he said that 'idealism' was a 'bourgeois philosophy' and 'materialism' a 'proletarian philosophy'. The statement, taken literally, is a lie; and Marx knew it for one. At least, I do not suppose him so ignorant as not to have known that Holbach, the best-known materialist of the eighteenth century, was a baron; or that there had never been a 'proletarian philosophy' of any kind whatever.

33. 97. What Marx wanted for purposes of herd-worship was to deny the freedom of the will: and that denial he found ready-made in the materialists. It is true, but it would not have been politic to confess it, that the same denial was typical of certain theologians. When it comes to the implications of the formula 'Deus sive Natura' Marx always plays heads I win, tails you lose.

33. 98. Marx hated the 'bourgeois' because (having forgotten, if he had ever known, what feudalism was) he thought of the bourgeois as a man specially addicted to entering into free partnerships: the kind of man who 'knows he is free, and there's an end on't' (13. 17). Marx's loyalty to the German tradition of herd-worship makes him spew out of his mouth as a sinner and a blasphemer whoever thus thinks and thus acts.

33. 99. The same loyalty explains why he converted the Hegelian dialectic into a materialist dialectic. He did not think he had cured the fault of the Hegelian dialectic (33. 9); he did not know it was a fault. He was obsessed by the idea that the freedom of the will must at all costs be denied. That obsession led him to reject Hegel's dialectic. The substitution of a materialistic dialectic, if it changed nothing else, did constitute a denial of freedom of the will and an act of submission to the great German god, the omnipotent herd.

PART III

CIVILIZATION

XXXIV

WHAT 'CIVILIZATION' MEANS: GENERICALLY

34. 1. WE have now to consider what civilization is.

34. 11. Civilization is a thing about which a good deal has been said by many persons over a space of many years. It is not a new subject of discourse. Something has already for a long time been called by that name; the word is established.

34. 12. A word is a linguistic habit (6. 12) of the community using it; the habit of conveying a special meaning by using any member of a certain class of auditory and visual vehicles (6. 17), the class (namely) of which any member is an example of that word.

34. 13. The right method of starting an inquiry into the nature of civilization, then, is to ask what persons have used the word 'civilization' and what they have meant by it.

34. 14. Civilization is a thing of the mind (1. 21); an inquiry into its nature, therefore, belongs to the sciences of mind, and must be pursued by the method proper to those sciences.

34. 15. The principle of this method is that sciences of mind teach men only what they had already reflected on as features of their own consciousness (1. 77).

34. 16. All science is based on facts. The sciences of nature are based on natural facts ascertained by observation and experiment; the sciences of mind are based on mental facts ascertained by reflection.

34. 17. These mental facts are one and all facts of consciousness in its various forms; these being the only constituents of mind (4. 14).

34. 18. Since all thinking is done in words (6. 22), and since every specialized form of consciousness is done 'in' a correspondingly specialized form of language (6. 32), the scientific study of any special class of mental facts must be accompanied by a study of the special language used by men reflecting on those facts.

34. 19. This is why, surprising though it may be to a man who has experience only of natural science, and has not considered how a science of mind would resemble it and how it must differ from it, any scientific study of a thing like civilization must begin with an historical study of the word which has been used as its name; if none has, no data are to hand from which a scientific study could begin.

34. 2. This study must not be abstractly etymological. Etymology inquires into one aspect of a word's history and only one; and not only are its results incomplete unless other aspects are borne in mind, they are not even reliable so far as they go unless they are checked by reference to other aspects.

34. 21. Etymology by itself tells us very little about the meaning of a word like 'civilization', and what little it tells us is not trustworthy.

34. 22. It may tell us that civilization should mean the process of rendering something civil, or the process of becoming civil; or alternatively the state of being civil which is the result of either process.

34. 23. And civil should mean of or belonging to a townsman; so that the process should be one of conversion into, or becoming, a townsman or like a townsman.

34. 24. But this is very little, even granted it is right so far as it goes; far less than we could find out by examination of actual usage. It tells us that civilization implies certain resemblances to a townsman; but it does not tell us what resemblances, nor whether the resemblances are real or imaginary.

34. 25. Nor is it trustworthy. The same etymological argument would tell us that 'circularization' should mean the process of rendering something circular or the process of becoming circular; and the fact that it actually means the process of rendering persons the recipients of a kind of advertisement called a 'circular' throws doubt upon the whole argument.

34. 26. Etymology, in fact, is a good servant to the historical study of language; but a bad master.

34. 27. It is a good servant when it helps to explain why words mean what in fact they do mean.

34. 28. Here it is valuable because it solves a problem arising from the .acts of usage.

34. 29. Unless the facts of usage are known, such problems cannot arise; and there is no worse kind of pseudo-science than that which offers solutions for non-existent problems.

34. 3. We have to inquire into the history of the word 'civilization'.

34. 31. Into the history of some of its usages: not into the history of all.

34. 32. Here is one with which we are not concerned. There is civil law and there is criminal law; there are processes of civil law and there are processes of criminal law; there are cases of the one which have a certain resemblance to cases of the other; enough, perhaps, for them to share a name: for example, libel may be either 'civil libel' or 'criminal libel'.

34. 33. By the effect of a given statute, or a given judgement, or the like, a process of criminal law may be converted into a process of civil law.

34. 34. This conversion of a criminal case into a civil case is called in legal terminology the 'civilization' of that case; and in general the assimilation of criminal to civil law is called 'civilization'.

34. 35. This is one sense in which the word 'civilization' is used, namely as a technical term in law; it is actually the oldest sense of the word to be recorded; but it does not concern us.

34. 36. In the sense which concerns us the word 'civilization' certainly denotes a process, or perhaps the result of a process. Where there is a process there is something which undergoes the process; and it is often possible to know what it is that can undergo a certain process even without knowing what the process is.

34. 37. It is sometimes possible to say that a certain sense of a word cannot be the sense we propose to investigate because, though each sense refers to a process, the sense we propose to investigate refers to a thing of one kind as that which undergoes the process, and this sense refers to a thing of another kind.

34. 38. For example, what undergoes the process of civilization in the legal sense (34. 33) is a criminal case or, in general, criminal law.

34. 39. This, therefore, cannot be the sense we propose to investigate: because in that sense what undergoes the process of civilization is a community.

34. 4. Civilization is *something which happens to a community*.

34. 41. It does not happen, that is to say, except to human beings; and to them it does not happen individually, it happens collectively.

34. 42. To know this is to know something about the usage of words. A man need only know in what kinds of context the word 'glanders' is used in order to know that glanders is something which happens to horses.

34. 43. He need only know in what kinds of context the word 'civilization' (in the sense we are investigating) is used in order to know that it stands for something that happens to men and not any other animals, or to anything not an animal; and to men not singly but in groups; as talking a certain language is a thing that happens to men not singly but in groups.

34. 44. We do not yet know what this thing is.

34. 45. Nor do we know whether the community to which it happens need be a society as opposed to a non-social community, or a non-social community as opposed to a society.

34. 46. If it is a society then (in that case at least) the process of civilizing is an immanent process (20. 38); if it is a non-social community the process is a transeunt process (20. 39). If it may be either, the process of civilizing may be either immanent or transeunt.

34. 5. Civilization is a *process of approximation to an ideal state*.

34. 51. To civilize a thing is to impose on it or promote in it a process; a process of becoming; a process in something which we know to be a community (34. 4), whereby it approaches nearer to an ideal state which I will call *civility* and recedes farther from its contradictory, an ideal state which I will call *barbarity*.

34. 52. These are ideal states, not actual states. No society is just *civil*; no society is just *barbarous*. The state in which any society is actually found to be is a mixture of civility and barbarity, just as the state of the paint in 24. 64

at any given moment was a mixture of white with some other colour.

34. 53. If the paint were getting paler and paler as more and more white was mixed in, the white would gradually predominate, and the other colour would be gradually prevailed over, though it never vanished.

34. 54. There would be an *asymptotic approximation* to white.

34. 55. So in the present case, if the process of *civilizing* is at work, the civil elements in the life of the community are gradually predominating and the barbarous elements are being gradually prevailed over, though the community's condition never becomes one of pure civility and the barbarous elements never vanish.

34. 56. The process of civilization would thus be one of *asymptotic approximation to the ideal condition of civility.*

34. 57. The same would be true of the process at its other end. Just as the community which undergoes civilization never will be purely civil, so it never was purely barbarous and if the process is reversed can never become purely barbarous.

34. 58. All mental processes have this *asymptotic* or *approximative* character. A spatio-temporal process from t_1 to t_2 or from p_1 to p_2 really begins at t_1 or p_1 and really ends at t_2 or p_2; it really begins at its 'initial' point and really ends at its 'terminal' point. But a mental process from ignorance to knowledge or from fear to anger or from cowardice to courage never begins simply at the first term, but always at the first term with a mixture of the second; and never ends simply at the second term, but always at the second term qualified by the first.

34. 59. It is only a victim of wish-fulfilment fantasies who thinks that a mental process from ignorance to knowledge, for example, begins with pure ignorance and ends in pure knowledge. These are 'ideals': they lie outside the process of change leading towards the one and away from the other. To mistake them for 'facts', or terms in that process, is self-deception.

34. 6. I have distinguished (34. 51) *civility* as the name of an ideal state from *civilization* as the name of a process

directed towards that ideal state and leading not to the state itself but only to an approximation to it.

34. 61. This is how Samuel Johnson distinguished them. Boswell has left it on record that he objected to the distinction and urged Johnson to adopt the word 'civilization' for a state opposed to barbarity, which Johnson himself in 1772 wished to call civility. (O.E.D., s.v. 'civility'.)

34. 62. Johnson's use of words showed the finer and more scrupulous correctitude; what justifies Boswell in usurping the name of a process for the name of a state is that in the life of mind there are no states, there are only processes.

34. 63. Every case of mental 'being', so called, turns out on examination to be a case of mental 'becoming'. To describe a community as being in a state of civility, or any state approximating thereto, is a way of saying that it is undergoing a process of civilization; or perhaps, in certain cases, the reverse: a process of *barbarization*.

34. 64. Boswell has triumphed; and the state Johnson wished to call 'civility' is now in standard English called 'civilization'.

34. 65. If I have preferred in a previous paragraph (34. 51) to follow Johnson's usage, it is not that I grudge Boswell his success or seek to put the clock back, but only that I wish to set clearly before the reader certain distinctions often confused in the current English of to-day.

34. 66. Whether civility is one ideal or many ideals I will not yet ask; but even if it is one ideal there may be many approximations to that ideal, differing among themselves as shots on a target may differ not only as being at different distances from the centre but as being distant from it in different directions.

34. 67. Each shot is called a 'civilization'. Different communities, each of which has undergone the process of civilization in a certain way and to a certain degree, exhibit different conditions as the results that this process has severally achieved in them.

34. 68. To borrow the name of a process, as Boswell did, for the name of the ideal aimed at in the process, is one thing; and only with difficulty defensible.

34. 69. To borrow the name of a process for the result

arrived at in an instance of the process is a different thing, amply supported by precedent in many languages, and (if any defence is needed) easily defensible.

34. 7. '*Civility*' is the name I use (following English custom established for several centuries) for the ideal condition into which whoever is trying to civilize a community is trying to bring it.

34. 71. '*Barbarity*' I use for the condition out of which whoever is trying to civilize a community is trying to bring it.

34. 72. To '*civilize*' a community is to try to bring it into a condition of civility.

34. 73. To '*barbarize*' a community means bringing or trying to bring a community into a condition of barbarity.

34. 74. '*Civilization*' I use, as I find it used, in three senses.

34. 75. In sense (I) it is used for *the process itself* (Johnson's sense).

34. 76. In sense (II) it is used for *the condition to which in a given case it leads*: the result of the process.

34. 77. In sense (III) it is used as *equivalent to* '*civility*' (as in 34. 7; Boswell's sense).

34. 78. For symmetry's sake I admit as justifiable three corresponding senses of the word '*Barbarism*'.

34. 79. (I) as a name for *the process of barbarizing*; (II) as a name for *the condition to which in a given case that process leads*; (III) as *equivalent to* '*barbarity*'.

34. 8. The only possible method of constructing a terminology suitable for use in a science of mind is by using words already current in the language you are adopting, and using them with scrupulous attention to the facts of usage as already established in that language.

34. 81. These are the facts upon which the science is based (34. 19); and the surest way of knowing whether a professed exponent of the science is a scientist or a charlatan is by finding out whether he treats them respectfully or contemptuously.

34. 82. A man who, professing to expound a science of mind, defines terms belonging to that science as meaning what they do not mean in the language to which they belong is poisoning the wells of truth.

34. 83. He is falsifying the facts on which his science depends like a hydrographer who, when soundings give him fifty fathoms, should take his pen quickly and write down a hundred; or like a meteorologist who, when his thermometer reads sixty, should write thirty.

34. 84. His motives are no doubt intelligible. Inquiries into the history of word-meanings are laborious; except to a man who has exercised himself in them for many years, they present almost insuperable difficulties. And men are expected to pose as masters in these sciences without spending time on such inquiries; just as men were once expected to teach anatomy without spending time on dissecting corpses.

34. 85. For the most part these motives are frankly discreditable. Most of them proceed from the vested interests of ignorance and error; some from the innocent delight in fantasy, the personal fantasy of an individual or the collective fantasy of a school of thought, guiltily usurping the place due to the very different delight in scientific work; others from the desire that a system of errors which brings in a pretty good return to the conservatives or agitators who trade upon it should be exempted from criticism.

34. 86. Other motives are almost laudable. Natural science has won a long battle for recognition; and naturally it persecutes in its turn. Naturally, too, its persecution is decently cloaked beneath a veil of sweet reasonableness.

34. 87. 'Falsify a sounding or a thermometer-reading? Monstrous! No one, of course, would do such a thing; if he did, hanging would be too good for him.'

34. 88. 'But why should anybody care if the word "civilization" is used in three senses? What is there about that fact which demands our respect? People use a word in as many senses as their whim dictates. Surely the study of whims can never lead to science.'

34. 89. Thus professed friends of natural science, representing a vested interest now for once allied with the vested interests of ignorance and error, argue that a science of mind ought not to be attempted because, if the thing were done, the monopoly of natural science as the only form of organized knowledge in existence would be infringed.

34. 9. The definitions I have propounded above (34.

7–79) are in harmony with modern usage as regards the plurality of senses (three are in fact recognized) ascribed to the word 'civilization'.

34. 91. They are also in harmony with modern usage in recognizing that, whether or no the civilizing process everywhere and always aims at the same ideal, it leads in different places and at different times to different results.

34. 92. For we speak of 'Bronze Age civilization' as a constellation of historical facts different in character from 'Neolithic civilization'; of 'Chinese civilization' as different in character from 'Indian civilization'; and so on, where the word 'civilization' is used in sense II.

34. 93. In speaking thus we neither assert nor deny that the creators of one such 'civilization' are trying to do at bottom the same kind of thing as the creators of another, namely to bring a given community into a condition of 'civility'.

34. 94. We are free to assert this and equally free to deny it. The denial would only involve striking an admittedly obsolete word, 'civility', out of our vocabulary, and out of our thought whatever it stands for.

34. 95. If we deny it, we maintain that all the creators of a particular civilization aim at creating is the civilization they do in fact create.

34. 96. If we assert it, we maintain that there is a difference between the civility they aim at creating and the civilization (in sense II) which they create; somewhat as men who create a particular society aim at creating a universal society but, owing to facts over which they have no control, find it turning under their hands into a particular society (21. 54).

XXXV

WHAT 'CIVILIZATION' MEANS: SPECIFICALLY

35. 1. THE preceding chapter has shown that 'civilization' is primarily the name of a process whereby a community (34. 4) undergoes a mental (34. 14) change from a condition of relative *barbarity* to one of relative *civility*.

35. 11. Let us ignore for the present the fact that the same word is also used for the result of this process (34. 76) and the ideal towards which the process is directed (34. 77) but which it never fully realizes; to which it makes what I have called (rather disgustingly) asymptotic approximation (34. 56).

35. 12. When once we know what the word means in the first sense, the other two will present no difficulty.

35. 13. The preceding chapter has not told us what the word means in any one of its various senses: it has only told us what it means 'generically', leaving this chapter to settle what it means 'specifically'.

35. 14. It is as if we had wanted to know what a caracal is, and the preceding chapter had told us it was a kind of cat.

35. 15. We should still want to know what kind of cat.

35. 16. 'Civilization' in sense I, we know, means a process taking place in a community of asymptotic approximation towards an ideal condition.

35. 17. We still want to know how it differs from other such processes.

35. 18. Towards answering that question we have as yet no information.

35. 19. We know that another ideal condition called barbarity is opposite to the one in question; but that, too, is a word whose meaning we do not know.

35. 2. I find the word used in two ways, with the implication that the two things to which it applies are not two kinds of civilization (still less two senses of the word 'civilization') but two constituents of civilization.

35. 21. The generic formula for any definition of civilization in the first of the three senses above distinguished runs as follows.

35. 22. ' "Civilization" in sense I of the word means the process whereby a community, whether by its own efforts or by the efforts of something other than its own corporate will, becomes more x.'

35. 23. The missing word x will be differently filled in according as the specific character of the process (or, which amounts to the same thing, of the ideal condition at which the process is directed) is differently identified.

35. 24. Finding it currently identified as a compound containing two constituents (let us call them a and b), I substitute $(a+b)$ for x and proceed to evaluate a and b.

35. 25. A community is to its own members a 'we'. Now a self, an 'I', is always correlative to a not-self, a 'not-I' (8. 16). Similarly a 'we' is always *correlative to a 'not-we'*.

35. 26. A thing that is not myself may be an absolute 'not-I', not a self at all but a piece of unconscious matter; or it may be a relative 'not-I', a self in its own right, an 'I' to itself, but an 'I' other than myself.

35. 27. Similarly a 'not-we' may be an *absolute 'not-we'*; not a community at all; something of which no one thinks as 'we'; a whole of parts each of which is a piece of unconscious matter.

35. 28. Or it may be a *relative 'not-we'*; a community, but one of which I am not a member; something which is a 'we' to one of its own members but which to me is a 'you' or a 'they'.

35. 3. Let us regard the first constituent (a) of civilization as concerned with the relation of a community to itself; the relation of its members to one another.

35. 31. Then the second (b) will concern the relation of the community to what is outside the community.

35. 32. This will be subdivided into b_1 and b_2. First comes the relation between any member of the community and anything which forms part of the natural world, a piece of unconscious matter.

35. 33. Second comes the relation between any member of the community and any member of a different community.

35. 34. According to the view I find expressed in books I have looked at, and in the mouths of persons I have questioned to find out what the thing called civilization is commonly thought to involve, civilization has something to do with the mutual relations of members within a community; something to do with the relation of these members to the world of nature; and something to do with the relation between them and other human beings not being members of the same community.

35. 35. In relation to members of the same community, civilization means *coming to obey rules of civil intercourse.*

35. 36. In relation to the natural world civilization means *exploitation*; or, to be more exact, *scientific or intelligent exploitation.*

35. 37. In relation to the members of other communities it means something more complicated than that; something I would rather not try to summarize in half a dozen words. I will return to the question in 35. 6.

35. 38. The two constituents of civilization which I called *a* and *b* (35. 24) have now turned into three: civilization within the community as affecting the relation of any one member to any other; civilization outside the community as affecting the relation between members of the community and things in the world of nature; and civilization outside the community as affecting the relation between members of the community and members of other communities.

35. 39. Let us consider these separately.

35. 4. If the civilization of a community means the process of bringing it into a condition of civility (34. 72), and if the first constituent of civilization concerns the relation between any one member of that community and any other (35. 38), the first constituent is the process of bringing members of the community to *behave 'civilly' to one another.*

35. 41. Behaving 'civilly' to a man means respecting his feelings: abstaining from shocking him, annoying him, frightening him, or (briefly) arousing in him any passion or desire which might diminish his self-respect (13. 31); that is, threaten his consciousness of freedom by making him feel that his power of choice is in danger of breaking down and the passion or desire likely to take charge (13. 67).

35. 42. How the word 'civil' came to have this meaning I will not inquire. It had already done so in ancient Latin. The meaning is not peculiar to the medieval and modern development of a Latin word.

35..43. To behave towards a man in such a way as to arouse in him uncontrollable passions or desires, with the resulting breakdown of his will, is *to exercise force over him* (20. 5 seqq.).

35. 44. The ideal of civil behaviour in one's dealings with one's fellow-men, therefore, is the ideal of *refraining from the use of force towards them.*

35. 45. The first constituent of civilization is thus a system of conduct so determining the relations of members within a civilized community that each refrains from the use of force in his dealings with the rest.

35. 46. Or rather, refrains so far as possible; for civility is only an ideal condition to which the process of civilization brings about an asymptotic approximation (34. 56).

35. 47. Complete civility between all members of the community is a counsel of perfection, not susceptible of realization in practice or as a first-order object.

35. 48. Circumstances arise in which there is no doing without force; and there are no circumstances in which a certain degree of force, open or concealed, is not needed for the very existence of a community. A community must be a community before it is a civilized community; the degree and kind of force which the existence of a community demands, though it involves a departure from the ideal of civility, must be provided for in the rules of civilization.

35. 49. Civilization is not civilization but barbarity unless it insists that you shall treat every member of your community as civilly as possible; it is not civilization but Utopia unless it distinguishes occasions on which you simply must be civil from others on which you may (and indeed, even for civility's sake, must) be uncivil.

35. 5. A community that is 'civil' in relation to the natural world is one which (*a*) gets from the world of nature what it needs in the way of food, clothing, and satisfactions for the other demands it makes upon that world; (*b*) not merely gets these things but gets them as the fruit of its own industry; not receiving them as gifts but earning them by its own efforts; (*c*) gets them not merely by labour but by intelligent labour: a labour directed and controlled by scientific understanding of that natural world which it aims at converting into a source of supply for man's demands.

35. 51. The first of these three conditions, so far from entitling a community to be called civilized, does not even entitle it to be called animal. The grass of the field gets from the natural world what it needs in the way of food, clothing ('Even Solomon in all his glory. . .'), and so forth. If it dies in the heat it has no grievance against Nature, who promises none of her creatures eternal life, or even long life, but only death.

35. 52. The second condition, so far from entitling a community to be called civilized, does not even entitle it to be called human. Bees and ants, the early bird and the lion roaring after its prey, get what they need of the world around them by their own labour.

35. 53. The same is to some extent true even of man, in so far as he is what we call 'savage' or devoid of civilization. What we mean by a 'savage' community is one which can only get out of the natural world what it can extort thence through sheer labour unmitigated by thought; one which has not learned to save its muscles by using its brains. To learn that lesson, piecemeal as alone it can be learned, is to become civilized relatively to the world of nature: to progress in the second constituent of civilization.

35. 54. I have used the word 'civil' (35. 5) for the ideal towards which this involves an approximation. The ideal is to get out of the natural world everything you need of it by a combination of labour and science, or muscle-work and brain-work.

35. 55. Unlike the sense of the word 'civil' previously mentioned (35. 42) this is not an old Latin sense; it is a modern sense, found especially in such derivatives of the Latin word as 'civilità', 'civilité', 'civility', a Renaissance group of words whose central idea is that man can increase his ability to get what he needs out of the natural world by coming to understand it better, and that to advance in such understanding of the natural world is to become more 'civilized' in relation to it.

35. 56. I have spoken of man as getting from the natural world what he needs in the way of food, clothing, &c. (35. 5). It would be well to explain what is meant by the word 'needs'.

35. 57. There is a superstition to the effect that some

things are *necessary* to man; and that when he demands them of Nature or of his fellow-man he is only demanding what he has a right to receive. Among these are, for example, enough food to support life. If he demands anything in excess of these necessaries what he asks for is a *luxury*, a thing which it is pleasant to have, but one to which he has no peremptory claim or indefeasible right.

35.58. This is nonsense. There are no necessaries. Nature recognizes no more right to live in a man than in a wild flower (35. 51). What man needs of the natural world is what he thinks he can get from it. His catalogue of these needs undergoes expansion as his consciousness of power over the world of nature expands. As men become, in this second sense of the word, more 'civilized', what passed for luxuries are constantly being transferred into the list of necessaries, and new luxuries are constantly being invented.

35. 59. And what is a luxury to a higher civilization is not a luxury to one at a lower level of development; which may answer its boasts with an 'incredulus odi'. I spoke once with a peasant who lived in what I thought the extreme of poverty on the plains of Estremadura, and shamefacedly confessed, in answer to his question, that I owned no donkeys. 'Now I know', said he, with the smile of a man whose leg is unsuccessfully pulled, 'that you are amusing yourself at my expense; for if you had no donkeys how could you bring water from the river?'

35. 6. To the members of a given community the question whether civilization involves an increase in civility *towards members of other communities* is a difficult one to answer (35. 37).

35. 61. How they answer it depends on how they answer the notoriously difficult question: 'Are foreigners human?'

35. 62. If the answer to this second question is 'yes', the ideal of civility comes into operation as regards our relation to foreigners.

35. 63. For civility requires civil demeanour to whatever is recognized as possessing it. If foreigners are human, civility requires that we should treat them civilly; and in proportion as we are civilized the rules of our civilization give them a right to civility at our hands.

35. 64. If the answer is 'no', foreigners are a part of the natural world; and are there to be exploited as scientifically as possible.

35. 65. It makes no difference whether they share our home or not; in neither case does our civilization put us under any obligation to treat them civilly.

35. 66. *Strangers* (i.e. foreigners not sharing our communal home) are in fact often treated with the utmost incivility; often, for example, murdered with impunity and a clear conscience even by peoples who enjoy a relatively high civilization.

35. 67. This happens in spite of a conviction that all human beings ought to be civilly treated; all that is lacking is a conviction that strangers are human beings.

35. 68. How does this conviction arise, if and when it does, where at first it is lacking? Through experience of common action with the erstwhile strangers, setting up a social consciousness on our part in virtue of which we recognize them as part and parcel of ourselves.

35. 69. One kind of common action is commercial action. A community accustomed to trade with strangers is commonly accustomed to treat strangers with civility.

35. 7. *Metics* (to use the Greek word for foreigners who share with us our communal home) are often, even by communities with a relatively high civilization, no better treated. Cases are too common to need quotation; I will refer only to C. M. Doughty's life as a metic among the Arabs.

35. 71. The cause is the same: the metic is not thought altogether human. And, once more, this opinion can be changed by engaging with him in a course of common action, sustained until it generates a social consciousness.

35. 72. The social consciousness on my part towards a foreigner, which brings him from my point of view within the circle of human beings and converts him from something I exploit or even, if so disposed, murder with a clear conscience into something which in proportion as I am a civilized man I have to treat civilly, and see to it that others shall treat civilly, is an entirely different thing from an affectionate or expansive emotion, what is called 'liking' him or 'being fond of' him.

35. 73. The first (promoted, as I say, by trading with

foreigners) is promoted by travelling among them; the second is so far from being promoted by foreign travel that a cynic might be pardoned if he described men as travelling in order to make sure that foreigners really deserved their hatred.

35. 74. Conversely, people who keep pigs love them tenderly, but that does not prevent them from murdering the objects of their affection.

35. 75. And people may be fond enough of foreigners (whether subjects of a nation, or members of a class within the same nation, other than their own), yet never think of them as really human and never treat them with civility.

35. 76. In short, 'being fond of' an object is quite consistent with an uncivil demeanour (i.e. the use of force) towards it, or even an uncivilized demeanour (i.e. the use of force where there is no need of force) towards it; even though the object is in fact human and therefore, according to the ideal of civility, entitled to civil treatment, or according to the rules of civilization entitled to civilized treatment.

35. 77. And understanding the obligation to civil or civilized treatment of an object is quite consistent with disliking it; so much so that a man who excuses himself for incivility towards *x* on the ground that he loathes, hates, or fears *x* is offering no excuse whatever.

35. 78. It may be right to distinguish *incivility* from *cruelty*. For though 'the utmost incivility' may amount to murder (35. 66) there seems to be a difference in kind between even the grossest and beastliest incivility, the sort that would not trouble to warn a man before firing a shot where his head happens to be, and the cruelty of killing or hurting him for the sake of killing or hurting him.

35. 79. That is true; but from the victim's point of view the distinction is too refined to be of much interest. And in any case the ideal of civility excludes both.

35. 8. These considerations do not excuse us from dealing with the question. The point of view with which we are concerned is that of the civilized man, not those towards whom his civilization prescribes his demeanour.

35. 81. Granted a civilizing process which has not gone very far, or one whose results have been to a great extent destroyed by a counter-process of barbarization (34. 73), the ideal of treating men outside the community as human beings, or treating them civilly, may have been to any extent (short, I suppose, of completeness) superseded by the ideal of treating them as parts of the natural world: that is, forcibly.

35. 82. According to the degree of civilization (or barbarism) thus produced the community will treat non-members with a more or less complete lack of civility; in all cases, more or less, where civility could be used, replacing it by force.

35. 83. This will involve a more or less ruthless exploitation; or, to be more exact, scientific or intelligent exploitation (35. 36) of the stranger (35. 66) and the metic (35. 7).

35. 84. And such exploitation will be justified and indeed prescribed by the rules of the civilization adopted by the community.

35. 85. Our question is this: Granted that a civilization of admittedly low type can make it a rule to reduce non-members of the community to this servile state and to justify it as a rule and as part and parcel of a way of life, can we say the same about reducing non-members to the status of whipping-boys, objects of cruelties practised for the sake of cruelty?

35. 86. Members of such a community might answer: 'Such employment of metics or other aliens is a legitimate article of our civilization. The exploitation of the alien is barred, by your own account, only from a civilization of Utopian purity. In all civilizations that actually exist in an imperfect world, such as ours (for we are no hypocrites) it goes on unrebuked.

35. 87. 'How you exploit the world around you depends on what you think you can get out of it. We have a psychological need to inflict suffering. We are sadists. Explain it if you can, but at least face it. What we need of the world around us is victims for our sadistic impulses. We need someone to torture. You admit that we may legitimately exploit our aliens. Torturing them is our way of exploiting them.'

35. 88. If I should allow torture to be called exploitation (which I do not) I should still draw the line at calling it scientific or intelligent exploitation (35. 83).

35. 9. What is this 'psychological need to inflict suffering'

(35. 87)? Is it something like the ungovernable impulses of passion and desire? or is it the fruit of calm deliberation, a thing under the control of the will?

35. 91. If it is the second, why do they plead it as an excuse for a course of conduct they have reason to think unpopular? It is, of course, the first. They confess to acting in an unpopular way from uncontrollable impulse.

35. 92. We can pity a sadist, but we cannot allow him to be observing the rules of his own civilization. He has no civilization. He is nearer akin to a Yahoo than to the *animal rationale* that obeys the rules of a civilization, whether high or low.

35. 93. To be a human brute of that kind is a hideous fate. But it is human brutes, not votaries of a peculiar civilization, that gave us the answer (35. 86–7) to our question (35. 85). This is not a civilization; it is a barbarism.

XXXVI

THE ESSENCE OF CIVILIZATION

36. 1. GENERICALLY, civilization is a mental process which goes on in a community (35. 1).

36. 11. Specifically we have found it described as a combination of two such processes or perhaps three.

36. 12. The first is a process whereby the members of that community become less addicted to force in their dealings with one another (35. 4).

36. 13. The second is one whereby they become more able to get what necessaries or luxuries they demand for the maintenance and amelioration of their life by the intelligent or scientific exploitation of the natural world (35. 5).

36. 14. The third is one whereby, originally treating men outside their own community under the second head, as natural things to be exploited for their benefit, they come to consider them under the first head, as human beings and therefore as much entitled to civility as if they had been members of the community.

36. 15. It does not much matter whether we reckon these as two characteristics of civilization (one concerned with man and one concerned with nature) or as three (one concerned with man, one with nature, and one with what may be treated either as man or as nature); or even as four.

36. 16. In any case we are reckoning them as more than one.

36. 17. I have protested (6. 11 seqq.) against the doctrine that a term is rendered fit for scientific use only by being defined. What renders it fit for scientific use is having its usage settled.

36. 18. But, as against the irrationalists who believe in 'indefinables', or in other words claim licence to unsettle usages and use terms arbitrarily at the dictate of any momentary whim, I have insisted (6. 16) that wherever the usage of a word has been settled it can be described, that is, the word can be defined.

36. 19. According to the traditional logic a definition must state the essence of the term to be defined: and the essence of a term (in this case the term civilization) can only involve one differentia.

36. 2. Where there are two differentiae (e.g. 'an isosceles triangle has two sides equal *and two angles equal*') the definition is faulty; one of the two ought to be shown to follow as a necessary consequence from the other.

36. 21. But is not this whole doctrine of definition, as it stands in the old logic-books, abrogated by the Principle of Limited Objective (31. 61) with its destructive consequences to the idea of essence?

36. 22. No, it is not abrogated; only modified. According to the Principle of Limited Objective, indeed, it is no longer held that the properties of a given thing can be exhaustively deduced from one single essence, but there is still what may be called a 'relative essence', an 'essence from our point of view', where 'we' are the persons engaged in a certain kind of scientific inquiry such as the mathematical physics of the 'classical' physicists.

36. 23. 'We' use a given term in a definite way, and the 'relative essence' is the essence as corresponding with that usage. From this 'relative essence' can be deduced, not indeed all the properties of the thing in question, but all those with which our special kind of science is able to deal.

36. 24. Whether they are two or three in number, the characteristics of civilization, regarded as its 'differentiae', must be reduced to one.

36. 25. What connexion is there between a spirit of civility towards our fellow-men and a spirit of intelligent exploitation towards the world of nature?

36. 26. If we can find that connexion, we shall be able to treat the two (or possibly three) characteristics mentioned above as 'properties' of civilization, or logical consequences of its essence (36. 23).

36. 27. Moreover we shall perhaps be able, when we begin looking for them, to detect other logical consequences and thus increase our brief list of the characteristics of civilization; which as it now stands is merely the outcome of reading and conversation (35. 34) of a desultory kind.

36. 28. Increase it, but not complete it. There can be no completeness in an inquiry of this kind.

36. 3. The intelligent exploitation of the natural world involves the scientific study of the natural world, that is, natural science.

36. 31. Not necessarily a highly technical form of natural science; it may well be one wholly innocent of laboratories and differential (or even simple) equations; a natural science more akin to folklore than to mathematics, riddled with superstition, and from the point of view of a twentieth-century 'scientist' lamentably unscientific.

36. 32. The sort of natural science which is inseparable from an intelligent exploitation of the natural world means watching, and remembering, and handing down from father to son, things which it is useful for a hunter or a shepherd or a fisherman or a farmer or a sailor or a miner or the like to know: things about the seasons, the weather, the soil, the subsoil, the habits of game and fish and domestic animals and vermin; how to get materials for the implements needed in these various crafts, and how to work them up into finished articles and how to use and keep and mend these articles when made: the sort of 'natural science', if I may call it by that name, which was mostly discovered in what we call the Neolithic Age, and of which the chief masters among ourselves are what we call (I suppose for a joke) Unskilled Agricultural Labourers.·

36. 33. If a community has attained any degree, high or low, of civilization relatively to the natural world, it is by acquiring and conserving an incredible amount of this sort of natural science. Partly, no doubt, by improving on it; but in this kind of science improving on what is handed down to us is far less important than conserving it; a fact which it is well to remember.

36. 34. The proportion between the two things has been much misunderstood in the last century or two when for accidental and temporary reasons Europeans have attached too much importance to invention and too little to conservation.

36. 35. Consider knots. The life of every sailor, the catch of every fisherman, and a thousand other things of varying importance, depend on knowing that a knot you have tied will not come untied until you set out to untie it, and will quickly come untied when you do.

36. 36. There are forty or fifty knots; less than twenty are in regular use.

36. 37. None has been invented at any known time, in any known place, by any known person. All are of immemorial antiquity.

36. 38. For some thousands of years at least, therefore, the tradition of tying a quite small number of simple and reliable knots has been conserved; no new inventions have been added to it, because the purposes for which knots are needed are few and adequately provided for.

36. 39. There is nothing to be gained by inventing a new knot; there is almost incredibly much to be lost by failure to conserve the tradition of knot-tying that we have.

36. 4. The 'arts' or 'practical sciences' which are the basis of all man's civilization relatively to the natural world are common property.

36. 41. I do not mean that no one man invented the bowline. Any one accustomed to knots will agree that some one man did; a man in whose presence a fellow-inventor consisting of Archimedes and Gutenberg and George Stephenson and Edison, rolled into one, would hide his diminished head.

36. 42. I mean that to perpetuate an invention like this has been the joint work of nameless and numberless millions of men combined by doing so into a vast and mutually unknown society whose members owe, this his life (how many times over?), that his catch of fish, the other his protection from the weather, to the nameless genius whose knot they have learned to use.

36. 43. Think of the society assembled; imagine its resurrection in response to a Last Trump signalling: 'This way, all who can tie a bowline.'

36. 44. 'Will they hold torches, and pass them from hand to hand as they ride the race?'

36. 45. The gradual building-up and storing of all this knowledge of which the bowline is an infinitesimal fraction is the gradual building-up and garnering of human civilization relatively to the natural world.

36. 46. The mainspring of the whole process is the spirit of agreement. So vast a body of knowledge (I call it knowledge, but it is not the kind of thing logicians call knowledge; it is all practical knowledge, knowing how to tie a bowline, knowing how to swim, knowing how to help a lambing ewe, how to tickle a trout, where to pitch a tent, when to plough and when to sow and when to harvest your crop) can only be brought together in a community (for it is too vast for the mind of one man) whose custom is that everybody who has anything to teach to anyone else who wants to know it shall teach it; and that everybody who does not know a thing that may be useful for the betterment of living shall go frankly to one who knows it, and listen while he explains it or watch while he shows it, confident by custom of a civil answer to a civil question.

36. 5. There. It is out. We have the connexion for which we were looking (36. 25). The missing word is civility.

36. 51. Civility as between man and man, members of the same community, is not only what constitutes the civilization of that community relatively to the human world; it is also what makes possible that community's civilization relatively to the natural world.

36. 52. This is a thing we take too lightly. We are the beneficiaries of an ancestral, prehistoric civility which we take too much for granted.

36. 53. A character in a dialogue of Plato addresses another, famous for his store of information: 'I beg you, if you know the answer to this question, tell it me; be generous of your knowledge; don't grudge me your treasure (μὴ φθονήσῃς)'.

36. 54. How civilized! we exclaim. How enlightened of these ancient Greeks to talk about mere knowledge as if it were gold or silver!

36. 55. Centuries later we find Chaucer writing of his poor clerk: 'And gladly would he learn, and gladly teach.'

36. 56. How admirable, we think, and how strange! Here we are in the howling wilderness of fourteenth-century England; and here, depicted by the poet who of all poets is least given to paint fancy pictures, to flatter any man or any class of men, rides a threadbare scholar whose only passions are a miserly greed to acquire knowledge and a princely generosity to share it.

36. 57. But in the times we lightly call barbarous, then and for many centuries earlier, unless men had been in sober fact

as greedy of knowledge and as generous of it as Chaucer and Plato describe them, there would never have been any civilization at all; none of the arts of civilization would have been discovered, or, if once discovered, imparted.

36. 58. Do you suspect me, Reader, of refurbishing the old stories of the Golden Age? Do you brush aside my fancy picture of a distant past when men were glad to teach and glad to learn with the latest catchword of bogus anthropology: 'No savage ever invented anything; all they possess is decayed scraps from the cultures of more civilized peoples'?

36. 59. Origins do not matter. Who invented the bowline? *Ignoramus, ignorabimus.* How did he invent it? *Ignoramus, ignorabimus.* I cannot conceive how anybody ever did anything so brilliant. Nor (confess it) can you. But how, once invented, was it transmitted? In general terms I know the answer. The conditions for such an event are that there should be a community in which inventions are not hoarded, but taught; that there should be men who know them and are willing to teach them, and men who do not know them and are willing to learn them.

36. 6. If that is a Golden Age, the picture (I mean) of a condition so different from our own that we cannot soberly believe it ever to have existed, then God help us as anthropologists; for we cannot explain, with all our myths about diffusion, how any civilization, however low, ever continued in existence for more than a single generation. We are diffusionists who do not believe in diffusion.

36. 61. And God help our children; for if we have really lost the will to teach, then of all the civilization our ancestors have left us they will inherit nothing.

36. 62. It is not a Golden Age. The passion for learning and the passion for teaching have not disappeared from humanity. They still live.

36. 63. It is as true as when Aristotle wrote it that all men have a natural desire for knowledge.

36. 64. It is true, too, that all men have a natural desire to impart knowledge.

36. 65. That there is also a desire, at war with this, to gain power over men by monopolizing knowledge I do not deny.

36. 66. But although there is certainly an eristic of know-

ledge, a tendency to make it a matter of contention and competition and monopoly, there is also a dialectic of knowledge, a tendency to make it a matter of agreement and co-operation and sharing.

36. 7. This is the origin and essence of civilization. Civilization, even in its crudest and most barbarous form, in part consists in civility and in part depends on civility: consists in it so far as it consists in relations of man to man; depends on it so far as it consists in relations of man to nature.

36. 71. Hobbes thought (utilitarian that he was, like all the men of his century) that men were naturally enemies to each other, but that reason taught them to avoid the frightful consequences of mutual enmity by deciding to make friends.

36. 72. He was right to think that men are 'naturally' enemies to each other; so they are; but they are 'naturally' friends too.

36. 73. Human co-operation does not rest, as Hobbes thought, on so feeble a foundation as human reason.

36. 74. Reason supports it, and powerfully; but it does not originate it.

36. 75. There is no aspect or cross-section of human life in which we do not find, inextricably confused, the need of man for man and the hostility of man for man.

36. 76. They first appear as a feeling of pleasure in human propinquity to ourselves and a feeling of pain in human propinquity to ourselves. They reappear in appetite as an inclination to associate with our fellow-men and an inclination to separate ourselves from our fellow-men.

36. 77. We try to segregate these two appetites by focusing our affections on human beings we 'like' (with whom we want to associate) and others whom we 'dislike' (from whom we want to dissociate ourselves). But this is a poor compromise. If we look at ourselves with a keen eye we notice ourselves disliking the persons we think of ourselves as liking, and vice versa.

36. 78. When we come to the level of desire the cat is out of the bag. The self, we now know, is correlative with the not-self. Whether we like other people or dislike them is correlative to the question whether we like or dislike ourselves. We do both.

36. 79. The more energetically we try to believe that we are very well pleased with ourselves and other people, the more probable it is that we are in secret deeply dissatisfied with both. And if we pretend that we love our neighbour and dislike ourselves, or love ourselves and dislike our neighbour, our self-deception is pitiable.

36. 8. This is the tangled skein we inherit when we reach the level of will. The situation might seem hopeless but that in a sense we make a fresh start.

36. 81. It is true, but it does not so terribly matter, that our feelings and appetites and passions and desires are inextricably confused and hopelessly contradictory; because, within limits, we can ignore them and make decisions.

36. 82. We cannot prevent ourselves from having these confused emotions of friendliness and unfriendliness to our fellow-men. We cannot prevent them from impelling us towards an 'eristical' life in which we try to hurt and crush and destroy other men, glutting our lust for power on the death and blows we distribute among them, and towards a 'dialectical' life in which we try to live at peace with all men, forming ourselves with them into societies for the prosecution of common purposes arrived at by dint of discussing the situation in which from time to time we find ourselves and the possible methods of dealing with it.

36. 83. But we can now choose which of these two courses, or what compromise between them, we shall adopt. We can now use our wills instead of being blown about by the veering winds of emotion. We can think which we will do, live eristically or live dialectically.

36. 84. Here, with the appearance of free will in human life, begins the process of civilization.

36. 85. Hitherto men have lived in a non-social community held together not by their own wills (hitherto they have none) but by something else; perhaps by psychological forces within them which we call 'instincts', perhaps by the brute force of some human beast or group of human beasts forcing them to live in a kind of harmony.

36. 86. Now they reach intellectual maturity (I am describing it as if it were an event that happened quickly, but it commonly happens piecemeal and very slowly) and realize

that in the non-social community, under the confused rule of emotion, they were being friendly and unfriendly to one another as the fit took them. They will now make up their minds which they are to be.

36. 87. If they decide to make friends, this awakening to free will is an awakening to a process of civilization.

36. 88. The essence of this process is the control of each man's emotions by his intellect: that is, the self-assertion of the man as will.

36. 89. Civilization is the process in a community by which the various members assert themselves as will: severally as individual will, corporately as social will (the two being inseparable, 21. 1 seqq.).

36. 9. Barbarism is a process too. It is the process in which the non-social community, instead of drifting as before on the winds of emotion, accentuates the non-social, non-voluntary, character of its life; hands itself over to the control of emotions which it has contemplated controlling but has decided not to control.

36. 91. The non-social community, to speak in a paradox, resolves itself into a society for the realization of the Yahoo herd (30. 52 seqq.). Whereas civilization means that the non-social community resolves itself into a society for the promotion of free will.

36. 92. A paradox, because the Yahoo herd (being the negation of free will) is the negation of sociality; and there cannot be a society for the suppression of sociality.

36. 93. The will to civilization is just will. The members of any non-social community who, awaking to free will, decide no longer to drift with their emotions, but to take charge of the situation in which they corporately find themselves and do something with it, whatever in particular they decide to do, have embarked on the process of civilizing themselves.

36. 94. The will to barbarism is a will, for otherwise it would not, as it does, break down the non-social community from which it begins; but it is a *will to do nothing*, a will to acquiesce in the chaotic rule of emotion which it began by destroying. All it does is to assert itself as will and then deny itself as will.

XXXVII

CIVILIZATION AS EDUCATION

37. 1. THE process whereby a community becomes civilized is the process whereby its members become free agents: agents possessing and exercising free will (36. 88).

37. 11. To have free will implies being conscious of freedom (13. 18).

37. 12. This consciousness of freedom is self-respect (13. 31).

37. 13. Recognizing one's own freedom is inseparably bound up with recognizing the freedom of others with whom one stands in social relations (21. 19).

37. 14. To recognize the freedom of others is to respect them.

37. 15. The civility about which I have said so much is respect for others as shown in demeanour towards them.

37. 16. Civility towards others is, therefore, inseparably bound up with self-respect.

37. 17. This enables us to distinguish two different kinds of demeanour which are often confused: *civility*, or the demeanour of a self-respecting man towards one whom he respects, and *servility*, or the demeanour of a man lacking self-respect towards one whom he fears.

37. 18. The will to civilization is the will to earn one's own self-respect and the respect of the other members of one's own community; and this is done (36. 93) by the sheer exercise of will, joining with these others to do something about the situation in which you find yourselves.

37. 19. The will to barbarism (a paradoxical phrase, 36. 92) is the will to servility: the will to treat others in a servile spirit and produce in them a servile spirit towards oneself; and this is done by the suicide of will (36. 94).

37. 2. Civilization (34. 4) has been generically described as a process which happens in a community.

37. 21. What kind of community? For a community is either social (a society) or non-social (20. 2, 20. 32); or else it is a complex community (22. 1) like the family or the body politic, part of which is social and part non-social.

37. 22. The preceding chapter has answered this question. Civilization is the process of converting a non-social community into a society. For 'to convert into a society' let us say 'to socialize'; then *to civilize is to socialize.*

37. 23. No reference is here implied to what is called 'socialism'. In that connexion a verb 'to socialize' is sometimes used, but in a sense quite unrelated to this.

37. 24. I have used the name 'civility' (34. 7) for the ideal condition into which whoever is trying to civilize a community is trying to bring it.

37. 25. We now know what civility is. It is sociality. It is the condition in which every member of the community, as a free man in a community of free men, respects himself and all his fellow-members, treats them accordingly, and expects them to treat him likewise.

37. 26. Why call this an 'ideal' condition, and insist that an attempt to realize it can only lead at best to an asymptotic approximation (34. 56) to it?

37. 27. 'For surely' (you may urge) 'it is easy enough to take a non-social community and insist that every member of it behaves civilly to every other'.

37. 28. It is not easy. It is impossible. You may work as hard as you like to turn a non-social community into a society; but you can never finish the job. Every particular society has about it a trace of the non-social community out of which it has emerged (21. 5).

37. 29. You can promulgate rules of civility and punish anyone who breaks them; but at best this will only produce an approximation to civility, and (enforced as it is by punishment) there will always be about it more than a trace of servility.

37. 3. How in fact do people socialize, or civilize, non-social communities?

37. 31. The problem exists in its purest form in the family; for the dialectic of family life involves the augmentation of the parental family-society by incorporating into it the growing children; that is to say, converting the nursery from a non-social community into a society or briefly *civilizing the children.*

37. 32. The reason why, in the tradition of family life as known to us since the Neolithic age at least (36. 32), this business of civilizing the children has on the whole been satisfactorily done (far more satisfactorily than by the public educational institutions which are in essence departments of the nursery managed by specialists) is that *it has not been done by specialists*.

37. 33. It has been done by parents; and parents have an enormous advantage over specialists in two ways.

37. 34. First, *their power over the child is much greater*. To the child, the parent stands for omnipotence as a specialist can never do. The mere division of power between the parent and the educator puts each in a position of vastly diminished strength.

37. 35. Even if, as in Plato's city, the child is taken right out of the parent's hands and put unreservedly into those of the professional educator, and if the professional educator educates him in all subjects and not, by a fatal division of power, in one only (a most important provision if the educator is to have any power over the child) the 'deracination' inflicted on the child by transferring him from the hands of the parent to those of the educator must leave him emotionally disorientated for the rest of his life.

37. 36. Secondly, *the parent as educator has the resourcefulness, the versatility, of a non-specialist*. He is tied to no particular methods; he is judged by no particular results. No specialist can say to a child as, in effect, the parent can: 'It doesn't matter what you do; you are free to do anything you like; all I ask is that you shall do *something*, and try to do it better than you did it last time.'

37. 37. For these two reasons the parent as educator, if he understands the barest elements of his job, *has no failures*. His power over the child enables him to make the child want to do well; his versatility in finding subjects for the child to study, or letting the child find them for himself, enables him to ensure, as nearly as anything in human life can be ensured, that a subject of study will be forthcoming from day to day at which, with that incentive, the child shall do well, and daily progress in the self-confidence of one that knows he can do well.

37. 38. It is pitiable to see men who have 'devoted their lives to education' struggling against overwhelming odds to run schools in such a way that in favourable cases, and granted exceptional ability on their own part, they can excite in pupils a very small fraction of the enthusiasm and the self-confidence that any ordinary parent can excite in his own very ordinary children by taking hardly any trouble at all; and to hear their admirers hailing them as great reformers in the world of education.

37. 39. It is more than pitiable, it is ghastly (if you can think a thing ghastly that happened so long ago) to see Plato, after his long and heroic struggle against the professional educators or 'sophists', enthusiastically giving in to them on what he knew to be the vital issue of all politics, the care of children: taking children out of their parents' hands and turning them over to state-employed professionals, as pleased as Punch because the idea was a nasty knock for 'democracy'.

37. 4. Plato is the man who planted on the European world the crazy idea that education ought to be profession-alized; and, as if that were not enough, the crazier idea that the profession ought to be a public service.

37. 41. The first idea has come true. The loss of power and efficiency it has brought about is beyond my calculating; I will only suggest that this is what is wrong with European civilization.

37. 42. It has entrusted the conservation of its own tradi-tions to a class of persons who, owing to their position, have not the power to conserve them. By doing this it has put itself as much at a disadvantage, as compared with peoples it calls barbarous, as if it were a tribe which threw away the paddles of its war-canoes, set sail, and employed crews of professional medicine-men to whistle for a wind.

37. 43. William Cobbett has described how he brought up his children *mutatis mutandis* precisely as 'savages' bring up theirs; by joining in their daily lives and encouraging them to join in his own.

37. 44. 'The book-learning crept in of its own accord. Children naturally want to be like their parents, and to do what they do; and as I was always writing or reading, mine naturally desired to do something in the same way. Fond of book-learning, and knowing well its powers, I naturally

wished them to possess it too; but never did I impose it upon any one of them.

37. 45. 'I accomplished my purpose indirectly. Health was secured by the deeply interesting and never-ending sports of the field and pleasures of the garden. Luckily these things were treated of in books and pictures of endless variety; so that, on wet days, in long evenings, these came into play.

37. 46. 'A large strong table in the middle of the room, their mother sitting at her work, used to be surrounded with them, the baby, if big enough, set up in a high chair. Here were inkstands, pens, pencils, india-rubber, and paper, all in abundance, and everyone scribbled about as he or she pleased . . .'

37. 47. 'All the meddlings and teasings of friends and, what was more serious, the pressing prayers of their anxious mother, about sending them to school, I withstood without the slightest effect on my resolution.'

37. 48. ' "Bless me, so tall, and not learned anything yet!" "Oh, yes, he has," I used to say, "he has learned to ride, and hunt, and shoot and fish, and look after cattle and sheep, and to work in the garden, and to feed his dogs, and to go from village to village in the dark." '

37. 5. 'Cobbett could do it; he made his living by farming and writing at home. He was not tied to an office all day like us.'

37. 51. Very true; but is that really your reason for not doing like him? Or is it that you have not the courage to educate your own children; but prefer to hand it over to professionals so that, in time, they can wear a recognizable old school tie?

37. 52. You don't know. Very few people do know as much about themselves as that.

37. 53. Cobbett's method is so vastly more efficient than any method which can possibly be used in a school, that a very little of it would produce better-educated children than a far greater amount of even the best schooling.

37. 54. You probably think the opposite; you probably think that the professional is more efficient. Look back at

37. 34–7.

37. 55. But in a world of office-drudges and factory-drudges to ask for even a little of Cobbett's method is to ask for the moon.

37. 56. That is, no doubt, a good reason for smashing a world of office-drudges and factory-drudges. Not simply that it is a world unfit for men to live in; but it is a world consuming its own capital of civilization through having wantonly thrown away the power of educating its young, and is heading straight for bankruptcy.

37. 57. And what are we to have instead? Not the world of Fascist or Nazi dreams; that is simply our present world with bankruptcy brought nearer.

37. 58. Not the world of Marxian socialism; that is a world committed not only to the first Platonic error of professional education but to the second Platonic error of bureaucratizing the educators. Any relics of efficiency left intact by the first error will inevitably be dissipated by the second.

37. 59. Nor do I advocate standing bogged in the world of capitalism bolstered up by what they call cold socialism; a world infested by the Juggernauts of big business preserved from the bankruptcy fairly earned through their own incompetence by subsidies paid for out of taxation.

37. 6. These are the alternative forms of ruin which by now confront a civilization where men have been fools enough to hand their children over to professional educators.

37. 61. (What is all this about professionalism, anyhow? Does anyone think that if a man marries he should marry no one but a whore, or that if sleeping or eating is done it should be entrusted to professional sleepers or skilled prize-winners in eating-competitions?)

37. 62. The future of the world lies with peoples among whom there are no professional educators and every man educates his own children.

37. 63. And if I were Mr. H. G. Wells or one of these highly-paid Utopia-mongers I should draw up a list of the Rights of Man beginning with the right to educate one's own children.

37. 64. And a lot of good that pious wish would do to me or to anyone else.

37. 65. Let us think seriously what can be done and what

must be done to liberate European civilization from the stranglehold of this Old Man of the Sea, the professional educator.

37. 66. It is not necessary to imitate Sindbad the Sailor, make him drunk, and after untwining him liquidate him (as they say) with a big stone.

37. 67. A civilized community does not liquidate its oppressors; it finds them an occupation in which they can use their talents to the common advantage.

37. 68. The professional educator is certainly the caterpillar of civilization; but he may prove, properly handled, its silk-worm.

37. 69. Handling him consists first in making him harmless; secondly in making him useful.

37. 7. But there is something to be done before we begin. As a preliminary step we must make up our minds that whatever is done must be done individually.

37. 71. There must be no waiting for legislative help, and no attempt to do what we want by legislative action.

37. 72. Legislation is controlled by the Old Man of the Sea in his own interest.

37. 73. The sort of professionalized, bureaucratized education which is our Old Man of the Sea is the only kind politicians can produce.

37. 74. If you want a different kind, don't go to that shop.

37. 75. 'Come to ours instead' clamour the totalitarians on one side and the communists on the other; 'of course you get a rotten education from the corrupt representatives of parliamentary politics. Leave that shop and come to ours.'

37. 76. Why should you go to theirs? Because they are not politicians or because they are?

37. 77. If they are not politicians, dislike of your own politicians is no more a reason for crossing the road to their shop than discontent with your tailor is a reason for getting your next suit from the ironmonger over the way.

37. 78. If they are politicians, a wise man will hardly ask them to help him in getting rid of a politicians' system of education and starting to educate his children himself.

37. 79. The 'Revolution' of one kind and another, which these gentry agree in proclaiming, is only the fire to your

frying-pan; it is in either case only the event piously expected by herd-worshippers when the herd shall be all in all and the Old Man of the Sea shall rivet every man of us in permanent chains.

37. 8. This preliminary stage (37. 7) is the difficult one. That accomplished, all will be simple; but that is very difficult indeed.

37. 81. The difficulty is that we are so deeply accustomed to leaving things to the professional that we have no longer the self-confidence to do anything in which we are not experts, except when we forget this frightful fact and do the thing irresponsibly, for the fun of it.

37. 82. Failing that irresponsible attitude, we do things at which we are not experts partly with a conviction of sin (as when a man who 'can't sing' lifts up his voice in others' hearing) and partly with a conviction of being sinned against (as when he is asked to scrub a floor).

37. 83. But there is a vast region of experience in which the irresponsible attitude of doing things for fun resists all the onslaughts of professionalism.

37. 84. For every man who indulges himself in games and sports and pastimes, this region includes all those things. For almost every human being it includes eating and sleeping and making love.

37. 85. ('Philosophers' have traditionally belittled these things. More fools they. Look closely, and you will see in them the sheet-anchor of civilization.)

37. 86. This region includes almost all that is enjoyable in life, and almost all that people do well for the excellent reason that they have no motive to shirk it.

37. 87. The way to accomplish this preliminary stage is to reflect on the region of experience; to see how much it contains and how important it is.

37. 88. Then we must think how vastly life would be impoverished, brutalized, uglified if everything in it were handed over to experts and the spirit of irresponsibility banned.

37. 89. And lastly, we must resolve that this blessed region shall be not only defended against all comers but enlarged by all possible means: and that, first, it shall be

enlarged by a resolution on the part of all men and women neither to be shamed nor cajoled out of playing with their children.

37.9. The first move in our campaign against the Old Man of the Sea is for every man or woman who has a child to decide in future to spend more time in its company.

37.91. Every parent can do this, and do it now. Have the child share your meals or, if you are an office-drudge or a factory-drudge, the meals you have at home. Have it share your bedroom. If doctors say that it is unhealthy, they lie; they are paid to lie by the Old Man of the Sea.

37.92. If you are rich enough to have a nurse, sack her and look after the children yourself. If you are a delicate lady, trained to be idle, and find the work too much, cut it down. If you don't positively enjoy the work of keeping the children clean, let them run about dirty. They will not be a penny the worse if nothing is done for them but what you find it fun to do yourself.

37.93. Fathers, if you get promotion in your job, try to arrange matters so that promotion shall give you more time with your children. And when you are with your children don't always be thinking about doing them good and keeping them in order and all that; enjoy their company and make them enjoy yours. It is surprisingly easy to get fun out of children, once you make up your mind that fun is what you want.

37.94. Mothers, if you are rich enough to pay a governess, sack the governess and have the children to yourself. If you are too ignorant to teach them, don't try; all modern children are grossly and criminally over-taught. Read to them out of any book they enjoy or play with them at any game they like, the sillier the better; if you are young enough to have little children you are young enough to enjoy romping with them. If they 'get on your nerves', neglect them a bit; don't take them so seriously; be irresponsible about them. Above all, remember that you must be mistress in your own house. You must never allow a granny or an aunt or a neighbour to bully you about the way you bring up your children.

37.95. There need be no general massacre of schoolmasters and school-inspectors and university teachers. Their power is an illusion to which we are unhappily subject, fostered by parental dislike of responsibility for the care of their children: the wish that they shall be educationally efficient is father to the thought. Once parents take the step (a bold one, I admit) of deciding to enjoy their children's company, the illusion will vanish like a dream at waking.

37. 96. The second question now stares us in the face. The professional educator having been rendered harmless, how can we render him useful? By *keeping him as a pet*; when you will find him to possess many engaging and even profitable accomplishments.

37. 97. These will be in the main, of two kinds. First, *let him go on teaching*. There may be things a child wants to know that its parents cannot teach. Let it be sent to learn them from a professional teacher. And the parent, if it wants, can go too. Every professional teacher in the country will jump at the chance of getting quit, once for all, of pupils who do not want to learn and getting pupils who do.

37. 98. Secondly, *let him go on researching*. Every community that is to any degree civilized needs that research in a vast diversity of sciences and branches of learning shall go on. Let us keep our educational institutions or as many of them as are needed for the purpose, partly as teaching institutions where specialized teaching is on tap for all comers who want it, and partly as institutions of research where science and learning shall be kept alive instead of being, as they too often are in our educational institutions of to-day, dead.

37. 99. Such a distribution of functions as between the amateur and the professional is already customary for the medical profession, where nobody has ever demanded its abolition; why should it not work as well in the educational profession? Children do not leave their homes for medical reasons to reside for half the year in a doctor's house or in a clinic. They live at home, and if they have a cold or bark their shins their parents give them first aid. If they want more, they go to a doctor.

XXXVIII

CIVILIZATION AND WEALTH

38. 1. A COMMUNITY that becomes relatively civilized becomes relatively good at exploiting the natural world in a scientific or intelligent way (35. 36).

38. 11. This does not mean that what it needs of the natural world remains the same but its power to get it increases.

38. 12. What it needs of the natural world is constantly changing; and, if its power to get things from the natural world increases, constantly increasing; for need is correlative to power (35. 58); what men have no power to get from nature they learn to do without, docking their needs to match their powers.

38. 13. Man's demands upon the natural world, if his mastery of 'natural science' as defined in 36. 32 is increasing, increase concurrently with his power to satisfy them; and it makes no difference whether civilization is defined in terms of increased demand or increased power to satisfy demand.

38. 14. What, then, is meant by the word 'wealth'?

38. 15. A wealthy community cannot mean one whose power to win what it needs from the world of nature is sufficient to satisfy its needs; for in a sense every community is in that condition, and in another sense none is.

38. 16. Every community is well-to-do in the sense that every community learns to adjust its needs to its powers, going without what it cannot have.

38. 17. Alternatively, none is well-to-do, because if you have less than you need you find the process of adjusting your needs to your powers a painful one.

38. 18. It means (as the case may be) doing without a second motor-car or exposing your baby, or going to bed supperless, or just lying down and dying of hunger.

38. 19. And you cannot distinguish between going without 'luxuries', which does not matter, and going without 'necessaries', which does. There are no necessaries (35. 58); consequently there are no luxuries.

38. 2. *Wealth is a comparative term* like largeness. Nothing is simply large, and nothing simply small; this watch is larger than this pin and smaller than this table.

38. 21. One community A may be wealthier or 'better off' than another community B, but each may be 'ill off' as compared with a still wealthier community C.

38. 22. What does this mean? We are making a supposition; what supposition?

38. 23. We are not supposing that one community A has such a degree of 'natural science' and industry combined as will enable its members to satisfy a higher percentage of their demands for food and the like than B, but a lower percentage than C.

38. 24. For there can be no such difference between communities; because a type of demand which a community lacks even the power to satisfy soon ceases to be a demand (38. 16).

38. 25. And contrariwise a thing which a community is able to produce creates a demand for itself by the mere fact of being produced.

38. 26. This may seem so odd that persons who do not understand economic processes are tempted to blame it on the cupidity of capitalists marketing trash for their private ends. But that is demonology, not economics.

38. 27. What we are supposing is that the community A, owing to its superiority in 'natural science' and industry combined, *demands more of the natural world than B and is able to get more.*

38. 28. At the same time a third community C demands still more, and is able to get still more.

38. 29. How much a community demands of nature and how much it gets from nature is the measure of its wealth, and thus one measure of its civilization.

38. 3. *Wealth* must be carefully distinguished from *riches.*

38. 31. The more carefully because the two are sometimes confused: the substantives 'wealth' and 'riches' being treated as synonymous, and the adjectives 'wealthy', 'well-to-do', 'well off', being carelessly used as equivalent to 'rich'.

38. 32. Sometimes they are used as nearly equivalent, though not quite; as referring to a high and a moderate degree of the same thing; 'rich' meaning very wealthy, and 'wealthy' meaning almost rich.

38. 33. Thus a man with an income of x pounds a year is classified as rich, one with an income of $\frac{x}{2}$ pounds a year is classified, according to this usage, as wealthy or well-to-do.

38. 34. This usage is not current among persons who speak good English. Let the reader attend to the following points.

38. 35. The adjective 'wealthy' applies primarily to a community and only in a secondary sense to its individual members. What is wealthy is the community; individuals are wealthy only as members of a wealthy community.

38. 36. 'Rich' applies in the first instance to individuals and not the community of which they are members; a community can be rich only in its capacity as an individual community related to poor communities.

38. 37. Adam Smith wrote of 'the Wealth of Nations', making this very point in his title: wealth is something that belongs primarily to a community, riches something that belongs primarily to an individual man.

38. 38. In the second place, *'wealthy' is a comparative term, 'rich' a relative term.*

38. 39. I mean by a *comparative* term one which involves *reference to a standard.*

38. 4. For example, if I say: 'This is a good book', I am very likely thinking of other books that are bad; but I am not simply thinking of this book as better than they; I am thinking simply that *it comes up to my standard of goodness.*

38. 41. I mean by a *relative* term one which involves *contrast with its own correlative,* no reference to a standard being necessarily implied.

38. 42. For example, a motor-car is called a 'fast' car only by contrast with other cars which are slower. There is no standard velocity of which it is said: 'Whatever car exceeds that velocity I call a fast car.'

38. 43. Where terms are comparative, a lowering of the standard will bring over into a higher class what previously stood in a lower class.

38. 44. A man may say: 'this is what I used once to call a bad dinner; but my standards have changed and now I call it a good one.' 'Good' and 'bad' are here comparative terms, referring to a standard of goodness.

38. 45. Terms are often both relative and comparative at once; but when they are purely relative there is no standard, and therefore the standard cannot change; but what stood in a low class may still be transferred into a higher class, or vice versa, by a change in the other terms of the relation: a lowering of them in the scale is automatically a raising of it, a raising of them is automatically a lowering of it.

38. 46. A rowing coach may say to his crew: 'You are not good enough to enter for the Leander; try for the Ladies' Plate; there you will do better.'

38. 47. Excellence in rowing, as it affects these events, is (he means) a purely relative matter. It does not consist in coming up to any standard; it consists only in doing better than your competitors.

38. 48. Granted your own form as a *datum*, you can place it higher or lower on the scale of excellence by choosing low-grade competitors, or by handicapping them.

38. 49. 'Well off' is a comparative term, the opposite of 'ill off'; but the level of wealth prevailing in a community affords a standard by reference to which it is possible for every member of that community to be well off.

38. 5. There might be a community, for example, in which every member was sufficiently fed to keep him in good health, sufficiently clothed to keep him from rags and vermin, and sufficiently housed to shelter him from the weather.

38. 51. The community would be wealthy as a whole; as a whole, that is to say, it would satisfy a standard of wealth, no matter what other community did or did not come up to that standard, which might be called a comfortable standard and one which a community might well be glad to have attained.

38. 52. The individual members of that community would have severally attained a corresponding standard; no one, perhaps, would have risen very much above it, but no one would have fallen below it; the wealth of the community would have been so distributed among its members that every member could be called well-to-do.

38. 53. 'Rich' is a purely relative term. To call a man rich

means that he is rich in relation to others who are poor. It refers to no standard. It only refers to the contrast implied in that relation.

38. 54. The relation here implied is an economic relation: the relation of parties to an economic transaction, which is always some kind of purchase on the one part and some kind of sale on the other.

38. 55. To say that a person A is well off, or well-to-do, or wealthy implies that you recognize a standard of wealth, whether that standard implies the possession of three motor-cars or the command of one good meal a day, and that A comes up to that standard.

38. 56. It is consistent with A's being a member of a community whose every member comes up to the standard.

38. 57. To say that A is rich implies that there is some-body, perhaps a whole group of persons, in relation to whom he is rich, and who are poor in relation to him.

38. 58. It also implies that this person or these persons stand in economic relations with A, selling what he buys or buying what he sells.

38. 59. Persons standing to each other as purchaser and seller in the same transaction must be members of the same community; therefore it is impossible for all members of the same community to be equally rich; where A is rich to a certain degree B must be poor to the same degree, and they must be members of the same community.

38. 6. To be rich is to stand in a certain relation to another party with whom one is connected by economic relations, this other person being poor in proportion as you are rich; but what relation?

38. 61. A relation of *power*; for power (21. 77) means the exercise of force. The word 'riches' means *economic force*, or force as complicating economic transactions.

38. 62. Uncomplicated by force, an economic transaction or exchange is a transaction between two or more parties in which each engages of his own free will because he thinks he will be better off for doing so.

38. 63. Where A has more cheese than he thinks he will need to eat, and B has more honey, they may agree to ex-change some cheese for some honey, each becoming better off by the exchange; the wealth of the community $A + B$ and the wealth of each member being thereby enhanced; for wealth can be created not only by 'production' but also by 'distribution'.

38. 64. If A 'exercises force' over B in respect of this same transaction, that means he compels B to make an exchange by which he thinks he will not be better off; perhaps compelling him to exchange honey he would rather keep, perhaps compelling him to exchange it for less cheese than he thinks it worth.

38. 65. This brings us to the conception of a 'just price'. It is this. When A says 'the first price for x is y' he means 'y is the price for which I am willing to sell x when no force is exercised upon me.' The conception of a just price is logically dependent upon the conception of free will as exercised in economic transactions or exchanges.

38. 66. But how can A force B to make an exchange by which B thinks he will not be better off? The answer has already been given in general terms, 20. 5 seqq. A arouses in B emotions which he cannot control and which prevent him from making a genuine bargain or exchange with A.

38. 67. The result is what I will call a 'pseudo-bargain'; that is, a pretended exchange wherein B is forced or defrauded into accepting, in return for value really given, what he does not judge its fair price. If the bargain were a contract (and *emptio-venditio* is recognized, not only by Roman law, as a kind of contract), then a pseudo-bargain is a leonine contract (19. 54) and at Roman law invalid.

38. 68. To implement this admitted legal principle is a matter (to say the least) of extreme difficulty.

38. 69. That obtaining money by false pretences, or by menaces, is against the law is generally allowed; but by what legal reformation it can be made illegal to buy labour for less than its just price by taking advantage of one's own economic power and the unemployed labourer's economic weakness I do not know.

38. 7. I suspect that it cannot be done by law at all; that if once the contrast between riches and poverty is allowed to exist a force is set up which henceforth it is idle to resist.

38. 71. However men work to minimize that result, there

will always be one law for the rich and another for the poor; for that is what being rich and being poor are.

38. 72. The ideal of civil behaviour is the ideal of refraining from the use of force in one's dealings with one's fellow-men (35. 44).

38. 73. Civilization implies a set of rules so determining the conduct of members of a given community that each refrains to some extent (a small extent for a low civilization, a larger extent for a high one) from the use of force primarily in his dealings with other members of that community (35. 45) and secondarily in his dealings with men outside it (35. 63).

38. 74. The existence of the contrast between rich and poor is an offence against the ideal of civility; for it involves the constant use of one kind of force by the rich in all their dealings with the poor; economic force; the force whose essence it is to compel the poor to accept or give unjust prices in all their dealings with the rich.

38. 75. Though this is an offence against the ideal of civility, it is not necessarily an offence against a particular civilization.

38. 76. Any civilization, we know, is only an approximation to that ideal, and in many respects so far departs from it as to permit and even demand the use of force.

38. 77. Those responsible for the institutions of a particular civilization, then, must recognize clearly that the existence of a contrast between rich and poor, even a slight contrast, is an element of barbarity in it; but if it is only a slight contrast they may judge it sufficiently paid for by the service done to the whole community by the rich as the class charged with maintaining the communal wealth.

38. 78. The community in which the contrast between rich and poor exists, therefore, will not, if it is wise, waste the ingenuity of its lawyers in trying to abolish the evils resulting from that contrast (38. 7).

38. 79. It will examine its economic life very carefully, to decide whether that contrast is necessary to the preservation of what it regards as a tolerable standard of living.

38. 8. If it decides that the contrast can be diminished (for it can never be wholly abolished, any more than any other of the forms in which force appears as a feature in political life) without a greater inroad on its income or capital than it can afford, it will take the necessary steps to that diminution.

38. 81. For the *raison d'être* not only of bodies politic but of every community is that men should live, as Aristotle says, a good life; and in our terminology Aristotle's 'good life' is called civilization.

38. 82. This is the only motive for which men accumulate wealth: in order to pursue civilization.

38. 83. To accumulate wealth in order to create by its means a contrast between rich and poor is to use it for the destruction of civilization, or the pursuit of barbarism.

XXXIX

LAW AND ORDER

39. 1. BEGINNING this Part with a study of the meaning commonly attached to the word 'civilization', we began (xxxiv) by finding that generically it denotes a process taking place in a community.

39. 11. Specifically it denotes (xxxv) a process of becoming more civil; a word which, we saw, has two meanings. Where it refers to a man's relations with his fellow-men it indicates abstention from the use of force; where it refers to his relations with the natural world it indicates a combination of industry and intelligence whereby man gets more in the way of food, clothing, and the like out of the natural world, and at the same time forms the habit of expecting to get more.

39. 12. We then found (xxxvi) that the connecting link between these two ideas was the notion of dialectical thinking, or thinking together with others who are thinking about the same subject and intending to come to an agreement with them.

39. 13. If men mean to reach agreement about the relations between themselves they treat each other civilly (36. 12). If they mean to reach agreement about their relations with the natural world they build up among themselves a body of shared knowledge or opinion about things in the natural world and of traditional methods for dealing with them (36. 3).

39. 14. This, then, is the essence of civilization; the essence of what the word, as currently used, actually means.

39. 15. *Being civilized* means *living, so far as possible, dialectically*, that is, in constant endeavour to convert every occasion of non-agreement into an occasion of agreement. A degree of force is inevitable in human life; but being civilized means cutting it down, and becoming more civilized means cutting it down still further.

39. 16. Having discovered the essence of civilization we can cut ourselves adrift from the dictionary. We are no longer obliged to follow established usage. In chapter xxxv we were following it slavishly; now we can leave it.

39. 17. We can argue deductively from the essence of civilization (as now discovered) to 'properties' of civilization which ordinary usage does not recognize. Two examples of such agreement have now been given.

39. 18. It has been shown that one example of civilization, and a very important one, is the *education of children*, by which a civilization keeps itself alive from one generation to the next; and that this is a job for the family, which only a civilization bent upon suicide will leave to professional educators (xxxvii).

39. 19. It has been shown that in proportion as a community becomes civilized it becomes *wealthy*; not by an increased power of production which overtakes or outstrips its needs, but by increasing its needs and its power of production concurrently; that a diffusion of wealth throughout the whole community (for the term 'wealthy' applies in the first instance to the community as a whole (38. 35)) entails the abolition of poverty; and that the abolition of poverty entails the abolition of riches (xxxviii).

39. 2. I will now conclude this theoretical account of civilization with some remarks gathered up under two heads: the first 'Law and Order', the second 'Peace and Plenty'.

39. 21. Both are familiar phrases. Each is a name for civilization in one of its main aspects. The first is a name for *civilization as a task*: it is a name for what you have to do to be civilized. The second is a name for *civilization as a product*: it is a name for what you get by being civilized, the fruits of the civilized life.

39. 3. *Law and Order* is a name for a feature in the life of any civilized community, otherwise called *the rule of law*. According to European standards a community that does not exhibit the rule of law is not civilized at all; it is barbarous; but barbarity itself is a sort of civilization, though a low sort; and civilization of a sort may be enjoyed without a rule of law, though too low a sort for Europeans to call it civilization: for example, the sort that is enjoyed under the rough justice of a barbarian despot, who may be an admirable fellow in his way.

39. 31. The rule of law means, first, that there is a law; not necessarily that there is legislation, for there may be a rule of law either where the law is only customary; or where the law is merely what a despot decides from time to time that it shall be; but even so there may be a rule of law on condition that the law he makes to-day shall remain law until he abrogates it.

39. 32. Secondly, the rule of law implies that those who are under the law can find out what it is. How this is done will differ in different cases; perhaps by consulting the repositories of an oral tradition; perhaps by reading books; perhaps by bringing a test case in the courts; but unless the thing can be done somehow there is no rule of law.

39. 33. Thirdly, there must be courts where judgements are given according to the law. For a law that is not applied to individual cases is not a law but a dead letter.

39. 34. Fourthly, there must be equality before the law. What differentiates a law from an executive action or decree (28. 28) is its universality: the fact of its applying to every one of an undetermined number of defined cases. Anyone who comes under the definition comes under the law, whatever characteristics he may otherwise possess.

39. 35. To deny that all men are equal before the law is to say that a law admits of exceptions; to say that a law admits of exceptions is to say either that it has been carelessly stated (e.g. by someone who said 'The law prescribes death by hanging for certain crimes' and forgot that for certain classes of criminals it prescribes other forms of death) or else that it has been corruptly administered (e.g. by a Bench that said 'We don't fine the Squire for riding his bicycle without a light').

39. 4. Why (the reader may ask) does the European mind set up a standard of civilization which includes, as an essential condition of anything it deigns to call civilization, the rule of law?

39. 41. I will not answer by detailing the possible consequences of allowing the rule of law to die out. Such a catalogue would not answer the question.

39. 42. The real answer to the question: 'Why does the European mind set up this standard of civilization?' is: 'Because that is the standard to which it is accustomed.'

39. 43. It became accustomed to that standard under the tuition of Rome.

39. 44. The Greco-Roman city-state accustomed not only its members, but even (especially Rome) the foreigners resident within its limits, for whom Rome set up a special legal machinery and devised a special system of law, to settle their disputes by legal methods, and to make the rule of law a presupposition of their daily life.

39. 45. The Roman Empire convinced the peoples of Europe and hither Asia and north Africa, so far as they came under its sway, that the rule of law was among the elements of any civilization they could accept.

39. 46. The part of the Greek city-states in this process was confined to their share (a considerable share) in the creation of Roman law; so that what Rome gave to her empire included a good deal that was Greek.

39. 5. Foolish people do not always understand that the law is a part of civilization. They think that going to law is a way of quarrelling with a man, and that litigation belongs to the eristical side of life.

39. 51. But going to law with a man is meant for a way of settling your quarrel with him. No one goes to law except in the hope of coming away reconciled. Litigation belongs to the dialectical side of life.

39. 52. The rule of law means the substitution, in every quarrel which the law can handle, of dialectical for eristical methods.

39. 53. Take away the rule of law and you let in the vendetta, the blood feud, and all the forms of violence from which the rule of law has delivered us.

39. 54. The error that going to law with a man is an eristical thing to do, instead of a dialectical thing to do, is deliberately encouraged in the twentieth century by certain parties who want to destroy the rule of law and reintroduce the vendetta and the blood feud; and by others who act as their jackals.

39. 6. The habituation of Europe to the rule of law by Roman government did not take place only within the limits of the Roman Empire.

39. 61. The 'barbarians', as the Romans called them,

living outside those limits, to some extent as time went on
adopted Roman ways of thinking and living; and to some
extent as time went on found themselves enlisted under the
Roman standard and even paid for their services by being
transplanted in large bodies to settle on Roman land.

39. 62. The value of the rule of law consequently impressed itself not only on the provincial populations inside
the frontiers of the Empire but to some extent on the 'barbarians' outside them as well; who thus came to form an
outer ring of partially Romanized tribes between the fully
Romanized provincials and the un-Romanized outer world.

39. 63. From this outer ring came most of the barbarians
to whom historical ignorance attributes the break-up of the
Roman Empire: Goths and Vandals, Lombards and Franks
and Burgundians, Angles and Saxons, Picts and Scots.

39. 64. It was owing to the efficiency of these tribes as
buffers between Rome and the outer world that the rule of
law survived in Europe as it did.

39. 7. Here is what no less an authority than Maitland
has written about the general character of law in some
'successor-states' of the Roman Empire.

39. 71. The Anglo-Saxon laws 'deal . . . in particular with
the preservation of the peace . . . The family bond is strong;
an act of violence will often lead to a blood feud, a *private
war*. To force the injured man or the slain man's kinsfolk to
accept a money composition instead of resorting to reprisals
is a main aim for the lawgiver' (*Constitutional History of
England*, p. 4).

39. 72. 'To *force* the injured man'. The lawgiver uses
force; but he uses it for the sake of agreement. He uses it
against an injured party who did not begin the quarrel but
suffered aggression, perhaps unprovoked aggression, from
somebody else. Here is a *casus belli* for a private war. But
the lawgiver makes no fatuous distinction between aggressor
and aggrieved. He wants to stop private wars; and he does
it by forcing the aggrieved party to accept a money payment
instead of prosecuting the customary blood feud.

39. 73. Here is force justifiably used for the discourage-
ment of force and the promotion of agreement. The Anglo-
Saxon king uses force against the injured party in a quarrel

because there is no other way to keep the peace; and the king's law has for its object the maintenance of the king's peace.

39. 8. The rule of law does not only mean that the king, or other head of the executive, uses the power at his disposal for compelling the weaker among his subjects to drop a quarrel and to accept nominal compensation for injuries received.

39. 81. It also means, since all are equal before the law, that this same technique for checking an eristical process and initiating a dialectical process applies to the entire community without exception.

39. 82. The institution of wergild (since that is what we are discussing) was certainly law of a primitive and barbarous kind; but the men who were responsible for it had learned from their Roman masters one thing at least: that there was no rule of law unless all men were equal before the law.

39. 83. This did not mean that every man's wergild was the same as every other's. It was not. What it meant was that, whatever a man's wergild was, it was the same for anyone who might happen to kill him. It was neither increased for a friendless killer, who could not bring any graft to bear on the court, nor diminished for a very famous gangster who dined in exalted circles. The Anglo-Saxons may have been barbarians, but they were not barbarous enough to forget that if distinctions of that sort were made the rule of law was at an end.

39. 84. And one night last year a noble lord said to a constable who took him up for driving with the wrong headlights in the black-out: 'Is this all such —— —— as you have got to do while gentlemen like me are fighting for their country?' But they fined him ten pounds at Camberley on the 11th of July 1940.

39. 9. Fools have been heard to argue that if so much time and trouble and money were not spent on keeping the weak alive we should have a stouter people, with the unfit naturally weeded out by natural causes or healthy competition, and the fit surviving as Nature meant they should.

39. 91. I say nothing about that argument. But there is a similar argument to the effect that if natural causes had their way strong masterful men like his lordship here would come to the top and run things in a strong masterful way; and low fellows like this constable who go sneaking to hide behind the skirts of Justices of the Peace and the protection of the law would get a smack in the face, and a good thing too.

39. 92. Let us get this clear, for it is the most important thing in the book. *Law and order mean strength.* Men who respect the rule of law are by daily exercise building up the strength of their own wills; becoming more and more capable of mastering themselves and other men and the world of nature. They are becoming daily more and more able to control their own desires and passions and to crush all opposition to the carrying-out of their intentions. They are becoming day by day less liable to be bullied or threatened or cajoled or frightened into courses they would not adopt of their own free will by men who would drive them into doing things in the only way in which men can drive others into doing things: by arousing in them passions or desires or appetites they cannot control.

39. 93. This is a lesson of history and a very familiar one; everybody knows it, and the more history he knows the better he knows it. There have been peoples whose enemies have gnashed their teeth to find them sitting unshakable on the top of the world. These have been peoples who honoured law and order. The times when they won their greatest victories have been the times when they most scrupulously observed the rule of law.

39. 94. There is nothing mysterious about this. It is a simple case of cause and effect. It has always been so in the past; if the reader has followed the argument of this book he knows that it will always be so in the future.

XL

PEACE AND PLENTY

40. 1. 'Peace and plenty' (one of those brief alliterative phrases in which, as Otto Jespersen has remarked, the English people loves to express its ideas) is a familiar name for the fruits of civilized life (39. 21).

40. 11. 'Law and Order' (another phrase of the same type) is what civilization demands of you, in the form and up to the standard which Europe learned from Rome (39. 43).

40. 12. 'Peace and Plenty' is what civilization in that form and up to that standard promises you.

40. 13. To call them means and end respectively would be a blunder. Means properly so called have no value in themselves; their only value is utility, that is their relation to an end as what serves to procure the end.

40. 14. But the rule of law has a value in itself. It is justice. The fruits of justice may be peace and plenty; but by itself, independently of these fruits, justice has a value of its own, and a man or a community that values it values it for its own sake; one that values it only as means to peace and plenty does not value it at all.

40. 15. Moreover peace and plenty can be had (to some extent), though less completely, without the rule of law. What can be had otherwise than through a certain thing is not the end to which that thing is means.

40. 16. 'Law and order' is characteristic of a communal life which in itself, even apart from by-products or consequences, is already a good life and (since a good life is necessarily a happy life) already a happy life.

40. 17. As a by-product or consequence, a life of law and order is a life of peace and plenty. For peace and plenty may be had to some extent without law and order (40. 15); but with law and order they are ensured, and abundantly.

40. 18. I will remind the reader, merely to warn him against it, of the argument that law and order may be deprived of their just reward in the shape of peace and plenty (and hence do not ensure them without fail) when a good man, just in all his dealings, is robbed by the wicked.

40. 19. Civilization is something which happens to a community (34. 4); law and order, peace and plenty, are therefore communal things; if in a certain community virtue is oppressed, that community is defective in respect of law and order. If it did justice between its members there would be in it no oppressed virtue.

40. 2. Let us consider the meaning of 'peace and plenty'.

40. 21. A life of peace and plenty does not mean a life of stagnation or quiescence; it means a life of activity and exertion; what kind of activity and exertion we shall see.

40. 22. Let us take the two words separately.

40. 23. A life of peace does not mean a life of static quiescence and somnolence, a life in which no occasions for quarrels arise. That is not peace but stagnation, and a life of that kind is a slow death.

40. 24. Peace is a dynamic thing; a strenuous thing; the detection, even the forestalling, of occasions for quarrels; the checking of the process by which the non-agreements thus constantly generated harden into disagreements (29. 53); the promotion of a counter-process by which disagreements (not without the use of force, are softened into non-agreements; and the dialectical labour whereby occasions of non-agreement are converted into occasions of agreement.

40. 25. Unintelligent or envious spectators of this strenuous and complicated process think from time to time, or pretend to think, because the work is done efficiently and without fuss, without broken bones and waving of flags and firing of guns, that no work is being done; and mistake peace for death, or pretend so to mistake it.

40. 26. They are like ignorant visitors to some great building, who think because the building has stood firm for many years that it is at rest; not knowing that its component parts never sleep but are always moving this way or that, the movements always being watched and measured by the architects in charge, ready if a movement should exceed the fraction of an inch they allow it to take measures against the strain.

40. 27. Because it is all done without fuss, a sufficiently unintelligent or sufficiently spiteful visitor might think: 'These architects earn their salaries very easily. All that is going on is a little eyewash.'

40. 3. The peace which a community enjoys is partly internal and partly external. Enough has been said of external peace in chapters xxix and xxx; here I will add a few observations about internal peace.

40. 31. Internal peace involves the suppression of civil war; but that is only a very small part of it. Taken as a whole it is a much more complex thing, a much more difficult thing, a much more strenuous thing, than that.

40. 32. A situation that might lead to civil war is one in which a community is already divided into factions (30. 39). moved by conflicting interests, hostile to each other, each desirous not of agreement with the other but of victory over the other, potentially or actually armed for a conflict.

40. 33. A situation of this kind would never arise, and in fact has never arisen, except in a community ruled by men unfit for the job. Otherwise the process leading to it would have been long ago nipped in the bud.

40. 34. The two means of doing this, corresponding to the two types of men who bring about such a process, are repression and conciliation.

40. 35. The first type is the 'gangster': the ambitious criminal who, being mentally unfit for the strenuous life of peace, hopes to make his mark in a reign of violence and disorder.

40. 36. A community that wants law and order will see to it that it has a system of criminal law fit to deal with these, and courts prepared to administer it.

40. 37. The second type is the man with a grievance; the man who rightly or wrongly thinks himself ill-used and despairs of obtaining justice.

40. 38. A community that wants law and order will never wait for him to proceed to extremes. It will search into his grievances and remedy them long before there is any danger of civil war.

40. 39. In a community with a vigorous political life, where the Third Law of Politics operates directly, aggrieved persons to some extent rise above the status of a ruled class into one of co-operation with their rulers, and show this new status by becoming able and being encouraged to formulate their grievances and propose remedies.

40. 4. The gangsters (40. 35) hate and despise this sort of co-operation, as they hate and despise everything symptomatic of a vigorous political life.

40. 41. They do not want redress of grievances; they want civil war, because they feel themselves unequal (40. 35) to the mental strain of a civilized life.

40. 42. For being civilized is living dialectically (39. 15), that is, constantly endeavouring to turn occasions of non-agreement into occasions of agreement.

40. 43. This implies constantly overcoming one's own passions and desires by asserting oneself as free will.

40. 44. This, again, means living at the somewhat high and arduous level of mental adultness; impossible for men who, for one reason or another, have never grown up, and intolerable to them in others as implying contempt for their own immaturity.

40. 45. Just as war means a breakdown of policy when men encounter a problem in external politics which they have not the political ability to solve (30. 47) and retreat from the arduous business of keeping the peace into the easier job of fighting, so gangsterism means a breakdown of mental maturity when men are psychologically unable to go on behaving in a grown-up manner and collapse into the easier business of behaving childishly.

40. 46. They are likely to 'camouflage' this collapse either by disguising themselves in the sheep's clothing of the 'grievance' type (40. 37), pretending to have a grievance when they have none, or by using the 'grievance' type as a stalking-horse and posing as defenders of the oppressed.

40. 47. It is important to know how these disguises can be tested. The question to ask is: 'How do they stand towards attempts to redress grievances dialectically, by mutual agreement between the parties concerned?'

40. 48. If favourably the sheep's clothing is genuine. If unfavourably it conceals a wolf: an enemy of peace and plenty, an enemy of law and order, an enemy of the people whose friend he claims to be.

40. 5. It is not only quarrels which might lead to civil war that a peaceful community will nip in the bud.

40. 51. Endless opportunities arise for disagreement on

questions of policy among the rulers; non-agreements on such questions may harden into disagreements and so give rise to quarrels, or their occasions may be dialectically dealt with as they arise by converting them into occasions of agreement.

40. 52. The former method is an infallible sign of political incompetence in rulers and a fertile source of weakness in their rule.

40. 53. A community whose rulers quarrel, especially if they are so childish as to let their quarrels lead to violence, is an ill-governed community, unable to provide a life of peace and plenty for its members at home and unable to make itself respected abroad.

40. 54. It may be feared abroad, because it cannot be trusted; other communities can never know where they are with it; but it will never have the strength to pursue a policy.

40. 55. Among the ruled there are endless occasions of non-agreement on questions concerning economic life, domestic life, and so forth, resulting in endless opportunities for quarrels.

40. 56. These range in degrees of triviality down to the squabbles of children in the nursery.

40. 57. Relatively speaking these may be trivial; but absolutely, as indications of an eristic habit in the community, they are highly significant.

40. 58. So much so that there ought to have been, if there never was, a sage who advised the proverbial young ruler, his pupil, to investigate the nursery life of a people on whom he thought of making war: 'If they allow their children to quarrel, they will be unable to resist you; if they keep the peace in their nurseries beware of them.'

40. 6. I spoke above (40. 33) as if keeping the peace in a given community were the business of its rulers. In a non-social community this is true so far as its non-sociality is unimpaired by any taint of sociality; but this it can never actually be.

40. 61. Granted that a non-social community, being unable to rule itself, must be ruled from outside itself, by rulers who are not members of it (20. 36); nevertheless, when a complex community, whether of the family type or of the political type, is formed by the symbiosis of a social ruling class with a non-social ruled class, a dialectical process is set up whereby the non-social community changes by degrees into a society.

40. 62. This process of *socializing* the non-social community is the process of *civilizing* it (37. 22).

40. 63. In the case of the family, the agent in this process is the parental society, and the name of the process is education.

40. 64. In the case of the body politic the agent is the joint will of the rulers, and the process is called ruling.

40. 65. It is by the operation of the Third Law of Politics that the non-social community gradually approximates to the character of a society.

40. 66. So far as this happens every member of the ruled class comes to share in the civilization of the community as a whole and hence in the work of keeping the peace.

40. 67. To throw the whole work of keeping the peace upon the shoulders of 'the state' means that 'the state' is conceived as doing its work so inefficiently that the Third Law of Politics never comes into operation, and no share in that work is ever taken by the ruled.

40. 68. This is fully recognized by the tradition of English law: which makes a distinction between the king's peace and the peace of the individual subject, and requires every man to keep his own peace and thus co-operate in keeping the peace of the community.

40. 69. To take the education of children out of their parents' hands and put it in the hands of the king (or, as we nowadays say, 'the state') demonstrates a charming loyalty to the king and trust in his omnipotence; but it is taking a job away from those who can do it and handing it over to those who cannot (37. 37).

40. 7. This dodge for the avoidance of responsibility is very common to-day and is becoming commoner. I shall call it 'PASSING THE BABY'.

40. 71. A community among which the peace is adequately kept by converting occasions of non-agreement into occasions of agreement and thus averting quarrels before they happen is called a *wellmannered* community.

40.72. I will ask the reader to think how a tradition of good manners comes to exist in a community.

40.73. For myself, the most beautiful manners I have met with are in countries where men carry knives and, if anybody gives them a nasty word or a nasty look, stick them into him.

40.74. I have also been deeply impressed by the good manners I have found all my life in English public-houses, where I have never had a cross word or a cross look myself and never seen or heard one addressed to anybody else. I wish I could say as much for what is called polite society.

40.75. English manners are the product of English fisticuffs. They are not so polished as manners in Crete or Spain; but fists are not so polished as knives.

40.76. But in each case the tradition of good manners is the outcome of a tradition that in one way or another men keep their own peace.

40.77. A tradition of this sort, once established, is easy to maintain. No man need use his fists in a modern English public-house, or even look as if he could. Unless he is exceptionally clever with them, he had better not try.

40.78. It is not (as might be thought by confirmed baby-passers) that the chucker-out keeps men polite, any more than the policeman keeps them honest.

40.79. They keep themselves polite and honest. They have been civilized up to that point; and being civilized they value their civilization and keep themselves by their own free will up to the standard they now recognize.

40.8. So much for peace; now for plenty.

40.81. Plenty does not mean a life of full bellies and soft sleep, any more than peace means a life where no occasions arise for quarrelling (40.23).

40.82. Plenty means a life of mutual adjustment between the positive or commodity-creating elements of the economic process and the negative or commodity-destroying elements.

40.83. This does not mean simply striking a balance between them. Somehow or other a balance is always struck; a producer must somehow get rid of all he produces, whether by eating it (if it consists of eatables) or by selling it or by reinvesting it or by letting it spoil or by throwing it away;

and a consumer must somehow balance what he consumes with what he gets, perhaps by getting more, perhaps by consuming less.

40. 84.   It means striking such a balance as shall give him the result at which he aims; enable him to carry on his business, keep his health, bring up *x* children, or the like.

40. 85.   A civilized community will aim at striking such a balance in its economic life as shall enable it to keep up the civilization for whose sake it exists.

40. 86.   For example, it will devote a certain amount of its wealth to arming itself against enemies.

40. 87.   It will not condemn this as 'unremunerative expenditure' or 'waste', because unless it met that expense it would not be providing the indispensable conditions of its own civilized existence.

40. 88.   Plenty is obtained in part by exploiting the natural world in a civilized way, a way at once laborious and intelligent (35. 5).

40. 89.   But what is thus produced forms a contribution to plenty only so far as it is rendered available for consumption, not (for example) thrown away to keep prices up, and for a consumption which goes to promote a civilized life, not (for example) the consumption of bank-notes for pipe-lighters.

40. 9.   Plenty is also in part procured, therefore, by controlling distribution and partly by controlling consumption: canalizing these in such a way as to promote the civilized life of the community.

40. 91.   As with keeping the peace, so with the procuring of plenty, there are some things that can be done publicly (to parody an old phrase one might speak of procuring or infringing 'the king's plenty' as of keeping or breaking the king's peace) and there are some things that can only be done privately.

40. 92.   The labour of procuring plenty I call *thrift*: using the word not merely for restricting consumption (saving instead of spending and the like) but also for increasing production and for improving distribution: in general, for the commodity-producing elements in the community's economic life.

40. 93.   And I shall distinguish between *the king's thrift*,

or measures of this kind publicly undertaken on behalf of a given community by its rulers, and *private thrift*, or measures of the same kind which members of the community take each for himself.

40. 94. If the ruled class in the community had remained utterly non-social and uncivilized through bestiality in itself and incompetence in its rulers, there would be no private thrift; whatever plenty the community enjoyed would have to be procured solely by the rulers, and 'the king's thrift' would be all the thrift there was.

40. 95. Such bestial or incompetently ruled subjects would take no measures of thrift except what their rulers forced them to take. Left to themselves, they would always be unthrifty. In production they would never take the trouble either to work hard or to think hard. In distribution they would never have the energy to think where commodities were needed and to take them there. In consumption they would be gluttonous for themselves, indulgent to their kindred, and wasteful through idleness and stupidity. And if checked for these habits they would cheerfully pass the baby: 'Thrift is the king's business; let the king see to it.'

40. 96. From this Yahoo condition they would by degrees be elevated through the work of any body politic worthy of the name. From a brutally passive or non-social condition the mere fact of being ruled, if it were done with the least competence, would to some extent civilize them, socialize them, and endow them with a conviction (or as it is called a 'sense') of responsibility.

40. 97. However little way this process went, it would lead them to distinguish what I have called 'the king's thrift' from 'private thrift', and to see that, just as every man has a peace of his own, so every man has a plenty of his own which it is for him to procure by his own thrift and to avoid infringing by his own unthriftiness and prevent others from infringing.

PART IV

BARBARISM

XLI

WHAT BARBARISM IS

41. 1. I DISTINGUISH two ways of being uncivilized. I call them savagery and barbarism, and distinguish them as follows.

41. 11. Savagery is a negative idea. It means not being civilized, and that is all. In practice, I need hardly say, there is no such thing as absolute savagery; there is only relative savagery, that is, being civilized up to a certain point and no more (34. 52).

41. 12. By barbarism I mean hostility towards civilization; the effort, conscious or unconscious, to become less civilized than you are, either in general or in some special way, and, so far as in you lies, to promote a similar change in others.

41. 13. The reader will perhaps pardon me for reminding him (16. 11) of the correct meaning of verbs in '-ize'. They are loan-words from ancient Greek, borrowed, I suppose, by persons anxious to display their learning; and in ancient Greek such a verb means: 'I imitate a so-and-so.'

41. 14. 'To barbarize' is found more than once in ancient Greek, meaning: 'behave like a barbarian', or in particular 'talk like a barbarian'.

41. 15. I propose so far to follow the Greek as to make verbs in '-ize' and their derivatives always contain a reference to imitative action, the first part of the verb naming the thing imitated.

41. 16. There are two classes of derivatives from such verbs: first, abstract substantives in '-ism', denoting an act of imitation; second, concrete substantives in '-ist', denoting an imitator.

41. 17. I should not trouble the reader with so trifling a matter but that lately, reading a book which purported to be in English, I found the word 'scapegoatism' evidently intended to mean not 'behaviour modelled on that of a scapegoat' but 'tendency to treat people like, or make them into, scapegoats', as Nazis treat Jews, or as Russians treat kulaks.

41. 18. This will not do, and it must not be allowed to pass unchallenged; or the English language will die, as the German (in which my author was thinking) has long ago died, into one no longer capable of accuracy.

41. 2. Being civilized and being uncivilized are two correlative ideas, neither of which is thinkable without the other.

41. 21. We have come across such correlatives before; for example, the self and the not-self (10. 15), which are correlative abstractions from the experience of reflection upon passion.

41. 22. Such abstractions are always to some extent vague (7. 56); for example, I may think that the action of something upon me is what makes me angry, but what this thing is I have only a vague or indeterminate idea.

41. 23. If that does not satisfy me, if I want to replace it with a less vague and more determinate idea, how can I do so?

41. 24. By closer examination of the *datum* from which it is derived: my anger itself, the source of all possible information about its cause.

41. 25. Such information is not to be had directly from inspection of a first-order object; it is derived indirectly from that object; that is, from the answers to questions asked about it; it is the answers to these questions, intelligently asked, that are the *data* from which the information must be drawn.

41. 26. What is the *datum* by examining which we can render less vague our ideas about the civilized or uncivilized character of a given act?

41. 27. There must be some *datum*, some ground for describing this act as civilized and that as uncivilized. A man challenged to explain why he classifies this act as civilized and that act as uncivilized will hardly hesitate to admit that it is a thing he does for some reason, even though he does not know what that reason is.

41. 28. But this *datum* is not anything so simple as the fact of passion, which I have here (41. 24) quoted as a parallel case.

41. 3. It is something known as 'the sentiment of approval or disapproval'. What this is I will now proceed to inquire.

41. 31. A *sentiment* is something partly emotional and partly intellectual. It begins as an emotion; as a feeling of comfort or discomfort, for example, which you experience in the company of certain persons; or as something still vaguer, an impulse, you do not know what exactly, moving you towards or away from forgathering with them; it ends as the conviction that they are good or bad people and live in a good or bad way.

41. 32. But it is practical from beginning to end of its development. It begins in an emotional form as an impulse moving you in this direction or in that; it ends with what may be called a *rationalization* of the same emotional impulse, viz. a reasoned case for going deliberately in this direction or in that.

41. 33. If the reader should press me to say whether a sentiment as such should be classified as an emotional thing or an intellectual thing, I should answer: 'As both. It ought not to surprise you to be told that emotions may turn into thoughts or that thoughts may originate as emotions. Sentiment is the name of this process; the process in which the same thing begins as an emotion and ends as a thought.'

41. 34. To describe the sentiment of approval in merely emotional terms is to say too little about it; for it is more than merely emotional. My approval of a man's activity, for example, is not merely the pleasurable feeling with which I contemplate that activity; it is more than that; it is this feeling of pleasure in the course of developing into an entire moral theory.

41. 35. I have said (41. 32) that such a theory may be called a 'rationalization' of the emotional impulse from which it started. But that word should be used with caution. As vulgarly used to-day, it is complicated by the suggestion that the conversion of a sentiment from an emotional thing into an intellectual thing is somehow illegitimate; the thing has a right to life in the first form, but none in the second; what is called a rationalization is a dog called by a bad name as a preliminary to hanging it.

41. 36. These suggestions do not deserve to be taken seriously. I shall not waste time in further discussing them.

41.37. To describe the sentiment of approval in merely intellectual terms is, again, to say too little about it; for in its character as a sentiment it has a vigour, an elasticity, a liveliness which it only stands to lose by conversion into the drier, more brittle, form of a theory.

41.38. Whether there are any sentiments other than what were called in the eighteenth century the 'moral sentiments' of approval and disapproval I shall not ask; nor whether there are any which are not concerned (as these are) with man's social life.

41.39. At any rate there are moral sentiments, whether or not there are any others; and there are social sentiments, whether or not there are any others. For brevity, then, let us omit the epithets and speak simply of sentiments.

41.4. What makes a sentiment social is that it is concerned with acts done by a society. My sentiments aim, so to speak, at controlling not only the things I do but the things we do; the things done by a society to which I belong.

41.41. What makes it moral is that it is concerned with free action; action for which every member of the society in question is jointly responsible. Indeed, unless the action were free, it could not strictly speaking be social; it would at most be communal (20.23).

41.42. Sentiments make it their primary object to reduce the actions done in common by the societies in which they exist to the type of free and moral activities; that is to say, to civilize them.

41.43. Let us consider how a sentiment operates in the mind of a member of the society which it is thus civilizing. Such operation is not necessarily conscious; the man in question does not necessarily think why he is doing the thing he feels driven to do; but on the other hand it is not necessarily unconscious.

41.44. When the sentiment is near the emotional end of its scale, the agent in whom it works is relatively unaware of its working; he does what it bids (if he did not, it would not be working), but without thinking that he acts at the bidding of sentiment, let alone a sentiment which is civilizing his actions.

41.45. When the sentiment approaches the intellectual

end of its scale, the agent in whom it works is relatively aware of its working; he does what it bids no less and no more than he did, but he does so in the awareness that he acts under the influence of sentiment, and to this may be added the further consciousness that this influence is a civilizing influence.

41.5. A civilized man or relatively civilized man can work unconsciously at promoting civilization; that is, he can promote civilization without any clear idea of what he is promoting or why.

41.51. He can do this because he is working under the influence which in this case is operating near the emotional end of its scale (41.44).

41.52. In a conflict between civilization and barbarism it is only civilization that can fight in this unconscious way.

41.53. Barbarism can never be in this sense unconscious. The barbarist, as I will call the man who imitates the conditions of an uncivilized world (41.16), cannot afford to forget what it is that he is trying to bring about; he is trying to bring about, not anything positive, but something negative, the destruction of civilization; and he must remember, if not what civilization is, at least what the destruction of civilization is.

41.54. Concentrating his mind on this question as he must do, the barbarist feels himself to be in one sense at least the intellectual superior of his enemy, and prides himself upon it.

41.55. For if he knows what the destruction of civilization is, he knows what civilization is; but his enemy does not have to worry about that question; on that subject his mind is relaxed and effortless, in so far as the work he does for the cause of civilization is left to the operation of sentiment at the emotional end of its scale.

41.56. A community fighting against civilization must work very hard not only at fighting but at thinking what they are fighting against.

41.57. Their intellectual labour is in fact futile, for the promotion of civilization does not require that it should be done, and (as we shall see) the destruction of civilization cannot be done by its means.

41.58. It does not even give the barbarist an advantage

in his warfare against civilization; though it seems to do so. It means that the barbarist has all his ideas cut and dried and his answer ready for any challenge.

41. 6. But this is a very dangerous position; and a belligerent who takes pains to put himself in it is doing a more foolish thing than merely wasting his labour; he is cutting his own throat.

41. 61. He is giving away the initiative; and this is a loss no belligerent can afford. It is no compensation for losing the initiative to be ready with an answer to every problem with which the enemy may confront you; it means always being one jump behind him.

41. 62. Where the barbarist scores is at the beginning of his career. His plans have been matured in a peaceful world; when they begin to yield him a harvest, it is from his enemies' point of view too late; they are a world of unprepared victims.

41. 63. He has one advantage over his victims, and only one: their unpreparedness. This advantage can be protracted for as long as he can keep the situation fluid. What he must not allow is that the ice should pack round him.

41. 64. The rules for success in barbarism, therefore, urge the barbarist above all to keep the ice moving and to reproduce every day, so far as possible, the fluid conditions that prevailed at the beginning of his career.

41. 65. For the barbarist plays a losing game. The cards are stacked in favour of civilization, and he knows it. At least the more intelligent barbarists have always become aware of it at an early stage.

41. 66. Why should this be so? Why are the rules for success in barbarism only rules for staving off defeat?

41. 67. Because the conditions under which the barbarist decides to fight are such that any victory he may win in any temporary engagement makes his defeat *in the long run* more probable; so that in the long run the odds against his success mount up to infinity.

41. 68. But once more, why should this be? It is because *there is no such thing as civilization*. If there were, it could be exterminated, and the barbarist would have won; but in fact there are only innumerable and variously distant approximations to it, a kaleidoscope of patterns all more or less akin to the ideal I have depicted in Part III.

41. 7. What ensures the defeat of barbarism is not so much the enormous diversity of existing civilizations, too numerous for any conqueror to dream of overcoming; it is the literally infinite possibility of varying the nature of the thing called civilization, leaving it recognizable in this diversity; a possibility which will be exploited as soon as success in a barbarian attack stimulates the inventive powers of civilization to look for new channels of development.

41. 71. For example, under the destructive energy of barbarism's first onslaught it may seem dreadful that the monuments of civilization in brick and mortar, in paint and canvas, in human customs and institutions, should be destroyed. But these things are not civilization itself, they are only examples of what it can do. What made them once can make them again; their destruction is a challenge to such remaking; it can be an ineffective challenge only if the creative power is already dead.

41. 72. It may seem dreadful if the same fate has overcome the means of subsistence for a whole country-side; but few countries, if any, and perhaps no civilized countries are fertile by nature; it is civilization that has made them fertile in the past; and civilization, working by degrees, as civilization always works, can make them fertile again.

41. 73. The defeat of barbarism, I say, is always certain in the long run (41. 67). Under what conditions is the defeat of barbarism assured? What is the meaning of the phrase 'in the long run'?

41. 74. It means that there must always be partisans of civilization who are ready to go on defending it, *whatever happens*, until its cause is victorious.

41. 75. This condition is at any rate likelier to be fulfilled than the opposite, namely that there should continue to be partisans, and harmonious partisans, of barbarism: an alternative hardly possible of fulfilment.

41. 76. For barbarism implies not only a quarrel between any barbarist and any civilized man; it also implies a quarrel between any one barbarist and any other; and that any state of harmony between them is merely this quarrel suspended.

41.77. Quarrels, pushed to the point of war, are normal as between one barbarism and another. But between a barbarism and a civilization they are exceptional, because peace is a fundamental object of any civilization (40. 1).

41.78. Any two belligerents who agree in regarding warfare, whether overt or suspended, as the normal condition of bodies politic, are more nearly in agreement than any two belligerents one of which regards war as the normal condition of bodies politic, the other peace.

41.8. Where, as in the latter case, the war is between a civilized body politic and a barbarous, it is like a war between parties each inhabiting an element of its own: let us say an eagle and a dolphin.

41.81. Each can defeat the other only by wearing it out: but each has its own method of doing this.

41.82. The eagle tries to force a decision by the fury of its attack; hoping to bleed the dolphin to weakness and submission.

41.83. The dolphin cannot attack the eagle directly, because it cannot fly; but it does not want to; it is the eagle, not the dolphin, that wants to fight.

41.84. How is this consistent with saying (41. 61) that the barbarist has surrendered the initiative?

41.85. Both statements are true; the two together constitute a criticism of *war as waged by the barbarist.*

41.86. In a military sense he thinks of himself as armed and equipped for aggression, and is proud of it; but in a psychological sense he thinks of himself as a peaceful, domestically minded eagle protecting himself against a sea of bloodthirsty dolphins; and prides himself on that, too.

41.87. This is not hypocrisy; he really does think of himself in both ways, inconsistent though they are; if he did not, he might have, if not a chance of winning, at any rate a chance of coming to terms with his notoriously peaceful antagonist.

41.88. It is the eagle's persecution-mania that drives him into prosecuting a hopeless war. The war might be brought to an end at any moment; but this it cannot be as long as that persecution-mania dictates the eagle's policy.

41.89. The dolphin tries to turn the eagle's onslaughts to the eagle's own destruction; if that can be done (and history has many cases) the dolphin's victory has about it a dream-like quality of rapidity and unexpectedness; a moment ago the eagle was at the height of a prosperous attack; now it is inert, drowned, dead, a corpse at the bottom of the sea. Round such events legends grow.

41.9. It is time we turned to the history of the various barbarisms which have from time to time pitted themselves against European civilization.

XLII

THE FIRST BARBARISM:
THE SARACENS

42. 1. BEFORE there could be any revolt against civilization there must first be civilization itself; not so much a system of conceptions but a body of functions, practices, habits, holding good, roughly speaking, over the entire world.

42. 11. What does 'world' mean in this context? It means that some group of people thinks of itself as inhabiting a continuous tract of earth and sea which is for it an οἰκουμένη, 'where people live'.

42. 12. Such a phrase, and the idea for which it stands, were already current in the Hellenistic period, and thereafter never lost to sight.

42. 13. The conception of an inhabited world carries with it, at least in potentiality, the conception of a world-wide manner of life; and that conception may be found coming into existence more in practice than in theory, under the Romans (cf. their conception of '*ius gentium*').

42. 14. Thus from the Roman age onward there was such a thing in people's minds as the idea of a pattern or shape of human life, world-wide as the conception of the world then went, against which a revolt could arise.

42. 15. Such a revolt would have been essentially a revolt against Rome, the leader or organizer or at any rate the centre of this world-wide pattern of human life.

42. 16. Hatred of Rome, we may be sure, would have been the central motive of any revolt against a form of life whose centre was Rome.

42. 17. There appear on the stage of Roman history characters called 'barbarians' or more strictly, as I have defined the term (41. 1), 'savages'. They appear especially on and beyond the Empire's northern frontier; it has been fashionable, though inaccurate, to regard them as the corrupting influence to which the weakness and collapse of the Roman Empire were chiefly due.

42. 18. There are several reasons why such a view is unsound. I will mention only one; a proof that these so-called barbarians were not barbarists.

42. 19. They were in no sense inspired by hatred of Rome or the civilization for which Rome stood. You may find one here and there like Ataulf,[1] who cherished anti-Roman feelings in youth; but was taught by experience that the only status either possible or attractive to a 'barbarian' leader like himself was the status of a *restitutor orbis Romani,* a 'restorer of the Roman world'.

42. 2. With this pro-Roman policy went a pro-Christian policy; for the cause of Rome, from about the end of the fourth century, was the cause of Christendom.

42. 21. True, these European 'barbarians' for the most part received the Arian heresy, not Christianity in its true or trinitarian form, which alone could appeal to an intelligent man; but this divergence from what ultimately became the accepted form of Christianity was not enough to turn them against Rome.

42. 22. But in the seventh century a movement inspired by hostility towards everything Roman (or let us now call it after the fall of the western Empire 'Byzantine') and everything Christian, flared up on the south-eastern frontier of the Roman world.

42. 23. Mohammedanism would not have presented so definitely anti-Christian a guise if Mohammed had been able to read the books, numerous by now, in which Christian writers had expressed in many different languages their ideas of any sort of Christianity, even the most heretical sorts.

42. 24. The hostility of Mohammed, which was directed against Christianity by a strangely crude misunderstanding on his part of what Christianity was (for he thought, and taught, that trinitarianism implied believing not in one God but in three), appears to have been originally directed not against Christianity but against a kind of primitive idolatry which surrounded him in his Arabian home.

42. 25. It is hardly conceivable that Mohammed should have so grossly misunderstood Christianity. But, genius though he was, he was also an illiterate man living in a

[1] J. B. Bury, *Invasion of Europe by the Barbarians* (1928), pp. 98–9.

country outside—just outside—the bounds of civilization; and in places and by people of that kind that is the kind of mistake that is constantly made.

42. 3. It was in 622 that the Moslem conquest of Arabia began; in 634 that they first invaded Syria; Damascus fell in 635; in 641 they took Alexandria; in 673 they besieged Constantinople for the first time, and for six months tried to take the capital of the world.

42. 31. The new force that had sprung up in Arabia reached and passed its zenith within the limits of a single generation from its birth; for the Moslem failure to take Constantinople was a final failure; it was not redeemed by the success of the Turks in 1453, to which it was irrelevant; it meant that the Saracens (as we will now begin to call them) could not enter Europe by the front door but must seek a back entrance by Gibraltar, which leads in its turn to the field of Tours (732) and defeat by Charles Martel (42. 54).

42. 32. The Arabs were a desert race, and the European ideals of peace and plenty disgusted them rather than the reverse. Whether they devastated the whole of North Africa deliberately or otherwise (one need hardly take seriously the tale that the Berbers did it) is not known; but, apart from the tale I have dismissed, they did devastate it; and ever since then it has been a wilderness watched over by the ruins of Roman towns.

42. 33. With devastation went treachery; or rather in advance of it; for treachery, the means by which from the first the Moslems captured cities or fortresses, became a feature of Moslem warfare before the devastation which first became a feature of it in North Africa.

42. 34. There was a reason for this treachery: viz. the superior attraction of Mohammedanism as compared with Christianity for simple minds which, if not actually deceived by Mohammed's misunderstanding (42. 25) of Christianity, were ready to think of Islam as a simple uncorrupted faith, in fact, a fool-proof version of whatever was best in Christendom itself, fittingly united with the fanatical valour they admired in the desert-bred Moslems.

42. 35. We have evidence of this. 'It is true', wrote an African governor to the Emperor Heraclius, 'that the enemy are not nearly so numerous as we. But one Saracen is equal to a hundred of our men. Of the enjoyments of the earth they desire only simple clothing and simple food, and yearn for the death of martyrs because it leads them to Paradise, while we cling to life and fear death.'

42. 36. 'The Greeks wish to fight on', writes the same governor in another context; 'but I wish to have no dealings with the Greeks in this world or the next. I renounce for ever the tyrant of Byzantium and the orthodox who are his slaves.'

42. 37. These, however, are the words of a Monophysite heretic, whose readiness to join hands with the invaders (though not to renounce his faith[1]) might, as Gibbon thinks (Bury's ed. v. 448), have been stimulated by worldly motives.

42. 38. Whatever the motives, however, it is clear that in Egypt at least what we should call the 'heretic vote' constituted a pro-Islam vote. 'The Saracens', says Gibbon, 'were received as the deliverers of the Jacobite [Monophysite] church.'

42. 39. That Islam should have profited by the divisions of Christendom was not surprising; seven centuries had produced in Christendom such divisions as at that time still lay for Islam in the future.

42. 4. This was not the only way in which Islam showed its youthful or inexperienced character.[2] During the conquest of Syria Mohammed, then still alive, granted to all who should surrender to Islam personal immunity, freedom of property and trade, and religious toleration; and early in the same campaign his successor Abu Bekr warned his followers to spare monks, women, and children, not to destroy fruit-trees or crops, and never to break their word.

42. 41. We know so little about the course of the campaign leading to the devastation of North Africa that we cannot say why, on that occasion, the example of the Prophet and Abu Bekr was so signally flouted.

[1] And the Moslem conquerors, in those more tolerant days, did not insist.

[2] Elsewhere (25. 3 *seqq.*) I have protested against certain modern revivals of the doctrine that a body politic, after being young, becomes by degrees adult, then senile. But I should never deny that a society, as it pursues the business for which it exists, gradually builds up and corrects a tradition as to how that business should be done; which is what I am here talking about.

42.42. That campaign, beginning under Abdallah in 647 and ending in or about 710, when the Moslems first traversed the Straits of Gibraltar under Tarik, has left behind it at least a hint of growing exasperation on the part of Moslems and hardening resistance on that of the natives. Much may have happened in those sixty years.

42.43. Not until 711 did the Saracens (as the Moslems are henceforth called) cross the Straits in force enough to threaten the Gothic monarchy of Spain. The numbers were now augmented by many Christian malcontents and African recruits; of the latter enough to impress upon the Spanish mind, ever since, the name of Moors, not Arabs nor even Saracens, for their conquerors.

42.44. A desperate battle which lasted for a week on a river-bank near Xeres was decided in the Moors' favour only by the defection of the royal princes and the Archbishop of Toledo on the field of battle; and Tarik lost no time in occupying first Cordova and then Toledo.

42.45. I will not linger over the operations consequent upon a decisive victory. 'Spain', says Gibbon, 'which in a more savage and disorderly state had resisted two hundred years the arms of the Romans, was overrun in a few months by those of the Saracens.'

42.46. 'Yet', he continues, 'a spark of the vital flame was still alive; some invincible fugitives preferred a life of poverty and freedom in the Asturian valleys; the hardy mountaineers repulsed the slaves of the Caliph; and the sword of Pelagius has been transformed into the sceptre of the Catholic kings.' (Gibbon, ed. Bury, v, p. 479.)

42.47. Islam came out of the Spanish war victorious by a very narrow margin. Not only had the main attack on Europe by way of Constantinople failed (42.31), with what loss in life and prestige we can only guess, but now the second choice, the attack on Europe by way of Spain, was showing signs of failing.

42.48. The Saracens must have been alive to the danger. For in 716 they renewed the attack on Constantinople on a large scale.

42.49. A great armada was used for this attack; but after a siege of thirteen weeks, resisted by the Greeks with a remarkable combination of resource and bravery, nothing was left of it.

42. 5. The Saracens (aware, it would seem, that the attack by way of Spain was their second string and that the first had again failed them) in 721 attacked France over the Pyrenees.

42. 51. The French monarchy was no less degenerate than the Spanish. Power had passed from the Merovingian kings to the mayors of the palace; but it was a duke of Aquitaine on whom fell the honour of first defeating the new invader.

42. 52. The victory of Eudes over the Saracens at Toulouse was followed by rapid Saracen raids, legendary in French history, as far afield as Arles, Lyons, and Besançon.

42. 53. But Charles Martel, assembling the entire strength of Europe on the hills between Tours and Poitiers, was not to be hurried.

42. 54. The battle to which history has given the name of Tours was carefully prepared against an enemy who had already tried his strength to the limit, and it was decisive. For Europe the Saracen peril was over.

42. 55. Henceforth the Saracens were for a long time, it is true, well known and heartily feared in Europe; in the ninth century they conquered Sicily and Crete, and sacked Rome, no longer in those days the centre of civilization; but in the following century the Greeks recovered Crete and conquered Syria and Cyprus.

42. 6. Let us sum up the main features of this episode in European history.

42. 61. It was the first experiment in barbarism and therefore in many ways the mildest, the least removed from the spirit of civilization itself.

42. 62. In a sense Islam was more like a Christian heresy than an anti-Christian religion, being an attempt to make Arabs more Christian than the Christians themselves.

42. 63. It started with everything in its favour: a peaceful world in which to make its début; a home on the outskirts of the Roman world which Roman arms ever since Trajan had tried in vain to penetrate, which might reasonably, therefore, be regarded as impregnable; and among its neighbours many ill disposed to the prevailing religion and ready to look to Islam for protection against it.

42. 64. What I may call its youthful characteristics were also in its favour; I mean its tolerance, its tendency towards mercy (even Allah is merciful in the Koran, and it is only in a guilelessly youthful religion that men imitate the virtues of their God), its insistence on the duty of keeping one's word, and above all its emphasis upon its own central points and refusal to take an interest in comparatively unimportant details.

42. 65. With the logic of its position as a barbarism it had no option but to aim at the conquest of the world. No agreement with any other body politic was possible; like all barbarisms it did not believe with any firmness of conviction that any body politic other than itself existed at all; with the characteristic of barbarism which is called fanaticism, it craved to be surrounded by a completely empty world, a world containing only itself and God.

42. 66. This impulse to surround itself with an empty world exposed Islam to the crowning test of all barbarisms. This was what led it to failure twice over at Constantinople and at Tours. The reader who looks at the story of these failures will detect in both the dream-like quality I have mentioned (41. 89) affecting even the hard-headed Gibbon.

42. 67. The failure of Islam to conquer Europe would have been, by a tougher God, unforgivable; but Allah is merciful, in other words if Moslems fail they can be content with minor successes such as the devastation of Africa, the psychological substitute for the uncompleted conquest of the world.

42. 68. This is the one thing that Islam in its whole history has done. It is a negative thing, as whatever barbarism does must be; a feat of destruction (41. 53); but there it is for all to see, the desolation of Africa.

42. 7. The intellectual labour undertaken by Islam, when once it had reconciled itself to accepting defeat, was considerable; but it is interesting rather as having provided our medieval forefathers with an introduction to Aristotle than on its merits.

42. 71. And here once more Islam presents itself as something only half barbarous. Acting as a link between Aristotle and the Middle Ages, it has in effect abandoned barbarism under the scourge of that double defeat.

42. 72. Finally, it is emphatically true that in the seventh century 'there was no such thing as civilization'. All that modern people recognize under that name lay in the future; even the word itself was only invented centuries later.

42. 73. Early Islam was a revolt against civilization only in the rather special sense that it was a revolt against something that had not yet happened; a revolt against the embryonic form that civilization had not yet quite taken, but was beginning to take.

42. 74. The ancients said that the infant Herakles strangled the snakes that had been sent against him. Borrowing the legend, we may describe the infant civilization as a not yet mature Christendom strangling the barbarism which threatened it so early with destruction.

XLIII

THE SECOND BARBARISM:
THE 'ALBIGENSIAN HERESY'

43. 1. THE next barbarism is what is known as the 'Albigensian heresy'.

43. 11. Not that all heresies either were or involved barbarisms. In an age when civilization assumed a distinctively Christian colouring, a heresy implied a proposal to alter the characteristic tone of a civilization; but to alter it is one thing, to destroy it another.

43. 12. What is called the 'Albigensian Heresy' might be legitimately described as neither Albigensian nor a heresy. It took its name from Albi in the south of France, where it was especially rife; but it did not originate there or anywhere in Europe. Strictly speaking it was not a heresy. Its form was modelled on that of Christianity; but its spirit was not so much pseudo-Christian as anti-Christian.

43. 13. It was a Near Eastern religion something like Christianity, but in many essentials different from any possible form of Christianity; it was in fact more akin to Manichaeism, that offshoot of the Zoroastrian faith which at one time in his youth attracted the attention of Saint Augustine. Of this faith something survived to put forth fresh roots and disguise them in a Christian dress in the twelfth and thirteenth centuries. No kind of Manichaeism could be like enough to any kind of Christianity to deceive a close scrutiny.

43. 14. The difference, if I may dare to put briefly what calls for much subtlety, is that for the Manichee good and evil are equal and opposite, each utterly and eternally antagonistic to the other; for the Christian, good is stronger and, so to speak, older than evil. The struggle between good and evil, which both believe to be real, is for the Manichee a struggle that can never have an ending; for the Christian it must end in the victory of the good. From this pregnant principle many consequences arise.

43. 15. Among others, there arises one with which we are

already familiar; the distinction between what Plato calls
'eristic' and 'dialectical' discussions (24. 57). Any discussion that aims at the victory of one disputant and the defeat
of the other is an eristical discussion (24. 58); and discussion
in which the originally antagonistic parties aim at reaching
an agreement is dialectical (24. 59).

43. 16. This is why it is straining a word to speak of the
Albigensian 'heresy'. The thing was not a heresy. 'Heresy'
is the Greek for 'choice', in the special case where choosing is
choosing to think, and 'my heresy' or 'what I choose to think'
is peculiar in being what few other people think.

43. 17. Imagine that someone were to say: 'You must not,
shall not choose. No choice is open to you. Either accept
our doctrine exactly as it stands, or else . . .' Yes? Or else
what? The man is speaking foolishly; he is pretending to
confront you with an alarming alternative when in fact no
alternative is offered. He is bluffing. There is no purgatory
for repentance, no hell for punishment; nothing but the
emptiness of a mind that pretends to have something to say
and has nothing.

43. 18. That is what Albigensianism is; not a heresy, but
a megalomania.

43. 19. The Bogomils (by which name the Albigensians
were more properly, though less politely, known) are said by
Gibbon's editor, J. B. Bury, to have held the following
doctrines. I quote Bury's edition of Gibbon, vol. vi, p. 542,
verbatim; I do not think it appears in any other edition.

'(1) They rejected the Old Testament, the Fathers and
ecclesiastical tradition. They accepted the New Testament
and laid weight on a number of old apocryphal works.

'(2) They held two principles, equal in age and power;
one good (a triune being = God); the other bad (= Satan);
who created the visible world, caused the Fall, [and] governed
the world during the period of the Old Testament.

'(3) The body of Christ the Redeemer was only an
apparent, not a real body (for everything corporeal is the work
of Satan); Mary was an angel. The sacraments are corporeal, and therefore Satanic, symbols.

'(4) They rejected the use of crucifixes and icons, and regarded churches as the abode of evil spirits.

'(5) Only adults were received into their church; the ceremony consisted of fasting and prayer, not baptism, for water is created by Satan.

'(6) They had no hierarchy; but an executive, consisting of a senior or bishop, and two grades of Apostles.

'(7) Besides the ordinary Christians there was a special order of the Perfect or the Good, who renounced all earthly possessions, marriage, and the use of animal food. These chosen few dressed in black, lived like hermits, and were not allowed to speak to an unbeliever except for the purpose of converting him.

'(8) No Bogomil was allowed to drink wine.

'(9) The Bulgarian Bogomils prayed four times every day and four times every night; the Greek seven times every day, five times every night. They prayed whenever they crossed a bridge or entered a village. They had no holy days.

'(10) They had a death-bed ceremony (called in the west *la convenensa*). Whoever died without advantage of this ceremony went to hell, the ultimate abode of all unbelievers. They did not believe in a purgatory.'

43. 2. One need only glance at the ideas here expressed without troubling about niceties of expression to see what their source must be. They cannot be derived, however distantly, from the repertory of Christian beliefs and practices. At every crucial point, as I will not insult the reader by showing, they bear the well-known marks of Manichaeism.

43. 21. In 1898 the late F. C. Conybeare threw further light on the Bogomils by publishing one of their liturgies, apparently drawn up by the beginning of the ninth century and representing tendencies known to have survived in Spain to the eighth and ninth centuries.

43. 22. This fact, says Bury 'suggests the conjecture that it' (viz. the form of Bogomil worship recorded in the passage I have quoted in ten numbered sentences) 'also lingered in southern France'.

43. 23. The material in Bury's appendix to Gibbon, to which I have directed the reader's attention, is not mentioned (as it might, perhaps, advantageously have been, but for the inexpediency of referring readers to writers who have the enormous prestige of a Bury but are not Roman

Catholics) in a work of Roman Catholic Apologetics: *European Civilization, its Origin and Development*, edited by the late Edward Eyre, one of whose authors, Monsieur Jean Guiraud (vol. iii, pp. 354–409), has evidently devoted special attention to the records of the Holy Office.

43. 24. That the Inquisition 'did not punish for the sake of punishing', whatever that means, but used force to resist the force of a well equipped and formidable adversary whose attacks would doubtless have proved fatal, Monsieur Guiraud may be admitted to have proved.

43. 25. He has proved, too, that official Christianity was stirred to the point of using this force only when it became evident that force of a corresponding kind was being used, and would continue to be used, by the Bogomils.

43. 26. 'The suppression of heresy', says Monsieur Guiraud[1] (p. 390), 'was no new thing'; it was a very old thing; in fact, an example set by the Emperor Diocletian against the Manichees and later revived against the same enemy. For you need not be a Christian (Diocletian was not) in order to find the Manichees intolerable.

43. 27. 'When the [Bogomils] spread throughout his Empire,' says Monsieur Guiraud (p. 390), 'the Byzantine Emperor, Alexius Comnenus, renewed in the eleventh century the decrees of the Roman Emperors against the Manicheans.'

---

[1] Some readers may possibly be unfamiliar with some of the following facts relating to the *history of persecution*.

Under Greek paganism the 'city state' was a church. The distinction between 'church' and 'state' had not been made. What we call religious persecution was a normal and natural thing; it was simply society carrying out the duty of educating its members in their religion; if necessary by forcible means and on the person of a recalcitrant pupil.

Under Roman paganism the same principles held good. 'Persecution' of Christianity was regarded as a perfectly natural punishment for denying the 'city's' religion, with all that it implied.

Under early Christianity we encounter a novelty: a non-persecuting religion. The Fathers are unanimous on this point, viz. that a Christian cannot persecute.

In the Middle Ages this Patristic doctrine was abandoned. The Church knew what it was doing and why: it was consciously reacting to the Bogomil danger.

In modern times Spinoza's *Tractatus Theologico-Politicus* may be described as the classical restatement of a case for toleration.

43. 28. Why this special savagery against Manichees? It was not a peculiarity of the Christians. Christians and pagans agreed to regard Manichees as intolerable. It is worth asking why.

43. 3. Between the Manichees and certain other persons who included both the early Christians and certain of their pagan contemporaries there was a relation of 'kill or be killed'; and that without any will to do either. The mere coexistence of Manichees with Christians (and some non-Christians, for that matter) set in motion a double threat by each to the life of the other; a threat which might operate involuntarily.

43. 31. Where such a state of things obtains, there are two groups of persons each constituting a danger to the other's welfare, yet without either having a hostile intention towards the other.

43. 32. It is easy to understand the psychological conditions giving rise to such a situation. Each group is equipped with sentiments different from, and hostile to, those of the other. How such sentiments work near the emotional end of their scale, and therefore unconsciously, we have already seen (41. 5 seqq.).

43. 33. Let us assume it for a fact that medieval Christianity was based on the sanctity of the oath. I do not mean that it was based on assuming that oaths were not in fact sometimes, or even frequently, violated; I mean that it was based on assuming a certain hesitation or unwillingness to violate them.

43. 34. Place this hesitation as low as you like (and sometimes, among certain sorts of people, it was doubtless low), still, so long as the conditions of life are recognizably medieval, it would not sink to zero. It was only under what I will call a certain 'inducement' that a medieval man would be willing to break an oath.

43. 35. This inducement was a variable quantity. The pressure which would be required to induce a given man in given circumstances to break a given oath had to be stronger in proportion as he was a relatively well-brought-up, decent, god-fearing man.

43. 36. Moreover he is assumed to be a man whose

upbringing was of a Christian kind, and whose decency and god-fearingness were judged by Christian standards. Unless we are told what kind of upbringing is in question, nothing is gained by using colourless phrases like 'well-brought-up, decent, god-fearing'. We must know what kind of God he has been taught to fear.

43. 4. For example, Bogomils regarded churches as the abode of evil spirits (43. 19, § 4). Christians regarded them as the abode of spirits friendly to man, though, no doubt, to be approached with caution.

43. 41. The two systems of thought, therefore, involved not only different but opposite answers to the question 'how would a decent, well-brought-up person behave in church?'

43. 42. The answer to this question differs according as it is asked about a different person. If the person is a Christian he will go into the house of his God with rejoicing; if he is a Bogomil (assuming that we have been correctly informed about their liturgy) in the spirit of one who believes and trembles.

43. 43. To resume: The basis of medieval society was the sanctity of the oath (43. 33).

43. 44. A Christian man's oath was better than his word because it has a special solemnity which was absent from his mere word as such; it was his Christian upbringing which brought about this distinction (43. 36).

43. 45. The Bogomil system of conduct, as we happen to know, was hostile to this distinction between a man's word and his oath. This emerged from the testimony of the 'Cathari', or arch-members of the sect, giving evidence before the Inquisition that 'any oath, true or false, is unlawful' (Guiraud, op. cit., p. 360).

43. 46. Even if we did not possess this testimony, or disbelieved it, the same inference would emerge from what we know of the Bogomils.

43. 47. If a man's word is not enough to command our credence (so runs the Bogomil train of thought) neither is his oath; and if his oath is sufficient, his bare word is sufficient.

43. 48. It is a train of thought familiar to all who are Christians enough to catch at certain New Testament sayings and pride themselves on exaggerating them.

43. 49. So the injunction: 'Swear not at all' (Matt. v. 34) can be easily twisted into a prohibition of all such customs and usages as depend on the distinction between a man's word and his oath; a prohibition that impoverishes his discourse by banishing from it (to take one example) whatever is not intended to be 'taken seriously'.

43. 5. It was in the thirteenth century that the 'Albigensian heresy' was stamped out, too completely for us now ever to discover in detail what it was like.

43. 51. Through the mists of antiquity it seems to have been a barbarism, in particular a religion of a Manichean sort existing in a Christian world. If it was a barbarism, it was the only one known to us whose career came to an end in early and complete failure.

43. 52. The mere idea of its being a failure inclines us to sympathy with it; that sympathy with failures as such which they earn at the hands of sentimental posterity just by being dead.

43. 53. If we are careful how we bestow this sympathy, confining it, in fact, to what is really dead, there is no harm in it; but are we ever careful enough? By lavishing undeserved sympathy on the dead, do we not call them or their likes back to life?

43. 54. If that is the danger into which we run by extending to the dead a sympathy they did not deserve when they lived, we ought to be careful how we extend to them the privilege of lying quiet in their graves.

43. 55. It was the piety of Gibbon's hand, when writing his fifty-fourth chapter, that extended that privilege to the Bogomils.

43. 56. Since Gibbon's time the curiosity of the learned world has worked insatiably to lay bare a little more of the facts he left half-revealed.

43. 57. In consequence we know too much about the Bogomils to be content with a Gibbonesque, eighteenth-century picture of them as simple, philosophically minded innocents; but only very little too much.

XLIV

THE THIRD BARBARISM:
THE TURKS

44. 1. No complete list of barbarisms will be offered here or elsewhere. All that is claimed for those which appear on the list here given is that they have a right to appear on the present list. That this right is such as to countervail any objections is not suggested.

44. 11. Nor does this convey any suggestion as to what is intended by appearance in the present list. It does not convey a suggestion, for example, that this list, or indeed any other, is a list on which any barbarism worthy of the name will appear.

44. 12. That there could be in this sense a complete or exhaustive list of barbarisms that deserved the name, or indeed that there could be any competition for the name, I do not believe.

44. 13. Nor am I prepared to admit that there are any characteristics generally present in barbarism; whether 'generally' means 'sometimes' or 'always'. I need not, perhaps, labour the point that 'generally' has both meanings.

44. 14. Savagery is a negative conception (41. 11), and there are theoretically any number of different ways of being uncivilized, between which there need be nothing in common.

44. 15. If this is true of savagery, it is equally true of barbarism. Hostility towards civilization might exist in an infinity of different forms having nothing in common but the name.

44. 16. It is quite possible, however, that barbarisms intrinsically different might undergo a kind of assimilation, like what an entomologist will call *mimicry*, where one insect, without having what I will call any 'reason' to be like another, is actually like it through sheer superfluity of scientifically inexplicable morphogenesis.

44. 17. If anything analogous to protective or other mimicry happens as between one barbarism and another, we must conclude that barbarisms may exhibit not only well founded resemblances but resemblances of a freakish or erratic kind, like, for example, those which connect a twig with the caterpillar that 'imitates' it.

44. 18. So much by the way of preface.

44. 2. The third barbarism on our present list is that of the Turks: but I must begin by distinguishing the Seljuk Turks from the Ottoman Turks who in the later Middle Ages succeeded, with no very clear title, to the name which the Seljuks had made glorious or nefarious in the earlier Middle Ages.

44. 21. The Seljuks (Gibbon, ch. lvii) were a pastoral and predatory caste whose warlike feats first established their fame about the end of the tenth century on the waters of the Oxus.

44. 22. In the year 1050 they invaded the Roman Empire; that is, the Eastern Empire.

44. 23. Their chief, Togrul Beg, embraced Islam; perhaps after being a Christian: for the evidence see Bury's *Gibbon*, vol. vi, p. 232, note 19.

44. 24. After migrating westward to the head-waters of the Euphrates his son, Alp Arslan, conquered Armenia and established himself on an equality with the Emperor of Constantinople; in 1071 he defeated the Romans at Manzikert, between Erzerum and Van.

44. 25. Malek Shah, the successor of Alp Arslan, divided the Seljuk Empire into the four provinces of Persia, Syria, Kerman, and Roum.

44. 26. The next phase of the Seljuk expansion was the partial, and incomplete, conquest of Asia Minor. This involved the removal of the Seljuk provincial capital (viz. the capital of Roum) to within a hundred miles of Constantinople, and the loss to the Byzantine Empire of almost all its Asiatic territories.

44. 27. The conquest of so large an area by the Seljuks implied a merely forcible conversion of its inhabitants to Islam; their governors, in some cases at least, meeting trouble half-way by surrendering to the conqueror.

44. 28. In 1076 the Seljuks captured Jerusalem, forbade Christians access by pilgrimage to the holy places of their faith, and desecrated these places themselves. By this time, however, the Seljuk Empire was in a state of decay, and the history of the Crusades need not command our attention.

44. 3. Two hundred years later, to quote Gibbon, 'the decline of the Moguls gave a free scope to the rise and progress of the OTTOMAN EMPIRE'; where the use of capitals is a typographical salute accorded by Gibbon to the name of TURK, reappearing in his narrative.

44. 31. What Gibbon (vii. 25; the edition quoted is Bury throughout) attractively calls 'the obscure fathers of the Othman line' whose origin is in fact unknown, used to pitch their tents near the south bank of the Oxus at a time when the Seljuk dynasty was already a thing of the past; later they moved in a westerly direction to the upper waters of the Euphrates.

44. 32. This brought them to the outskirts of the Greek Empire; in fact, to the plains of Bithynia, which had at that time recently been patrolled after the Roman fashion by the local militia, half soldiers and half farmers, who had been paid in their military capacity by remission of the rents which they owed in their fiscal capacity as tenants of the Empire.

44. 33. Gibbon did not understand this arrangement, though it is a commonplace to modern students of the Roman Empire; and he attributes its breakdown, which was obviously due to depopulation, to an imaginary cause, 'the political errors of the Greek emperor'.

43. 34. Any attentive reader of his narrative from the 57th chapter to the 64th will notice abundant evidence that the Seljuk inroads into Asia Minor (43. 26) were followed by a sharp decline in its population. What we encountered in the eleventh century as a populous upland plain has gone back by the beginning of the fourteenth century to steppe.

44. 35. The depopulation of a once rich country-side produces in it a variety of famine phenomena, notably shortage of tax yield and consequent inability to meet the cost of soldiers' pay. Gibbon realized that about the year 1300 something happened on the plateau of Asia Minor as a result of which the Empire became unable to keep the peace; what he did not realize was that, by a vicious circle, they became less able to keep it at the moment when, owing to Seljuk invasions, it most urgently needed to be kept.

44. 36. A barbarian inroad into Europe, especially into a highly civilized part of it, such as Asia Minor was in the eleventh century, would inflict an injury primarily on the part of the European organism immediately affected, and secondarily on those more remotely concerned; the nature of the injury, in broad and general terms, being as follows.

44. 37. *The country undergoes impoverishment.* This is the most general name of which I can think for the shrinkage of all the activities that go on over any part of the country-side; the most general name for the fact that, whatever people are doing over a given tract of country, they become on the whole less able to do it after a certain time than they had been before.

44. 38. In the second place *its recovery is retarded.* A given country-side depends for its efficiency in any activity you like to name on having a sufficiently dense population to pursue that activity with reasonable efficiency; for part of the vigour a population has at its disposal is used in keeping up its own strength.

44. 39. Two factors may thus be distinguished in considering the waste or destruction produced by war or the like in a given country-side. There is damage done, and there is hindrance to any form of positive or constructive activity, no matter whether this takes the form of re-making something old or making something new, so long as the thing is needed.

44. 4. The Turks from the beginning of their history established themselves in a parasitic position relatively to their Christian neighbours. From Orchan's time onwards it was their habit to select the likeliest of their Christian captives, all of them being young men, convert them forcibly to Islam, educate them in the use of arms, and entitle them Janissaries ('bright faces').

44. 41. It was not until in 1826 that the total body of Janissaries then living were abolished, characteristically, by massacre.

44. 42. The Turks' conquests began with the taking of Brusa (1326), which from that time became the capital of Othman and his son Orchan.

44. 43. The whole of Bithynia up to the Bosporus and Hellespont was conquered in 1340.

B b

44. 44. In 1346 Orchan married the Greek princess Irene and became an ally of the Emperor her father; but the alliance was precarious from the start; Orchan looked upon the Greek world merely as so much prospective plunder, and never intended that any treaty he had made with its members should bind him for a moment after it had outlived its utility to himself.

44. 45. If anyone doubted this, he need not wait long for evidence. Before the negotiations for the marriage of Irene were complete, Orchan had been in treaty for the hand of Anne of Savoy, whom he threw over when a richer alliance offered; but in the meantime he used the earlier negotiations as an opportunity for obtaining permission to hold a slave-market at Gallipoli.

44. 46. This permission gave him a formal claim, which he retained in spite of renouncing the intended marriage, to occupy positions on the European side of the Dardanelles. This is how the Turk obtained his foothold in Europe.

44. 47. Henceforth the reader may consult the relevant chapter (ch. iii) of the *Cambridge Modern History*, and the authorities there quoted.

44. 48. At this juncture Orchan died, his son Soliman predeceasing him; to be succeeded by Amurath I (1360–87).

44. 49. With the sons of the Emperor John Palaeologus in forced attendance, Amurath marched against the hardy and warlike peasantry of the Balkan highlands; his successor Bajazet I (1389–1403) defeated his rival not only in the east but in the west as far as the pass of Thermopylae.

44. 5. It was now that Europe first realized her danger, and saw that unless she destroyed the Turks the Turks would destroy her.

44. 51. Sigismund, King of Hungaria, preached a crusade; the knights of France and other countries took it up eagerly; Bajazet in reply threatened to feed his horse on St. Peter's altar at Rome; and in fact at the battle of Nicopolis (1396) routed a hundred thousand Christians.

44. 52. In the course of this battle the Janissaries, amounting to half the Turkish army, were destroyed; and Bajazet, infuriated by his loss, seems to have threatened death to any prisoner who refused to abjure his faith.

44. 53. When the prisoners were at length ransomed, they brought home strange tales of the state in which Bajazet lived, his violence, cruelty, and contempt for human life.

44. 54. In the year 1400 a new luminary suddenly appeared on the eastern horizon of Europe; for this was the year in which Aleppo was taken by Timur, and in 1402 Bajazet was conclusively defeated at Angora, and died in the following year.

44. 55. Towards the end of the fourteenth and the beginning of the fifteenth centuries the career of the Turks as representatives of barbarism, as opposed to the civilization for which Europe stood even in a relatively uncivilized period of her history, was at its height.

44. 56. The battle of Kosovo was fought in 1389; and from that time until the fall of Constantinople (1453) and even later the fortunes of the Turkish arms were attended by almost monotonous success.

44. 57. By degrees as time went on these successes came to be more and more cheaply won, as the Turks came to count upon easier victory and the Christians to reckon upon a more certain defeat.

44. 58. To analyse the conditions which went to make these correlative and opposite states of mind in the two belligerents would be tedious. I will only say that an important factor was the difficulty, for a long-civilized subject of the Eastern Empire, of believing that there was, and in particular that there was for him in the near future (as we should call it) a Turkish peril.

44. 59. It thus came about for one reason and another that the period in which the Turks brought to an end the long history of the Byzantine Empire was one in which the glory of the Turkish arms was already somewhat overblown.

44. 6. Constantinople was won, in fact, by superiority in gun-fire, which levelled the walls attacked by a force 'fifty, perhaps a hundred times, greater' than the defenders (Gibbon, vii. 191); but the Turkish superiority in gun-fire was due to a disgruntled Hungarian gunner named Orban.

44. 61. This represents only one of innumerable ways in which the siege of Constantinople was lost by treachery before it was begun. To crown all, the Pope, Nicholas V, foretold the ruin of Rome's hated rival.

44. 62. After the fall of Constantinople the Turkish successes are not, indeed, less monotonous, but they are cheaper.

44. 63. Perhaps the historian may be justified in detecting a change of tone consequent on the three weeks' siege of Belgrade in 1456 and its brilliant relief by John Hunyadi, with 50,000 Turks killed and wounded; it may be that casualties on this scale were regarded by the Turkish high command as excessive.

44. 64. At any rate, the next event in the Balkan war shows the Turk once more master of his old form; in 1458 he took by treachery the fortress of Semendra and deported its inhabitants.

44. 65. Three years later they invaded Bosnia and attacked the fortress of Bobovac. Its defender, Prince Radak, was a Bogomil (for there were still plenty of Bogomils in the Balkans in the Middle Ages, and naturally, as enemies of Christianity, they were well disposed towards Islam) and [naturally] handed the fortress over to the Turks.

44. 66. But Radak did not understand the game of treachery as the Turks played it. He thought it was a game in which you made up your mind which side you would be on, and then you would be on that side and against the other side. So when he handed the fortress over to the Turks, the Turks cut his head off.

44. 67. The rules of the game, as understood by the Turks, are that there are no sides; you play, as children call it, all against all. In such a state of things one player may have a kind of ascendancy over another, such that this other obeys the orders he gives him, strictly speaking they are not orders but what I have called (20. 5) *force*, and the giving of them I call not the giving of orders but the bringing of force to bear on someone.

44. 68. It is only parental discipline that keeps such games from ending not only in tears but in grim and murderous bloodshed.

44. 69. It was in 1456 that the Acropolis was surrendered by Franco, the last Duke of Athens, who was privately strangled for his pains; and Greece was by degrees reduced to the most miserable province of the Turkish Empire.

44. 7. This shall suffice for a narrative of Turkish history. It would add little to extend it over the time when the Turk was celebrated for his piratical exploits up and down the Mediterranean, and even farther afield; less to come down to living memory, recall the melancholy figure he cut as the sick man of Europe, and remind ourselves of the occasion when Mr. Gladstone threatened to turn him out of Europe bag and baggage.

44. 8. The Saracens' intention to destroy Christendom was based on a too fanatical interpretation of Islam; for there is room for it and Christianity, as posterity has now seen, in the same world. It was based on a misunderstanding by the Saracens of what they themselves stood for.

44. 81. The Albigensians, according to our evidence, were at daggers drawn with Christianity, and therefore with civilization; which the earlier Moslems at least were not. The Christian Church, however, recognized this in time, and so far as Europe was concerned stamped them out.

44. 82. The Turks were the first to conceive the idea of barbarism as we know it to-day, and to see how it could be carried out. When it came to the actual carrying out, they failed; and why? Because the odds against success in doing it were too long.

44. 83. At Brusa in 1326 the Turks were in a good way to be victorious (44. 42); again at Nicopolis in 1396 (44. 51); and again at Constantinople in 1453 (44. 56); but at Constantinople they lost their last chance and committed themselves to a career as the sick man of Europe.

44. 84. The fact that the Turks were never able, even at the height of their power, to register upon the body of Europe the knock-out blow that they needed for a decisive victory was fatal to their attempts at a mastery of the world; every struggle they made during those long years was another failure to keep the ice from packing round them (41. 63) until at last civilization triumphed.

44. 85. The result is visible in the Turkey of to-day, a country no longer to be tempted by a recollection of her ancestors' thievery, but leading an honest and upright life.

44. 86. Those who remember the operations of 1915 and 1916 in the Dardanelles and in Mesopotamia may be glad that the Turks, who were then against us, are now for us.

44. 87. What is the cause of this change? It was because, during the same years in which the Germans turned to thievery, the Turks turned to honest ways.

44. 9. This brings us to the fourth and last part of our history of barbarism, viz. the history of German barbarism.

XLV

THE FOURTH BARBARISM:
THE GERMANS

45. 1. THE fourth and last barbarism which we have to study, that of the Germans, appears to be in one way unique, or at least uniquely situated.

45. 11. We shall find that this appearance of uniqueness is an illusion due to the presence, in other cases, of sources of error that are absent in this.

45. 12. The other barbarists whom we have hitherto studied presented us with a delusive appearance of having been always barbarists; they seem to have been born without any manners, as Mongols are born without any beards.

45. 13. But the barbarism of a German, at least one whom we know personally, does not seem to be innate; it seems to have grown in him as his reaction to a peculiar situation in which a certain element in him, his nationality, was involved at a certain time. It is as if something had happened corporately to the Germans (and nothing parallel, we suppose, to, for example, a Seljuk) endowing them with a peculiar kind of bumptiousness.

45. 14. I do not say that anything of the sort ever happened; only that if it happened in the one case it is reasonable to suppose that it may have happened in the other as well.

45. 15. For consider what assumptions must otherwise be made in order to explain the facts already known. It is arguable that Germans have always been what may be called bad neighbours, but the characteristic has remained latent until recently, when conditions have arisen favourable to its display.

45. 16. If the question is asked: What conditions in particular favour the display of a latent ill-neighbourliness or (let us speak plainly and call it) latent barbarism?

45. 17. The answer will be given by any thoughtful man: No condition in particular. Any condition will favour the display of barbarism in one kind or another. A man who is going to behave barbarously will always find opportunities for so behaving. No conditions will impede him.

45. 18. In what way, then, is the barbarism of Germans peculiar? Only in this: that we look at it with the eye of a contemporary observer, whereas we look at the barbarism of a Seljuk (for example) with the eye of one who fancies that Seljuks and the like belong to an age of portents and miracles which differed *toto caelo* from the world that you and I know.

45. 19. What makes anybody think so strangely (for strangely it is) about Seljuks? No reason whatever. As Dr. Johnson said to the lady, 'Ignorance, Madam, sheer ignorance.'

45. 2. We look at the records of these ancient barbarisms as people look at what they call history, with eyes half shut, blurred into something romantic; but you and I, if we know what we are about, have to look at the German barbarism (which concerns us, because it is happening now) with our eyes wide open and all sources of error removed; there is no other way of fighting it efficiently (45. 11).

45. 21. What is the general nature of this German barbarism which claims our attention as something now going on?

45. 22. It is something historical (the word is now being used in its proper sense, not an ironic sense, 45. 2), like anything that forms a part of the contemporary world; not something that 'is' but something that 'becomes'; something that happens and takes time to happen, happening more and more completely according as it takes more and more time to happen.

45. 23. You may give a date to the occurrence of this barbarism; you may say that it exhibited itself in the age of Bismarck in the third quarter of the nineteenth century; and I should not quarrel with that; but that would not mean that it had never displayed itself before that time, or that by that time it was fully formed.

45. 24. German barbarism came into existence, as historical things do, gradually; at first despite the opposition of a great deal that was civilized in the country, at last sweeping away this opposition in a flood.

45. 25. Much of the process goes on underground; no one outside Germany, and very few at most inside it, know in detail how it goes on; it is essential to the process that no one should know; I do not mean because interested parties keep it secret, but because no one could explain it thoroughly even if he wished to.

45. 26. The thing is a landslide; and no one knows exactly how a landslide happens. All you can do is to name certain marks and say: 'Now that mark is standing firm', and a little later 'now that mark is gone'.

45. 27. What is there between these two times? In the case of which I am thinking, there is oblivion; unconsciousness; an interval in which your head is lost. This, at any rate, is the Nazi theory, expounded in some detail by the Nazi psychologists.

45. 28. 'And why not? What Nazis call thinking with your blood is a much quicker way of thinking than the old-fashioned way of doing it with your brains.'

45. 29. Certainly, provided that you sometimes have someone with brains at your elbow to check your results and see that they are right; or, failing that, do not care whether they are right or wrong.

45. 3. I am not sure that Nazis understand what logic is for; at any rate they talk as if they were proud of believing a lot of nonsense about it.

45. 31. Everyone who has digested Locke's *Essay* knows that it is a great mark of folly to over-estimate the value of logic, or to think that anything can be done with it that cannot be done just as well without it.

45. 32. But the Nazis advocate 'thinking with your blood' as if it were a new and revolutionary idea; which it could only be for a generation slavishly taught, in sheer defiance of Locke to think exclusively with their brains.

45. 33. Exclusively, I say; for therein lies the whole difference between thinking like a sane man and thinking like a Nazi.

45. 34. A sane man thinks just as fast or as slowly as he finds it expedient to think, granted the peculiarities of the work on which he is engaged. If it is especially important to think fast, he allows no consideration to induce him to think slowly; if it is especially important to think slowly, he lets nothing induce him to think fast.

45. 35. Suppose there were a generation, say, of Germans, who happened to have been educated by the most pedantic of professors, against whose teaching, like good little boys, they had never risen in revolt.

45. 36. Suppose the professors had never heard of Locke, but fancied in a stick-in-the-mud sort of way that a good little boy must mind not only his book but two kinds of book in particular: his logic and his grammar; wishing to turn him into a gerund-grinding little boy.

45. 37. Suppose one day the little boys turned naughty, and barred out their schoolmaster-professor; should we not commend them for showing a proper spirit and bringing about what I dare say they would be ignorant enough to call a 'revolution' (26. 7) in their school?

45. 38. If we did, I only suggest that we should be careful to praise them for the right things and not for the wrong. In the course of their so-called revolution their apple-stealing will perhaps have greatly improved, but their lessons will have gone to glory; instead of getting better, their school-work, by which it is likely that these good little gerund-grinders would set exaggerated store, would get very much worse.

45. 39. And they could not know that it had got worse; because in the 'revolution' they had got rid of the only men who were both able and trusted to mark their papers and tell them how they were doing.

45. 4. I said (45. 23) that the German barbarism could be dated, not too inaccurately, to the age of Bismarck. Here is a typical example of it, which I quote from *The Italian Alps* by D. W. Freshfield, published at London in 1875.

45. 41. '"In all our German Alps", writes a learned doctor, "there is hardly a more forsaken or unknown corner than the Adamello."'

45. 42. This gets Dr. Freshfield's goat, and he bursts into expostulation, thus.

45. 43. '"In unseren deutschen Alpen!" There is not in the whole Alps a region which is more thoroughly Italian than the mountain-mass of which the Presanella is the highest, the Adamello the most famous, summit.'

45.44. Dr. Freshfield is angry with his author for the childishly boastful way in which he calls a mountain a 'German' mountain when by any test internationally used it belongs to another country; the implication being not that the 'learned doctor' is ignorant what country he is writing about, but that he is lying about a little-known region, pretending (in 1864), in order to gratify a sort of national vanity for which Germans had an evil reputation, that the country on which he was writing was a part of Germany when it was not.

45.45. I call it 'childishly boastful' to attach the epithet 'German' to things which you and your readers know are not German, but enjoy pretending to think of as German. By the middle of the nineteenth century this had established itself as a 'bad habit' of the German mind.

45.46. Of what was it a symptom? The answer will depend on how you classify mental diseases. In one way, it is a symptom of lunatic greed or envy, which drives you to claim ownership in what you know to be your neighbour's property.

45.47. In one way it is a symptom of cowardice, for it is essential to these claims on your neighbour's property that they should be only make-believe claims; you would regard yourself as grossly injured if anyone took them seriously.

45.48. However you decide to classify it, you will classify it as something at once morbid and infantile; something which, if you regarded it as the product of a grown-up mind, you would be obliged to condemn as the product of an evilly distorted mind (think, for example, of *Max und Moritz* or *Struwwelpeter*); but you are ashamed to regard them in that way, because it means imputing obscenities to babes and sucklings. So you hesitate.

45.49. In brief, the Bismarckian age exhibits German barbarism in an ambiguous form. It is something that comes very near to being a downright barbarism, but the question whether it is or not is a question most non-Germans will hesitate to answer. Or rather, would have hesitated in the time of Bismarck; no one would hesitate now.

45.5. Except a man who is tarred with the same brush. And it should surprise nobody to learn that there are many of these; in a sense, too, deservedly respected.

45. 51. It is the time-factor that makes the difference. What is mere childish boasting in 1864 (45. 44) may be confessed barbarism a generation later, by (say) 1897; and if at that stage it is still a thing at which a spectator who is resolved to be as sympathetic as possible can look with sympathy, the time-limit for that attitude might come in another generation; say 1910.

45. 52. To estimate (you cannot call it measuring) large-scale psychological changes by taking events a generation apart on a time-scale is certainly rough; but it gives us a reasonable approximation to the quantity we wish to evaluate.

45. 53. It gives us ground for saying that a non-German who, living at the time of the Boer War, ascribed the contemporary state of German feeling towards England to barbarism was probably wrong, unless he had a specialist's knowledge of the German political atmosphere; but that to say the same thing ten, twenty, or thirty years later would be increasingly likely to be right, and would need correspondingly less shrewdness.

45. 54. Now an Englishman (say) is liable to a certain time-lag between barbarism's arriving at a certain stage of maturity in Germany and that fact's becoming known to him in England; perhaps a longer time-lag than we might expect, perhaps not; it does not matter.

45. 55. Let us call the lag between the time at which German barbarism becomes a danger to the world, and the time when an average Englishman makes up his mind that it is a danger to the world, x.

45. 56. An Englishman who is more intelligent or better informed than the average will take less time than this, other things being equal; say the time he takes is y, where $y < x$. In the opposite case more time will be needed, viz. z, where $z > x$.

45. 57. At a time when a given barbarism is taking shape by degrees, for example in the Bismarckian phase of German barbarism (45. 49), there must in any non-German country be a large number of persons who think it would be wrong to take that barbarism seriously. What kind of government the country has makes no difference.

45. 58. As the barbarism accentuates itself, hostility to it will increase *pari passu*, but subject to the above time-lag (45. 54). Various communities, at various times because of differences in the time-lag, become aware that the barbarist country is an enemy to each one of them.

45. 59. If they all found this out at once, the barbarist would have a hard time; his only hope (in fact a pretty good hope) is diplomacy, to prevent his enemies from working together.

45. 6. The barbarist, while being in fact everyone's enemy, must work at exacerbating the enmity between this party and that, pretending to be, himself, a good friend to each, or at any rate to the one he is at the moment addressing; *les absents*, says the proverb, *ont toujours tort*, so no harm is done.

45. 61. The German barbarist has rediscovered the great rule of barbarist warfare originally laid down by the Turks: that among barbarists there are no allies; all fight against all (44. 67); a principle qualified, but not abrogated, by that other great rule providing for a sort of make-believe command based upon what I have called force (21. 72) as distinct from authority.

45. 62. When the barbarism in question has taken shape and consolidated itself as a conscious and self-confessed barbarism (to continue 45. 57) there is still a time, not yet elapsed, during which this or that person is unaware that it has so taken shape.

45. 63. There not only may be such a time for any given observer of the process, there must be such a time for any given observer of the process; it will be longer or shorter according to his length of time-lag (45. 54) for that event, but it can never shrink to zero for any observer and any process.

45. 64. While there is any part of this time (45. 62) not yet elapsed, there are members of the body politic in question who cannot be expected to scent danger through the ambiguous form in which a neighbouring community expresses its immature leanings to barbarism (45. 5).

45. 65. Even when it has become clear to most people that the thing is a public danger, there may still be members of a given body politic whose time-lag relatively to that

danger is so large that at a given time they still think it innocuous and even laudable. They are likely to be very stupid people; but by the method here expounded the stupidity of a given person is expressible algebraically as a function of the average time he takes to grasp a new idea.

45. 66. The Bismarckian age, I said (45. 49), exhibited German barbarism in an ambiguous form. Not even the Germans themselves could clear up the ambiguity. No one knew, and the Germans could not have told you, whether they were a nation of simple-minded innocents, gazing wide-eyed at the world around them, or a nation of heroes, ready at any moment to sacrifice their lives for the Fatherland. No one can be both.

45. 67. If a man is as muddle-headed about himself as this implies, there is only one thing about him of which you can be certain. He is a liar; or if you prefer it, a man addicted to self-deception; a man whose judgements about himself, and therefore about everything else as well, are likely to be wrong with a probability that increases as he grows older.

45. 68. Please observe, Reader, that I am not talking about all Germans. I do not say that all Germans are liars. I know of some who are not; those heroes, for example, who continue in spite of everything the Nazis can do to run their secret wireless station and keep on printing *Das Wahre Deutschland*.

45. 69. Even about these, however, I say that there are not enough of them; there ought to be, not barely enough to keep the flag of the 'True Germany' flying, but enough to sweep the flag of the false Germany from all the lands and waters of the world.

45. 7. It would no doubt be right and proper that Englishmen should help in this process. But in a general way it is a mistake for one person, A, to interfere with another, B, in the doing of what is called his duty (for this sense of the word 'duty' cf. 17. 63).

45. 71. This is because the obligation here in question is not only an obligation that the act should be done, it is an obligation that it should be done by B; if A puts in his oar and takes it upon himself to do it, the result may be (must be, if the obligation is one of those which admit of being discharged only by one irreplaceable agent) that A does what he is under no obligation to do, and that what B is under obligation to do is not done.

45.72. And that is what comes, according to the homely proverb, of people's not minding their own business.

45.73. Within what limits it is necessary that everyone should mind his own business and prevent others from interfering I do not know; though I know very well that the principle is one which I, like other people, neglect at my peril.

45.74. I have learnt, too, by experience that Germans who have taken refuge in this country from Nazi oppression and made use of that hospitality to pursue the work they had been doing at home by writing books against the Nazi tyranny may be doing a very ill service to their hosts, because they do not understand the conditions under which that tyranny can be exercised.

45.75. I have learnt this because while writing this book I have read a great many books on political subjects by German refugees.

45.76. There are some wines which, they say, do not travel. The same is true of these samples of modern German politics. On reflection, it seems only natural that an author who has taken part in a long and nerve-racking political battle in one country should arrive in another with his nerves shot to pieces and a determination (very likely unconscious) that his new audience should fully realize how invincible is the man or party or machine that defeated him.

45.77. And the fact remains that what he is offering is an article which has already been offered on the market, and failed. Is it surprising that he comes before his present audience in the attitude of a defeatist?

45.78. It is not surprising, it is perfectly natural, if you accept the account given in the last few pages of German barbarism.

45.79. According to that account, there was once, before the time of Bismarck, a time when the Germans were a pedant-ridden nation; a nation whose nose was ground to its book by the strong hands of an entire generation of professors.

45.8. Do you remember when Germany was like that? If not, ask any old man, and he will tell you.

45. 81. And do you remember how a whole herd of school-inspectors, of whom Mr. Matthew Arnold was the chief, scolded us for not being like that, and threatened us with the direst penalties that a schoolmasterly mind could invent for contumaciously refusing to be like that?

45. 82. To satisfy yourself that it was so you need not depend on anybody's memory; Matthew Arnold's books are extant; if you don't know which to look at first, I suggest *Friendship's Garland* (1871).

45. 83. To resume. According to the same account this prehistoric age of innocence (45. 2) was followed by an age of iron, into which the ambiguities of the Bismarckian period (45. 49) were resolved. That was when the Prussian armies marched victoriously over the soil of France; and when the French people, not realizing that they had to deal with a nation of wide-eyed innocents, all, to a man, laying down their lives for the Fatherland, learned to call them 'les sales Boches'.

45. 84. In this chapter I have considered the barbarism of the modern Germans as if it had been a phenomenon that first appeared, in an ambiguous shape, under Bismarck in the nineteenth century (45. 23); or, to be accurate, I said that such a date might be given to it and that I should not object. I had in fact already written something on the same subject in chapter xxxiii; and I knew that a careless or malevolent reader might fancy the two inconsistent.

45. 85. In chapter xxxiii I pointed out that the classical politics was unadvisedly and unsuccessfully transplanted into the soil of Prussia by Frederick the Great, who, in the hot-house atmosphere of the universities he planted under glass, did not succeed in reproducing (indeed, never tried to reproduce) conditions like those which had produced Locke or Hobbes.

45. 86. The conditions under which the royal patron would say to one beneficiary: 'Be another Locke', and to another 'Improve upon the work of Hobbes', were conditions of which the first was to do what you were told; to practise in a spirit of piety the good old German religion of herd-worship (33. 35).

45. 87. There is no inconsistency between saying that the Germans were addicted to herd-worship in the time of

Bismarck, and saying that they were addicted to it in the time of Frederick the Great; or, for that matter, saying that they were addicted to it in the time of Martin Luther or Thomas à Kempis.

45. 88. If herd-worship is in fact, as it appears to be, an immemorial condition of the German people, a condition out of which no process of civilization has succeeded in bringing them, then we know what is wrong with the German people and what is wrong with the world that harbours them. What is wrong is insufficient civilization; not absolute non-civilization or savagery, for there is no such thing; but a defect in civilization where more civilization was needed.

45. 89. We know, I say, what is wrong with the German people. It is that incivility of which all who know them have at one time or other complained, and which in these last days has been exaggerated to the point of a mania. That it should be a mania is what makes it intolerable; but what makes it acceptable to the Germans in their present frame of mind is the fact that it is a mania.

45. 9. There is nothing new or unexpected about this. Ever since the world began, if anybody has become intolerable to his neighbours, what has made him intolerable has been something maniacal or fanatical about his demeanour. The lesson of making oneself tolerable, the lesson of cultivating a type of demeanour which other people find they can stand, often depends on distinctions which in themselves are slight; a little more here, and a little less there, may suffice to convert what no man can stand into something tolerable.

45. 91. It is distinctions of this kind which are systematically pursued by the man who makes a point of coming to an agreement with everyone from whom he might have differed; that is, what Plato calls the dialectical man (24. 59). I have warned the reader that this does not mean the 'pacifist'; that to be what is called a 'pacifist' is to be a war-monger in whom war-mongery is complicated by defeatism (29. 98); if what Plato calls dialectic is peace, such a peace is not to be pursued under the conditions which prevail in this world except by one resolved, if need be, to fight for it, and fight hard.

45. 92. In the chapters preceding this I have given some

account of the activities and fortunes of certain notable barbarists; that is, people, who have thought it an easy matter,
or at any rate a possible one, to destroy civilization and
batten on the proceeds. I make no claim to have considered
them all; in fact, I have been at pains to explain that I do not
even know what that phrase would mean; but I have considered claimants for the position of what may be called arch-
barbarists who have appeared in certain ages and have received a strong backing from certain historians whom I will
not name; and have found that they did not come up to the
standard which I had already set myself (44. 1). In this connexion I will mention the Magyars and the Vikings.

45. 93. The best claimants whom I can identify for the
place of arch-barbarists are the Turks; not the genuine Seljuks who petered out long before they reached the Bosporus, or at any rate before they crossed it, handing on their
claim, if claim it was, to the Ottomans (44. 3); nor even the
Ottomans as they finally declined into the 'sick man of
Europe' (44. 83); but only the Ottomans in the moments of
glory which repeatedly, at an early stage of their career, they
promised but never won (44. 84).

45. 94. The Turks are no exception to the rule which
elsewhere, to the best of my knowledge, is unbroken: the rule
that barbarists in the end have always been beaten; a rule
which I state here merely as the conclusion arrived at by the
inductive study of cases. The reader already knows that an
inductive conclusion to the effect that, given a certain group
of conditions c, the effect e will be forthcoming, entitles no
man to say that if c is given e will be given. That is a universal proposition, and inductive inquiries never provide a
foundation for universal propositions. What induction does
is to provide reasons for thinking that something, for example e, is likely or unlikely to happen; never that it is
certain to happen or not to happen. As I said in an earlier
chapter, an inductive proposition 'tells you what to expect'
(16. 21).

45. 95. I do not know what the reason is why barbarists
have always in the end been beaten. I do not even know
whether there is a reason, that is, a single reason, the same in
every case; it might very well be that one was beaten for one

reason and one for another; or even that of various portions into which a single barbarist army was divided one part was beaten for one reason and one for another. At questions like these imagination recoils; but that is no reason for refusing to ask them. The only valid reason would be that you saw through the fallacy they involve.

45. 96. That, again, I do not profess to do. I profess only to be a plain man telling a plain story, the story of various successive barbarisms as I find it told by Gibbon and a few other authors whose works happen to be on my shelves; and venturing to put it before the public because, plain though the story is, I think it not wholly without interest to read once more how the professed champions of barbarism, embattling themselves time and again to make an end once for all of the thing we call civilization, have not so much perished at the stroke of lightning from heaven as withered away in the very hour of their victory, or even after it, until those who once feared their rage come first to despise, and then utterly to forget, those who once set themselves up as champions of that which needs no champion, and would not even tolerate a champion if it was the sheer force it pretends to be.

CPSIA information can be obtained
at www.ICGtesting.com
Printed in the USA
BVOW04s0737020617

485821BV00002B/139/P